Dreadful Pleasures

DREADFUL PLEASURES

An Anatomy of
Modern Horror

JAMES B. TWITCHELL

New York   Oxford
OXFORD UNIVERSITY PRESS
1985

Oxford University Press

Oxford   New York   Toronto
Delhi   Bombay   Calcutta   Madras   Karachi
Kuala Lumpur   Singapore   Hong Kong   Tokyo
Nairobi   Dar es Salaam   Cape Town
Melbourne   Auckland

and associated companies in
Beirut   Berlin   Ibadan   Mexico City   Nicosia

Copyright © 1985 by Oxford University Press, Inc.

Published by Oxford University Press, Inc.,
200 Madison Avenue, New York, New York 10016

Library of Congress Cataloging in Publication Data
Twitchell, James B., 1943–
Dreadful Pleasures.
Bibliography: p.   Includes index.
1. Horror in art.   2. Arts, Modern—20th century—
Psychological aspects.   I. Title.
NX650.H67T95   1985   700′.9′04   85-13812
ISBN 0-19-503566-6

Printing (last digit):   9 8 7 6 5 4 3 2 1

Printed in the United States of America

For my family

Acknowledgments

I regret that because of a deprived childhood (no gum, no *E.C.* comics, no state fairs until after the vaccine, no frightening movies, no pulp fiction, no sugar drinks) I am unable to write the standard reminiscence of a lifelong addiction to horror. I cannot thank Bela Lugosi or Christopher Lee for scaring the daylight out of me, or Universal Studios for getting me safely through Saturday, or *Tales from the Vault* for explaining the dark mysteries that surrounded me. Instead, I came to this subject ten years ago when I was teaching Keats' "La Belle Dame Sans Merci" and a young lady who had never spoken all semester raised her hand to declaim that this femme fatale was no fairy maiden, no personified Muse, no projected Fanny Brawne, nor any other possibility I had ever considered; she was in truth a female vampire, a lamia. I thought this was preposterous and did what instructors do in such situations. I asked the student to write a paper about it. She did; I think she was right, and, although I have long forgotten her name, I would like to thank her for the insight.

Since that time I have consumed the stuff of horror in bulk. The gothic novels were easy enough to get to; the movies were a different matter. So I should like to thank the estate of Samuel Kipnis, whose collection of films is at the University of Florida; the American Philosophical Society for a travel grant to visit the Library of Congress film collection; and the inventors of the coaxial cable and video cassette recorder which allowed me to get to bed at a decent hour. Although the viewing has not always been pleasant—in the last five years I have seen a surfeit of heads blown off, brains eaten, bodies chainsawed, eyes poked with splinters and sliced with razors, human flesh seared and eaten, and, most of all, women stabbed, hacked, raped, disembow-eled, and generally treated hideously—it has been full of surprises. I have seen Humphrey Bogart as a blood fiend in *The Return of Dr. X,* James Arness as a vampiric vegetable in *The Thing,* Michael Landon as a sophomoric wolf-boy in *I Was a Teenage Werewolf,* and Jack Nicholson as an overeager den-tal patient in *The Little Shop of Horrors.* I have heard such great lines as the doctor to his young patient in *I Was a Teenage Frankenstein:* "Answer me, you have a civil tongue in your head. I know, I sewed it in there myself"; or the sheriff in *Night of the Lepus:* "There's a herd of killer rabbits heading this way!"; or Lou Costello's response to the Wolfman's pathetic confession that he turns into a wolf every night when the moon is full: "Yea, you and 50 million other guys." I have marveled at slime and alligator people, wasp and jungle women, leopard and fly men, human snakes, crab monsters, giant leeches, killer tomatoes, lots of apes, and even more nasty but pathetic mutants.

I clearly owe another debt to the scholars who preceded me: Prawer, Evans, Glut, Dillard, Wolf, Greenberg, Clarens, Punter, and many others whose insights I have often cannibalized. I am grateful as well to *The Geor-gia Review* for permission to reprint Chapter 4, and to the Museum of Mod-ern Art, the American Academy of Motion Picture Arts and Sciences, and Universal and Hammer studios for their still images. Gary and Pam, and Larry and Gayl have given me more than I can properly acknowledge.

Gainesville, Florida   J.B.T.
June 1985

Contents

Dreadful Pleasures

Introduction

We are currently enjoying—or better yet, enduring—a revival of horror in popular culture. Like the Blob, the stuff is oozing out everywhere: in music (the monstrous make-up of KISS is now a commonplace), in music videos (Michael Jackson's "Thriller" cassette has set sales records in every possible category), in books (Stephen King and his confreres have dominated the best-seller lists for the past five years), in painting (in 1977 the Bronx Museum of the Arts had an exhibition, "Images of Horror and Fantasy," the descriptive catalog for which has been issued as a trade paperback and has proved a startling success), on television (not only the Friday Nite Fright Flicks and Saturday morning cartoons, but almost half the made-for-TV movies are ter-ror-jerkers), and even breakfast cereals ("Count Chocula," "Frankenberry"). And if you have looked at newspaper advertisements for movies recently, let alone been brave enough to see such offerings as *The Exorcist*, *Carrie*, *Alien*, or the "slice-and-dice" variety such as *Halloween*, *Friday the 13th*, *He Knows You're Alone*, you know there has been a veritable rash of horror films.

It is tempting to think we are the only ones infected with the germs of horror; concomitantly, we may feel we should be a bit ashamed of ourselves for contracting it, let alone scratching it. But it won't go away. As with much

pornography, contemporary formulaic horror sequences are so rife with misogyny, incest, rape, and aggressive antisocial behavior that we are almost
frightened to take it seriously. Most of us know it still incubates behind the
theatre doors, at the drive-in, in comics, in rock videos, in gothic novels, and
we know that at one time we may have been eager to get close to it, but we
rarely—if ever—think it worthy of careful observation. After all, it's kid's
stuff. When the critic John Simon recently commented on the horror film:
"It is the lowbrow's delight, the middlebrow's camp and the highbrow's
trash," he did not have to add the self-evident. The stuff of horror is not the
stuff of scholarship. He may very well be right, but when we look back over
the past two centuries we see that certain images and sequences have plagued
popular culture. Surely it must be important that these motifs won't go away.
Surely it must be important that these nightmarish figments have became
fantasies we all recognize. What we have experienced since the 1960s is a
swelling of forms exploited in the films of the 1930s, which were in turn
scenarios often based on novels of the 1890s, themselves the outgrowths of
the "shilling shockers" which had evolved from the gothic novel. And where
did the gothic novel come from? It came from the profound shifting of sensibilities that first characterized romantic, and then modern, art. Essentially,
modern works of artificial horror originated in the late eighteenth-century
discovery that by inducing extreme feelings of dreadful pleasures, both print
and illustration could arouse and exploit powerful feelings deep within the
human spirit. Whatever first directed our attention toward the macabre, the
mis-shapen, the barbarous, and the deformed, it has yet to be expunged. No
amount of repetition, exploitation, or censorship can dislodge it.

To be sure, we can trace the artifice of horror back well before the turn of
the nineteenth century. Think only of Elizabethan and Jacobean "blood and
thunder" tragedies, of the more morbid morality plays, of Greek drama, or,
for that matter, of the first images ever imagined and then etched by the
human hand. I suppose the place to start any comprehensive study of horror
(of which this is not one!) would be back in the cave, where doubtless our
Aurignacian and Magdalenian ancestors nestled among the rocks to watch
the flickering shadows play on the walls, pretending that they were watching
the forms of charging beasts, the first "creature features."

People, unlike animals, have been drawn to re-create their fears in pictures
and then pass those images on, almost as if they believed that art could control present and future anxiety. When the cave people tried to freeze the
forms they found frightening, they re-created an exaggerated reality deep
inside the cave, usually at the farthest point from the entrance. We can still
see the results of their efforts in the "Salon Noirs" in southern France and
northern Spain, for there the so-called "hunger artists" engraved and then

Well Scene, Lascaux, c. 15,000–10,000 B.C. (Institut Géographique National)

painted with chunks of red and yellow ocher the scenes that affect us still: big monster forms surging in our direction. We don't know exactly who was allowed into these subterranean theaters, but there is evidence the audience went to participate, not just to view. Sharp gouges appear on the sides of the bison drawings at Niaux as well as on other animals at other sites, suggesting that young hunters may have thrown spears at the images. We still enact this kind of homeopathic magic as we wiggle and scream in the dark, watching the molesting monsters on the screen, hoping that we, too, can survive our fears, knowing what will happen if we don't.

Considering Cinema Eight at the local shopping mall as the modern cave may be a bit too McLuhanesque, but a similarity in function is clearly evident. We have gone into both to witness the transformation of real horror into artificial horror, and to practice controlling one of our primary impulses—the impulse to flee. It is surely important that in the earliest cave art the image of man is almost completely excluded, for the subject was the outside world, not narcissism; self-protection, not self-knowledge. When the figure of a man does appear, as he does in the puzzling paintings at Lascaux, he has fallen between a wounded buffalo and a slouching rhinoceros. He is a stick figure with arms akimbo and mouth gaping wide with awe, and although no scholar knows what has occurred (has he been struck by the rhino, or is he about to be charged by the wounded buffalo?), this much is clear: the first image of man in art is one of man either dead or absolutely terrified. Equally interesting is the weird humanoid found on the cave walls at Trois Frères in the Pyrenees, except that now the monster seems to be one of us. This so-called "Sorcerer" is a composite of wolf, bear, and man which possibly excited his audience just as the zombie, werewolf, mummy, and vampire continue to upset us. It is a human shape, all right, but it is not human.

If we could fathom the purposes of these paintings, we could probably uncover why we are still drawn to re-create them and, in so doing, re-experience them. This much, however, seems clear: when the earliest artists reconstructed scenes that produced the sensation of fright, they heightened the monstrous character of the beast (big horns, big hooves, big tusks) and approached the human form, if at all, only as an image to be outlined. Was this because they feared that filling in the human form would mean it was "captured" and eternally stabilized? I suspect not; I think it was because the palliative powers of art let us vicariously experience what we are horrified of, make us small and our fears large, and then allow us to purge ourselves in the paralysis of terror by resolving the tension.

The fascination of the abomination, the gut-tightening, hair-raising frisson of confronting objects of phobia, the narcotic of adrenalin and the exul-

Sorcerer, Trois-Frères, c. 15,000–10,000 B.C. (American Museum of Natural History)

tation of escape or triumph, are still very much part of the experience of artificial horror. In *Dreadful Pleasures* I pick up the imagery of horror in the mid-eighteenth century because it is here that diffuse fright figments converge into repeatable sequences, into modern myths. Three monsters on the wall of the modern cave are especially fascinating: the vampire, the Frankenstein monster, and the transformation monster. I intend to track them from the cave walls to the dream-life of individual artists, and from there into print, and then back out onto the modern cave wall—the silver screen. Although many approaches are possible—political, sociological, historical, semiotic, structural—I intend to study these stories as if they were one continuous text, unconsciously repeated regardless of medium, always directed to the same audience for the same unacknowledged reason.

By not distinguishing the "art" renditions from, say, the crassly exploitative ones, or those just meant to entertain, I hope to show that horror sequences are really formulaic rituals coded with precise social information needed by the adolescent audience. Like fairy tales that prepare the child for the anxieties of separation, modern horror myths prepare the teenager for the anxieties of reproduction. They are fantastic, ludicrous, crude, and important distortions of real life situations, not in the service of repression (though they certainly have that temporary effect), but of instruction. These fever dreams do more than make us shiver; they are fables of sexual identity. Horror myths establish social patterns not of escape, but entry. Night visitors prepare us for daylight.

1

The Dimensions and Evolution of Modern Horror Art

I want to make your skin crawl.
The Fat Boy in *The Pickwick Papers*

Horror art is not, strictly speaking, a genre; it is rather a collection of motifs in a usually predictable sequence that gives us a specific physiological effect—the shivers. As movies from Luis Buñuel and Salvador Dali's *An Andalusian Dog* (1928) to David Lynch's *Eraserhead* (1978) have shown, horror can be very one-dimensional and fast-acting. We do not have to know what is going on to be affected; in fact, ignorance may be essential. Or to put it in a more modern way, artificial horror is what an audience searches for in a verbal or visual text when it wants a particular kind of frisson without much intellectual explanation or sophistication. Horror art demands audience participation or, better yet, conspiracy. Those archetypical children huddled around the campfire asking for "just one more scary story" before going to bed are really part of the same audience queueing up at Cinema Eight to watch some variation of "Son of Dracula Meets Frankenstein and the Wolfman." Both audiences passionately want to be frightened and they will give up a great deal of control to make sure it happens. I make this point now because I have no interest in real horror: images of human distortions, suffering Biafran children, the eating of human flesh, elephant men, captives at concentration camps, "snuff" films, survivors of nuclear explosions, the decomposition of human bodies, and all manner of the "really" atrocious and hideous are quite beyond the pale of this book. They are always "out there," to be sure, off on the horizon, but Charles Manson's "helter-skelter" is in no way my heebie-jeebies. Instead, what I am interested in is why we have been drawn to certain images in art and popular culture that we would find repellent in actuality, and how, in the last two hundred years, this interest has helped create two veritable industries of transmission—the gothic novel and the horror film.

The modern interest in artificial horror is a chapter in cultural history that is only now being written, in part because, thanks to recent developments in criticism, the canon of literature is being expanded. Historically, many critics have wandered off into the mire of the gothic novel: Edith Birkhead, *The Tale of Terror* (1927); J. M. S. Tompkins, *The Popular Novel in England, 1770–1800* (1961); Montague Summers, *The Gothic Quest* (1938); Devendra Varma, *The Gothic Flame* (1957); Robert Kiely, *The Romantic Novel in England* (1972); Coral Ann Howells, *Love, Mystery, and Misery* (1978); Elizabeth MacAndrew, *The Gothic Tradition in Fiction* (1979); Eve Kosofsky Sedgwick, *The Coherence of Gothic Convention* (1980). Lately, movie critics have attempted to study the horror movie as a specific genre: Ivan Butler, *The Horror Film* (1967); Carlos Clarens, *An Illustrated History of the Horror Film* (1967); Roy Huss and T. J. Ross (eds.), *Focus on the Horror Film* (1972); David Pirie, *A Heritage of Horror* (1973); A. G. Frank, *Horror Movies* (1974); W. K. Everson, *Classics of the Horror Film* (1974); R. H. W. Dillard, *Horror Films* (1976); Charles Derry, *Dark Dreams* (1977); David Soren, *The Rise and Fall of the Horror Film* (1977); Richard Meyers, *The World of Fantasy Films* (1980). But until very recently no one had attempted to trace the iconography and conventions of modern horror art as they were first transformed from images of dream-life into the plots of the gothic novel and then solidified into the visual forms we so often see flickering before us. And with some reason—critics of the gothic novel have, with the exception of Summers, been academics trained in the rigors of literary scholarship, while critics of film have been aficionados who usually don't care about the provenance of the images they view. With some exceptions, interpretations of novels are as larded with footnotes as the explanations (often "appreciations") of the film are loaded with pictures. Les Daniels' *Living in Fear: A History of Horror in the Mass Media* (1975) attempted to interrelate film and literature, but it was hardly a rigorous study and more a series of assertions about "fabricated fright," followed by excerpts of first Poe, and then Bierce, M. R. James, Machen, and Lovecraft. Even S. S. Prawer, Taylor Professor of German Language and Literature at Oxford, who really could have written an intertextual study, was more concerned in *Caligari's Children: The Film as Tale of Terror* (1980) with what has been called a "psychophenomenological analysis" of his favorite movies than in any systematic inquiry into the origins and the migration of archetypes and motifs.

Thanks in part to the successes of structuralism, approaches may now be changing. First, Gérard Lenne's *Le Cinéma fantastique et ses mythes* (1970) attempted to build an intricate taxonomy of horror rituals based on the linguistic and anthropological studies of Saussure, Lévi-Strauss, and Jakobson, and then David Punter's *The Literature of Terror: A History of Gothic Fictions from 1765 to the Present Day* (1980) concluded with a short chapter discussing "Gothic in the Horror Film." The easy-to-read *Danse Macabre* (1981) by Stephen King illustrated a practitioner's sense of modern image transposition between verbal and visual media, and the almost-impossible-to-read *Powers of Horror* (1982) by Julia Kristeva proffered a viscous Lacanean commentary on abjection. But no one has ever tracked the major carriers of horror—the vampire, the werewolf, and the "hulk with no name"—from their lairs in the subconscious, up through folklore, into the printed text (*Dracula, Dr. Jekyll and Mr. Hyde,* and *Frankenstein*), and then out into what is now a veritable jungle of cinematic monsters. And so it is onto this relatively uncharted territory that we now set foot.

Perhaps because it is too pedestrian a place to start, critics have uniformly neglected the word they so readily invoke—horror. It is a difficult word primarily because we think we know what it means: what is horrible is what we are frightened of, and what we are frightened of usually has to do with the invasion of the abnormal into the world of the normal. Give any journeyman moviemaker a razor and a young lady, or a lumbering beast and a shrieking ingenue, and he should be able to scare the wits out of any audience. This is true as far as it goes, but horror really refers to a rather specific effect of that fright. To understand the meaning of "horror" we are initially taken back to the Latin word *horrēre*, which means "to bristle," and it describes the way the nape hair stands on end during moments of shivering excitement. In fact, the shiver we associate with horror is the result of the constriction of the skin that firms up the subcutaneous hair follicles and thus accounts for the rippling sensation, almost as if a tremor were fluttering down our back. From this comes the most appropriate trope for horror— creeping flesh or, more simply, the "creeps." This physiological phenomenon clearly has self-defense as its biological purpose, for we pause momentarily in horror, frozen between fight and flight, ironically at our strongest and yet most vulnerable. Medical science is now exploring the biochemical substance, corticotropin, that triggers this response by signaling the pituitary gland to produce hormones, but for our purposes just the hair on the neck will do.

Hence both real and artificial horror are oxymoronic—a moment of ecstatic dread, a second of full-passioned fixity, of panic and exultation. It is in this moment, incidentally, that theologians like Rudolf Otto located the sense of awe that leads to the evolution of spiritual consciousness. In fact, in

The Idea of the Holy (1917), Otto even argued that it is from this shiver ("dae-monic dread") that the visionary and mystical experience (*"mysterium tre-mendum"*) emanates. My concerns are thankfully less transcendental; still, this same mysterious sensation Edmund Burke argued could form the aes-thetic basis for a new artistic category—the sublime. So if only because the sensation of horror seems to have religious as well as aesthetic significance, let us magnify it further.

That the experience of horror is first physiological, and only then maybe numinous, remains encoded in all its hybrid and mutant linguistic forms. The word "horripilation," for instance, is still used in zoology to describe the condition commonly known as gooseflesh. What we call gooseflesh is usually caused by abrupt changes in body temperature and is the warm-blooded ani-mal's attempt to shove up its thermostat. Our teeth chatter, knees knock, and skin shivers when we are either cold or frightened. It is almost as if the body is saying, "Move, you fool, move!" But we don't. We stand still and shudder, suddenly paralyzed.

The shivering sensation, so prominent as the effect of horror, even found a pathway into medical terminology; in the nineteenth century and earlier, "horror" described the sudden tremors associated with the plummeting body temperature as a fever receded. So a patient experiencing a "horror" was just at that moment of transition between the sensation of a boiling fever and the chill that follows, caused by the evaporation of sweat. This same sense of static turbulence even migrated into nautical jargon, where "horror" became a graphic term used by sailors to catalog the cresting of a wave in a rough sea; it describes the topmost oscillation of surging water, the foam.

In this context I am reminded of the great impresario of horror schlock, William Castle (or the "King of Horror" as he preferred to call himself), who back in the early 1960s, when horror movies were temporarily out of fashion, made a limping clone of *Psycho* called *Homicidal*. *Homicidal* was one of those movies for which you had to arrive on time and then wait in line to buy your ticket and then wait again to be let inside. Only after the crowd had twice swelled and twice been made jittery were you at last able to be seated.[1] The movie finally began and ran until, at the crest of the horror effects, it suddenly stopped and Mr. Castle's voice intoned: "Ladies and gentlemen, this is William Castle. You are cordially invited, if you're too frightened to see the last sixty seconds, to be my guest and go to the box office and get your full admission price refunded." No one moved and not because, if you left, you had to wait awhile in "Coward's Corner," but because you were caught at the crest—the moment where to know what comes next is as terrifying as not to know.

Mr. Castle knew how important the crest of horror is, how important it is to keep churning the foam, and he made another movie called *The Tingler*,

(Above) The Tingler: lobby poster, 1959 (Columbia Pictures)

(Right) Edvard Munch, *The Scream,* 1893 (Nasjonalgalleriet, Oslo)

which unfortunately will never again be properly appreciated. Here is the gist of the story: at the opening, an avuncular Mr. Castle appears on screen to tell us that at the height of horror we *must* scream or the tension, the pressure inside us, will cause us to go insane. An exemplum follows but what we really see is a spoof of horror images played out by the arch-spoofer, Vincent Price. Price is a scientist convinced that unexpressed fright causes a microorganism—the tingler—to pinch the nerves at the base of the spine. This constriction ultimately leads to, first, a collapse of the body and, then, to death. The only way to exorcise the tingler is to scream like a frightened monkey before it latches on. Price then gives us proof by way of a tale. One day a deaf and dumb woman is in her bathroom and finds that blood flows from her bathroom faucets. But that's not all. She then sees a hand reaching toward her from out of her tub, and witnesses her own death certificate, fully filled out, in the medicine cabinet. Everything short of *Jaws II* inhabits the commode, but since she can't scream (she's deaf and dumb), she crumples to the floor, presumably "strangled" from inside by the tingler. After Dr. Vincent Price himself is revealed to be the culprit (who else could it have been in 1959?), an autopsy is performed and the "tingler" escapes, escapes right off the movie screen and, as a matter of fact, lands in the theater near us in the audience. At this point, certain theater chairs, which have been prewired, start to vibrate and (gasp!) the horror has been translated from art to life. The spine tingler is literally loose and we'd better scream and scream again to keep it at a distance.

Castle obviously knows a lot about the operation of horror (he went on to produce the minor classic *Rosemary's Baby*) and knows how it involves both the image and our physiological reaction to it. *The Tingler* violates all our expectations: what is the real movie producer doing there on the screen, why is that blood flowing from the water tap (here the black-and-white film becomes color), and, especially, how does the tingler escape the fantasy world up there on the screen and get down here with us? Although some post-modernist critic could have a field day with this movie, it is too late for us in the audience to intellectualize let alone deconstruct; the tingler is loose and exactly what are we going to do about it? We're going to ride out that crest and scream. Edvard Munch's *The Scream* so vividly shows us what to do.

To stay with modern art a moment longer, there is a visual analogy for the implosive threat to well-being that can be seen in many of the paintings of Francis Bacon. Bacon is able to tap the same reservoir that Castle attempted

Francis Bacon, *Triptych*, 1967 (Hirshhorn Museum and Sculpture Garden, Smithsonian Institution)

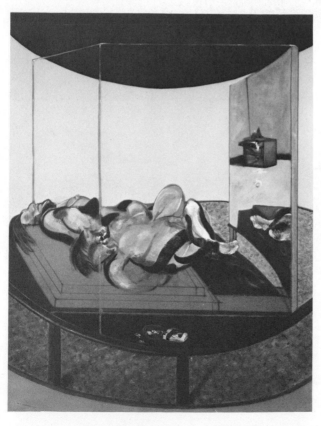

to pump dry. For instance, in a painting simply called *Triptych*, Bacon is typically preoccupied by the painful distortions of bodily parts.

This is a totally amoral, erratic, inexplicable, and confusing scene: on the left, two women, bodies tangled, lie exhausted; while on the right, two men are frantically intertwined, and far to the right, in the same scene, a third man casually answers the phone. In the middle frame a scene straight from that poor deaf and dumb woman's apartment: a bloody, amorphous mass of living goo, perhaps some victim's remnant, that is almost organic and growing. When we look at this image the only thing we know for sure is that somehow the tingler is loose and moving toward our spine and we want very badly to scream. Those who saw *The Blob* when they were teenagers can tell you that the scariest moment by far was not when Steve McQueen was trapped by the ooze in the hash-house, but when the goo came dripping down from the projection booth and onto our surrogate selves watching a horror movie at the downtown theater.

Thankfully most horror art does not oscillate at so high a pitch as Bacon's or we would be frazzled, but it does show us something central about the nature of this experience. Horror results from a brutal irreconciliation of opposites, a jerking displacement of understood visual signs that shocks our nervous system, producing specific, locatable, physiological symptoms. We voluntarily sit in Mr. Castle's vibrating seats. In the experience of make-believe horror we willingly stick our fingers into the electrical socket knowing full well that we will be jolted and, if it is really effective, we cannot get our finger out soon enough. Inside we feel profoundly vulnerable and cold; outside we are all aflutter and hot. In horror art we are transported to the threshold, to the margin, to the crest, to be caught in what Jean Cocteau has called *la zone*. The art of horror is thus the art of generating breakdown, where signifier and signified no longer can be kept separate, where distinctions can no longer be made, where old masks fall and new masks are not yet made. If images of horror often do not make intellectual sense, that is precisely because they are, in part, images of the uncanny, images from the subconscious, full of exaggeration and distortion. Horror art is, indeed, so informed by the dynamics of the nightmare that it may finally only be understood as "dreaming with one's eyes open," as dreamwork made real, the cinéma vérité of the psyche.

The word that has journeyed along with "horror" is "terror" and, although a distinction was attempted between the two back in the eighteenth century, they have since slid back together. We now talk about the terror-novel and the horror-movie as if only the noun-stems were different. I would, however, like to separate them again, at least for the time being, because it seems to me that terror describes something rather different. Maybe this difference is only a distinction of degree, but the level of dreamlike distortion and displacement in terror seems much lower than in horror. Terror is external and short-lived; horror is more internal and long-lasting. Terror will pass, as in the Reign of Terror or acts of terrorism, but horror will never disappear, no matter how rational we become about it. In fact, just the opposite is true: the more rational we are, the more exasperating it becomes. Horror has no end, no closure, no conclusion; terror always has an end. Extended horror can become a ritual, an endless loop. This is why, I think, horror novels, horror movies, horror myths are never really satisfying intellectually, for we never get them under control. To a considerable extent this may explain why horror art has never been systematically studied.

Let me briefly illustrate the ramifications of this horror/terror dichotomy in literary history. Until very recently, literary scholars have implied that the English novel was debased around the turn of the nineteenth century. By this they really meant that the traditional novel had somehow lost its appeal, and that a new sensationalism had "captured" both the traditional form and the traditional audience, which was then being swelled by the newly literate middle class. The "degenerate" forms: the sentimental novel, the historical novel, and, to a lesser degree, the novel of manners, were all thought to be corruptions of "the great tradition" that began with Fielding and Richardson and was to be blessedly revived by "the great Victorian novelists" like Trollope and Dickens. Chief culprit in the corruption of the English novel (this was never said, but it was a donnée of criticism nevertheless) was the *Schauerroman*, the shudder novel, the gothic. And so when the late-eighteenth-century and early-nineteenth-century novel was taught, Walpole's *Castle of Otranto* was the inappropriate choice. Nothing is so ludicrously funny as contrived fright images, especially if they are in the service of high sobriety, and *Otranto* certainly delivers these. The sign of failed horror art is always the guffaw, which we can hear whenever pretentious horror films are unearthed from the forties (*Calling Mr. Death, The Spider Woman*) or fifties (*House of Wax, The Mole People*). *Otranto* is important because it was written by Walpole, not because it is a gothic novel of any substance.

More often than not, the father's frisson turns out to be the son's frolic, especially if the motifs were originally intended to terrify. But when the same motifs (say, situations of incest, madness, burial, torture, as well as specific images like the haunted house, the severed limb, the threatening knife, billowing curtains, faces pressed to windows, to name just a few) are used to describe certain human interactions as well as to startle the audience, then horror may result. Although the conventions of horror and terror may well share the same iconography, the uses are radically different. *Otranto* develops neither images nor situations; in fact, what is included seems to be more the result of happenstance and of occasional good luck than of design. The great horror novels (*The Monk, Frankenstein*, and *Melmoth the Wanderer*, from the first cycle of the romantic novel, and *Dracula, The Strange Case of Dr. Jekyll and Mr. Hyde, The Picture of Dorian Gray*, and *The Island of Dr. Moreau*, from the second) have survived in spite of academic neglect, let alone disdain, because they still frighten *and* edify. Exactly how they edify is something I will discuss in the next chapter, but for now it is enough to recognize that the instructions embedded in horror resist literary, especially formalist, interpretation for the same reason that the "meaning" of pictorial horror art has proved elusive. Who knows how to interpret Goya, Munch, Kubin, Blake, Bosch, Grosz, Ruppert, when they clearly insist on creating images of threatening confusion rather than resolving them. Greek tragedy and Jacobean drama follow many of the same conventions. Yet most of us would agree, I hope, that these conventions are more often a strategy in the former and a device in the latter.

To return again to literary criticism, when Robert Kiely in the best book on the early gothic, *The Romantic Novel in England* (1972), complained about the critical problem of not being able to apply traditional apparatus and vocabulary (linear causality, characterization, logical development, narrative complexity) to the texts at hand, he was absolutely correct. But this is not because the novels themselves are inhospitable to a "close" reading, but because the gothic is a vehicle for transporting horror images and these images are not drawn from the "real" world but from the "land of dreams." Kiely resolves these "problem texts" by psychoanalyzing them, and he succeeds. For as critics like Railo, Varma, Summers, and even MacAndrews and Punter have shown by inadvertent examples, it is hard to say anything insightful about what exactly it is within the gothic novel that gives it coherence unless the methodology is psychological. And so usually the critic ends up at wit's end happy to catalog stock situations or tidy up historical loose ends.

The same is true of modern film criticism, except that here, since Susan Sontag's *Notes on "Camp"* (1964) and the passing of Bosley Crowther from the *New York Times*, it has become fashionable not just to like horror films, but to relish them. Words like "pulp," "sleazy," "lurid," "mannered," and "decadent" are not words of opprobrium, but praise. "Intellectual" means just the opposite as Vincent Canby recently explained: an "intellectual horror movie . . . means it's a movie that contains a certain amount of unseemly gore and makes no sense whatever" (October 28, 1983, *New York Times*, p. 18). These movies don't tingle the spines of critics the way they do those of the audience, and so the critic usually evaluates them only in terms of technique. It is not coincidental that recently the horror film has achieved critical acclaim at the same time auteur criticism was gaining popularity. Yet the tone of appreciation for the substance of horror films is usually condescending and often too insipid to be taken seriously.

Have a look at the critical reception of Brian De Palma's *Dressed to Kill* (1980), for example. Here is a slick little movie that plays on the genuine horror of a deranged father figure (Michael Caine, the psychiatrist), turned compulsive killer, and the adolescent boy who must destroy the menace with the aid of an older good, but gruff, mentor, Detective Marino. This configuration perennially has been a hot-wire in horror art, as the enduring voltage of Dracula attests, but listen to what the professional film critics have to say. David Denby in *New York* magazine praises it as

The First Great American Movie of the Eighties!

Violent, erotic, and wickedly funny. De Palma releases terror in laughter. Even at his most outrageous, Hitchcock could not have been as entertaining as this.

> De Palma is sensational, he heads straight for what's gorgeously lurid, for what appeals to the senses as pure excitement. The violence of this movie, so wildly improbable, leaves one exhilarated rather than shaken. (August 28, 1980, p. 44)

Pauline Kael in *The New Yorker* calls it "one of the most sheerly enjoyable films of recent years" because it is so splendid visually (August 4, 1980, p. 68); Shelia Benson for the *LA Times* claims that, "The brilliance of *Dressed to Kill* is apparent within seconds of its opening gliding shot; it is a sustained work of terror—elegant, sensual, erotic, bloody, a directorial tour de force" (August 25, 1980, part 6, p. 1); and even Vincent Canby at the *Times* says it is: "a witty, romantic, psychological horror film … [with] one succeeding spectacular effect after another" (August 25, 1980, p. C10). No one really discusses what makes the "psychological horror"; they much prefer the cinematic effects. And the reason the critics like this rather ill-conceived film (Are we really supposed to believe the teenager has all that electronic stuff in his bedroom? Or that Michael Caine is so asymptomatic? Or that Nancy Allen is such a happy hooker?) is because the film is so well-cut and crafted. True, the two shower scenes, the half-hour at the museum, and the elevator ride are gorgeously lurid and make for almost too much visceral excitement. And true, Brian De Palma can track the camera the way Thomas Love Peacock could wiggle the pen. The filming and editing *are* superb, but there has to be more to lasting horror than quick fingers and sharp scissors.

As Stephen Farber argued in "Why Do Critics Love Trashy Movies," the culprit here is partly the auteur theory itself, which essentially holds that film artistry can be judged independently of narrative responsibility. Hence "dynamite film tricks" (as *Time* magazine said in high praise of David Cronenberg's *Scanners*) become ends in themselves, and such emphasis on pyrotechnics threatens the horror film today the same way that fictional claptrap, like hidden doors and banks of fog and a host of other "devices," took over the early-nineteenth-century gothic novel and turned it toward melodrama, the thriller, and the mindless bloody pulps of the 1850s. The current reliance in horror films on special effects in lieu of plot or character development presages the same problem faced over a century ago in the gothic novel. You can only spin Regan's head around so many times per generation, or drop that gigantic helmet so many times on Manfred's son, before the act simply becomes a device, and the shock is gone. Some other story beneath the authorial or directorial virtuosity, some fairy tale waiting to be told, some ritual about to be performed, must coalesce with the surface story for the terror images to become horrible.

To reiterate the distinction between horror and terror, the etiology of horror is *always* in dreams, while the basis of terror is in actuality. Thus, while the images may be similar, the interpretation of horror will finally be psychological while the interpretation of terror will be contextual. Terror must start anew in each generation, not because the objects of fear are so changeable, but because images of them are. We now don't fear space invaders; we fear what we might bring back from space. We fear the Russians and not the Germans; computers and nuclear waste, no longer microfilm and carbolic soda. In 1985 a pastiche of the most successful recent terror-shockers (*Jaws, The Shining, Scanners, Klute, Marathon Man*, to name just a few) was assembled and released as *Terror in the Aisles*. Accompanied by genial Donald Pleasence and perky Nancy Allen, the audience in the theater joins an audience in the film to view, or better yet re-view, what is essentially an endless series of trailers. While the simulated crowd in the film may act shocked, the real audience seems more interested in reviving and recalling past shocks. The intellectual pretensions of this movie aside, what was informative was that the shocking images could be so successfully excised from the storyline without disturbing our need for context. After all, these are "our" films; we knew the routines by heart. A generation from now there will be a different "terror in the aisles." But horror is different. We will keep returning to watch the werewolf transform, or the vampire bite the virgin, or Dr. Frankenstein experiment in the laboratory, or Dr. Jekyll meet Mr. Hyde, and we will probably continue this interest until we resolve whatever it is in these myths that is unresolved within ourselves. The distinction between horror and terror has nothing to do with violence and grue; it has everything to do with the psychological resonance of sequence and imagery.

Fuseli's *The Nightmare*, a wonderfully apt image of horror, became almost iconic in the nineteenth century. We still react to this even though no one can explain precisely why. Who is that incubus on the dreamer's midriff, what has he done, what has she done, is she even alive? And what about that horse—a visual pun on the word "nightmare," or a weird atavistic beast peering in from another world? Horace Walpole, who might have missed the mark in *Otranto*, was certainly right when he called the painting "shocking." We know he is right because in a strange, subliminal, subconscious way we have been there in that bed, been there in that world of dreams, in *la zone*, and we know the horror that awaits us. There is, I think, no terror here, only horror.[2]

If horror is accessible only through psychoanalysis, then why has it not been studied by depth psychologists? From time to time it has been, but without much success. Certainly one of the problems has been a lack of critical vocabulary and methodology. For while horror is clearly related to what Freud called "the uncanny" (*unheimlich*, literally, "unhomely"), the English term is a woeful equivalent. Tzvetan Todorov in *The Fantastic: A Structural*

Henry Fuseli, *The Nightmare,* 1781 (Detroit Institute of Arts: Gift of Mr. and Mrs. Bert L. Smokler and Mr. and Mrs. Lawrence A. Fleischman)

Approach to a Literary Genre (1973) attempted to resolve this by comparing the imagery of the uncanny (explainable) to the imagery of the marvelous (inexplicable). But I think terror is a more appropriate counterpart because the uncanny, the horrible, and the marvelous often are inseparable. However, terror is always "real"; it is always objectifiable. We know where it came from, what it's going to do to us, and then where it's going next. Usually we even know how to destroy it, and if we do know, the method of destruction assumes that it is organic, just like ourselves. If we see a female victim on film being stalked by an ax-murderer with the requisite cleaver in hand, de rigueur in the 1970s, or even a big bug with teeth, as was the fashion in the 1960s, our sensation will be terror; but let that murderer be a zombie, a vampire, a werewolf, or anything akin, and our response is horror. Horror vehicles are different from terror carriers not so much in what they do— they both aggressively invade privacy—but in how and why they are doing it. Horror monsters are literally marvelous, truly fantastic. The myth will never explain them, but one thing is certain: they are not atomic mutants, unloved children, jilted lovers, or schizophrenics. They just *are*, and always have been.

It is this lack of information that ties horror not just to the marvelous but also to the occult, for horror art is essentially the art of occlusion. In make-believe horror there is always something hidden, something still and ever-concealed, some forbidden knowledge, a kept secret. What is "the horror, the horror," that Kurtz has seen? We don't quite know. What really is inside the vault beneath the House of Usher? We would like to find out if we could do so safely. This mystification does not mean, however, that horror is more exciting than terror, only that we will always have a sense of closure with terror and indeterminancy with horror. *The Monk* is not a better novel than *The Castle of Otranto* because it is a work of horror, not terror; it is just a different book. So in this context the bogeyman in John Carpenter's *Halloween* is an object of horror (will he keep coming out of that house, forever, each Halloween?), while the revenging crew in *The Fog* is also supernatural, yes, but well under control (the lepers had reason to attack the townspeople and we are satisfied that they'll not do it again) and hence are objects of terror.

I am arguing for this distinction between horror and terror because one of the shifts in sensibility that has informed the modern world has been the acknowledgment that horror is not just an aspect of human experience, but a central part of it. We can no longer claim with Alexander Pope that "discordia concors" is an appropriate explanation of aberrancy. We are not bees in Mandeville's hive or cogs in Pangloss' perfect clockwork. And, of course, for us to become sensitive to horror as an integral part of modern experience, the neoclassical world of just form and proper order had to crumble. Had Newton really been right, and had there really been laws to govern all change, there could be no horror; only temporary ignorance, only terror. But Darwin and Marx and Einstein and especially Freud made modern horror not just possible, but unavoidable. Sweet reasonableness is not enough. So it is not happenstance that horror art first developed in romanticism as part of the growing awareness and acceptance of the irrational; it is something quintessentially modern.

The sleep of reason, contended Goya in 1798, produces monsters and, it might be added, monsters have always been the prime carriers of horror, projections of dissembly. By their very definition monsters are just beyond the pale of the normal. They are always "out there" at the last grid and meridian of psychic cartographers, rising from the ooze of the subconscious, like sea-beasts on the horizons of ancient maps. Because they are on the seam where our rational world meets the next, they are never totally nonhuman. Instead, they usually combine some major human attribute with some truly

Francisco Goya, *The Sleep of Reason Produces Monsters,* 1796–98 (Museum of Fine Arts, Boston)

bizarre element. Thus the ancient monsters—the centaur, the sphinx, the minotaur, the griffin—are partly brute and partly human, and the brute part is not in itself frightening. So too the modern monsters—the vampire, the Frankenstein creature, and the werewolf—imply two incomplete systems of signs. In part, they are images of horror not because they do dreadful things to us (although they may well), but because they block our attempts to classify, categorize, and hence control them. They are uncanny; unable to be kenned. Once again, our fears are carried within the word itself, for "monster" in medical terminology refers to a fetus that is abnormal, combining human with something else, literally grotesque. But such "monsters" clearly threaten our classifying systems not our well-being. H. G. Wells generated intense horror in *The Island of Dr. Moreau* (1896) simply by dispassionately describing the harmless mutants created by the "mad scientist" who infused human forms and attributes into the animal world; Victor Hugo achieved the same effect by "crossing" Quasimodo with the gargoyle. Western folklore is full of such graftings, but in non-Church art they are a relatively recent development.

The king of shape-shifting monsters, the werewolf—as well as the vampire, Frankenstein monster, and all sorts of "things with no name"—did not rise from the graveyards of eighteenth-century literature like the hand of Carrie at the end of the movie, but were instead the result of the disintegration of Augustan order and the ensuing awareness of alienation. I don't mean to give a Marxist interpretation of the rise of nineteenth-century horror (man alienated from exploitative church, state, home, work, is made monstrous). For as Patricia Meyer Spacks has argued in *The Insistence of Horror: Aspects of the Supernatural in Eighteenth-Century Poetry* (1962), the seeds of horror were always just beneath the loam of the Enlightenment. Alexander Pope, Dr. Johnson, and George I may not have had much use for "things that go bump in the night," but John Ogilvie, William Hayley, and Erasmus Darwin certainly did. These popularizers of folklore monsters, who ended up with a far greater popular audience, were then just as neglected in criticism as H. P. Lovecraft, Robert W. Chambers, and Mervyn Peake have been until very recently. These writers were thought to represent the barbaric in what should be the *belles lettres* of culture—and, of course, they did.

It would be nice to think, as did philosophers like Thomas Hobbes, that a proper education could rid one of a hunger for horror, but theologians like John Wesley have always known better. "Giving up witchcraft," wrote Wesley, "is, in effect, giving up the Bible," but it is more than that—it is giving up both a sense of ourselves in nature as well as a cultural heritage that stretches back well before classical mythology. Horror images have always been more than just fear-jerkers to the culture that animates them; they are invariably the most subtle projections of buried and repressed fear. When it comes right down to it, the fascinating question is not why monsters were so suddenly obvious in the late eighteenth century, but how they could have been suppressed with such success for so long.

The invocation of horror, the fabrication of fright, has always been present in the English tradition from *Beowulf* on. But what separates "old" horror from what I call "modern" horror is that, prior to romanticism, horror monsters were usually the means by which the artist held his audience's attention while he prepared his protagonist for heroism. The monster was there to be destroyed, and if it could scare readers first that was fine, because they would then appreciate the hero even more. Pre-romantic monsters were in the text, much as Sidney prescribed, to show by their destruction the power of *virtù*. So here is the Grendel family, terrible ogres to be killed by Beowulf, the grotesque green knight to be decapitated by Sir Gawain, the fire-belching dragon to be dispatched by St. George, or, if you will, the pamphlet-spitting Foule Errour done in by the Redcrosse knight. The pre-modern story is usually the same: monsters are there to be removed by the hero, thereby illustrating his superiority, as well as our need to follow him. In modern versions we forget the victims and even the hero, but we remember the monster. Who, for instance, kills Dracula? How is the Frankenstein monster destroyed? Are we sure the werewolf is dead? Monsters have become bogeymen, and as the child in *Halloween* says, "Ya can't ever kill the bogeyman." Also curious is that now the monsters have become aristocrats (Count Dracula, Baron Frankenstein, Doctor Moreau, Doctor Jekyll, and so forth), and the victims are no longer "ladies in distress," but buxom young girls of the bourgeoisie. The hero is still a young man, but without much personality and with precious little *virtù*.

When these pre-modern horror monsters started to make their way into high art, they behaved somewhat like villains on the soap operas; they invariably knew the truth, but not what to do about it. The witches in *Macbeth*, Caliban in *The Tempest*, Marlowe's Mephistopheles and, most important of all, Milton's Satan had infernal wisdom but could easily be brought under control by the Courtier, be he a prince or Christ. What these Renaissance aberrations had in common with their folk brethren is that they were still included in the text primarily as foils to reflect the brilliance of their more illustrious foes. Jacobean drama may indeed be "supped full of horrors," but it was also supped full of a dynamic aristocracy. With the exception of Milton's Satan, monsters had no integrity, no life of their own.[3]

Any number of purely practical reasons can be offered to explain why modern horror monsters seem to have been carried into the nineteenth-century skies like triffid spores. The repressions of first the Puritans and then of the evangelical empiricists pent up the natural desires for the horrible. The Puritans, especially Milton, made the devil as nastily attractive as any classical horror monster; later the empiricists made him still more attractive by attempting to deny his palpable existence. And no doubt the political uneasiness at the beginning of the eighteenth century made startling shifts in the objectification of evil inevitable as the whole courtly tradition was being turned inside out. Members of the rising bourgeoisie, especially sensitive to any perversion of order, were caught between the castle and the field—two images that still resonate in the iconography of horror. This same middle class, now rapidly growing literate as well as affluent, lifted the buried texts of folklore horror into the realm of art, just as it leveled the aristocratic chivalric codes of protection and made them part of popular culture. The medium through which both traditions passed was the new mode of print transmission—first the broadside ballad and then the gothic novel. Most of the monsters we still know made at least cameo appearances first on the sheet, then in the printed page, and finally on the painted stage. Almost all of them—the vampire, the nameless hulk, the transformation beast (to become Dr. Jekyll and Mr. Hyde as well as Dorian Gray), and, to a lesser degree, the werewolf—were inducted here into the modern culture of the irrational.

What the novel did for horror monsters in the early nineteenth century, the movie did in the early twentieth: it provided a medium without equal. For if horror depends on occlusion, on not being able to know enough, then what makes the printed page and the flickering film so powerful is that the audience is always kept from complete knowledge, held in an almost hypnogogic state of suspended disbelief, in dreamland, in the dark. And so the theater, the medium for transporting the shivers from the time of Aeschylus to the heyday of the Jacobeans, simply collapsed. It turned into stage melodrama. Admittedly, it was helped by Puritan censorship but, even so, something is lost when you know the actor is carrying around a bladder of sheep's blood, or lurking under a sheet, or going through a trapdoor, or wiggling behind the arras unseen by the damsel but in full view for us. And if critics in the nineteenth century were still debating the mothy question of whether graphic horror is more frightening than suggested horror (a subject still debated by students of the film), they were missing the point. If you really want to experience the shock of, say, the blinding of Oedipus, it can be achieved with more effect in the novel or, better yet, on the film. Even

Gloucester in *King Lear* has to drop down out of sight to be blinded and immediately the play must go on. But see Dali and Buñuel's *An Andalusian Dog* and you will experience how shocking the act of lacerating the eye is when viewed with no cutting of film. The artist's imagination is stronger than our own: that's what makes him an artist and us an audience. Effective make-believe horror occurs when we can no longer trust our own senses to register reality, when we can no longer protect our own pressure points. And that is precisely what happens in the narrative complexities of the gothic and the visual illusions of the movie.

The English novels of Fielding, Richardson, and Sterne did not "degenerate" into the gothic of Radcliffe, Lewis, Mary Shelley, Hogg, or Maturin any more than did the "classic" cinema of Griffith, von Sternberg, or Ford become "corrupted" by Whale, Lewton, Hitchcock, and now Carpenter, De Palma, and Romero. It is in the nature of the medium that the novel and the movie became prime habitations for horror images, not in the fact that print or film were somehow corrupted by their presence. In fact, just the opposite is true: instead of decay, the production of horror has been one of the most important stimuli for innovation in both print and film. A case could even be made that both media were initially vehicles of horror: it is not by happenstance that when Defoe published his proto-novel "The Apparition of Mrs. Veal" in 1706 he chose what amounts to a horror story format, or that when Christian Huygens constructed his revolving magic lantern, one of his first spindles shows a drowsy man pursued by a monster. The early experiments of Georges Méliès were full of what is now known as *cinéfantastique*, a combination of horror and fantasy. The narrative demands of both linear print and unwinding film are very similar. The hidden control of speed and focus, the conscious excision of information, the manipulation of point of view, depth of field, characterization, the cross-cutting between "chapters," even the staging and the lighting, all are designed to destabilize the viewer and render him more susceptible not just to shock, but to profound confusion.

The gothic novel was really one of the most technically innovative of forms—think of the radical imagery of *The Castle of Otranto*, the symbolic characterization of *The Mysteries of Udolpho*, the intricate plotting of *The Monk*, the outrageous fantasy of *Vathek*, the decomposition of point of view in *Caleb Williams* and *Confessions of a Justified Sinner*, the virtuoso short-story form of Poe, the multiple points of view in *Dracula*, the china-box narrative of *Dr. Jekyll and Mr. Hyde*. Consider, too, that the horror film was the first to exploit expressionistic sets in films like *The Cabinet of Dr. Cali-*

gari, the Universal Dracula/Frankenstein/Wolfman series, and later the Corman films of the late 1950s. Think only of the subjective camera work in Mamoulian's *Dr. Jekyll and Mr. Hyde*, the optical printing in *King Kong*, the two-color process in *The Phantom of the Opera*, made yet more sophisticated in *Mystery of the Wax Museum*, the 3-D in *House of Wax*, and this is to overlook technical innovations in makeup, material developments in special effects (especially front and rear projection), and of course the old standby of horror films—the traveling matte. The list would still continue today: the Steadicam, Dolby-enhanced stereo, the Dykstraflex camera, Trumbull's "slit-scan" process, blue screens, all manner of computer-driven optical effects, latex prosthetics, and pneumatically operated transformations of body forms.[4] As long as horror art depends in part on jolting expectations, the novel and film will continue to consume innovation. For obvious reasons, the movie industry has been as hesitant to award the technical achievement of the horror film as the literary establishment has been slow to acknowledge the contributions of the gothic novel. High art is supposed to influence popular culture, not vice versa.

To see the context in which these innovations occurred as well as to have a sense of the modern rhythms of horror art in the last two hundred years, let me rather schematically reconstruct a literary and visual chronology of what has given us the shudders. This will be reductive and exclusionary, but I hope to show that the development of horror has been one of the most far-reaching and dynamic thrusts of Western imagination, and that, far from being idiosyncratic, it has characterized an important strain in the modern temper.

If I had to pick a specific text in art history where make-believe horror becomes modern, I would say it is in the engravings of William Hogarth. This is a statement worthy of Swift's Laputans, who wanted to graph the Music of the Spheres, but this date, or at least the mid-eighteenth century, is important if only because we usually think of Walpole's *Castle of Otranto* (1764) or better yet his Strawberry Hill estate, as the beginning of a new mise-en-scène associated with the gothic. If your taste runs to turrets, helmets, and other such grotesqueries, then Walpole's works are pivotal; but twenty years earlier Hogarth was giving form to what has really become the stock in trade of the modern horror: specific and highly located images of human perversion and transformation. His vision is still shocking where Walpole's is now only ludicrous.

Hogarth's scenes of urban exploitation and cruelty are uninformed by any aesthetic tradition, yet prescient of what is to come. Although he was ignorant of the continental painters of savagery, and it would be almost a decade before Burke could make a claim for "terror" on the basis of sublimity, Hogarth knew what his audience wanted to see. His mid-century prints may be satirical and topical in subject matter, but his vision was not; his serial engravings like *Marriage à la Mode* are almost documentary film strips recording the life cloaked behind Augustan good manners and genteel decorum. *Beer Street* and *Gin Lane* show the other side of town, the part "across the tracks" or, for us, the ghetto hidden by the skyscrapers. Here horrors can no longer be masked by powdered wigs; here we see the face of the barbaric; here degradation and degeneration are a way of life. If the city is the metaphor of modern experience, then the slum is where we play out the anxieties of our dream-life. Ezekiel may have observed that "the city is full of violence," but it was only halfway through the eighteenth century that the proverbial man-in-the-street knew how true it was.

As with all horror artists, Hogarth purposefully distorts images of the normal to exploit his middle-class audience's sensitivity. He knows the pressure points and doesn't just press them; he pinches them. Only the "graveyard poetry" of his contemporaries—Edward Young (*Night Thoughts*, 1742–43), Robert Blair (*The Grave*, 1743), James Hervey (*Meditations among the Tombs*, 1745–47), and Thomas Wharton (*The Pleasures of Melancholy*, 1747)—can compete with his imagery where the audience's response is so aggressively primed. In these poems we must confront bats on leathern wings, creeping shadows, weeping willows, occluded moons, vaulted arches; all described with the funereal drone of an "Il Penseroso" poet in an especially dour mood. Although Hogarth's imagery is equally contrived, the shock is more effective because his vision is so immediate. He wastes no space. He doesn't take us to the countryside, but into the claustrophobic space of the city—the slum as haunted house.

Although we may never have seen those foreground figures in *Gin Lane* before—that man battling the dog for a bone, that drunken, bare-breasted mother with syphilitic sores on her legs, that babe just thrown away, discarded, while the mother pinches snuff, that skeletal gin peddler with eyes rolled back and mouth agape, that other mother quieting her child with gin—we still recognize the scene as modern. It is a vision we will see again from Goya's Madrid to Crane's New York, from Dickens' London to Hugo's Paris. We are enclosed in the city; there is nowhere to hide; there are bad things hidden in this place; they are going to hurt us. Here we have the cave wall being readied for the urban setting that we see from German Weimar films to *Rosemary's Baby, Repulsion, Looking for Mr. Goodbar, Fanatic, It's Alive, Escape from New York*, and countless more.

What makes Hogarth's vision so shocking? Not the collection of derelicts

William Hogarth, *Gin Lane*, 1751 (British Museum)

nor the perversion of motherhood, but the look on that toppling baby's face—a look so central to horror—the look of complete helplessness. Why me? This is a character seldom seen in Sophocles or Shakespeare, but omnipresent in modern horror. That wide-eyed, open-mouthed look is on the face of every victim in every gothic novel and horror film. Of course the baby is naked. What makes the shower scene so shocking in *Psycho* is not just the virtuoso cutting, or the phallic knife plunging, or the blood streaming down the drain—it is also that we know poor Janet Leigh is all the time naked. From the age of five, we know exactly how vulnerable pants down, shirt up feels; stark nakedness makes stark fright.

A far more arresting, and certainly less explicable, sequence of modern horror can be seen in Hogarth's *The Four Stages of Cruelty*. I am especially interested because the images here "read" almost as a storyboard for modern horror film: low on narrative complexity and high on iconic manipulation. Hogarth certainly intended them to shock, and in a manuscript gloss (#49 in the British Museum) he mentions his radical "in Terrorem" technique that can affect "even the most strong heart." He wants to deliver the shivers to us—to unloose the Tingler.

This is the visual story: it is the Ur-text of downtown horror. In *The First Stage of Cruelty* we are introduced to Tom Nero, our nascent street monster, who will develop from urchinry to the psycho-killer we can still see in the "stalk-and-slash" genre like *Friday the 13th*, *Last House on the Left*, *When a Stranger Calls*, *Don't Go in the House*, *He Knows You're Alone*, *Silent Scream*, and so on. But before Tom has the opportunity to brutalize women, he has a chance to practice in the city streets.

Here he is attempting to stick an arrow up a dog's anus, aided by child-hood chums. Some of his cohorts are poking out the eyes of a bird or throwing a winged cat out of a window or hanging cats or playing "Throwing at

William Hogarth, *Gin Lane:* blow-up (British Museum)

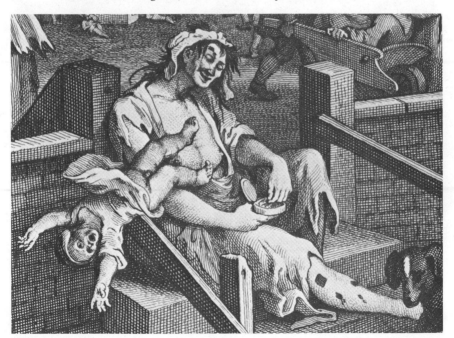

FIRST STAGE OF CRUELTY.

William Hogarth, *The First Stage of Cruelty*, 1751 (British Museum)

William Hogarth, *The Second Stage of Cruelty*, 1751 (British Museum)

Cocks," a game consisting (as far as I can learn) of heaving sticks at roosters. One especially nasty act is occurring in the lower right as a chum is tying a bone to a dog's tail, a tail soon to be torn off by other street dogs, yet ironically the dog is licking the hand of his tormentor. This is an image we will see again and again for the next two hundred years—an image embedded in horror art of the innocent conspirator. Meanwhile, Tom is doing nothing to repress his own bestiality—or is it his "humanness?"—because not only is he being abominable, he is also spurning the bribe proffered by the young gentleman in the frock coat. As we learn in the caption below the picture, Tom is being offered a candy, a tart, if he will just stop.

> Behold! a Youth of gentler Heart,
> To spare the Creature's pain
> O take, he cries—take all my Tart,
> But Tears and Tart are vain.

Tom won't stop, of course, and the young artist at Tom's left knows what the future holds in store. Before that future hanging is realized, however, Tom has an apprenticeship to serve.

In *The Second Stage*, the second reel, so to speak, we see Tom again beating an animal, this time a collapsed horse, and this act is duplicated by the peasant bludgeoning a sheep. The caption queries

> Inhuman Wretch! say whence proceeds
> This coward Cruelty?
> What Int'rest springs from barb'rous deeds?
> What Joy from Misery?

And, as in the horror art to follow in the nineteenth century, we are not going to be given an answer—at least not within this work. To do so would give the acts explanation and resolve our anxieties. Acts of such sadism simply *are*, and this is what makes them so uncontrollable. Horror monsters exist without explanation. Jack the Ripper, The Boston Strangler, and Charles Manson just are; likewise, the vampire, the Frankenstein monster, the werewolf, the zombie. It took a long time for artists of horror to learn what Hogarth knew so well. To explain, as did Mrs. Radcliffe, Horace Walpole, Sophia Lee, or Clara Reeve, is to dilute, to make horror into terror and terror into the predictable and the predictable into the reasonable. We know that Tom is getting worse, but we don't know why.

Once again, it is clear Tom is not alone. The pompous barristers who have overloaded the coach are implicated as much as the drowsing drayman who is just now running over the child playing with a hoop. Once again we encounter the requisite good man (noting the acts in his account book presumably to be reported) as impotent as the frock-coated young gentleman earlier with the candy. The good man is as important as the monster in the gothic scene, not as the victim, but as us—the helpless observer, the audience. This supernumerary on the horror stage does what we would probably do; he tries to stop the maniac, the psycho, the vampire, by reporting it to "the authorities." But in a sense, he too is trying to remove himself from the scene, to buy the monster off with words, to gain distance. The authorities will, of course, be far less fierce and concentrated than the fiend—they are, after all, salaried—and anyway, they would probably have to check first with their superiors. Monsters are usually destroyed by young men aided by a Professor Van Helsing character, or by an unruly mob, but rarely by a police lieutenant. In a sense, we see both the social drama and the psychodrama of horror here played out in front of us: how can the superego (the notetaker) succeed when the ego (the law, those barristers) refuses to confront the id-infested horror (Tom) that surrounds them. There is simply no resolution, at least not yet.

The Third Stage of Cruelty finally exhibits still more of the images resonant in horror art today. Here for the first time it is dark, and now for the first time the victim is no longer animal but human, and a very specific human—the young woman. This is the first female to appear in the masculine world of urban cruelty and she is not at all the passive colluder in violence as, say, the corpulent mother in *Gin Lane*. No, this poor innocent is the Jamie Lee Curtis of the eighteenth century, the schoolgirl victim of male aggression. The violence here is all-encompassing, and the plate is called *Cruelty in Perfection* for a reason. For not only has she been butchered at the neck (the very cut seems to cry out), she has also been sexually abused, or at least that is hinted at by her pregnant condition. Tom has used her first as sexual object and then as an accomplice in crime. For the letter addressed "To Tho. Nero at P . . ." reads

Dr Tommy
My Mistress has been the best of Women to me, and my Conscience flies in my face as often as I think of wrongdoing her, yet I am resolv'd to venture Body & Soul to do as you would have me so don't fail to meet me as you said you would. For I shall bring along with me all the things I can lay my hands on. So no more at present but I remain yours till Death.
                                                        Ann Gill.

William Hogarth, *Cruelty in Perfection*, 1751 (British Museum)

William Hogarth, *The Reward of Cruelty*, 1751 (British Museum)

She has served her purpose as vehicle for Tom's bestial and material lusts, and he has dispatched her. In doing so he has been caught—not by social design, but by forces beyond human control. The gloss reads:

> To lawless love when once betray'd
>   Soon Crime to Crime succeeds:
> At length beguil'd to Theft, the Maid
>   By her Beguiler bleeds.
>
> Yet learn, seducing Man! nor Night
>   With all its sable Cloud,
> Can screen the guilty Deed from Sight;
>   Foul Murder cries aloud.
>
> The gaping Wounds, and bloodstain'd Steel
>   Now shock his trembling Soul:
> But Oh! what Pangs his Breast must feel
>   When Death his Knell shall toll.

This penultimate scene is filled with archetypes of graveyard horror still alive and well in Hollywood: the tombstone inscribed "Here lieth the body," the bat "on leathern wing," the hooting owl, the startled watchman complete with lantern ("who goes there?"), the clock at the bewitching hour, the skull and crossbones, the crescent moon and skyful of swaggy clouds, the haunted house with escaping figure, the knife, pitchforks, the heavenly gaze of the man behind Tom ("Can such things happen in Our Town?"), and especially that mouthlike wound on the maiden's neck. Anyone who has seen Roger Corman's movies of the 1950s knows it well.

In the last plate we have a scene worthy not just of American International Pictures, but of some more crafty master like Terence Fisher at Hammer Studios. We find one freshly dead monster being dissected by another monster; the second made all the more horrible by virtue of his social and ethical position.[5] Instead of Vincent Price, it is now Peter Cushing. Tom is being coolly dissected by a team of worthy surgeons, his eyes gouged out, his feet slit, and his guts drawn out like a hose, to be fed—with poetic justice—to the very beast on whom Tom had himself worked such unspeakable acts back in Giles Parish. This is indeed *The Reward of Cruelty* and the gloss makes note:

> Behold the Villain's dire disgrace!
>   Not Death itself can end.

> He finds no peaceful Burial-Place;
>   His breathless Corpse, no friend.
>
> Torn from the Root, that Wicked Tongue,
>   Which daily swore and curst!
> Those Eyeballs, from their Sockets wrung,
>   That glow'd with lawless Lust!
>
> His Heart, expos'd to prying Eyes,
>   To Pity has no Claim:
> But, dreadful! from his Bones shall rise,
>   His Monument of Shame.

The gothic novel, as well as the pictorial arts, carried make-believe horror to the people, yet a purely mechanical invention, the printing press and stereotype, made both engraving and the novel so accessible. It was here, in the mid-eighteenth century, as the result of repeatable image-making, that modern horror art could have begun, and indeed did begin. One significant fact: there were sixty printing houses in London by the Restoration, seventy-five by 1724, and almost two hundred by 1757. These presses, especially the second-generation, steam-powered presses after the turn of the century, transformed the language of Grand Guignol into the vernacular. Cheap paper and new, quick-drying ink made the first mass audience for horror possible, just as, say, sprocketed film, the local theater, sound, and color projection allowed thousands of people access to another new medium of popular culture. This new low-brow, but literate, audience has always supported professional horror producers in style, as millionaires from G. W. M. Reynolds to Stephen King can attest.

The other impetus for modern horror art came from a most unlikely quarter, the aesthetic musings of Edmund Burke. If the printing press made the gothic novel possible, Burke made it respectable. Burke was the Susan Sontag of the eighteenth century. Not only did he know what he liked, he could explain why it should be liked—no mean trick for an aesthetician to praise the art of hoi polloi and get away with it. While Hogarth felt the need to explain his method in Latinate terms (his "in Terrorem" technique), Burke came right out and said it—the shivers are good for you. To do this Burke had to construct a new aesthetic category, the *sublime*, but he was not alone in doing this. He was unique, however, having no religious ax to grind: the sublime simply extended the territory of sensation beyond the beautiful and the picturesque into a state of excitement accessible, in part, through the experience of fright. Here is the *locus horrendus* from *Origin of Our Ideas of the Sublime and Beautiful* (1756):

Whatever is fitted in any sort to excite the ideas of pain, and danger, that is to say, whatever is in any sort terrible, or is conversant about terrible objects, or operates in a manner analogous to terror, is a source of the *sublime*; that is, it is productive of the strongest emotion which the mind is capable of feeling. (I.7)

.   .   .

The passion caused by the great and sublime in *nature*, when those causes operate most powerfully, is Astonishment; and astonishment is that state of the soul, in which all its motions are suspended, with some degree of horror. (II.1)

The sublime took on more than just religious connotation in romanticism, for here was a level of experience just below (*sub*) the transcendent (the *liminal*), yet above the normal and the natural, into which one could literally be shocked. Little wonder the gothic was soon assimilated by the intellectual as well as by the common reader. Wordsworth, Coleridge, Shelley, Byron, and Keats would all try their hand at producing that frisson, each with varying success. This much however is clear: the shudder was fast becoming as fashionable in literary circles as the tear had been a generation earlier. As a matter of fact, in the novels of the first third of the nineteenth century, you see the wholesale substitution of a Miss St. Aubert in sexual distress for a young Mr. Harley in the midst of a lachrymal attack. The story remains essentially the same (threats to the well-being of the young), but here was a new tuning fork for sensitivities and a new sensation.

I shall not catalog the hundreds of gothics produced during this first cycle of horror—that has been done often enough—but I will briefly mention a few of the image clusters and plot developments that still form the matrix of modern horror mythography. First there are ghosts, and although the early gothic is full of apparitions, most early forms of fright are firmly anchored (with the exception of Beckford's *Vathek*) in the reasonable world. They are in no way works of fantasy, although parts of them are often fantastic. Ghosts are too amorphous to be physically threatening and so they must be explained away. They shock us and attract us because they circumvent death, but after that what do they do? Clara Reeve dispatches them quickly; Ann Radcliffe has the grace to wait until the end. Ghosts will reappear later in the works of high Victorians, but as Jack Sullivan has argued in *Elegant Nightmares: The English Ghost Story from Le Fanu to Blackwood* (1978), their function is more antiquarian and spookish than gothic and horrible. Second, the images of the early gothics, from the bleeding statue to the creaking door, were already shopworn clichés by the turn of the century. The iconography had come from the Jacobean stage and more recently from German shudder-art and it was no longer, in itself, startling. In this sense the gothic was, and still is, mindlessly conservative; few chances are taken with delineation of scene or character. Third, the setting of these stories is almost always in the not-too-distant past and the characters almost always form a family—either literally or figuratively. In the archetypical story, a young lady plays the victim and, although there may be many males, an older, paternal male plays the victimizer. These characters are set in motion by a conflict that is usually sexual, probably tabooed, very often incestuous. This sexual transgression will often be expressed in terms of the violation of social convention. As I will show later, the enduring rituals of horror always revolve around a concussive family romance. And finally, the early gothics all share a major technical problem, one that still remains in horror art: they cannot be efficiently told; they cannot be properly framed. Especially at the end, they are narrative flops. As Coleridge said almost two centuries ago, horror stories are "fever dreams," and like nightmares they don't fit symmetrically. Structurally, they are unaesthetic, anti-artistic, preserving only the unities of the subconscious.

With the exception of Walpole's too silly and all too famous *Castle of Otranto*, the best of these novels in the first cycle of gothic fiction are Ann Radcliffe's *The Mysteries of Udolpho* (1794) and *The Italian* (1797) and Matthew Lewis' *The Monk* (1796). I should point out here something I will develop in the next chapter—purveyors of horror art are, like their audience, quite young: Radcliffe was thirty when *Udolpho* was published, Lewis was twenty when *The Monk* appeared. They were both joyously unaffected about transforming their dream visions into print. The coherence of their narratives need not concern us—they really did not concern either the reader or the author, although they certainly bothered the critics, as they still do today. Story lines are shallow and characterizations are flat; what is primary is the generation of "sublime" effect. This is accomplished almost entirely with images, with blue smoke, mazes, mirrors, and trapdoors. The image that was the most crucial, and still is, was the image of the active sexual molester. The old fustian fiends of Jacobean drama had finally dragged their clanking chains away and new, palpable antagonists were introduced. At last we have modern monsters, the great-grandfathers of the current stalkers.

In *Udolpho* this role is played by Montoni, in *The Italian* by Schedoni, and in *The Monk* by Ambrosio. The young lady, the virgin, is played by Emily, Ellena, and Antonia, all very passive, one-dimensional females, almost interchangeable. The older male carries most of the energy; the female carries most of the sensitivity. Seen from this point of view, these stories are almost fairy tales in which the older man, literally or figuratively, imprisons the young girl, abuses her, and is then eliminated. Sometimes he goes over a cliff or to jail, any device to get him out of the story line and save the damsel. Much has been made of the fact that Radcliffe explains, while Lewis accepts, the horrors of transgression. Who really cares? It is rather like arguing about the "proper" ending of "Little Red Riding Hood." What is important is that these are fables of adolescent identity in which the young are inducted into "the facts of life" through physical encounter. The old wolf tries to get the young girl into bed; if she is lucky her version includes the good woodsman. Although plots vary and dreck abounds, the focus is exactly where it will be for the next two hundred years—on scenes, often completely implied, of sexual violation.

The sexual assault usually takes place in a relatively confined social setting and, whereas later in the century the monster may travel from family to family, in the early gothics he usually stays at home. In fact, the early gothic usually tells the story of a single and specific family romance run amok: "father" has become monstrous to "daughter." It seems to make little difference if the father role is shunted to uncle, priest, duke, landlord, devil, as long as his relationship with the young female is one of paternal dominance. Nor does it seem to make much difference how he is introduced or dispatched as long as he can confront her and, in so doing, dislocate her already vulnerable sense of sexual identity. This often barely-disguised incestuous interaction forms the core of horror art which continues unabated to this day.

Although I will say much more about how this core will "heat" the great romantic horror stories—the vampire myths, the Frankenstein story, and even the Dr. Jekyll/Mr. Hyde archetype—I should reassert that the insistence on horror and its sublime effects was a major aspect not just of the novel but of romantic poetry as well. This is an aspect we have chosen not to anthologize; it still exists outside the official canon in academic limbo. We emphasize the lyrical and subjective aspects of romantic poetry, neglecting to note that the gothic was spreading into all genres. In part, our neglect of the gothic is the result of the last generation's virtual canonization of Wordsworth. Although influenced by the changing temper as seen in a work like *The Borderers*, Wordsworth had little use for its claptrap. For sublime effects, he went to the evangelical tradition of "natural" Christianity where he found a more acceptable symbol system to express the "sense sublime/Of something far more interfused," and I think it is because of Wordsworth's startling success that we have neglected the gothic tradition elsewhere in romantic poetry. Until very recently we have preferred Blake's symmetrical

Songs to his more gnarled works like *The Mental Traveller*, Coleridge's polite Conversation Poems to his more macabre works like *Limbo*,[6] Byron's travelogs and satires to his verse dramas like *Lara* or *Giaour*, Shelley's sonnets and odes to his more asymmetrical works like *The Revolt of Islam* or *The Triumph of Life* or, better yet, *The Cenci*. We all but neglect Keats' rude works like *Isabella* in favor of the high finish of the Great Odes.

Perceptions are changing and maybe someday the aggressive distortions and absolute horrors of Blake's *Prophetic Books* will seem more "romantic" to us than the relatively well-set contours of Wordsworth's *Prelude*. We haven't really appreciated the gothic in romantic poetry, not because the imagery is not there, but because we have looked elsewhere for other things more in keeping with our preconceptions. When this poetic intensity was directed toward prose, archetypes evolved that we recognize all too well and all too often today. We tend to limit our cultural legacy from romanticism to the noble savage, the divine child, the loyal dog, the reclusive poet, but far more important in terms of cultural impact is the imagery of potent monstrosity. Again and again we still find the demonic male set on the template of the hot-blooded, Mediterranean molester of Radcliffe and Lewis. In poetry, he becomes first Orc, then a host of Byronic heroes, Count Cenci and, at last back in the novel, the grand menace of Heathcliff, Count Dracula, Frankenstein's nameless creature, Wagner the Werewolf, Varney the Vampire, Doctor Moreau, Mr. Hyde, and their hooded brethren.

In the midst of these dynamic villains are scoundrels whom we have pretty much neglected like Melmoth in Maturin's *Melmoth the Wanderer* (1820) and Gil-Martin in James Hogg's *Confessions of a Justified Sinner* (1824). The novels that present these reprobates are admittedly lesser works in the romantic cycle of horror art and have suffered a fate rather like William Godwin's *Caleb Williams* (1794): often mentioned, seldom read. While they are important in the poeticization of the monster, in giving the fiend intensity, they are often insufferably dull and tedious. This dullness comes partly from self-conscious and ill-advised experimentations with gothic narrative. These novels are almost devoid of sexual violations, or even females to be violated. Hence there are no invasions of privacy, no transgressions of taboo, in short, no explosive conflict. Instead, the stories are wound around such themes as neurotic persecution, demonic pacts, revenge, and especially the disintegration of consciousness. In this respect they look forward to the claustrophobic works of Henry James, Dostoevsky, and Kafka as well as "intellectual" horror films like *Repulsion* in which compulsive narcissism animates the beasts in the subconscious jungle. *Melmoth, Confessions*, and

Caleb Williams proved too tame and too cumbersome to keep a popular audience spellbound, and too thin intellectually to keep academic critics interested. They are closer to ghost stories than to the mainline gothic and, like ghost stories, have had a way of degenerating into "elegant nightmares."

Still, the intensity of Falkland, Melmoth, and Gil-Martin had an effect on the development of horror art. These three maniacs were more interested in torture than in sex. This interest in sadism presages so much of what will transpire at the end of the century. It is almost as if Godwin, Maturin, and Hogg were trying to get only one aspect of the experience of horror in focus—the victim's fright at becoming unhinged—while forgetting to provide the apparatus for unhinging. Shivers become an end in themselves while the causality is neglected. In these works we are taken up the creaking stairs to the dark door, and then told to stay there with the protagonist while the author figures a way to get us downstairs again. So we stand there listening to our terrified compatriot, but not really feeling the shakes ourselves. The door never opens and so we wander away. In *The Literature of Terror*, David Punter has called these works "paranoiac texts," which correctly implies no real shocks in narrative and only short-lived identification with the male victim. Male maniacs do best with female victims, and since there is no implied or stated physical violation, no fears of sexual violation can threaten us. The only thing that changes is the protagonist's degree of persecution from manic to hebephrenic. No horror exists unless we have taken the victim to heart, and it is hard to sympathize with a quivering milquetoast. What we learn from these novels is that, without the damsel to put into sexual distress, the monster cannot be horrid and the novel as a vehicle for heebie-jeebies loses its concentration.

One can see the same loss of impact in the American gothic as it became absorbed by the dynamics of persecution, not violation. The dark worlds of Charles Brockden Brown or Nathaniel Hawthorne are intellectual worlds that cannot be breached by palpable monsters, only disturbed by projected ones: personified obsessions take the place of plasmic monstrosities. This is not to say that the "fear of going crazy," of losing control, cannot be genuinely terrible, but only that it will not last unless tied into some broader, mythic context. The worlds of *Edgar Huntly*, *Wieland*, *The House of the Seven Gables*, and *The Scarlet Letter* are simply too cerebral and contrived to frighten us for long, too erudite to disquiet. Things are explained away in terms of science, or history, or family, or even psychology, but they don't really need to be because we aren't really frightened, because we aren't really threatened. In fact, we might not be disturbed if the books had more pathetic, even tragic, endings. The villains are simply no threat to our well-being:

Chillingworth, Carwin, Ethan Brand, and the rest of this moody lot, are taciturn and dour, but not very daunting. They don't hunger for us. They are more concerned about themselves and about righting old wrongs than in violating damsels. These are great novels, but not (as they are often advertised) great horror novels. Many of the motifs are there, but not the method, and certainly not the monsters.

The great exception in American literature is Poe. Poe puts the monster back into the tale, fills him with libido, and turns him loose. In doing so, Poe saves horror prose from its arch-destroyers: the hack terror-jerkers on one hand, reckless in their exploitation, and the introspective intellectuals on the other, ruthless in their desire to understand and explain. Poe keeps all the subjectivity and all the mad powers of obsession carried in the literary tradition and adds, or rather reintroduces, the sexual violation. He does this so simply: Poe makes the teller of the tale into the invading monster. We now have the gothic story, not from the victim's point of view, but from the victimizer's. This switch in perspective more than anything else mandated a change in form that resulted in the development of a new genre well-suited to the gothic—the short story.

Surely this is a chicken-and-egg proposition—which came first: the first-person horror narrative or the short-story form? Both had been tried before, but not together. If you read Poe's *Philosophy of Composition* as a précis of horror stories, and his *Review of Hawthorne's "Twice-Told Tales"* as a survey of the field, you can see how perceptive Poe was about the aesthetics of fright. His insights have not been lost as such modern masters as Robert Bloch, Ray Bradbury, Jerzy Kosinski, Gabriel Garcia Marquez, Richard Matheson, Joyce Carol Oates, Peter Straub, and many, many others could testify. The horror movie, really the counterpart of the short story rather than of the novel, works on the same principles of enforced compression. In fact, Roger Corman almost made a whole career out of simply translating Poe's images to film. The reader of the short story has as little control as the audience in the theater: he can look away, get up and walk around, but not for long. The experience comes and goes fast; the movie lasts as long as the reading—the length of one sitting. We never have a chance to stop it and figure it out.

Poe knew that, although the exposition of detail can be long and the plot complex, the moment you get the reader up those stairs and over to that door of the forbidden room, you must let him see inside. The reader deserves this moment of what Stephen King calls "oogah-boogah." The shock must be provided or the reader will turn elsewhere. This shock is short-lived and cannot be stretched out or the effect will be lost. Poe also claimed that this concussion will be especially powerful if it involves the violation of beauty. Poe's favorite violatée, true to the conventional gothic, is thus young and female, not for misogynistic reasons (although these were probably there in Poe), but because "the death [the ultimate violation] of a beautiful woman is, unquestionably, the most poetical topic in the world." So here she is again, the damsel in distress. He did not say much about the perpetrator of horror, but it is clear in his stories that the victimizer, the monster, is always front and center so that we could see him if we wanted. He is not a projection: he is palpable, external, visceral. We often do not want to have to look far, because he is often very close to us—sometimes even telling us the story in the guise of the bereaved lover. In terms of modern horror, one of Poe's most lasting accomplishments is that he was able to get both the monster and the victim back into the story without sacrificing his reader's "suspension of disbelief."

In a later chapter I will discuss some of Poe's stories in more detail, but I think the lasting contribution of tales like *Ligeia, Berenice, Morella,* and even *The Fall of the House of Usher* is that here, at last, we are being given not the whole of the gothic novel but just the shocking part, not the unfolding but the enfolding, not the rising action but the climax. This is achieved so efficiently because Poe is not asking us to go over and stand by that forbidden door, he pushes us across the threshold in the first paragraph. The monster, the perpetrator of horror, is not around the corner; he is there beside us telling us the story, always in our confidence until . . . too late we turn and see him. It is the narrator of these stories who violates the women, Berenice, Ligeia, Morella (as well as possibly both Madeline and Roderick Usher). We are right there beside him all the time, being gulled by him until the story is over and we look down to see the knife, teeth, match, hatchet, or smoking pistol there in his hand.

One can see why Roger Corman was so attracted by Poe's imagery, if not his texts, for the motion picture can readily exploit this kind of febrility. We are the camera and it is us; it sees what we see; it turns, we turn. Just as the reader is synchronized with a first-person, nonintrospective narrator, so are we situated behind the lens. Poe's narrator always tells us that he can't tell us all (usually he can't remember for some drug-induced reason) and that is the same with the camera. We accept the limited view. The subjective camera that has been a hallmark of horror films since Mamoulian's *Dr. Jekyll* is still the most effective method of engaging us. In the last decade it has been almost shamefully overused. In the "stalk-and-slash" genre (*Dressed to Kill, Friday the 13th,* parts I and II, *New Year's Evil, I Spit on Your Grave, Terror Train, The Boogeyman,* to mention a few), the camera often shows us the violation scenes from the monster's point of view and naturally enough we find ourselves siding with him. We have slipped into his skin, almost werewolf style, and are doing his hideous and bestial deeds. We look down and see that the yak hair, long fingernails, and splattered blood are ours. The phallic knife is in our hands—both titillating and repulsive. It may be a cheap shock, but it still works just as it did for Poe.

Would that such narrative excitement had been assimilated into the novel (it was occasionally in Dickens and Collins especially as they experimented with the mystery genre), but for the most part the Victorian novel had other interests. The demands of melodrama, detection, historical fiction, bloody-pulp plotting, realism, fantasy, and, especially, social relevance—all these rest first on the stability of narrative point of view. Edward Bulwer-Lytton, G. P. R. James, William Harrison Ainsworth, and G. W. M. Reynolds were not interested in continuing the psychological thrillers of Hogg or Godwin, which would have required still more sophistication in narrative vantage point. They wanted to sell books that were easy to read. Clearly, what the audience, newly literate but socially confused, wanted was a continuation of "silver fork" fiction. So like Hollywood producers of sit-coms, genteel fiction is what so many mid-century novelists wrote. Class exploitation becomes the overriding mechanism of mid-Victorian violation, and the violator is now played by a morally effete and vapid capitalist. The laboring class is victimized via the soon-conventional motifs of the marketplace: mortgages, debtor prisons, and loophole legalisms like the statute of limitations or rights of domain. Horror is too intimate to be generated within the broad social context of the Victorian novel. While reading Dickens' *Edwin Drood*, a tantalizing novel in large part because it is unfinished, we tend to sit by and watch and gasp much as we do while watching the visual horror of some of the later Hammer productions like *Dracula Is Dead and Well and Living in London* (1973) or *Frankenstein and the Monster from Hell* (1973). There are moments of frantic action, lots of anonymous, upwardly mobile families being suppressed by a disdaining capitalist villain, and always the promise of a quick deus ex machina ending. This may make an interesting social exemplar, but not much in the way of shivers.

Such relevance was what the audience wanted a century ago and critics like Margaret Dalziel, *Popular Fiction 100 Years Ago* (1957), Avrom Fleishman, *The English Historical Novel: Walter Scott to Virginia Woolf* (1971), Q. D. Leavis, *Fiction and the Reading Public* (1968), and most recently Winifred Hughes, *The Maniac in the Cellar: Sensation Novels of the 1860s* (1980), have all agreed: here is the first upsurge of popular "taste" in the arts. It revolutionized the novel just as the coaxial cable promises to change the shape of television, because for the first time we have "variable reading," the precursor of "variable viewing." Never has so much fiction been produced in such profusion and of so little lasting value. This is largely because the new bourgeois audience with pennies in their pockets and a great curiosity could at last see themselves in print. "That's my town, my street, my house . . . me." This is, after all, the first time their story was told in print, and if they couldn't afford to buy the book at the railroad bookstore, they could borrow it from the lending libraries or a neighbor. Rather like primping teenagers, the young audience of the novel stood before the mirror of art, comb in hand, looking first this way, then that, rolling their eyes, mugging, then getting tired and moving on. There was plenty of reflective pulp to go around, plenty of channels, but little lasting horror art.

Thus the middle half of the nineteenth century was not a particularly eventful time in the spinning of horror fiction. Motifs from the first cycle of the gothic had either been jettisoned (ruined castle, fiendish monks, ghostly agents) or codified thanks to stage melodrama (bigamy, mistaken identity, inheritance plots, hulking idiots, violent crime—especially murder—and, of course, fiendish disguise). The stock allusions were so set in place that, by the time Dickens wrote *Little Dorrit* (1857), he could start working against the stereotypes by exaggerating them. Clearly the audience did not mind. One can see this even earlier in a work like *Oliver Twist* (1838) where Fagin is almost too purposefully the villain of the stage drama while Oliver is almost too much the "little orphan." No matter, Dickens understood the importance of violation, and if he exaggerated the extremes, it was only to make the confrontation more explosive. In retrospect, Dickens' great contribution to horror art is not that he could write great scenes of shock (who could forget Mrs. Boffin finding a house full of dead faces or Lizzie Hexham's intimation of her father's death in *Our Mutual Friend*), but that he really extended what had always been a donnée in the gothic: the more innocent the victim, the more shocking the assailant. No one has come close to creating victims like Dickens'. His Oliver, Little Nell, and her soul sister, Little Dorrit, are joined by the likes of Jo, Caddy, and Charley (*Bleak House*), Paul Dombey and sister Florence (*Dombey and Sons*), Jenny Wren and Lizzie Hexham (*Our Mutual Friend*), to live and die and live again, first in ink and now on celluloid.

Although Dickens could resuscitate the victims with virtuosity whenever he chose (as in *Bleak House*, where Esther's love does wonders), he could not save the "sensation" novel from triteness even if he had cared, because he was not willing to exaggerate the blackguard beyond the confines of Victo-

rian good taste. He was not willing to make him savage, facinorous, or barbaric. He wanted a scoundrel, yes, but not a monster. The only exception
may be John Jasper in *The Mystery of Edwin Drood*. Jasper is truly wicked
and sufficiently paranormal to invade the mind, but not body, of the heroine,
Rosa Budd. His telekinetic powers and his passion for evil do indeed presage
what is to come, and I suspect that had Dickens finished the novel it would
be one of the first modern masterpieces of horror art. Universal Studios finished it for him in 1935 by having Jasper kill Edwin (his surrogate son) in
order to possess Rosa (Edwin's intended bride). Ironically, Edwin and Rosa
had already canceled the wedding when they realized their relationship was
"like brother and sister." Jasper's incestuous design finally becomes apparent
when the mysterious Nevill Landless reveals the truth and wins Rosa's hand.
Dickens' Jasper is the exception. The more common purveyor of evil in the
Victorian novel, in the novels of, say, Wilkie Collins or Charles Reade, is
essentially a tame re-creation of Radcliffe's Montoni. Still human, he is still
a descendant of the master in the manor house, and he still works his willful
nastiness within a social context—be it family, town, or city.

What revived the Victorian gothic and made it once again an efficient vehicle for horror was that writers at the very end of the century were willing to
extend the limits of evil to the level of a John Jasper and beyond. The monster could come from the inside, as Mr. Hyde emerges from Dr. Jekyll, or
from the outside, as Dracula comes from faraway Transylvania. No matter
where he comes from, this much is certain—he cannot be controlled. His
powers transcend the human. If Dickens had shoved the victim to the limits
of innocence and vulnerability, then Wilde, Stevenson, Wells, and Stoker
pushed the perpetrator to the opposite extreme. This eidolon of evil simply
could not be stopped, and so it is here in the *fin-de-siècle* novel that we have
the second cresting of modern horror: *Dracula*, *Dr. Jekyll and Mr. Hyde*, *The
Island of Dr. Moreau*, and *The Picture of Dorian Gray*. Have there ever been
any other novels so neglected by academic critics, yet so enduringly popular?
They are rarely taught in classrooms, yet never out of print.

From the point of view of popular culture, the last twenty years of the
nineteenth century set the pattern for the next three generations of horror
art. We still mimic the forms, characters, and situations in both the novel
and the film; yet one should hasten to add that this period is still perceived
as the nadir of the "great tradition," a time of artistic decadence. Maybe it
is, but only because the "great tradition," rather like the "Augustan tradition" or the "chivalric tradition" before that, could not withstand the
changes in popular temper. Writers in the 1880s simply admitted what was

first implicit and then endemic in Victorianism: things were coming apart, and fast. The center—if ever there was such a thing—was simply not holding. Humpty Dumpty had fallen, or, in A. H. Whitehead's more polite, but no less biological metaphor—the "individual had become divided against himself."

As we witnessed with the initial rise of the gothic from the 1780s to the 1820s, and as we will see in the revival of this same spirit in the Hollywood movies of the 1930s and early 1940s, horror art seems to grow best in the soil of communal insecurity. If there is a real monster—a Hitler, for example—fantasy will migrate into less shocking forms. Just look at the World War II poster art and see the images of folklore horror made too real, and you can understand why Hollywood could not compete. Or, on the other hand, look at the illustrations in high Victorian novels or, better yet, the pre-Raphaelite paintings, and you see a pastoral world almost aggressively devoid of nastiness. In times of real stress or real complacency, the genres that seem to excite the popular imagination are melodrama or musical comedy, providing as they do both escape and social underpinnings. Such was not the case in the 1880s and 1890s, for here clearly the inside order was unraveling, but there was no real threat from the outside. Horror art was revived because, although in the long run it may drive for stasis, in the short run its emphasis is not on stability, but on rapid degeneration; not on greater coherence, but on insanity; not on health, but on neurosis; not on self-actualization, but on fragmentation.

It is almost as if the writers of the late Victorian era were trying to shed their respectability in return for some answers: How much could be peeled away from "the best that is known and thought in the world" to find out what man is really like? How many masks could be removed and still leave a recognizable human form? These *fin-de-siècle* monsters may well be syncretistic forms, combinations of the earlier gothic villains, but they have been animated by a whole new modern desire. Yes, they are still aristocrats on the surface, but just under the skin they are beasts driven by carnal lusts, and they will not be stopped by mere human defenses.

I suppose this end-of-century ferocity is influenced by the biological theories of Darwin as the libidinousness of their twentieth-century counterparts derives from the psychology of Freud. Late Victorian monsters emerge from the jungle just as modern monsters spring from the id. Dr. Jekyll, Dr. Moreau, Dorian Gray, and even Dracula bear the mark of the beast, the putrid, mephitic stench of the animal only slightly masked by gentlemen's perfume. Life near the Heart of Darkness smells of such sweat, and the hairy paw cannot be hidden for long under the manicured fingernails. Mr. Hyde is apelike; Dr. Moreau is a vivisector whose experiments deal specifically with beast/human transformations; Dorian Gray may be the smooth-faced innocent by day, but at night he is a predator, panther, reptile, snake; and Dracula has always the hairy palm, long talons, bat-cowl, and lupine habits. They are all *were*-animals. It is clear, in retrospect, that this atavistic imagery was as much the conscious acknowledgment of Darwinism as it was the unconscious extension of Victorian divisiveness. As literary critics like Jerome Buckley, *The Victorian Temper* (1951), Steven Marcus, *The Other Victorians* (1964), and Masao Miyoshi, *The Divided Self: A Perspective on the Literature of the Victorians* (1969), have amply illustrated, what seems a sudden profusion of doppelgänger motifs was actually the expression of both increased self-consciousness and the result of naturalism. These explanations are in no way mutually exclusive; in fact, quite the reverse is true. The look inside the self parallels the scientific look outside, the examination of the species: psychological ontogeny recapitulates social phylogeny.

However ontologically complicated these monstrous archetypes may have been, this much seems clear: whatever they expressed is something we are still very much interested in. We still must share their urge to "go native," to cross over the stream and re-enter the jungle, or at least we are still curious about what comes out of that "land beyond the forest," that figurative Transylvania. This may be because our own towns are becoming so metropolitan. And this returns us to the paradox articulated by Hogarth; while modern molesters are beasts, they are city folk as well. Dr. Jekyll is no country doctor, he is decidedly urban; Dr. Moreau is a model of gentility, having lived in London, who is isolated, true, but self-isolated on "Noble's Isle"; Dorian Gray is elegant and citified to the nth degree; and Dracula does not have a townhouse at 347 Piccadilly for nothing. These are men who know their way around town. They may well be the "fiend in the dark castle" or the "mad doctor on the deserted island," but their positions there are transitory. When they come to town, as each of them will sooner or later, we will not be able to recognize them. Even Dracula wears a straw hat and watches a cricket match unnoticed in London.

I will discuss these gentlemen/monsters in more detail later, for they only become complete when lifted from their relatively confined worlds in print and allowed to wander around on film. The popular imagination is continually finishing these stories, plugging loopholes, locating gaps, reiterating important characteristics, and, most important, introducing new players, especially victims. Each new audience tinkers with them, makes them personify different fears, propels them in assorted ways, like a child with a string toy, but they never get loose. Witness poor Dracula: in our century he has been sent from Transylvania into outer space, into corporate finance, into the antebellum South, into California encounter groups, and is still none the worse for wear. All these "decadent" monsters refuse to give up the ghost and are even now being transfused with new blood.

New monsters of this ilk are no longer being nurtured in ink and pulp. Although our century has been lush with images of make-believe horror, prose fiction has not been the vine; the real growth has occurred in film. Many will disagree, but I think what seeds have grown in the novel, especially in the short story, have not really flourished. There is a resurgence of the horror novel, as can be seen in any drugstore display of paperbacks. But the monsters created by authors like Peter Straub (*Ghost Story*), John Saul (*Comes the Blind Fury*), John Coyne (*The Piercing*), Catherine Breslin (*Unholy Child*), Gordon McGill (*The Final Conflict*), V. C. Andrews (*Flowers in the Attic*), and Stephen King (*The Shining, The Stand, The Dead Zone, Night Shift, Firestarter, Carrie, 'Salem's Lot, Cujo ...*) are not likely to endure. At best, they may become curiosities like the incredible shrinking man, or the invisible man, or the man with X-ray eyes—more at home with their brethren at E. C. Comics (Dr. Doom et al.) or Marvel (The Incredible Hulk et al.) than with a Frankenstein monster or a Dracula. I should mention, however, that the continuation of the American mythic kudzu germinated from Hawthorne and Poe and passed through the works of Ambrose Bierce and Robert Chambers, now seems to have expired in the compulsively macabre and uninteresting images of Lovecraft. On the other hand, we have the English tradition of heebie-jeebie art being subsumed by the mystery story, the thriller, the detective story, and especially the ghost story. Walter de la Mare, Arthur Conan Doyle, Algernon Blackwood, M. R. James, H. Rider Haggard, and now even William Peter Blatty and Ira Levin, have not revitalized the tradition of horror as much as they have exploited it. Traditional gothic imagery is now almost extraneous, like requisite gingerbread on the old Victorian home; there to attract the eye, not shiver the spine.

This is not to say that the imagery of horror is being debased in print; it is just being used, as it was a century ago, in the service of some "higher end." So here is William Burroughs (*Naked Lunch*) using it to describe drug addiction; Isak Dinesen (*Gothic Tales*) to explore female consciousness; John Hawkes (*The Cannibal*) to narrate; Nadine Gordimer (*Something Out There*) to criticize apartheid; Joyce Carol Oates (*Bellefleur*) to exaggerate character; Thomas Pynchon (*Gravity's Rainbow*) as a way to tell—or not tell—a story; even John Updike (*The Witches of Eastwick*) to send-up feminism. The list of simplifications could include such authors as Charles Williams, J. G. Ballard, Angela Carter, Shirley Jackson, and many more.[7] My concern is not to disparage; it's just that modern gothic fiction has become too complex to play the atmosphere, more specifically the *stimmung*, only to hear the squeals. Until very recently what had happened to horror imagery was rather like what happened when the "arthouse" movie caught up with the novel: the shudder images were used to serve the theme. Remember the playing children at the beginning of *The Wild Bunch*, the choreographed routines of violence in *Straw Dogs*, the surreal shudders of *Clockwork Orange*, the nightmare mise-en-scène at the end of *Apocalypse Now*, the shoot-'em-up scenes in *Scarface*, or the E.T. with teeth of *Gremlins*. These are shock sequences that have migrated into often totally different genres. This same appropriation of form without content also characterizes much in modern prose fiction.

Where we must go to find the innovations in modern horror is, of course, into the cinema, to what used to be called the "B movies." It is trite, but true, to say that as we sit in darkness we are returned to where horror began, into the world of dreams. Here at last shock image meets visual medium. We simply cannot control it. If the horror novel has tended to become either dimestore schlock or too intellectual and too convoluted to shock, then the low-budget horror movie has remained simple and direct, almost innocent by comparison. The horror novel and movie both still aim at the gut, but the former hits high while the latter aims below the belt, at Stephen King's "gross-me-out" level, and all too often succeeds.

The horror movie has never lost its punch (though it became complacent in the late 1940s and 1950s) for two straightforward reasons. First, it is produced by cost accountants who rarely underestimate the needs of the pubescent audience, and, second, it is assembled by directors who may not be great artists, but who always know their craft. When you look back at the various innovations in the horror film, you can see how these two forces have colluded. The same story gets made over and over again, and every time a minor change is successful it gets incorporated into the next rendition. To be derivative is to be successful. It has been said that of all movie genres the most predictably profitable—year in, year out—is the horror film, and the horror film has only about four different stories to tell. A few years ago this fact was celebrated with a message flashed at the beginning of *Student Bodies* (1981): "Last year, 26 horror films were released . . . none of them lost money." Such hubris . . . such truth. *Student Bodies*, misfiring a slice-'em-up, is now forgotten by all but its investors and their accountants.

Horror movies that don't hold up are in many ways as interesting as those that do. Let me explain by briefly alluding to some recent very popular films that I think will go the way of the "big bug" movies of the fifties, not because they are poorly made, but because the horror images are tied too closely with current fixations. The innovations did not stick even though the underlying myth was assuredly successful. In *Dracula A.D. 1972* the vampire is based on the then-current enigma of Howard Hughes; in *Frankenstein and the Mon-*

ster from Hell (1972), Doctor Frankenstein was Christiaan Barnard doing transplants; in *The Howling* (1981) the chief werewolf was a Dr. Get-in-Touch-with-Yourself from Esalen Institute; and in *Altered States* (1980), Dr. Jekyll was Timothy Leary. While these are all well-made movies and did quite well at the box office, they will, I think, be forgotten. Who still talks about my favorite film, *Black Friday*, because who now really cares any more about an English professor with a gangster's brain? Tell us something new, says the audience, but make sure it is tied into something important. As Andrew Tudor has contended in *Image and Influence: Studies in the Sociology of Film* (1974), the horror movie audience is unique in demanding such a high degree of relevance via very traditional iconography. No audience would make such demands of the Western, or the gangster movie, or the redneck road movie, but this is the case with the horror movie. If you try to make the imagery immediate, you run the risk of losing the next generation audience in a much more abrupt way than with other forms because objects of contemporary obsessions, especially political ones, have a half-life of about five years. This may explain why so many top-grossing "horror" films so soon run out of audience. Once in a while there will be a change that sticks, like Bela Lugosi's Transylvanian accent, or Universal's image of the Frankenstein monster, or the introduction of female victims into the Dr. Jekyll story, and the change will be so successful that all future retellings will treat it as a received part of the story. But such innovations are rare.

Recently, the drive for relevance and a "quick audience fix" has accelerated, thanks to the availability of cheap equipment and even cheaper scripts. Horror movies have been made the same way since the late sixties. Some small independent producer gets an idea (insect enlargements, telekinetic explosions, fetal monstrosities, drug aberrations, especially mutations made from careless nuclear-waste disposal), grafts it onto the old myths, makes a movie that is critically panned but somehow gathers a young audience, and is financially successful. Recent successes like *Eraserhead, The Texas Chainsaw Massacre, Friday the 13th, Night of the Living Dead, The Brood, Dementia–13, Halloween, Martin,* and *Rabid* are all renditions of the basic vampire, Frankenstein, or werewolf/Dr. Jekyll stories in which certain images are purposely distorted. Once the big studios like Twentieth Century Fox, Avco Embassy, EMI, and Paramount see the success of the upstart producer, they start producing mimics. Of course, this is not only the pattern for horror films but for all genres, and it results not so much from a dearth of creative activity at the large studios as it does from the expense and long lead time necessary "to put a product on line." Contemporary horror films are especially susceptible and may pay the price of super-quick obsolescence. The big studio also runs the risk of finding a hostile audience already in place as Tri-Star Pictures (Columbia, HBO, CBS) recently learned when they released *Silent Night, Deadly Night* (1984). After the now-standard television ad blitz, they were forced to "pull the picture" because of parental objections to yet another ax-murderer, this one posing as Santa Claus.

The other impetus for rapid change comes from technical developments within the medium itself. This is where the horror movie has outdistanced prose fiction, simply because print is still produced in lines, line under line. Horror films are so dependent on visual shock that any technical innovation that can unsettle visual expectations will greatly magnify our response. Until the forties the horror film was technically the most innovative, and it is fast returning to that status thanks to computer-driven optics and all manner of special effects, of which the most effective is the pneumatically operated mask. The only analogy for the excitement of watching heads spin 360 degrees, or explode into smithereens, or burst out into wolf faces, is to think how exciting it was to first see blood in technicolor in the 1940s, or prehistoric monsters battle in the 1930s, or birds landing on faces in the 1950s. The first few times we see such things it is a jolt, and such jolts are usually involved in horror films. The only other film genres that have been so technically innovative are biblical epics and science fiction, but these have been far more cyclical and, if I dare say so, ephemeral.

In retrospect, the most profound innovation was not technical but theatrical; it was the matinee. As Universal started to release its horror films to the Saturday afternoon crowd, it located what was to prove its most eager and dependable audience. In the films of the late thirties, one can almost see producer and consumer search for common ground as the sequels were tried out. In the first generation of films, gothic novels were adapted by adults to be shown to adults; next the monsters were separated from the text, then introduced to each other, then allowed to reproduce sons, until finally, by the late 1940s, the monsters found their milieu: they were paired with cultural equals—Abbott and Costello. These movies, *Abbott and Costello Meet . . .* , the last of the Universal cycle, were made by hacks to be shown *only* to kids. For a few years, Bud and Lou, the "boys," temporarily became bit players in the mythic sequences, chased by Dracula, the Frankenstein monster, Wolfman, the mad doctor, and the Mummy. No innovations followed because the process of vulgarization had stopped; there was no other more immature audience eager to "have a look." Thanks to the matinee, teenagers had "captured" the myths. Bud and Lou were soon excised, and the monsters frozen in their slightly exaggerated Universal forms in which they remain unto this day.

What cycles there have been in the transmission of cinematic horror roughly parallel the rhythms of the gothic novel, but while the initial icon-

Lou and Bud meet Dracula and the Frankenstein monster in *Abbott and Costello Meet Frankenstein*, 1948 (Universal Studios)

ography is Germanic, the development of imagery is not. If Bürger, Goethe, Naubert, Grosse, and the *Schauerroman* tradition set the temper for the first cycle of the English gothic novel, then Meyer, Reinhart, Wegener, Lang, and the Weimar cinema set the scene, quite literally, for the American horror film. The first great American horror films were more influenced by Teutonic silent horrors than by the English gothic tradition, simply because there were so many Middle Europeans in Hollywood during the 1930s. The early Universal films are almost formulaic recapitulations of the German films of a decade earlier—so full of enclosed space (often misnomered "expressionistic"), so full of light, shade, and mist, so textured and controlled with the angled camera, often giving a sense of perpetual disequilibrium. If you had to look at still photographs of, say, a scene set by Paul Wegener in the 1920s or one constructed by James Whale in the 1930s, you might be hard-pressed to tell which was which. It is impossible, for instance, to look at even a late film like *Son of Frankenstein* (1939) and not see the "psychological sets" of *Caligari* (1919). Yet it is relatively easy to distinguish the stock images of Universal from those of the RKO films of Val Lewton or the Warner films of Michael Curtiz. While the narrative subject matter and characterization are really quite similar, the visual vocabulary can be radically different.

Until recently, even though horror pictures had simple and repetitive themes, each successful studio tended to express its horror themes in the same visual language. They couldn't help it; they had the same technical and production staff, let alone the same props, stars, camera tracks, and sets. Universal first shot its scenes inside against flat backdrops of castle walls, laboratory walls, and haunted house walls; RKO went outdoors, but never far from the studio; Hammer shot everything in two studios and on a few sets outside London with no technical virtuosity other than pointing the camera first at the teeth and then the breast; AIP was more resourceful, but equally prescriptive—fog, staircases, cellars, graveyards, more fog, always more fog—usually in some other studio's backlot. With the rise of the director in the 1960s, it was the "look" not of the studio but of first Alfred Hitchcock, Terence Fisher, or Roger Corman, and more recently Tobe Hooper, George Romero, John Carpenter, Brian De Palma, or David Cronenberg, that gives a distinct visual lexicon to the slow-changing texts of horror.

Although I am going to confine myself to the cycles of Anglo-American filmic horrors, it should be noted that equally abrupt distinctions apply to other nations as well.[8] What characterizes the Anglo-American horror films, however, is that they have always been the most influential, exporting the imagery of Western shudders to the world. The first great unfolding of horror art in the American cinema occurred at Universal Studios in the 1930s under the aegis of the Laemmles, innovative father and consolidating son. From the start they simultaneously made complete English and Spanish versions, just as Hammer later made English, Spanish, and Japanese versions of the same film. Universal's "look" was German, the "stories" were English, and the actors were a combination—except for the women: they were usually red-blooded American girls, noteworthy mainly for their lung capacity. The early English directors (Tod Browning and James Whale) were essentially theater men working from stage plays and thus really not able to let the film scenes evolve; instead, they staged them to move mechanically. I think these directors, especially Browning, have been a little overpraised, in part because of the wash of auteur criticism, but I must admit that as directors of actors, they were unequalled: Bela Lugosi may have trouble acting any part other than Dracula, but in that part he is still the template; Lon Chaney, Jr., remains unexpectedly magnetic, even though critics usually praise him more for being able to sit up all night to be made-up than to act; and Boris Karloff had the unique genius for appearing both helpless and menacing. Without these three actors the iconography of modern horror would be profoundly different, and all three of them were first cast and coached by Universal directors.

If Universal was lucky with the monster actors, it was hard work that produced the visual context. The story itself was never enough; in fact, like us the audiences of the thirties already knew enough of the plot to feel somewhat protected—what they didn't recognize was the new configuration of forms. The Universal directors wisely let the story falter, almost too much in *Dracula*, in order to build the scene. And these scenes were so well done they now live independently of the films: the foyer in Dracula's castle, Frankenstein's laboratory, the monster's forehead and neck bolt, the vampire's horizontally lit eyes, the Wolfman's face, all have an iconic life of their own. These images created by the unacknowledged geniuses of Universal, Kenneth Strickfaden and Jack Pierce, have had a profound influence on our sensitivity to horror. They quite simply set the mold that has yet to be broken.

If Whale and Browning were the Horace Walpoles of American horror film (important, but overrated), then Michael Curtiz and Victor Halperin were the Ann Radcliffe and Matthew Lewis. Curtiz's underrated horror films of the thirties, *The Mad Genius* (1931), *Dr. X* (1932), *Mysteries of the Wax Museum* (1937), *The Walking Dead* (1936), as well as Halperin's *White Zombie* (1932), are really "knock-offs," and very good ones, of the Universal scenario. Here is the narrative borrowed from Universal: young boy, young girl, and old monster who chases young girl until young boy, helped by older man, destroys monster and gets young girl back. These movies have not lasted in the popular imagination in large part because the studios were not able to create any coherent language of images like Universal's, and hence had to rely on story and character. Stories don't carry horror; images do. And if you want to see this, look at the Universal horrors of the 1940s when the Laemmles were long gone and Jack Gross was in control. Budgets were tight and Universal employed a host of no-name actors (or worse yet, big-name, bad actors), but they kept the same mise-en-scène. They were still successful. All those *Abbott and Costello Meet . . . (Frankenstein, The Invisible Man, The Mummy,* and so on), in addition to the lesser *Son of . . .* and *Ghost of . . .* and *The Mummy's . . . (Curse, Ghost, Tomb,* et al.), continually played off images as trite as those in the early gothic novel. Critics may turn away in disgust from what Universal did in the forties, but the audience stayed and is still there every Friday night now watching the same clichés on television.

In a sense, what Val Lewton did in the RKO horrors of the 1940s was analogous to what happened with the second generation of gothic novelists. Like Godwin, Hogg, Brown, and even Hawthorne, Lewton dropped the image of external horror and replaced it with the projective fantasies of the protagonist. Lewton had had enough of Jack Gross' redundancies (he was reputed to have said that all Gross knew of horror was "a werewolf chasing a girl in a nightgown up a tree"), but he, too, had to struggle against the Universal text, the anxiety of influence. Lewton's resolution was to "get inside" the character, and most of his films seem dated now because of the rather too pat application of depth psychology. Monsters from the id appeal more to Freudians than to schoolkids. Only his *The Seventh Victim*, in which he was left alone to picture alienation and neurosis rather than portray devil worshipers as he was supposed to, packs a charge. When you look at the imagery of his more highly touted *I Walked with a Zombie* or *The Cat People*, what do you see? You see scenes right out of the Universal catalog: the castle scene in *Zombie* is Dracula's castle; the room scenes in *Cat People* are from *The Old Dark House*; and so forth.

All in all, the movies of the thirties and forties are best characterized by what Universal did first—the visualizing, without irony, of the images of childhood horror. All the scenes and characters—haunted houses, deformed hunchbacks, underground phantoms, werewolves, scarfaces, mad doctors, flour-white zombies, miniature freaks and overgrown apes, vampires and monsters-with-no-name—are still with us. They were first cast from the stuff of dreams into novels, and then from prose back into dream images on film. They are still settled there without the intrusive rearrangement of the grown-up intellect or the rigors of logic. They cannot, and will not, and probably must not be understood by the consuming audience. The enduring motifs are all profoundly paradoxical: Why does Dracula choose these specific victims, and why hasn't he overpopulated the world with vampires; why is the Frankenstein monster so big when all the parts come from regular-sized people; why do zombies not run into trees, yet march over cliffs like lemmings; why is there such a big door in King Kong's fence if he is not supposed to get out; why doesn't the werewolf sleep hidden from the full moon; why does the mummy always end up in the swamp, yet reappear in the sealed tomb? These early horror movies never mocked or reveled in their childishness, but instead, as James Agee said of *Curse of the Cat People*, they treated horror "poetically."

Would that this were so with the horror films of the late forties and fifties, but World War II pretty much ruined horror art with the real thing. In the last thirty years we see the same diffusion in the horror genre that earlier characterized the gothic novel from the late 1840s to the 1870s—a wholesale exploitation of imagery not in the service of innovation, but of titillation. Horror movies become thrillers in much the same way that gothic novels become shockers. True, there were many fine films within the various subsets: science fiction horror (*X, The Man with the X-Ray Eyes, The Fly*), outer space horror (*It Came from Outer Space, The Thing*), up-from-below horror (*Creature from the Black Lagoon, The Creature Walks among Us*), horror of neurotic women (*Whatever Happened to Baby Jane; Hush, Hush, Sweet Charlotte*), neurotic men (*Psycho, Peeping Tom*), and neurotic children (*The Bad Seed*), horrors of possession from without (*Invasion of the Body Snatchers, Night of the Living Dead*) and later from within (*The Exorcist, Rose-*

mary's Baby), natural horrors from big and little bugs (*Tarantula, The Swarm*), as well as actual cataclysms, usually more boring than horrible (*Earthquake, Tidal Wave*). However, these films offered few new complexities. One exception can be found among these desultory horrors and it developed into a new horror vehicle— the demonic child, the kiddie monster. In fact, until the mid-seventies, makers of horror films seemed content to wear the audience down by attrition. Rather like the literary generation of Edward Bulwer-Lytton, G. P. R. James, William Harrison Ainsworth, and G. M. W. Reynolds, movie producers followed the money, and when it dried up, they turned elsewhere.

In the late fifties Hammer Studios in London almost intuitively understood the lack of cohesion in horror imagery and attempted to return to the source—not the Universal horrors, but the literary texts of the romantics. Photographed in living color, especially red, and with plenty of plump cleavage, Hammer remade their Draculas and Frankensteins with one eye on the novels and the other on the pubescent audience. They were constrained, thanks to Universal's legal staff, which had wisely patented all the stock images, to create their own vernacular of forms, and they succeeded beyond their wildest dreams. Whereas Universal's black-and-white photography forced them to deal with the land of shadows, Hammer's brilliant color led them into the world of gore. Along the way, Hammer Studios developed their own Lugosi and Karloff in the personages of Christopher Lee and Peter Cushing, who still are wildly successful at box offices around the world. Hammer never could make a Frankenstein monster worthy of note, but their Faustian Dr. Frankenstein and libidinous Dracula can still make you tingle. Alas, in the mid–1970s Hammer proceeded to do what Universal had done— they wore out the imagery until only parody was left. What Mel Brooks' *Young Frankenstein* is to Universal, Jim Sharman's *The Rocky Horror Picture Show* is to Hammer. Even Woody Allen takes potshots in *Everything You Always Wanted to Know about Sex* when in one scene a gigantic breast, made by an explosion in the lab, attacks a young couple. (Things end happily, however, for the breast is captured in a brassiere.) Still, before Hammer was through, they had remade not just Frankenstein and Dracula but the whole entourage: zombie, phantom, mummy, werewolf, and brute in their own colorful and dim-witted way. The "House of Hammer" then collapsed as had "The Horror Factory" at Universal, as had "silver-fork fiction" and the "Newgate novel," not from desuetude, but exhaustion. The audience was tired of Hammer's formula.

There was other pabulum around. Jack Arnold was making some silly but successful films, and Roger Corman was doing something rather similar, except with more panache and certainly with more self-irony. Corman was returning to the sacred texts of American gothic—the works of Poe. He, too, knew what his ripe audience wanted to see: innocents in distress and young men to the rescue. He, also, found an older male actor—Vincent Price—around whom he could play out the violation motifs. Just as Hammer's Michael Carreas and Terence Fisher did not realize the power still left in the old gothic until *The Curse of Frankenstein* (1957) and *Dracula* (1958; *Horror of Dracula* in the United States), so too did Corman and the AIP front office never intend to spend so much time and money on what finally evolved into a whole cycle of Poe films. Once Corman started he was unstoppable until he ran out of not stories, but audience. His late Poe films of the mid-sixties did find an audience. From *The Fall of the House of Usher* (1960) through *The Pit and the Pendulum* (1961), *Premature Burial* (1960), and *The Raven* (1963), until finally *The Masque of the Red Death* (1964) and *The Tomb of Ligeia* (1964), Corman used the verbal text more for titles than for story line. The stories, often by writers of stature like Richard Matheson, were thin but amazingly lively. They were primarily narrative vehicles for the transmission of *stimmung*: a background of tombs, blood, skeletons, cobwebs, cellar dungeons, castles, rats, shadows, more blood, broken-off limbs, and a foreground of innocent nubiles with quivering breasts pursued by an always lugubrious Vincent Price. Corman's methods may have been slapdash (his *The Little Shop of Horrors* holds the record for the shortest shooting schedule for a full-length commercial feature film—two days), but he realized the importance of repeated shocks and made a number of anthology films (Corman calls them "fragments") in which independent short stories are subsumed in a collection. What was obvious in *Tales of Terror* (1962) was usually inherent in all his Poe films—the implanting of nonreferential subplots that take us outside the framing story for a good shock and then return us to the formal narrative. The short-story cycle had been used earlier in English films produced by Hammer, and after Corman, companies like Amicus produced many more. For a while this was a popular device simply because it made Poe's strictures about the effect of climax possible in film, but even this was not enough to resuscitate a bored audience in the late sixties. These framed stories proved so predictable, so mechanical, that they were no longer commercially successful, and by the early seventies they were abandoned to television where they now fill the spaces between commercials. However, the concept still works as George Romero's *Creepshow* (1982) recently showed by both its profit statement and the threat of a sequel.

Where Hammer and Corman moved backward to reread the lines of the gothic text to find imagery and story, others went inward, aided by the mythos of Freudian depth psychology, or else outward, informed by whatever national paranoia was lurking in the Sunday supplements. The psycho-horror had its early imagistic budding in the Lewton films at RKO as well as the *films noirs* of the forties, which flowered in Clouzot's *Diabolique* (1955) and then really blossomed in the "classic," Hitchcock's *Psycho* (1960). I am not really interested in these films because when they are good (*Hush, Hush, Sweet Charlotte, Whatever Happened to Baby Jane, Picture Mommy Dead, Play Misty for Me, Repulsion, Peeping Tom*) or when they are bad (*Mania, Twisted Nerve, Shock Treatment, Scream and Scream Again*), they are still concerned more in deranged personality than horror. They always drive away the images of disorder and violence (knife, ax, haunted house, stairway, basement, attic) to get at some rational explanation. Once that explanation is proffered, the story, which has depended on continually effacing our sense of security, ends abruptly. When we catch sight of the psychiatrist coming out of the insane asylum to explain what we've seen, we know the jig is up; we're off the hook. It has been this way since *Caligari*, and I think these endings are as unsatisfying to the nonanalytical horror fan today as the "Gee, I was only dreaming" motif was a generation ago. The open-ended story that attempts no resolution, like Roman Polanski's *Rosemary's Baby*, rightly becomes a favorite of contemporary directors like Peter Bogdanovich (*Targets*), John Carpenter (*Halloween*), Tobe Hooper (*Texas Chainsaw Massacre*), and David Cronenberg (*Rabid*), for these movies retain their frisson well past the safety of the house lights and signal what I hope to show in the last chapter is a new direction in modern shudder-art.

Along with psycho-horrors, the other thematic development of the last twenty years has to do with the literal invasion of our personal space by something or someone from far away. The sense of violation is almost always embedded in horror, but in this subset of the sixties and seventies, the intrusion is very often nonsexual, even in a metaphorical sense. The intruder is intelligent, but fundamentally nonhuman. Starting in the late forties and continuing for the next twenty years, we looked either up above the clouds or down below the seas to find intruding monsters. When the creature came to us from above as it did in *The Thing* or *The Blob* or *It Came from Outer Space*, the menace was simply too amorphous to be taken seriously. When it came from below (*The Creature from the Black Lagoon, The Beast from 20,000 Fathoms*) it was sufficiently anthropocentric to be recognized, but too fishy to be embraced, let alone violated by. How do you kiss a Martian or hug the gill-man covered with fish scales? The possibility of attack was intact and maybe frightening, but there was no real possibility of actual invasion even in the most forgiving of imaginations. King Kong got away with it, made us believe Fay Wray really was in trouble, in part because we knew he was really of this world. But we knew Julie Adams or Lori Nelson were safe all along because that fish-man really never existed. Although it is ludicrous to think that King Kong (so big) has sexual designs on Fay (so small) as he is fondling her there in his hairy paw, that is precisely what he has in mind. There is something believable in his form—something that I think can still horrify, as we see in all the *Planet of the Apes* movies. Alas, the implosive sexuality that was dormant in these ape-forms ironically returned in such ludicrous images as, of all things, a shark. In *Jaws I, II,* and *III* we have the threat from below, all right, but we can never really believe it is sexually motivated—its visage still too fishy. Sexual violation was so wildly metaphorical, so ludicrous, that without knowing the sexual infidelities of the first victim, without hearing the pulsating music, and without seeing the poster art (huge phallic shark coming from below to menace belly-down pubescent), we might well have missed it. I don't think this kind of scare can endure: it is either too political and fast-acting, or it is too intellectual and desultory. Although there are important exceptions, these films have already become more "dated" than the efforts of Hammer and Corman.

The only frontiers left, aside from below the earth and above the clouds, were either outside in nature or inside our bodies. I'll discuss the horror of bodily possession ("It came from within" as a modern horror) in the last chapter, but I should mention the natural horrors that were so prevalent in the environmentally conscious sixties and seventies. For more than two decades we were assaulted by bats, bees, snakes, plants, ants, spiders, killer tomatoes, and killer shrews. Once again it was a Hitchcock movie, *The Birds*, that set the pattern and provided the initial audience, but, unlike *Psycho*, the proto-story underwent dramatic revisions. *The Birds* is a movie of considerable horror, in part because it deals with an image usually devoid of aggression and makes it intrusive—not just by having it attack humans, but by having the attacks so unpredictable and fierce. The cinematic descendants of *The Birds* have been more concerned with explaining the act of violation than in exploiting it. Admittedly, such explanation was a part of *The Birds*—Tippi Hedren's callous behavior in the pet store—but still the consequences seemed wildly excessive. Good horror films are never predictable; they always violate expectation. Not so in movies like *The Deadly Bees* (1967), *Willard* (1971), *The Hellstrom Chronicle* (1971), *Ben* (1972), *Frogs* (1972), *The Swarm* (1977), *Piranha* (1978), all the way to current forgettables like *Blood Beach* (1981), *Alligator* (1981), *Snails* (1981), *Of Unknown Origin* (1983), and *C.H.U.D.* (1984), where what horror there is is sacrificed for terror.

In retrospect, we can see how much in popular culture has been dedicated to the construction and transportation of horror sequences. For whatever we may have gained by moving out of the cave and into the high-rise apartment, we have never lost our desire to look at these vibrant images. We continue to pass before them in awe because there is something still resonant in the iconography of horror, something not yet understood or categorized. But exactly what is it that makes us, especially for a time in our adolescence, not just susceptible to, but aggressively search for, specific image clusters and scenarios? It is one thing to point out the prolixity of horror imagery and note developments in presentation; it is quite another to explain why we should want to witness it at all. To paraphrase Walt Whitman's line that "great poets must have great readers," horror sequences must have an eager audience. And so, before I attempt to anatomize the most famous modern horror myths, I should like to explain specifically who the prime audience of artificial horror is, has been, and will continue to be.

2

The Psychological Attraction of Horror

What myths are to the race, dreams are to the individual, for in dreams, as in myths, there also appear those primitive emotions and feelings in the form of giants, heroes, dragons, serpents, and blood sucking vampires; representations of guilt, retribution, and fate; of lust and power; of monsters of the deep (the unconscious) and of unknown but overwhelming beings which fill our nights with nighmarish dreams and make us fear our sleep, but which, rightly used, can be fruitfully integrated into our personality.

J. A. Hadfield, *Dreams and Nightmares* (1954)

The attraction of horror can be understood in essentially three ways: (1) as counterphobia or the satisfaction of overcoming objects of fear; (2) as "the return of the repressed" or the compulsive projection of objects of sublimated desire; and (3) as part of a more complicated rite of passage from onanism to reproductive sexuality. However, as Byron said of Coleridge's murky metaphysics: the problem seems simple; it's these "explanations" that need a little explaining. So let me restate them in their popular shorthand. First, horror is like a roller coaster, pleasurable because it lets you be frightened without being hurt; second, horror "pulls the pop-top" off repressed urges to let them escape via the fizz of fantasy; and third, the horror art plays out the "do's" and "don't's" of adolescent sexuality explaining to the soon-to-be-reproductive audience exactly how to avoid making horrible mistakes—namely monsters. I find the last of these explanations the most interesting and I hope to show how it accounts for the ultra-conservative nature of horror myths as well as the remarkable lack of critical understanding on the part of both audience and storyteller. People who enjoy creating and consuming images of horror always claim they do it primarily "for the scares," but I think it's like the athlete who claims he competes just "for the exercise." Below the surface game of scares played around the archetypical campfire of Western culture, another match is being waged with the utmost seriousness. The game is played for nothing less than the social stability of the culture, but to see that game, let alone later to participate in it, the campers must pay a price, and that price is to be scared, sometimes shocked. The audience will return again and again to see the game (as well as variations of it) as it is played out in comics, on television, at the movies, or even in print, because they intuitively realize that their turn is soon to come. Then, inexplicably but predictably, they learn all the rules and take to the field, making way for a new audience. If you think back, you will probably recall with amazing clarity the first instance when you were shocked by horror images and then, after a few years, you ceased to be frightened and turned to other sights, other myths. Essentially, horror has little to do with fright; it has more to do with laying down the rules of socialization and extrapolating a hidden code of sexual behavior. Once we learn these rules, as we do in adolescence, horror dissipates. Lest this sound too grand, let me go all the way back to the first analysis, to the only thing we can scientifically observe, the primary audience for horror art.

Of all the various art forms, horror art has the most defined and most predictable audience. Whereas we all enjoy the comic, the epic, the pastoral, the detective, or even the tragic, and enjoy them throughout our lives, the audience for the horrific is both restricted and short-lived. Although the images often embedded in horror art are the same as those in the fairy tale—the damsel in distress, the beast, the wicked stepmother, the wise guardian, animals that act like men, men that act like animals—their manipulation in the horror scenario is uniquely appropriate for only one audience. While the characters who populate horror myths may be from Fairyland, their interests are startlingly new: they are concerned with sex and reproduction. I don't believe there is a horror myth in the West that is not entangled with the theme of procreation.[1] Tales of terror may go elsewhere, but not horror. Dracula wants those brides, Dr. Frankenstein wants to create life, and even the polite gentleman who just "wants to be left alone" has the werewolf/Mr. Hyde within him that, once released, must attack precisely those women he is supposed to care for. Like the fairy tale, the horror saga is remarkably rigid in prescribing behavior for its archetypes, but, unlike the fairy tale, the audience pays attention to them for only a few years and then seems to forget all about them. Once we stop listening to fairy tales we have to start telling them to our children and grandchildren, but when was the last time you thought about the vampire, Frankenstein monster, or werewolf? Are you still interested in stories about them? Do you want to read about them or tell your children about them? I would guess not. Like me you may be interested in learning about them, but not *in* them.

But you were; in fact, there was a time in your life when you were probably fascinated by them. It may be a little shameful to admit, but you still carry a vestige of that interest around in your memories about them. You have that knowledge because at one time the interest must have been important, but unlike the lore gleaned from fairy tales, it seems no longer relevant and so you feel no need to pass it on. It's not that we try to keep our knowledge of horror motifs a secret; it's just that it seems to have no use.

From time to time I have spoken to groups about horror monsters and what amazes me is that, while fourth-graders love to tell all they know and then ask for more, grownups only seem amused that they should be able to remember so much. Who do vampires attack? Where do they live? What do they fear? How can they be destroyed? Grownups know the answers to these and many other such questions because at one time knowing this was as important as knowing where the light switches were in the dark, or how to get out in case of fire. It made you feel much better knowing that you could make the sign of the cross and keep the night molester away, or that daylight was always safe. But nobody ever read you stories of vampires, zombies, and werewolves—other monster stories, yes, but not these. Even if you were a precocious reader you probably never read *Dracula, Frankenstein*, or *The Strange Case of Dr. Jekyll and Mr. Hyde* while you were an adolescent. Yet you know all about them because you had somehow found your way into the land where these wild things were, and you first made that trip somewhere between five and twelve. You were then in the prime audience for horror.

When you ask someone, especially someone who contends he has no interest in horror myths, to tell you what he knows about monsters, he invariably re-creates some scene from early adolescence or late childhood and then tells you it was one of the most frightening moments in his life. It is one memory that never seems to dim with time and everyone seems to have one. Ask any sixty-year-old what he remembers about horror stories and he will not tell you a tale from classical mythology; he will tell you about the Universal movies of the thirties and often he can re-create them almost scene for scene in specific detail. Those who saw, say, *Bride of Frankenstein* when they were twelve in 1938 do not forget it, just as those who saw *Horror of Dracula* when they were twelve in 1958 seem destined to carry it around forever. Yet both the current sixty-year-old and the thirty-year-old are now oblivious to the fact that right now the current crop of early teenagers is lining up to see the old horror myths made modern in *The Howling, Dawn of the Dead, Altered States*, and *Zombie II* and have what will be a life-long memory. Meanwhile their younger brothers and sisters are at home watching Michael Jackson's "Thriller" video and unconsciously learning to associate dating and sex with zombies, vampires, and wolfmen. As adults we are unaware that in the deluge of horror flooding adolescent minds as "entertainment," there is a flotsam that will be picked out and kept forever. We may now be uninterested in it, but that is because we have already assimilated it.[2]

Assuming an adolescent audience is the largest for horror art, how does this help us to understand the psychology of horror? Simply this: while we may not be able to locate what exactly it is within the horror myth that attracts its different audiences, we do know what is within this specific audience that keeps it interested. It needs information. Here anthropologists, sociologists, and psychologists all agree: the primary concern of early adolescence is the transition from individual and isolated sexuality to pairing and reproductive sexuality. It is a concern fraught with inarticulated anxiety and thus ripe for the experience of horror. And so it is here with this audience, not with the myth, that any study of horror should begin.

Freud unfortunately referred to preadolescence as the "latency period," a misnomer implying a sense of quietude, and he thought it primarily a time for the "dissolution of the Oedipus complex." (Freud used the phrase *Untergang des Ödipuskomplexes*, which even he realized was too passive, and so he occasionally substituted a stronger word, *Zertrummerung*.) A sense of apparent quietude and peaceful dissolution may well have characterized the surface behavior of Viennese youngsters a century ago, but we now know how mistaken Freud was. Pubescence is anything but contained and latent: everything seems aroused and furious, most especially sexual confusion. All of a sudden there is hair emerging in strange places, mysterious bodily fluids being secreted at unannounced times, breasts budding, voices cracking, and, most important, those disturbing, exciting urges welling up inside. For the first time in life the early adolescent has the biological ability to reproduce; now all that is needed is knowledge. There is nothing more frightening than power without knowledge, unless it be knowledge without control.

It is not remarkable that horror sagas and sexual anxieties should converge; what is remarkable is that we were then, and are now, so unaware of the convergence. But it is clear from even the surface story that horror monsters are every bit as anxious and confused about sex as their audience: King Kong and the Mummy and the Creature from Wherever only want the sexual attention of a young woman; Frankenstein's monster only wants a bride; Dracula only wants those young virgins; and the poor, young, repressed gentleman only wants to get the marriage over with, yet that Mr. Hyde part of himself is forever making him act like a "wolf."

Horror monsters may frighten, but that is partly because they are acting out those desires that we fear. When they come out in the nighttime, as monsters always do, they must move around using a body that has become a sexual weapon, a body full of power but so lacking in control. Monsters certainly are not happy about this, but they must do what they must do: Dracula would rather be dead ("to die, to be really dead, that would be glorious"); the Frankenstein monster wants to, and often does, commit suicide, as does Dr. Jekyll; the werewolf must beg to be destroyed, but they all, like us, must learn to be patient and wait. Maybe the nightmare will end and we will all wake, like the sleeping princesses of the fairy tale, to find that the world is full of goodness. But the horror myth warns, "maybe not," so you better learn about life as it really is.

Let us have yet another look at that ripening audience before turning to observe what it is they may find comforting on the screen. This time I venture a few personal observations because there has yet to be a careful sociological study of the horror movie audience, let alone the audience of other media dedicated to artificial horror.[3] The horror movie audience is the most feral of audiences. There is nothing like it in a classroom, in the military, or in any institution short of an eighteenth-century public lynching. You can watch the same horror movie on television or on a movieola, but it will not be the same show you see Friday night with the kids. This is a "live audience" if ever there was one, but it is also as self-conscious as the audience for pornography. Second, although most of the audience are in their early- to mid-teens, a number of older men (never women) are also present, usually sitting separately, often by themselves. I used to think these characters were all writing books on "The Aesthetics of Modern Horror." Then I went through a period of thinking they were simply late-bloomers, remembering Joseph Henderson's contention in *Thresholds of Initiation* that boyhood in America frequently ends at thirty-five. I now think otherwise. For these older men, rogue males, as it were, are so out of place that, although blacks and whites can sit together, young and old can't.

If you watch these men closely, you see they do not act in step with the rest of the audience. They are not there to be frightened, but to participate. So while the rest of the audience may shout and scream, these men make a lot of mumbling noises and may even push and shake the seats around them. Gene Siskel, film critic for the *Chicago Tribune*, has noticed them too and has concluded, on PBS's *Sneak Previews*, along with his colleague Roger Ebert of the *Chicago Sun-Times*, that these men have infiltrated the otherwise alien audience of youngsters because "one of the messages of these films [especially the stalk-and-slash variety] is that women should get back in line." In fact, in most of the stab-at-female movies the victim has been sexually "liberated" (read "promiscuous") and therefore should be "punished." Very often the attack occurs the night before she is to be married. These older men seem to be there in the audience to help dish out the punishment, something they seem to enjoy.

Often you can even hear these two audiences converse; the adolescents interested in the young lady's health, the male rogues interested in her demise. You can occasionally hear the young audience, especially the girls, squealing "watch out! be careful!" to the female protagonist, while the older males mutter, "yeah, get her, get even, knife her, punish her!"—everything but what they may really be thinking, which is "rape her! rape her!" As Mr. Siskel has contended, it is in such scenes that the contemporary director all too often obliges the older males by filming the sexual attack from the stalker's point of view, so whether we like it or not, we are forced to collude with the rapist. This was only rarely the case in pre–1970 horror movies.[4]

In the more traditional horror movie sexual violence was rarely countenanced, let alone even displayed. But it was always there; we're just now having a good look at it. What may be developing is yet another schism in modern horror myths as a different audience starts to compete for the traditional texts to be told "their way." One can almost see this happening within the theater. For although there is peace within the salt-and-pepper variety of the audience, there is almost a Darwinian struggle for space between young and old. The horror audience now often looks like this. The youngest viewers sit up front, almost on top of the screen, and are divided into small groups of five or six. Often a group will surround a couple that has managed to sit together, but usually they stay in little packs. Sometimes these are packs of all girls, but rarely, if ever, have I seen all boys. Behind them another audience forms, this one more neatly paired with partners, not necessarily older, but certainly better organized. There are also groups within this larger herd, groups which know both each other as well as members of the up-front ephebic audience, so there is much traveling around, up and back, before and during the movie. "A night at the movies" may have lost its meaning for those over thirty, but for the front half of the horror movie audience, it is certainly a social and participatory event. The back half of the theater seems dormant in comparison. For here sit disconnected young couples, intent on cuddling, not screaming; sometimes two or three older girls sit together; sometimes a few somber, single boys; older, well-dressed couples; and on the perimeter those rogue males. When the evening theater is full, one has the feeling that the audience has come in from the front and is pushing slowly backward as if to force out the supernumerary elders. I have even seen fifteen-year-olds prefer to sit in the aisle up front rather than be relegated to the back seats. It is all reminiscent of the campfire, except for those sour Humbert Humberts.

In audience participation films like *The Rocky Horror Picture Show*, the audience is restratified by having the very front made up of surrogate actors and their accomplices, behind them the still-active and partnered audience from the regular horror movie crowd, then larger groups of late adolescents who arrive and behave like a college fraternity, next a stratum of paired forty-year-olds who are rather shy and intent on finding out why they are there, and then finally the pros, the verbalizers, those who "know it all" and participate almost around the middle audience with the mimic actors up front. This audience is, as Bruce A. Austin tells us in "Portrait of a Cult Film Audience: *The Rocky Horror Picture Show*," intent on acting out behavior suppressed elsewhere. Yet the whole experience is rather like being in church. For the most part this audience has left the campfire and is now attending a different service.

I have tried to establish the contemporary audience for horror films for two obvious reasons: (1) to show that just as in, say, the classroom where students signal their designs by where they place their bodies and will fight for those places, so, too, adolescents here in the theater have a sense of a "spot" that may be equally revelatory and (2) to establish, if only by analogy, what the audience for the gothic may have been like. For one of the real puzzles in social and literary history is the determination of the specific reading audience for first the *Schauerroman*, and then the later sensation novel. For, as critics like Richard Altick, *The English Common Reader: A Social History of the Mass Reading Public 1800–1900*, Q. D. Leavis, *Fiction and the Reading Public*, and J. M. S. Tompkins, *The Popular Novel in England, 1770–1800*, all conclude that while we know the purchasing and lending audience of the gothic, we really have no fix on who was actively consuming the text. We know that it was not the subliterary audience of the "penny dreadful," nor the single-sex audience of the novel of manners, nor the highbrow audience of the *Quarterly*; instead, it seems to be, as Winifred Hughes recently pointed out in *The Maniac in the Cellar* (1980), the same audience that was to patronize the stage melodrama. I suggest that this same audience, now a little younger, is still in place, still stratified, still watching—as the Victorian stage handbills promised—"carefully selected horrors of every kind." For, as no less an observer than T. S. Eliot recognized, "melodrama is perennial and the craving for it is perennial and must be satisfied"; this is the same allure of horror art, which is after all melodrama made manic. So I think that the same audience that devoured *Wagner the Wehr Wolf* and *Varney the Vampyre*, leaving it in such tatters that the British Museum had trouble locating complete texts, probably later lined up to see their dramatic counterparts on stage and now wears out the sprocket-holes of *Night of the Living Dead*. It is not happenstance that Frankenstein, Dracula, the were-

wolf, Dr. Jekyll/Mr. Hyde all were transformed first from print into melo-drama and from there (*not* from the literary text) onto celluloid. Further-more, I suspect the young survivor of make-believe horror has always existed and has always passed around its important texts, whether played out in folk tales, or in print, or on stage, in rather the same manner that the modern horror audience now passes the "filmic" message from the eager front, through the interested middle, and then out into the back audience, into the repository of age. There were probably even those older males plundering the Victorian melodrama, not for excitement or information, but for vicar-ious revenge.

There is another, less obvious, reason for establishing this audience, and that has to do with the fluidity of horror stories. In no other folk or art form are conventions so actively re-created and embellished—not by the authors, but by the audience. Horror stories, like nightmares, never end; they are just re-dreamed. Surely it is important that, while all the major horror texts (*Dra-cula, Frankenstein, Dr. Jekyll*) initially came from specific, recorded dreams, they are then retold again and again until they *become* allegorical. As we will see later, Bram Stoker, Mary Shelley, and Robert Louis Stevenson have had their dreams become mythic only because the audience continually fills in what is missing and excises the dross. So let Stevenson retell his dream via a mystery story like *The Strange Case of Dr. Jekyll and Mr. Hyde* and let him try to make it "moral" (supposedly to please his wife), and the audience will repeatedly re-work the text until the women are added and the "moral" and other self-consciousness like the sophisticated china-box narration is removed. In other words, the apparent authors of this story are Stevenson, Sullivan (who did the stage play), Beranger (who did the screenplay for the Barrymore version), then Mamoulian, Fleming, and all the others who did remakes, including the Hammer versions and television versions, until the recent attempt by Paddy Chayefsky in *Altered States*. Each telling that suc-ceeds in conveying the tale does so because it is recaptured by the audience. Let Mary Shelley have her intellectual creature who can read Goethe and Plutarch. The audience, though, wants a monster and will play the melo-drama out until it is properly formed. Let Stoker have his "Bloofer Lady" and his Quincy Morris; the audience won't. These horror tales have become sagas because the audience knows where the thrills are and will only patron-ize the "proper" versions.[5] They have, after all, had these dreams on their own.

On this storytelling level, the entry level of make-believe horror, the "ick" and "boo" are what the audience wants. Invariably when critics investigate the allure of horror art, the analogy they proffer for the experience is the roller-coaster ride. This is not an inappropriate trope, for it is clear that the

audience that scours the carnival midway each summer looking for "the ride" is the same group that is patronizing the horror films each weekend. When they find the "right ride," they'll patiently line up and wait for the privilege of being pummeled, squeezed, bruised, battered, and, most of all, terrorized. Then ask them when they get off how they enjoyed it and they'll say, "It was really great; it was so awful." This is the same aesthetic criterion the horror movie audience applies. Jose Quinones, a young New York-born Puerto Rican, was asked by a staff reporter of the *Wall Street Journal* (December 11, 1981, p. 29) to explain why he frequents horror movies; he replied, "They're so disgusting, man. That's why I go to them." The *Journal* may muse that this is a strange commodity to build an industry around, but the transportation of shock also supports the carnival. Both businesses sell a strong feeling physiologically excited in the same places—the nape of the neck and the pit of the stomach.

The only other experience akin to the horror film for which shudders are value judgments is the fairy tale. Ask a child what she likes about "Jack and the Beanstalk," "The Three Little Pigs," or "Goldilocks and the Three Bears," and she can't say. This hesitancy is not simply because she is unsophisticated or inarticulate, but rather because she really doesn't know. All she recognizes is the feeling, and so all she says is "tell it again, and this time go slow over the scary parts." It is not that Mr. Quinones and his younger siblings don't follow the plot or don't understand the characterizations—they do; it's just that such understanding does not motivate interest. The interest is in being startled and then overcoming it.

One of the most illustrative aspects of horror art is the uniformly censorious comments made with regard to any claim for its artistic, let alone social, merit. Sooner ask the barker at the midway to explain the use of the "loop-the-loop" or the camp counselor the use of the nighttime fire-side story, than ask the horror artist why he does what he does, or if it is important. Deprecatory comments are made not only by critics, which is to be expected; such remarks are as likely to come from the practitioners as well. John Simon, the arch-Victorian on horror: "When you consider how little of the enormous body of horror fiction has artistic merit—and, further, how few films of any kind are works of art—the likelihood of there being a sufficient number of horror films for serious critical analysis is nil" (*Critical Matters*, p. 403). And in *The Gothic Flame* and *The Haunted Castle*, Devendra P. Varma and Eino Railo detail again and again how the tellers of the gothic tale from Radcliffe and Walpole, through Shelley and Maturin, and including Stevenson and Stoker, all treated their "bogey stories" (as Stevenson called them) as one-dimensional, lightweight, and superfluous. This self-chiding is especially true with the tellers of the late gothic tales—the ghost story—where academic practitioners like Le Fanu, M. R. James, Blackwood, and the rest, are downright apologetic about manipulating "those devices" and "that claptrap." Surely one does not expect the camp counselor to claim lasting merit for his bonfire tales, but wouldn't it be interesting if he were slightly embarrassed, perhaps even ashamed, of what he was doing? Yet most horror-tellers are.

I don't know why the teller of the horror tale should be so deferential unless he knows that he is doing something in public that really is rather private and it's also making him rich. In 1980 Dick Cavett had a two-hour Halloween special on horror art and he assembled four of the most successful contemporary arrangers of these "devices": George Romero, director of *Night of the Living Dead* and *Dawn of the Dead* (two zombie films) as well as *Martin* (one of the best and least appreciated modern vampire films) and *Creepshow*; Stephen King, author of *The Shining, Carrie, 'Salem's Lot, Pet Sematary*, and countless others, as well as the interpretive *Danse Macabre*; Ira Levin, who wrote *Rosemary's Baby* and *The Stepford Wives*; and finally a relative newcomer, Peter Straub, author of *Ghost Story* and *Shadowland*, and co-author with King of *The Talisman*. Cavett asked these full-grown men, all very successful camp counselors, to explain why they do what they do—what appeals to them in generating shock. It was clear from the tone and context that he was not trying to pry into their private lives ("now, tell me why are you still writing on the walls"); he was just curious. So were their answers. Mr. Romero said it was for the thrill of re-creating "the roller coaster ride"; King agreed, Mr. Straub concurred; Mr. Levin, if I remember correctly, wisely said nothing. It seems, if we can trust them, that they just want to startle people. They enjoy, in Mr. King's words, "Going oogah, boo-gah." Ride this, they seem to say, for the thrill of a lifetime.

Is there any other art form, or any other exchange in popular culture, in which both producer and consumer are in such agreement about the worth of their interaction? Alas, I don't think things are as simple as they maintain. The production of *lasting* horror is far more complex than just saying "boo!"—it's a very special "boo" said to a very special audience at a very special time. Terror, I hope I've shown, is something else, but these modern practitioners are certainly correct on one point: the fright must always be there; you must be able to see the little car loop the loop and hear those screams, or the audience will pass the ride by.

If the beginning of modern adolescence starts with the roller coaster ride at the fair and a trip to see *Dawn of the Dead* at the shopping center theater, then it ends a decade later with a ride on the mechanical bull at Country-and-Western saloon and a trip to the college cinema to see some send-up of earlier horror like *The Rocky Horror Picture Show* or *Pink Flamingos*, or yet another revival of *Eraserhead* or *Texas Chainsaw Massacre*. In such movies, all the horror shocks prescribed by Romero, King, and Straub are driven almost to parody: the roller coaster is shown to be not just safe, but contrived all along. It was built not by some madman, but by some engineer from M.I.T. and, worse yet, he did it with a computer. Let me describe one of these travesties, *Pink Flamingos*, because it does all the things that the War- hol/Morrisey *Frankenstein* and *Dracula* movies did—it plays the horror story and imagery against itself. And, as Mel Brooks's *Blazing Saddles* or *Young Frankenstein* also illustrate so well, parody is always part homage. So in these camp "horror" movies the late adolescent audience clearly delights in ridiculing the same roller coaster ride it had ridden in terror eight or so years before. And because it is such a caricature we get a chance to see "how it's done."

There is horror dreck aplenty in *Pink Flamingos*: incest, cannibalism, sod- omy, rape—you name it, it's all here to be unremittingly cartooned. It is, like many other contemporary horror films, so self-consciously kitschy that it almost disappoints the audience with contrived excess. But after all of the "oogah-boogahs" have been burlesqued, something really shocking does happen and it may be informative to see how the audience handles it.

In the film our protagonist, Miss Divine, a beefy, 325-pound transvestite, has dispatched her competition to be the undeniable "Queen of the Gross- out." She has performed some unmentionable acts on her family and others, yet it has been in wonderfully atrocious bad taste. At the end of the movie she prepares to leave Baltimore for a new life in the West. As she walks through the congested downtown to the bus station, we follow alongside as the film is clearly being shot from a slowly moving vehicle in the street. Nothing is now being staged—that is clear from the passersby who both gawk at this incredible hulk of womanhood and then stare at the film crew moving beside her. Nothing is being cut or spliced; the film runs continu- ously. Up ahead Miss Divine sees a dog defecating and turns to the film crew as if to say "I bet you don't dare me; well, I will." She waits for the dog to finish, and then she does; she first pauses and then stoops to pick up the feces. All the time she's talking to the camera crew, but we can't hear what she says. The camera, however, is shaking a bit and the off-center image jiggles on the screen. We wait to see where the splice will be made—the splice that is so important in the horror film—the splice you know will protect you from really being startled. After all, you are in your twenties now and you know movies are "just entertainment." The splice doesn't come. Miss Divine, now looking off-camera, puts the excrement in her mouth and her lips close. There is a gasp from the audience; an audience that has been yelling and hooting at the scenes that once made them shiver is now genuinely startled.

Divine of *Pink Flamingos*, 1972 (New Line Cinema)

This is just the way it was when we first saw horror films—it's not pretend after all. The film ends abruptly, and the audience that usually lingers after a show empties the theater like water through a sieve. As one wag has stated, *Pink Flamingos* is the only film made in which "shit-eating describes both a critical judgment and an on-screen activity." This scene is the last "boo" of adolescence, the last roll of the roller coaster.

But how much of the appeal of horror is in just being shocked? Is the roller coaster or the mechanical bull really the final analogy? For the few psychoanalysts who have studied horror, the answer lies partly elsewhere. That we want to be shocked is not as important as *what* shocks us and *why* we should seek to be shocked at predictable times. As in so many cases, while Freud provided the initial answer which seemed promising enough, his explanation still has not been challenged or developed. Admittedly, analysts have neglected this subject for more pressing interests, but it is also because, as

Freud himself cautioned, certain areas of aesthetics seem impermeable to psychoanalysis. Horror seems to be one such area.

As early as 1913, Freud became fascinated by the attraction of horror and, in particular, by one aspect that he referred to as *unheimlich* or the "uncanny." For the next five years he ruminated until, in 1919, he published "The Uncanny" as an article in *The Imago*. Along the way his fascination with this aesthetic cul-de-sac doubled back to take him to the path of his primary interests—the stages of sexual growth. Freud's suppositions about the iconography of the uncanny began to inform both his anthropological conjectures in *Totem and Taboo* and his cultural speculations in *Beyond the Pleasure Principle*. So what exactly is *unheimlich*? Freud explains:

> [The uncanny] is undoubtedly related to what is frightening—to what arouses dread and horror; equally certainly, too, the word is not always used in a clearly definable sense, so that it tends to coincide with what excites fear in general. Yet we may expect that a special core of feeling is present which justifies the use of a special conceptual term. One is curious to know what this common core is which allows us to distinguish as "uncanny" certain things which lie within the field of what is frightening. ("The Uncanny," p. 219)

Freud is clearly having the same problem we have had—the need to separate horror from terror, to move "the uncanny" out of the field of what is simply frightening so that it can be studied in isolation. To do this he argues first by semantic, then clinical, and finally by psychological evidence, that images of the uncanny are drawn from a combination of individual and group repressions. But repressions of what? Freud believes there are repressions of primary narcissism that have to be re-directed by increasing social demands if we are to become acculturated. In other words, desires—sexual desires—are safely abreacted in horror so that other growth can occur. So in a sense, a very important sense, horror is rather like humor; it is a discharge system for pent-up energy that, unless released, threatens to implode into neurosis. As an example of this process, Freud claims that the doppelgänger motif, always a staple of horror art, is really the projection and diffusion of infantile desires that slip past the superego censors so that the "double" can act independently of the central self. As Freud was well aware from his reading of Otto Rank, the double thus safely cathects desire by fantasy.

The uncanny seems clear enough so far—the process is analogous to displacement in dreamwork. The "incredible hulks" of horror stories, fairy tales, and nightmares all have the same etiology: they are the projected wishes of the young protagonist/dreamer. They act out his unscripted wishes even if it means, as it usually does, their own destruction. But Freud also wanted to account for the shared vocabulary of these motifs—why is it that certain images are almost always cast in the same sequences? Here he invokes his old standby—first learned from the study of dreams—the theory of compulsive repetition.

> For it is possible to recognize the dominance in the unconscious mind of a "compulsion to repeat" proceeding from the instinctual impulses and probably inherent in the very nature of the instincts—a compulsion powerful enough to overrule the pleasure principle, lending to certain aspects of the mind their daemonic character, and still very clearly expressed in the impulses of small children; a compulsion, too, which is responsible for a part of the course taken by the analyses of neurotic patients. All these considerations prepare us for the discovery that whatever reminds us of this inner 'compulsion to repeat' is perceived as uncanny. ("The Uncanny," p. 238)

So, according to Freud, we should be able to find a lexicon of repressed desires embedded in the cultural text of horror art that, *especially if often repeated*, will tell us something about the sublimated desires of both individual and race.

> Our conclusion could then be stated thus: an uncanny experience occurs either when infantile complexes which have been repressed are once more revived by some impression, or when primitive beliefs which have been surmounted seem once more to be confirmed. Finally, we must not let our predilection for smooth solutions and lucid exposition blind us to the fact that these two classes of uncanny experience are not always sharply distinguishable. When we consider that primitive beliefs are most intimately connected with infantile complexes, and are, in fact, based on them, we shall not be greatly astonished to find that the distinction is often a hazy one. ("The Uncanny," p. 249)

If horror is thus a kind of communal wish fulfillment, a kind of tribal dream made real, then why does it have to shock? Why does the audience have to ride the roller coaster to get to it? Presumably it shocks because this is the only way to play out these particular fantasies (whatever they exactly are—Freud is not specific) in daylight. So the shiver may be produced both because the wishes are tabooed and because we pay a price, so to speak, for transporting these wishes out of the subconscious, past the censor, and into a text. We think we get on the roller coaster to ride up and down, to be tossed about, and so we never pay attention to where the tracks really lead. We think we get off at the same place we got on, but that may not be entirely accurate.

To return to the earlier example, when we keep our eye on the monstrous double, we lose sight of exactly what it does once animated, as well as what is happening to the protagonist. We are almost stymied by just looking at it.

Although the double can appear as either a libidinous Mr. Hyde or a censorious William Wilson, it is not how he appears (the shock), but that he then performs specific tasks while his host dallies elsewhere. Freud does not say this, but monsters are *never* capricious; the projectors may be. Monstrous doubles do terrible things on purpose— the question is, whose purpose? They may not have a mind of their own, but that is only because they have the desires of the dreamer.

So in summation: the frisson associated with the uncanny may be powered by both the singular impulses of the secluded id and by the "sparking" between individual and collective desires of the species.[6] But, says Freud, the shock is not what is uncanny; what is uncanny is what the shock reveals.

One of the problems with psychoanalyzing modern horror films is that just as Freudian patients dream Freudian dreams, so Freudian directors make Freudian movies. They turn over the same rocks. It is hard to see a movie like *Countess Dracula* (in which the Oedipal conflict drives the mother to make a vampire of her son) or *Frankenstein and the Monster from Hell* (where the monster is obviously the id-infested projection of the repressed doctor) or *The Two Faces of Dr. Jekyll* (where the real monster is the repressed Jekyll) and not be a little put off by such self-conscious contrivance. The desire of moviemakers, especially since the 1950s, to project psychological relevance so often contorts the received myth that instead of projected fantasy we get only intellectual mish-mash. But let us take a quick look anyway at Fred McLeod Wilcox's *Forbidden Planet* (1956), for although it is a little out of the way (science-fiction horror) and somewhat contrived, it still details how images of the uncanny can infiltrate a text even when the author seems well in control.

Here is the plot in brief. Several centuries into the future a search party of American astronauts is sent into "deep space" to find the whereabouts of a lost party of colonizers sent twenty years earlier to the planet Altair. As they near the planet and prepare to land, they are warned off by a Dr. Morbius who claims he is alone and would rather not be disturbed. The astronauts, cooped up for months in their tiny capsule, land anyway and find that, while the latter statement is true enough (Morbius lives in 1950 Hollywood luxury—motorized curtains, Westinghouse refrigerator, conversation pit, indoor-outdoor carpet), the former is not. Morbius (played by the redoubtable Walter Pidgeon) has both a daughter named Alta (played by the voluptuous Anne Francis) and a friendly robot named Robbie (played by who knows who, but it had to be an actor because the union then demanded such for all speaking or squeaking parts). The nineteen-year-old daughter is as desperately oversexed and undersupplied with partners as are the spacemen and, since she knows nothing at all about sex and has no superego, both parties behave as expected. But when one of them, Commander Adams (the Edenic myth is too obvious to miss), finally kisses the young nymphet in her garden, her pet tiger is aroused, prepares to attack, and is zapped by the commander's dematerializing Buck Rogers ray gun. "He did not recognize me," explains Alta of the tiger, and she is right, for Adams' sensual kiss has changed her. No longer a girl, she is being transformed into womanhood.

Now that should tell us something about Mr. Wilcox's (actually screenwriters Irving Block and Allen Adler) reading of both the Bible and Freud, at least in Westwood, California, *circa* 1950, but he has still more to say. For later that night one of the astronauts is found mutilated and we soon learn that some wild beast with a leaping, tigerish shape is on the loose.[7] Dr. Morbius (who is not an honest-to-goodness doctor at all, but just a philologist) is now forced to explain.

It seems that Altair was originally the planet of the Krell, a hyper-intelligent, humanoid species. But the Krell became so enamoured of their intellect—the word used is "IQ"—that they constructed a brain-boosting machine so that they could know everything about reality. In addition, the machine allowed them to project mental images into reality, thereby closing the gap between imagination and action. It proved a tragic experience, for the price paid for this Faustian endeavor was the repression of their sexual desire, their reproductive instinct. All that they left behind was their brain-booster and it was with that machine that Morbius has been able to construct his Beverly Hills Xanadu. But, though the philologist may have used his language skills to break the code of the Krell, he is still encased in flesh and blood and hence not able to control his body—namely, his libido.

While Morbius is thus mulling over the human condition, the Commander's best friend, a lieutenant, sneaks off for an IQ-boost of his own and returns looking as if he has just swum through a whirlpool. The Lieutenant dies at our feet, but not before taking his Hollywood perquisite, the saying of the Last Words: "The monster," he gasps, "is from the id."

"The id—what's that?" queries the Commander, and Morbius, ever the patient instructor, explains. The id, he says, is an "obsolete term once used to describe the elementary structure of the subconscious." So it seems that the Krell were destroyed, not by Faustian overreaching, but by neglecting to care for the "mindless beast" of their subconscious. The monster now loose on Altair, that numinous tiger, the Commander concludes, is none other than Morbius' own projected id that has, thanks to the "brain-booster," been magnified to massive proportions. Adams and his party have to get off Altair, and fast, and he asks Alta to go with him. She accepts. Think of her alternative.

Now, it is never mentioned why Morbius' id-monster is attempting to intimidate the astronauts into departing, but let me mention a possibility in passing because I will return to it later. There is only one female whom this outer-space Prospero (the thematic and structural connections with *The Tempest* are also too obvious to miss) could possibly covet and that, of course, is his adolescent and uninformed and well-endowed daughter—his own Miranda. This little bit of the uncanny does not seem at all contrived; in fact, their father-daughter relationship is played out in the best bobby-sox tradition of "Father Knows Best." But if that brain-booster really has projected Morbius' id into the tiger-monster, we had better keep one eye on the cat.

Once Morbius sees that he is going to lose his daughter, there is no hope; he shuts down the booster, thereby deactivating the beast, and all is safe. The horror is over. Then, like Robert Young handing Betty over to her prom date, Morbius hands Alta over to Adams, calls the Commander "son," and wishes them godspeed. We cut abruptly to the spaceship to see all are safely aboard, including the well-behaved robot, Robbie (later to appear on "The Perry Como Show" and still later to be reincarnated as R2D2 of *Star Wars* fame), and learn that Morbius has chosen to be left alone on the Forbidden

Robbie, Leslie Nielsen, Walter Pidgeon, and Anne Francis in *Forbidden Planet,* 1956 (M-G-M Studios)

Planet. He is going to "shut it down." This he does quite literally. The whole planet explodes, but we are assured that his death has made the future once again safe for us all.

The obvious "message" of *Forbidden Planet* is social, not psychological. Do not neglect your family by striving for knowledge and power, for although you may get a lot of money and a higher IQ, you will be lonely and, worse, lusty. Next, it says, don't repress your emotions or you will become, like the Krell, self-consuming. Learn to live with your passions in moderation. Certainly, the price paid for two hours in the theater is cheaper than an hour on the analyst's couch. As Commander Adams, without the brain-boost but with plenty of Freudian savvy, informs both us and his father-in-law-to-be, Dr. Morbius, "We are all part monsters in our subconscious. That's why we have laws and religion." Desires, especially sexual desires, need to be controlled, not excised.

When that kind of statement is consciously made within a work of fantasy, there is not much for the psychological critic to do. Who needs a critic when the psychiatrist comes in at the end of *Psycho* to explain Norman Bates, or even a Dr. Loomis to explain the bogeyman in *Halloween II*? Only the most sensitive viewer will be unsettled by the inadequacy of such Caligariesque conclusions. The enduring horror motifs are invariably those most un-self-consciously developed and left unexplained. The vampire, the no-name creature, and the transformation monster are susceptible to psychoanalysis, while, say, King Kong, the Beast from 20,000 Fathoms, and the Krell are not, because the former monsters come pre-coded out of folklore, while the others have been contrived to fit modern theory. The modern manipulator of the vampire never has to say to himself, "OK, now I have to explain exactly where this thing spends his time between 8 A.M. and nightfall," or "shall I have my vampire attack a middle-aged matron." The myth does it all for him. Horror monsters have their own established habits, families, traditions, and tastes that cannot be permanently changed. You can set Howard Hughes on the template of the vampire, or Christiaan Barnard on Dr. Frankenstein, or even a Timothy Leary on Dr. Jekyll (all of which have been recently done), and you may entertain the mature audience, but the adolescent audience will simply remove the dross and reinstate the story they received somewhere in their past.

While there have been a number of psychological critics of the horror film, the most influential has been a practicing analyst, Harvey R. Greenberg, M.D. In his entertaining and informative *The Movies on Your Mind* (1975), Greenberg interprets our coterie of horror monsters as they, now in his words, "blow the lid off our id." So we deduce that Lawrence Talbot in Universal's *Wolf Man* (1941) is acting out an Oedipal battle in which the father is victorious; Mamoulian's *Dr. Jekyll* (1932) cuts loose the id-infested Mr. Hyde to act out the doctor's repressed misogyny; Whale's *Frankenstein* (1931) becomes a parable of sadistic masturbatory fantasies as well as the imaging of the primal scene, which then must be compulsively repeated; and Browning's *Dracula* (1932) disguises an erudite discussion of oral fixation. Admittedly, I am being unfairly reductive with Greenberg's interpretations, but my point is that he is not interpreting the myths of the Frankenstein monster, Dracula, the werewolf, and Dr. Jekyll; he is interpreting only a version by Whale, Browning, Siodmak, and Mamoulian. Such criticism is always susceptible to a version of the intentional fallacy because these men were consciously syncretizing received myth with then-contemporary psychology. This kind of category mistake will inevitably occur (and you can find it again and again in the articles collected by Huss and Ross in *Focus on the Horror Film* as well as in Margaret Tarratt's "Monsters from the Id") when the critic attempts to extrapolate meaning from a specific text only and not from texts *within* the broader myth. I admit this is an occupational hazard, and I admit Greenberg's intent is to study individual movies, but one needs to be cautious about forming general conclusions about horror from isolated samples.

Quite simply, the makers of these films were exploiting specific images and situations because they knew enough about psychology to calculate the pattern that ought to work. They made films for money and they knew which audience had the money. They usually adapted a stage play (*The Wolf Man* is the exception) in which the playwrights had already arranged most of the "devices" for them, so they already had tested the audience. I do not mean to imply that these directors were not first-rate artists, but only that their versions were just one step along the way. If we want to understand the horror myth, what we need to follow is the path, not what Dr. Greenberg studies, which is the footprint. It's important to know that Universal's Wolfmen have almost nothing to do with werewolf folklore, but instead came from the genius of Curt Siodmak, that Dr. Frankenstein's laboratory, complete with phallic lift, is nowhere in the novel or the Victorian melodrama, but rather the work of Kenneth Strickfaden, that the women who are now *always* in the Dr. Jekyll myth were nowhere in Stevenson's text, and that even the Transylvanian dialogue and stilted delivery of Dracula is now in the vampire saga because Bela Lugosi could not learn to modulate his voice in front of the camera—he had played the part only on stage. These "devices" are now part of the horror *stimmung*, but there is ever so much more carried by the myth.

Greenberg's psychoanalytic method, however, is useful in explaining the attraction of specific works, especially when those works were conceived ex nihilo or adapted precisely for the screen. When he discusses movies like *The Invisible Ray*, *The Forbin Project*, *Invasion of the Body Snatchers*, and *King Kong*, his interpretations make much better sense, if only because the distance from author to text to movie to audience is much smaller and more well-defined. These stories have a specific number of versions and we know them all. King Kong is a movie legend, pure and simple; what we see is what we get. So if you want to interpret the story as an allegory of capitalist mania (as Dino De Laurentiis did) or as a Caucasian nightmare of miscegenation, that certainly is more plausible than contending that the Frankenstein story is really a masturbatory fantasy. One version of it certainly may be, but there are a lot more that aren't.

The problem with the pop-top theory of interpretation ("it blows the lid off the id") is that the critic must never be allowed to settle on one text, unless of course he is interested primarily in the maker of that version. In anatomizing modern myths I am not much interested in specific, self-conscious texts; in fact, just the opposite: the more derivative and exploitative the version, the more revealing it may be. What is needed to explain horror is, I think, a broad approach, an ethnological approach, in which the various stories are analyzed as if no one individual telling really mattered, as if each version were but a chapter which may or may not be finally included. You search for what is stable and repeated; you neglect what is "artistic" and "original." This is why, for me, auteur criticism is quite beside the point in explaining horror. The myth may appear in a literary text and it may appear on the movies or on television, but it may also be told in comics, on bubble gum cards, on dolls, on Halloween masks, in toys of all description, even in the names of breakfast cereals. The critic's first job in explaining the fascination of horror is not to fix the images at their every appearance but, instead, to trace their migrations to the audience and, only then, try to understand why they have been crucial enough to pass along.

The most important thing we have learned about mythography, first from Jung and Frazer and now from Joseph Campbell and Northrop Frye, is that myths are anything but frivolous. On the contrary, myths embody and convey the most sacred truths a society can first produce and then protect. Myths are memories. Above all else, they are memories of what must never be forgotten, for without them there could be no lasting culture, and without culture there could be little meaning in life. If poets—or any artists, for that matter—"are the hierophants of unapprehended inspiration; the mirrors of the gigantic shadows which futurity casts upon the present ... the unacknowledged legislators of the world," it is only because their intuitive understanding of myth is so keen. They are the ones who make sure the truth is

kept fresh and vibrant so that the storytellers of a culture—those camp counselors—are never at a loss for words.

Modern ethnologists have shown that myths in all their manifold forms, from sophisticated religious ceremonies and complex magic to animal masks and mundane drinking cups, are not just adaptive; they are prescriptive. Myths inform an identifiable audience about a particular problem at a specific time. To endure, the myth must do more than inform or validate some social order; it must suggest specific behavior that maintains both the social order and bolsters the individual's sense of worth. Without these "fictions," cultural anthropologists contend, the members of the audience could truly go insane, not because they would do things wrong, but because there would be no wrong things to do. Myths convey alternatives and contrasts ("binary matrices and poles") that hint at what the myth-telling group considers optimal choices. People who need answers to resolve choices ask for myths. People who have learned the culture's responses tell them.

Because myths are lines of travel through difficult passages, we find them wherever confusion exists—usually in childhood and adolescence. As we mature we move from one myth audience to another; when we think we have found a "fix" on our choices, we close the book, leave the theater, or change campfires. As quickly as we move away from certain myths, we are drawn to others. By mid-life we are almost unconscious of the fact that we have come to understand the various "purposes" of life, not because whatever meaning it may have has burst forth like Athena from the head of Zeus, but because our heads have been slowly filled with hundreds of stories that have helped us create a sense of design. We have attributed meaning according to the designs of our culture. We may only have a dim sense of this design, but even this is far brighter than the confusion perceived by the child. We quickly forget how bewildering life was to us once and we may only remember this chaos when we turn to tell our children those myths that were told to us. And when we do, we may not even know why we tell these stories and we may not even know what the stories are about. We do know what the stories do: they make our children feel better just as they did us when we heard them. Little do we realize how much more they do. They help us find order.

Bruno Bettelheim was not the first to study the relationship between the surface "stories" told to children and the deeper social message they carry, but he has certainly been the most influential. From the romantic period onward, artists especially have been aware of the embedded wisdom of folklore (remember Schiller's "Deeper meaning resides in the fairy tales told to me in my childhood than in the truth that is taught in life"), but Bettelheim, in *The Uses of Enchantment: The Meaning and Importance of Fairy Tales* (1975), was the first to explain systematically those "deeper meanings." It was

not an easy task because, since the mid-nineteenth century, we have thought of the child as so delicate as to need protection and we therefore excised much of the horror from the ancient lore of childhood. As with the horror sagas I am interested in, however, we have lately restored the motifs of violence, revenge, bloodshed, cruelty, and especially sexuality, almost with a vengeance. The horror in fairy tales is no longer on the "high shelf," thanks in part to analysts like Bettelheim and practitioners like Maurice Sendak whose long arms have taken down the dragons, stepmothers, wolves, and all the other wild things and put them back where they were. Now that they are out in the open, the teratology of childhood is not so dreadful after all—in fact, the monsters that seemed images of such stark terror to Victorians are more likely the projected anxieties of childhood made real, not to frighten as much as to be controlled. And the fear that the youthful audience must want to exercise, or better yet, exorcise, is the fear most often resolved within the fairy-tale horror—the natural fear of separation and its consequences. The teller of the fairy tale, now usually the parent, has as much to gain in resolving this fear as the child, so these stories go on generation after generation—a kind of mutual therapy.

Bettelheim's method of exegesis is the essence of simplicity: look at the audience, look at the text, look at the teller; surely there must be some connection between all three. Let Mrs. Grundy or the Brothers Grimm or Walt Disney do what they will, the audience knows what information it needs and if left alone will separate fire from smoke. If the teller bowdlerizes a fairy tale in the service of censorship, the motifs will simply recede and reappear elsewhere.

The motifs inherent in the mythography of fairy tales are indomitable because these motifs are linked, not only to culture, but to biology—something in the physiological changes of the audience demands explanation or at least consolation. Traumatic changes need diagnosis, as Bettelheim contends, lest neurosis, essentially a dysfunction caused by an inability to find order, develops. So the fairy tale plays out the possible alternatives, telling the child that it is acceptable to be confused, separated, denied—the future will resolve the present; just wait and see. Others have felt the same way, be patient. In Bettelheim's words,

> While fairy tales invariably point the way to a better future, they concentrate on the process of change, rather than describing the exact details of the bliss eventually to be gained. The stories start where the child is at the time, and suggest where he has to go—with emphasis on the process itself. Fairy tales can even show the child the way through that thorniest of thickets, the oedipal period. (*The Uses of Enchantment*, p. 73)

Because we need myths when we need information, and because we need information when we are confused, fantasy structures are given by a society as maps—so to speak—by which a lost audience can find its way. The audience pulls over to the curb before a difficult turn and says "tell me again the story of Little Red Riding Hood and this time be sure you tell me a lot more about the big, bad wolf," almost as if they were inquiring about proper speed limit and route number. And so we tell them, because we too want them to make it around that corner, past the plotting wolf. Soon they stop asking and, when they are five or six years old, we may think they have lost interest, or even their fears, but they haven't. In a sense they are assimilating in latency what they have learned and are preparing for the next passage, the next trip, searching for a new list of route numbers and speed limits. We will not tell them these numbers. These numbers they will learn elsewhere, but they are every bit as important as the ones we've told them. These untold routes are the ones embedded in horror myths.[8]

The most important theory linking cultural mythologies and biological maturation was propounded almost a century ago by a French anthropologist, Arnold Van Gennep. The key phrase in his theories, the "rites of passage," has become so commonplace that whole schools of developmental psychology have been formed around it. Van Gennep studied the place and meaning of social ritual in a number of isolated communities and concluded that a definite pattern could be adduced: not only do similar rites occur at distinct stages of maturation, but there are divisions within rites, divisions he called *separation*, *transition*, and *incorporation*, which occur with more than coincidental frequency. In his words,

> The life of an individual in any society is a series of passages from one age to another and from one occupation to another. Wherever there are fine distinctions among age and occupational groups, progression from one group to the next is accompanied by special acts, like those which make up apprenticeship in our trades. Among semicivilized peoples such acts are enveloped in ceremonies, since to the semicivilized mind no act is entirely free of the sacred. In such societies every change in a person's life involves actions and reactions between sacred and profane—actions and reactions to be regulated and guarded so that society as a whole will suffer no discomfort or injury. Transitions from group to group and from one social situation to the next are looked on as implicit in the very fact of existence, so that a man's life comes to be a succession of stages with similar ends and beginnings: birth, social puberty, marriage, fatherhood, advancement to a higher class, occupational specialization, and death. For every one of these events there are ceremonies whose essential purpose is to enable the individual to pass from one defined position to another which is equally defined. (*The Rites of Passage*, p. 3)

In the last decade the study of these passages has moved out of academia and into popular culture as we have come to realize that "grown up" is really a misnomer for "still growing up." Thanks to life-span psychologists like Daniel Levinson, Roger Gould, George Vaillant, Gail Sheehy, Ellen Galinsky, and others, we are learning that the seasons of mature life are almost as cyclical, just as predictable, and thankfully a little less jolting than the passage from childhood into and out of adolescence. Maturation does not end the day your feet stop seeming farther and farther away from your head, or the day you become a parent or a grandparent. It ends when you do.

Still, the periods of greatest biological change are the periods in which the rites are most pronounced and mythologies most in demand. The period most studied in the last twenty years, especially since Yehudi Cohen's *The Transition from Childhood to Adolescence* (1964), has been late puberty. Cultural anthropologists are forever going off to study the semen transportation rites of the Nyakyusa in Central Africa, the impregnation rites of the Banaro of New Guinea, the circumcision and subincision rites of the Aranda in Central Australia, and wherever else on the globe there may be a tribe guiding its young past the anxieties of reproductive sexuality.

Ironically, what is interesting about the study of sexual rites of passage, and what some anthropolgist should really investigate, is why we have been so reluctant to study ourselves. What makes us so certain that we are not part of the same family of man that now struggles in the jungle of Africa or New Guinea—as desperate for tribal order as the "savages"? Aside from some studies of high school proms and college fraternity hazing, there has been very little study of our own adolescents. Here are some tidbits of modern anthropological sentiment. First, from Mircea Eliade in *Rites and Symbols of Initiation* (1965): "It has often been said that one of the characteristics of the modern world is the disappearance of any meaningful rites of initiation. Of primary importance in traditional societies, in the modern Western world, significant initiation is practically nonexistent" (p. ix). And here modern echoes from Joseph Henderson in *Thresholds of Initiation* (1967): "Initiation as a meaningful process of transition between Mother and Father, or between inner and outer worlds of experience, has been almost entirely lost in Christian tribes" (pp. 75–76). Or Solon T. Kimball in his introduction to Van Gennep's *The Rites of Passage* (1960):

> There is no evidence that a secularized urban world has lessened the need for ritualized expression of an individual's transition from one status to another. . . . The critical problems of becoming male and female, of relations within the family, and of passing into old age are directly related to the devices which the society offers the individual to help him achieve the new adjustment. Somehow we

seem to have forgotten this—or perhaps the ritual has become so completely individualistic that it is now found for many only in the privacy of the psychoanalyst's couch. The evidence, however, does not bear out this suggestion. It seems much more likely that one dimension of mental illness may arise because an increasing number of individuals are forced to accomplish their transitions alone and with private symbols. (p. xviii)

I suggest, however, that these rites of passage are occurring every day (or every weekend); that the myths of initiation are being carefully told at this very moment not just in our culture, but throughout the West. What makes the ceremony especially fascinating (and maybe this is what should be "mourned" as cultural hubris) is that, while the aborigine may not know what his rite celebrates, he at least knows it occurs; we, on the other hand, seem oblivious not just to the content of our myths, but to their presence in our lives. I hope to show that the adolescent crowd assembled at the theater on Friday night is up to something important—something both they and we don't understand. And while we may only see the plumage and hear the jungle drums in such "events" as *The Rocky Horror Picture Show*, *Dawn of the Dead*, *Eraserhead*, or *Pink Flamingos*, the stuff of sexual initiation inheres in all the major horror myths and informs the audience of important knowledge whether it be told in comics, on television, or especially now, on the screen. What the gothic novel carried via ink on paper to our grandparents, the horror movie carries via images on a screen to us. The myth informs because, as we have seen in the bedtime routine of telling the fairy tale, the pubescent audience needs its message and we acknowledge, perhaps unconsciously, its power. However much we would like them to be quiet and "join the scouts," we know that they have interests elsewhere—just as we had and our parents had before us.

It is a nifty paradox that in a culture that prides itself on openness, especially sexual openness, we should still send our children into the dark to find the truth. If the campfire has become first the novel then the movie, the bard has become first the novelist then the scriptwriter. Moving pictures parent us through adolescence. Try to remember again what you know about these horror sagas, for in learning the stories, you had to assimilate important sexual information. Better yet, ask a pre-teen of either sex, because he or she really has the information without even imagining the future use. In each myth a tale of sexual confusion is played out with implicit sexual directions. In the Frankenstein story the young "doctor" does something that creates monstrous life, and suffers the loss of his girlfriend because of it. The vampire has everything any adolescent could want (money, all-night parties, uncomplicated sex), yet must endure eternal agony because of some hunger. Mr. Hyde does something that Dr. Jekyll cannot do himself, and in so doing destroys the young doctor. The young man transforms into a wolf, the mummy comes back from the dead, the Phantom of the Opera needs a mask, all because they cannot do something they secretly desire to do. They all suffer terribly in order to do what should not be done.

Under all the confusion (i.e., "Frankenstein" now refers to the monster not the doctor, the vampire has become an unhappy monster, and so on), the core subject is invariably sexual. Usually this core is buried in what the myths promulgate as some "secret of life" or "forbidden knowledge," but it is clear from the creation and behavior of these monsters that the subject is reproductive conduct: be it in the creation of new life or the choice of partners or simply the responsibilities of being—for the first time—capable of reproduction. Where fairy tales end with the matrimonial prospect of a Prince Charming who is no longer a toad thanks to his Cinderella, horror stories begin by telling them they better be careful, because "happily ever after" is not a foregone conclusion.

While it might be predicted that latency sagas be spun around a core of sexual confusion, especially reproductive anxiety, why should horror result? Yet it most assuredly does. Can sex really be that frightening? Or unwanted babies? Or maybe, as has been suggested, the horror results from a deep-seated fear of venereal disease. We might approach the problem from an angle: what exactly is embedded in the imagery of horror that is seen and unconsciously processed by the audience in such a way as to produce those heebie-jeebies? A look at a few paintings that supposedly horrify, yet have no ostensible connection with the central modern horror myths, may help to clarify. Here are some examples of what was chosen in 1977 to be included in an exhibition assembled at the Bronx Museum of the Arts entitled "Images of Horror and Fantasy." There was no attempt in the exhibition to be chronological or complete, only an attempt to show what has horrified people since the mid-nineteenth century. I, too, picked these examples almost at random to give a sampling, because what one finds is that if a modern artist is attempting to horrify *without* being political (Goya, Grosz, Blake, Picasso, Dali, Dix, Gillespie), he or she will almost inevitably be drawn back to the unresolved sexual confusions of adolescence. The artist will be imaging sexual anxiety in terms that are, for us as well, still frightening.

We see again and again in these modern paintings the imagery of sexual chaos that started with the gothic and developed through romanticism. Doubtless we have experienced this anxiety for centuries, but only in modern horror art have we displayed it quite so publicly. In Paul Klee's *Outbreak of Fear* (1939) we see a dissembling of bodily parts that need to be reordered and made whole. And what is the part most imaged, the part off to the side

Paul Klee, *Outbreak of Fear,* 1939 (Museum of Fine Arts, Bern, Paul Klee Foundation, copyright © 1984 by COSMO PRESS, Genève and ADAGP, Paris)

Sibylle Ruppert, *The Last Ride,* 1976 (Collection of artist)

(*Above*) Miriam Beerman, *Untitled,* 1969 (Collection of artist)

(*Left*) Alfred Kubin, *The Ape,* 1903–6 (Albertina Museum, Vienna)

that needs to be centered? It is the phallus. In Sibylle Ruppert's *The Last Ride*
(1976) we see a compressed human upper form that has been mated (the toes
are human) with some foul reptile, while other hybrids, this time an owl with
scorpion legs and another bird head, hover above. To understand how these
atrocities were created we need only look at Alfred Kubin's *The Ape* (1906).
Somehow the bestial part, the King Kong part, has linked with the human,
the Fay Wray, and the situation is indeed horrible. But what if the beast in
the jungle is not really an animal, but a projection of some feral aspect of the
self? Clearly, such bestiality is only metaphoric. So, to go back even farther
on the chain of causality, to discover what produces monsters, we might look
at Miriam Beerman's *Untitled* (1969). Here we find two humanesque creatures in a state of torment, yet we cannot distinguish either sex or, more
important, who is the victim and who is the victimizer. All we know is that
they are in a physical position we recognize as one of sexual excitement. Yet
obviously they are in pain. Why? If it is the "sleep of reason that produces
monsters," as Goya said, and if it is sexuality that is irrational, especially to
the young, then exactly what specific aspect of sexuality is it that produces
horror? Bestiality might be an answer, as might sodomy, but neither seems
realistic: in fact, the ape/reptile/creature/monster is more probably a disguise covering something else. But what?

It would seem that (1) since the prime audience for horror is made of adolescents of both sexes, (2) since what we see in images of nonpolitical horror
are scenes of sexual confusion and frustration, and (3) since adolescence
seems characterized by a perplexity of strong drives and little knowledge,
horror art must present scenarios that are possible, but forbidden. "Monsters
are indeed from the id," as Commander Adams informs Dr. Morbius, and
Dr. Greenberg reaffirms, but they must be let out for some purpose.

From what we know about fairy tales, these latency sagas of initiation
ought to do more than let the fizz of shaken-up repression escape; they ought
to quench some thirst as well. That is, after all, what other myths do: they
conserve culture *and* protect the individual. Yet, at first glance horror sagas
perversely seem to do more than articulate the anxieties of puberty; they seem
to excite it. They appear to do more than acknowledge sexual frustration;
they almost encourage it. If these horror monsters are from the id, it is only
because the superego feels the necessity of letting them out to air, and then
presumably sends them back only after they have taught us something necessary. But what have they taught us? Whatever it is, it is information efficiently processed, for remember, if we don't repress quickly our Mr. Hyde
will do us in. If we give in to desire too soon, the vampire's life will be ours.
If we tamper with (pro)creation, we risk birthing a creature who will thwart,
like Frankenstein's monster, our every future sexual desire.

What is it that we sexually want to do that we must repress, subvert, sublimate—anything rather than express for too long? Psychoanalysts may speak of the "uncanny" and anthropologists may mention the lure of the "taboo," but specifically what is it that we must learn enough about so that we will not do it? What is the sexual act that must be feared (and is especially feared in cultures where initiation horror myths are the most vibrant), lest real horror result?

I think it is incest. I think that along with all the other phobic explanations for the attraction of horror (fear of insanity, death, madness, homosexuality, castration) the fear of incest underlies all horror myths in our culture that are repeatedly told for more than one generation. You can tell the story of the "incredible shrinking man" or the "leech woman" once, but not twice. The Blob, the Mutant, the Mantis, the Big Bug, don't live long, while the vampire, the werewolf, the manmade, no-name creature have stayed around awhile. I believe they enjoy a long life because, within the horror that surrounds these monsters, there is a sexual truth preserved by our culture: a truth about incest so important that we feel uneasy explaining it, let alone even dreaming it.

Freud certainly knew about the implosive dynamics of incest; in fact, he repeatedly referred to the "horror of incest" as if it were unique, and we are only now realizing how profoundly perplexed Freud was on this subject. Just why Freud changed his mind from believing in actual seduction to believing in imagined seduction is a subject of considerable current speculation.[9] In private correspondence with Wilhelm Fliess he first cites "seduction by the father" as the "essential point" in hysteria, but then a few months later, Freud concludes that "it was hardly credible that perverted acts against children were so general." Certainly he was not alone in being profoundly confused about interpreting the sexual energies surrounding the taboo on incest. In literary history, everyone acknowledges incest was a recurrent theme in Jacobean drama, then in the gothic novels, and in the *fin-de-siècle* novels. And yet literary critics are stymied as to the why and wherefore. Why should incest be, from time to time, such an important theme in art and at other times seemingly forgotten? Why should it be such a modern concern?[10]

First, what is incest and, second, why are we frightened and fascinated by it? Incest names a tabooed sexual union between close blood relatives, a relationship that is usually forbidden by both law and custom. The term "incest" comes from the Latin *incestur*, which means "impure" (*in* = not + *castus* = pure), but it is not clear exactly what is impure—the sexual act, or the results. Even more confusing is the fact that sometimes either marriage or sex between consanguineous partners can be considered incestuous. What is clear is that the act, sexual or social, so violates social mores that it is literally

abhorred by most societies. Incest is not a subject for action or even for conversation. What little is said about it is usually wrong. A generation ago, for
instance, it was thought that incest was one of the few acts (along with cannibalism) that inspired universal horror, or át least it was supposed to.
Actually, the act we really fear seems to be talking about it and thinking
about it, and so from the seventeenth century onward we have remained
rather mum. We may not even dream much about it.

Although we rarely talk about incest, we spend considerable energy fig-
uring out, and then explaining to our querulous youngsters, exactly whom
they should consider off-limits. We seem to most abhor mother-son union,
then father-daughter, then sibling, then maybe uncle-niece. Outside the
nuclear family, we rather lose interest—first cousins are not sufficiently consanguineous to activate the law in most states, but the relationship is still too
close for most of us to accept. In other societies, however, aunts, uncles,
cousins, and occasionally even nonblood relatives such as surrogate parents
or adopted relatives and mentors are too close for social comfort.

When we used to think a universal taboo against incest existed, the nag-
ging problem arose of explaining the instances where not only incest was
mentioned, but actually flaunted: for instance, among pharaohs of the Pto-
lemaic dynasty (Cleopatra was the product of eleven generations of brother-
sister incest), within the ancient Incan and Hawaiian societies, or still in
certain African tribes. In such cultures incest was both announced and doc-
umented by the participants. Were these exceptions that proved the rule or
were they simply the "way of the ruling class," a method to make sure that
nobility was not polluted? Or maybe the taboo was made to be broken as a
sign of the power, the *droit du seigneur*, a kind of unpunished violation by
the noble classes to show who controlled the law. Thanks to our deepening
concern with child abuse, we now realize that incest is far more prevalent in
our society than we had ever imagined and probably more prevalent elsewhere in the West as well.[11] It has probably always been this way. In 1979
the American Humane Society, which is the national monitor for the mis-
treatment of animals (if that gives any inkling of how bestial we consider the
violation of this taboo), reported 11,306 sexually maltreated children, and
this figure admittedly was grossly low because this kind of sexual violation
usually goes unreported. Still, from figures like these, as well as from other
etic research, Professor Alexander G. Zaphiris, a social worker, lawyer, and
Dean of the Graduate School of Social Work at the University of Houston,
has estimated that two or three children out of every thousand are sexually
abused. This would mean a national total of between 125,000 and 187,000 of
which, Zaphiris contends, more than 90 percent are victims of incest (*New
York Times*, June 15, 1981). The original Kinsey sample suggested that one

woman in sixteen had been the victim of incest, while a 1980 study by the chief psychologist at Nazareth Child Care Center in Boston argued that one in ten was closer to the truth. In 1980 even the *Harvard Medical School Newsletter* had a special insert in "The Medical Forum" on the widespread incidence and woeful lack of medical understanding of this problem, and a year later the Harvard University Press published the first comprehensive study of the subject, *Father-Daughter Incest*, written by a practicing therapist, Judith Herman.

Incest is present in all races and religions, income levels, and at much higher incidence than is usually supposed. Recent studies reveal that incest most commonly occurs in large families in which both parents are sexually jealous, timid, and passive. When questioned, the incest-committing father (mother-son is very rare) frequently says he was only teaching his daughter "the facts of life," while his wife claims she "didn't know what was happening." Very often sibling incest occurs as the continuation of the father's sexual conditioning. But, interestingly enough, incest rarely occurs between children raised together, a phenomenon known as the "kibbutz syndrome," because in all the studies of Israeli children there are no cases of marriage, much less reports of coitus, between lifelong companions. Extended close proximity usually breeds sexual inhibition bordering almost on bodily contempt, or as one waggish anthropologist has put it, "familiarity not only does not breed contempt; it does not breed at all." This conclusion is further reinforced by studies of Taiwanese "marry-a-sister" arrangements in which the bride and groom, who have been raised together, tend to be soon sexually disenchanted and nonreproductive. The fact of the matter is that most of us, most of the time, simply have no interest in committing incest.

Still more shocking, especially to those who, like Freud, have held that incest is an instinctive desire that must be capped by taboo, is that the victims of this "crime against nature" are not automatically candidates for neurosis. If the figures are correct, there are thousands of incest victims leading well-adjusted lives, at least in statistical proportion to what one could expect after encounters with a parent or a sibling who really was sexually disturbed. What does cause trauma for the victim, however, and there is plenty of it, is not so much the victim's revulsion, but the social stigma and ensuing guilt and confusion. I realize this is uncomfortably close to those chauvinist arguments that the rape victim is really asking for it and so deserves what she has gotten. By no means do I wish to imply that. However, we have to address the fact that, as Dr. Zaphiris and others have reported, if the victim (almost all females in his studies), is allowed to simply speak her mind, she may well see nothing wrong with the acts her father has described as a natural part of his affection.[12] Certainly, this is the same behavior reported by anthropologists who have studied incest in cultures with few social taboos. But what is interesting about our culture, in which there is a strong taboo against incest, is the treatment prescribed. Here is Dr. Zaphiris' advice based on studies of more than twenty years: "[The] customary procedure is to undo the father's conditioning and resolve the child's guilt by encouraging the child to discuss it and by making her aware that many others have had similar traumas. To help break the incestuous bond, her guilt for having enjoyed the incestuous sex must be strengthened" (*New York Times*, June 15, 1981, and Zaphiris' monograph *Incest: The Family with Two Known Victims*, 1978).

Now why should her "guilt for having enjoyed the incestuous sex" need to be strengthened? If the incest-avoidance mechanism were phylogenetically transferred, it would seem too late—an aberration has slipped through the protective sieve. But what we are now finding out is that there is no *instinctive* command either to do, or not to do, acts of incest. *The "grisly horror" of incest is socially learned*. It has to be taught, and shivers are a most efficient teacher. Guilt occurs after an act; horror, however, can occur before—and may prevent the action.

A generation ago it was thought that natural selection "prohibited" inbreeding because of resultant biological aberrations. It was common in the social sciences to point to those Russian and Greek princes who were hemophiliacs, or to those slack-jawed country folk isolated in the Appalachian valleys (who, by the way, have become almost stock characters in slash-'em-up horror since *Deliverance*) as proof. From what we now know about genetics and heredity, such aberrations were not caused primarily by inbreeding, but by the fact that a small breeding pool passed certain traits around without being able to have them countermanded by stronger traits. While incestuous mating does increase the probability of recessive alleles, this same homozygosity can also produce a counterbalancing hybrid vigor, especially in small populations. Think, for instance, how we breed race horses or beef cows. Harvard biologist Edward O. Wilson probably knows as much about the natural selection argument as anyone and has concluded the following in *Sociobiology* (1980):

> In summary, small group size and the inbreeding that accompanies it favor social evolution, because they ally the group members by kinship and make altruism profitable through the promotion of autozygous genes (hence, one's own genes) among the recipients of the altruism. But inbreeding lowers individual fitness and imperils group survival by the depression of performance and loss of genetic adaptability. Presumably, then, the degree of sociality is to some extent the evolutionary outcome of these two opposed selection tendencies. How are the forces to be translated into components of fitness and then traded off in the same selec-

tion models? This logical next step does not seem feasible at the present time, and it stands as one of the more important challenges of theoretical population genetics. (p. 39)

Simply in terms of adaptation, then, too much inbreeding can be as dele-terious as too much outbreeding; the two must be kept in a dynamic balance. And they probably have been, even though we have been unaware of it, thinking always that we were breeding outside of our clan because we have been exogamous for so long. Still, what is perplexing to Darwinian theorists is that, although a little incest will not do massive genetic harm, the social taboo (and in the centuries since Leviticus, the legal restrictions) has been applied as if even a little bit would do damage. Thus, our social tolerance is much lower than our biological threshold.

The incest taboo is cultural, not genetic: it does not protect the phenotype, it protects the society. So in the modern sociobiological explanations of incest, the center of logical gravity has shifted from incest-avoidance mech-anisms to the social process that establishes exogamy. In other words, cul-tures abhor incest not to protect the purity of the gene pool, but to enforce domestic stability. The advantages of exogamy are simple: kinship is extended well beyond the family and, on the assumption that blood is thicker than water, the chances for social tranquility are increased. "Marry out or be kicked out" seems to be the demand of the tribe. Doubtless the extension and then maintenance of kinship boundaries facilitated such tasks as migra-tion, hunting, harvesting, governing, and later, warfare. Yet, one wonders if even such a desire for social cohesion could really have powered so long-lasting and pervasive a taboo as the one countermanding incest.

The truth is that anthropologists, whatever their intellectual bias, do not really know why the incest taboo is so Procrustean; they are like English teachers explaining what makes a literary masterpiece. Ultimately, it is just because it has an audience that wants it and believes in it. Although we may not know much about incest, we are increasing our knowledge of various cultures and the exogamy myths they perpetuate. One of the most interesting connections made involves societies that are sensitive to, and hence usually repressed about, incest. In these societies specific initiation ceremonies for adolescents teach them to be wary, if not horrified, of incest. These rituals, as Harvard anthropologist J. W. M. Whiting and his colleagues detailed in their cross-cultural study on "The Function of Male Initiation Ceremonies at Puberty," tend to be elaborate and brutal. For example, in Australia a num-ber of tribes have such rigorous breeding rules that the genitalia of both sexes are mutilated in adolescence (circumcision, superincision, subincision for the boys; clitoridectomy and infibulation for the girls) as a way of hinting that the tribe's sexual expectations will be met or there will be no breeding allowed. In such cultures myths are often told to the boys that stress the need for the young men to leave the immediate family and go fetch a lion skin or human head or anything, just as long as the search takes them far away from the tribe. Only after much time has passed are the novitiates allowed to return home and enter the breeding population, for presumably by this time mother and sisters will have moved elsewhere. The same kind of induction ceremony occurs for the girls, except that their ceremony has them sequestered in a sorority of older females who presumably protect them from the advances of father and brothers.[13]

If we ever wonder about our own freedom from such myths, we might do well to pause and take a quick look at one of our favorite adolescent templates, Hercules. Hercules is not just the greatest hero Greece ever knew; he is arguably the greatest hero to early adolescents in the West. Here he is, the archetypical teenage male—forever misunderstood, forever confused, yet forever strong and mighty. The brain may not have grown much, but the biceps have. Hercules, the first "incredible hulk," presides over his own cinematic cottage industry (with Joseph E. Levine and the Italians) in such forgettables as *Hercules Against the Moon Men*, *Hercules in the Haunted World*, *Hercules and the Captive Women*, *Hercules Unchained*, and so on. He is still with us, continually being reincarnated as Superman, Tarzan, Mighty Mouse, Conan the Barbarian, the Incredible Hulk, and all the other big boys who must stumble their way through the vicissitudes of adolescence—namely, sex.

I won't dwell on the myth of Hercules other than to say that he was the result of one of Zeus' many indiscretions with a mortal, and that Hera cursed Hercules at birth by giving him an uncontrollable temper. It was so bad that in adolescence he was sent away to wander about until he came to the Oracle at Delphi where he learned he must perform the twelve labors in order to be relieved. He did, and in so doing, introduced us to the stable of monsters who have kept camp counselors and movie moguls in business ever since: the lion of Nema, the Hydra, the Stymphalian birds, the Geryon, among others. Hercules was still not at peace. He was off for yet more brawny adventures: he fought with Antaeus, dressed up as a girl, fell in love with a boy, hefted the earth, and threw huge objects around, but he was still melancholy. Finally, he destroyed himself in flames and, in death, was transported to the heavens where at last he found peace. He did what he never could have done on earth, the one thing that quieted him: he married Hebe, his half-sister; he committed incest.

I do not mean to make too much of this, if only because the myth itself doesn't and the ancient gods were notoriously heedless of human taboos anyway; but I do use it to point out that the incest-avoidance mechanisms, rites of passage, monster confrontations, and initiation myths are connected in our own cultural past and so may well be in the present. In fact, those monsters in the Hercules myth are still with us and the horror they engender is still palpable, at least to adolescents. Ray Harryhausen has made almost a career of just re-creating the visual imagery of the Hercules myth for one movie after another. But how does this classical heritage connect with the vampire, the nameless creature, the werewolf, and Mr. Hyde?

I think what animates these particular myths, these stories from our youth, is that beneath the horror there is a prescriptive text detailing the "do's" and "don't's" of breeding, especially as they pertain to incest. Make-believe frights may or may not protect the audience from real scares, but the one thing they clearly do is show consequences of socially inappropriate sexual action.[14] So let the young virgin have sex (even though it seems only a bite on the neck—her response is sexual enough) with that specific older man and the vampire's life will be hers. Let young Frankenstein tinker away in his lab attempting to create life on his own, and he'll make a monster who will then attack the boy's loved ones; in the novel the loved one is clearly his "sister." Let your "wolf" come out and you'll have to be destroyed by the girl you love most, lest you destroy her first. Remember that when the women get added to the Jekyll story, the future father-in-law postpones the young doctor's marriage, and this frustration, in part, causes Mr. Hyde to come out and maul not the supposed fiancée; instead, he attacks her displaced "self"— the sensual woman of the streets. Hyde will not touch Jekyll's intended bride, nor for that matter will Jekyll—she is off-limits to both. Or think about lesser myths, such as the Phantom of the Opera—is this a story of a disfigured musician who just wants to help a young soprano, or is it also a story of an older man who, because he wants this particular girl in a way he should not want her, has to become (rather like the vampire) a monster in the cellar, a phantom, a disfigured, but still polite enough madman?

There will be time to retell these stories later. Right now we might wonder whether, since they are all vaguely related to the subject of early adolescents being initiated into sexuality, there might not be a core myth from which they all descended. Could there be a story, now long since forgotten, that was the Ur-myth of adolescence, a tale still hidden, within these variants? I think so. And I think it was the "family romance" first propounded by Freud in *Totem and Taboo* (1913) and now recently made the startling thesis of Robin Fox's *The Red Lamp of Incest* (1980). Let me tell it again, for within it are the strains of what will become the modern symphonies of horror: the werewolf, the no-name creature, and, most especially, the vampire. Here is the tale of the primal horde told by Freud ostensibly to explain what he took to be the instinctive avoidance of incest, what he repeatedly called the "horror of incest," what he was convinced was the central primordial act that inspired civilization and all its discontents.

Long, long ago, at the edge of language and hence of history, we lived in small nomadic clans numbering about twenty members. We mated freely, with whomever and whenever we could, although probably not often in mother-son unions, for this was the only relationship in which both parties could be sure of an earlier physical proximity. But father-daughter and sibling incest certainly occurred, in no way self-consciously, because the breeding pool was small. There was some squabbling over the women and eventually the strongest male, most probably the father of many of the young boys, took control of several females and, rather like modern-day apes, forbade the boy-cubs to come close. These women were his; they were "taken"; the boys were driven out. Patriarchy begins. The young males were doubtless enraged by what seemed an arbitrary denial and bound together to fight the oppressor, their father. Freud continues the story:

> One day the brothers who had been driven out came together, killed and devoured their father and so made an end of the patriarchal horde. United, they had the courage to do and succeed in doing what would have been impossible for them individually (some cultural advance, perhaps, command over some new weapon, had given them a sense of superior strength). Cannibal savages as they were, it goes without saying that they devoured their victim as well as killing him. The violent primal father had doubtless been the feared and envied model of each one of the company of brothers; and in the act of devouring him they accomplished their act of identification with him, and each of them acquired a portion of his strength. The totem meal, which is perhaps mankind's earliest festival, would thus be a repetition and a commemoration of this memorable and criminal deed, which was the beginning of so many things—of social organization, of moral restrictions and of religion. (*Totem and Taboo*, pp. 141–42)

It is important to stress (as Freud really didn't, if only because there was no way for him to realize how he was to be misread) that the boys did not want to copulate with their sisters or even with their mother—even if they could have known who they were—they simply wanted to copulate, to release the pressures of their sexuality. But once the act was done, once they had destroyed, literally consumed, the father-oppressor and then had satisfied their carnality, they were intelligent enough to realize that they were now fated to assume his role. They would now have to battle among themselves as well as against a new generation of youngsters. And so over generations of intrafamilial turmoil a social contract, the first cultural agreement, was struck: certain mutually recognizable women were "put aside," made off limits to the males of the family, tabooed. They were tabooed *not* because they were objects of stronger desire than other women, but because relationships with *these* women would rend the fabric of the only society known, the clan. If there was an "original sin" in human culture, here it was.

Families that inbred squabbled themselves out of existence, while families that outbred were stable and eventually dominant. These successful groups felt the guilt of patricide (although presumably not of incest) as well as the abiding fear that they might be next, and so they saw to it that their young learned how the game was played before it was too late for both of them.

> The tumultuous mob of brothers were filled with the same contradictory feelings which we can see at work in the ambivalent father-complexes of our children and of our neurotic patients. They hated their father, who presented such a formidable obstacle to their craving for power and their sexual desires; but they loved and admired him too. After they had got rid of him, had satisfied their hatred and had put into effect their wish to identify themselves with him, the affection which had all this time been pushed under was bound to make itself felt. It did so in the form of remorse. A sense of guilt made its appearance, which in this instance coincided with the remorse felt by the whole group. The dead father became stronger than the living one had been—for events took the course we so often see them follow in human affairs to this day. What had up to then been prevented by his actual existence was thenceforward prohibited by the sons themselves, in accordance with the psychological procedure so familiar to us in psychoanalyses under the name of "deferred obedience." They revoked their deed by forbidding the killing of the totem, the substitute for their father, and they renounced its fruits by resigning their claim to the women who had now been set free. (*Totem and Taboo*, p. 143)

From this first communal renunciation came the sublimation of psychic energy that has, in a sense, separated us from the animals: it has given us religion, art, culture, history, politics, and neuroses.

Freud did not really believe the primal horde "scenario" took place; it did not have to, for we act as if it did. The "omnipotence of thoughts," our imaginations, our dream-lives, can produce effects every bit as real as any "reality." And these "thoughts," as Freud found—and modern anthropologists and psychologists have at least concurred with Freud here—are especially accessible in the fantasy life of neurotics, children, and savages. Often individuals in these groups believe the story is true, while the rest of us simply act *as if* it had happened. We act as if certain females really are forbidden; we act as if the fate of Oedipus would be ours if the taboo were violated. So we make sure the information does not get lost on the next generation even if it means, as if often does, that they be horrified.

The "universal horror of incest" is, therefore, a way of resolving the anxiety of sexual ambivalence. While we may be curious in late childhood about sex with a parent or sibling, we unconsciously recall the hopeless tangle of patricide and cannibalism. The jungle is worse than the town: linen is better than leaves. Freud had read his James Frazer: we have overthrown the king and we had best make sure our fate is not his. So we "celebrate" the grisly act by repeating the scenes via totems and myths as if to confess our own hostility while repressing that of our sons. This celebration eventually becomes one of the central events in the rites of passage through adolescence, for the young must be led across the mine field of sexuality not for their sakes only, but for ours. They must be taught not just "when," but especially "with whom," or they will send us all back to the bush. Turning away from incest and toward exogamy was the first step out of the jungle and into the meadow. So conscience was born; so culture began. In the words of Claude Lévi-Strauss,

> If social organization had a beginning, this could only have consisted in the incest prohibition, since ... the incest prohibition is, in fact, a kind of remodeling of the biological conditions of mating and procreation (which know no rule, as can be seen from observing animal life) compelling them to be perpetuated only in an artificial framework of taboos and obligations. It is there, and only there, that we find a passage from nature to culture, from animal to human life. ("The Family" in *Man, Culture and Society*, p. 278)

Freud did not come away with his "hypothesis ... of such a monstrous air" (p. 142) unscathed, for every cultural anthropologist from Marrett to Lévi-Strauss has had first to push the "primal horde" conjecture aside. Freud's grand theory has usually been attacked for its stark simplicity ("over-simplified") and lack of attention to data ("unscientific"). Here the critics were correct: most of Freud's psychological proof came from neurotic patients, while his anthropology came from Westermarck, Frazer, McLennan, Smith, and especially studies of Australian aborigines which were popular around the turn of the century and soon suspect. Additionally, I think what really detracted from his hypothesis was Freud's unorthodox style. In retrospect, he never should have told it as a horror story, but that, of course, is exactly what it was. So it is interesting to note that a quarter of a century later in *Moses and Monotheism* Freud flattened the tone, but to no avail. "Real scientists," as A. L. Kroeber, the dean of American anthropologists reportedly said of Freud's thesis, do not tell "Just-So stories," whatever the tone.

While Freud's thesis has never run short of supporters, especially among the orthodox, the two scholarly reservations—too reductive and too unscientific—have at last been partially resolved. Robin Fox, an English anthropologist whose expertise on kinship is considerable (*Kinship and Marriage*, co-author of *The Imperial Animal*, and author of three other books on biosocial development), has recently passed Freud's conjectures through a rigorous scientific cross-examination. Using what we now know about evolution, primatology, brain function, as well as psychoanalysis, Fox repeatedly documents how accurate Freud was, an accuracy that is almost eerie.

When he started his studies of incest, Fox did not intend to end on the side of what, for most academic anthropologists, is still the Viennese witch doctor, but as he himself ruefully admits, that is where he finally stood. In *The Red Lamp of Incest* (1980) Fox attempts only to account for the "universal horror of incest" as it reinforces certain specific evolutionary "preferences." From studies of kinship it is clear that there is no natural aversion to incest; from the biological pattern of human reproduction it is clear that incest-aversion is nowhere coded in the DNA; so the trait must be learned through generations of natural selection. We must unconsciously be teaching our children the proper multiplication tables because we must have learned that our culture, as well as our species, depends on it. But how did we learn this? We learned it, Fox contends, because "*something like it* [the primal horde experience] *must actually have taken place*" (p. 61; Fox's italics).

Here, then, is Fox's updating of Freud, working from the present backward. Kinship stability, which is the basis of all social stability, is achieved by the continual reaffirmation of certain sexual relationships and the taboo of others. We have forbidden incest, not because we really care about it, but because it is socially implosive—it will collapse the social and political structure of a group. It destroys not by producing mutants, but rather by producing strife. Thus the tribes who survived were not the most aggressive or the most sexually potent, but rather those "who knew best how to time and use their sexuality." Those who knew that staying alive was more important than being sexually active made it; those others, who were perhaps only incidentally incestuous, did not.

Fox then contends that as we evolved and populated ourselves into ever larger groups, a new kind of stability was achieved between the major human groups, an organization that almost parodies the nuclear family. This order is still operative. First, there are the established males who mate according to pre-established rules, then there are the females with children, and lastly those social satellites, the hot-blooded, unmated males. These males orbit around the reproductive females until they find those with whom they can be successful. But there is no Oedipal desire here, as Freud would have claimed, nor any incestuous desire between siblings, just the never-ending drives demanded by biology. So what separates us from the baboons, who will savagely attack a younger male when he makes an improper choice (i.e., a "taken" female) and then let him try all over again? We humans have developed a code—what Fox calls a "permanent pattern of memory"—to inform the prepotent males of the consequences *before* they can choose. This information is embedded into both the brain matter and the rites and myths of initiation with one simple message: have intercourse with a "taken" woman and you will be cast out. It is as simple as that—make a mistake and you will not breed for a while. Thus the rogue males as well as the independent females will not make it through the evolutionary grid because, *before* the iron law of natural selection rewards the independent and strong, it first protects the fruitful.[15]

Fox is not interested in how this message is inscribed onto what E. R. Leach has called the "rubber sheeting" of culture (an apt analogy to describe how certain human behavior is diagrammed into all of us as if on a flexible sheet that can be twisted, stretched, even knotted, yet always retains the same relative, not absolute, pattern); but I certainly am. I believe and hope to show (1) that horror stories, especially about Dracula, Frankenstein, and the werewolf (Jekyll/Hyde), carry the prescriptive codes of modern Western sexual behavior, (2) that horror stories owe their vitality to both the audience's need to know and the elder's need to inform and are thus a crucial conversation between generations, (3) that horror motifs have their *initial* appeal to both sexes during latency (ages five to twelve) and become part of more extensive rites of initiation, the "danse macabre," and finally, (4) that these sagas, while not necessarily making the *right* predictions about future life, are memory banks of social and sexual possibilities both for the individual and the group. They show exactly what will melt down the nuclear family. Just as fairy tales articulate a continuous range of future alternatives that deal with resolving the anxieties of separation, so horror tales announce the whys and wherefores of sexual reproduction and then attempt to resolve some of the alternatives. Horror art is not escapist fantasy; it is social history.

3

The Rise and Fall and Rise of Dracula

The story of the strangest passion the world has ever known.
Universal Studio's advertisement for Dracula, November 1930

The Strangest Love a Man has ever Known!
Universal marquee for Dracula, 1931

We are currently plagued by two vampires. The emaciated snaggle-toothed fiend, who is straight from folklore, is feral, mindless, and barbaric; the foppish gentleman, who is from the arts, is articulate, sensitive, and cultured. They both dedicate their waking hours to the same activity—draining blood and hence the life energy of innocent women. If ever Sir Philip Sidney wanted an example of the sugar-coating powers of art, this is it, for the suave gentleman is ever so much more palatable (if that is the right word) than the scruffy menace, the nosferatu. But like a china doll the nosferatu, literally the "not dead," is just under the skin of the gentlemanly Dracula, and what they both promise to do still lifts the hairs on the nape of our necks and sends ripples down our spines.

These monsters are vampires and the verb "plague" is not inappropriate, for they are members of a genus of monsters that, like the werewolf, reproduce themselves through their victims. In a most unsophisticated doppelgänger transformation, the vampire's victim becomes a second-generation vampire who, in turn, inducts a third, fourth, and so on. So it is no wonder that, although the vampire is one of mankind's oldest horror images, he really entered Western popular culture in the seventeenth century as a logical way to account for the geometric progression of deaths caused by the fast-acting plague bacteria. We now know that the toxic strain was carried to man from mice via fleas, but it was ever so much more logical, ever so much more plausible, to think that the vampire did it. Plague victims were burned for more than sanitary reasons: they were burned because incineration was one of the most effective methods of vampire disposal.[1]

But the only way for Occam's razor to cut so sharply through the medical confusion of the plague was for the vampire already to be considered alive and well. And indeed he was. Long before Christ, the vampire had roamed Middle European mythologies, migrating from the high steppes of India eastward into China and westward into Greece. The rise of Christianity, ironically, did as much to nurture the vampire as the plague would later do, for the Catholic Church found in the story of this fiend a most propitious analogy to describe the intricate workings of evil.

Aside from the devil, the vampire is the most popular malefactor in Christianity.[2] In fact, the competition is unfair, not just because the vampire is now probably more popular, but because the vampire really *is* the devil. The vampire is simply the husk of a human that has been commandeered by the spirit of Satan. The force of evil has gained control of the sinner's body and has trapped the psyche, or the soul, depending on the culture, and is sealing it off from eternal rest. In Christian worlds the devil has done this because the human sinner died unbaptized, was excommunicated, was buried in unhallowed ground, committed suicide, or—most commonly used today, but relatively unheard of before the seventeenth century—was the victim of a vampire's attack. The human form is simply the soma, the undead hulk, carrying around the demon and letting it pass through society undetected.

Or almost undetected, because this avatar still carries vestiges of satanic possession; for instance, the nosferatu/vampire stinks of putrefaction, has tufts of hair in the palm (a reminder of the lycanthropic transformation), has bloodshot, incandescent eyes, often a cleft palate, fingernail claws and, of course, those extended teeth. It has been appropriately pointed out that many of these traits were Victorian symptoms of sexual excess, particularly self-abuse. Little wonder the vampire should only feel safe alone at night. Incidentally, the vampire's fear of daylight seems an example of reasoning *post hoc, ergo propter hoc*, for he was a nocturnal molester in folklore first, a daylight despiser second. In pre-cinematic folklore the vampire was superpowerful in moonlight and only ordinary during the day. Hence Bram Stoker's Dracula walked undetected around London at noontime in a business suit and straw hat. We have, however, made the vampire so photophobic that for a while during the 1960s and 1970s it was a sure sign that the vampire's demise was near at hand when the string section of the studio orchestra was

Max Schreck as Count Orlock in F. W. Murnau's *Nosferatu, A Symphony of Terror*, 1922 (Prana Films)

Klaus Kinski as Count Dracula in Werner Herzog's *Nosferatu—The Vampire*, 1979 (20th Century Fox)

Bela Lugosi as the Count in the 1927 stage production of *Dracula*.

Frank Langella as the Count in John Badham's *Dracula*, 1979 (Universal Studios)

cued-up and the camera panned over to the rising crest of light on the horizon.

The other method of vampire destruction in both contemporary and ancient folklore was the stake. Here one sees the wonderfully concentrated logic of the folk imagination, for while the audience was unperturbed that, with the vampire's geometric population burst the poor fiends would soon run out of virgin blood to drink, they always demanded that the logic of vampire destruction be maintained.[3] Since the vampire is the devil inside an already dead human carcass, he must be destroyed, not killed. There is simply nothing alive left to kill. That is why he cannot be shot or knifed or bludgeoned to death. The husk is then either burned or staked to the ground, and often the head is cut off and stuffed with garlic for good measure. Once again the stake is not to kill, it simply holds the carrion in place. To a purist, this stake should be of the same wood from which Christ's cross was fashioned—aspen, buckthorn, or oak, depending on the culture—and the vampire should be placed chest down, so if the leech somehow revives, he will dig down to the center of the earth, not up to the crust.

For all the vampire's quaint habits, for all his serendipitous encounters with Satan and the plague, he might never have survived in Western horror art had he not been adopted by the Holy Roman Church. The results of this sponsorship are still visible in the myth as the principal symbols used in destroying the vampire: holy water, the sign of the cross, church icons of all sorts and, of course, the vampire's most common enemy, the parish priest. But the Church could have fostered other monsters—why not the zombie or the ghoul or some other already extant ogre? Why the vampire? What the medieval church found in the vampire legend was not just an apt mythologem for evil, but an elaborate allegory for the transubstantiation of evil. The reason this was so important was that the vampire myth explained the most difficult concept in the last of the sacraments to be introduced—the Eucharist. It explained the doctrine of transubstantiation in reverse. In the Middle Ages the Church fathers found their congregation understandably hesitant about accepting that the wafer and the wine were the actual, let alone the metaphoric, body and blood of Christ. How better could the transubstantiation be explained than on the more primitive level, the level the folk already knew and believed in—namely, the vampire transformation. For just as the devil-vampire drank the blood and then captured the spirit of a sinner, so too could the penitent drink the blood, eat the body, and possess the divinity of Christ.

There is every indication that, without this syncretic layering with Christian dogma, the vampire might have shriveled up to become a lesser monster as he did in most non-Christian cultures. But thanks to the Church, the vampire found a niche in the occidental chamber of horrors and has yet to be dislodged. By the Renaissance the folk myth had been almost completely expropriated by the Church. The vampire destroyer in folklore, usually the fiend's son, called a "dhampire," who intuitively knew how best to destroy the father, became the priest. Garlic and certain berries, which had been the bane of the vampire, evolved into holy water and icons. Decapitation and burning became staking, complete with all the rigamarole about the choice of proper wood. The folklore beast even made it into the register of the Inquisition, the *Malleus Maleficarum*, or *Witch Hammer*. This *vade mecum* of Church prosecutors did not name the vampire as such but acknowledged the existence of the blood-sucking undead and prescribed the requisite legal tests. Thus did the folk vampire, the nosferatu, slowly but surely become the Christian vampire, the dracula.

The vampire has now become such a part of the whole Christian ethos that in the 1960s Hammer Studios even attempted to make this the theme of one of its then-endless celluloid resuscitations. In *Dracula Has Risen from the Grave* (1968) we find that a village church in Middle Europe has fallen on hard times. The local priest has given himself over to liquor and gambling and neglected his flock. Atheists have flourished and so too has the neighborhood Dracula. When the monsignor comes to inspect the parish he is outraged and collars the backsliding priest, promising to straighten matters out. Together they climb up to Castle Dracula, which overlooks the town (Hammer seemed to use the same matte work for Castle Dracula or Castle Frankenstein or Castle Fu Manchu, and it always looked like cardboard), in order to "sanitize the devil's lair." The modern priest is clearly bored by all this superstitious fiddle-de-dee such as putting crosses all over—especially a big golden one in the door latch—spraying holy water and mumbling prayers. He is so blasé that en route home he wanders off the steep path and stumbles over a cliff. Meanwhile, the monsignor is so rapt in his prayers that he does not notice that his young charge has been cut on a jagged rock and that his blood is dripping onto the frozen body of . . . Dracula. The king vampire has lain there in an ice chunk since he was trapped in an ice flow at the end of *Dracula, Prince of Darkness* (1965). Dracula, now revived and furious, makes the priest erase all unsightly graffiti from his castle as well as remove the big golden cross from the door. The priest heaves it over the cliff. Dracula will have his revenge for this defacement of his castle and the now-powerless priest will be his instrument.

Dracula avenges himself in typical Hammer style: he "attacks" (seduces) the monsignor's full-breasted niece who is, of course, "almost a daughter" to the churchman. To make matters worse, just as the young priest should have protected his flock, so the requisite boyfriend, Paul, should be protecting his comely girlfriend. But Paul is an atheist! The monsignor clearly has his hands full, having a careless surrogate son in the church and a faithless surrogate son-in-law-to-be at home. Typically, the monsignor now dies of a broken heart and a punch or two from Dracula, but not before he has deputized Paul to collar the wayward priest and promise to destroy the evil patriarch. The girl must be saved before it is too late. The boys catch Dracula, but when they try to stake him it won't take—Paul is an atheist and can't pray; the priest is a coward and won't. So the vampire is on the loose once again.

Only luck saves them now. Dracula returns to make the girl his "bride," but Paul surprises him and is badly beaten for his troubles. The vampire is now able to take her to his castle to make a queen of her (she's not so unwilling), but who should appear at the gate but a revived Paul. Another fight, and this time it's Dracula who trips over the cliff, to be impaled on that big golden cross that the priest had earlier heaved over the cliff. Just happening to be passing by is that wayward priest. He sees Dracula fall, is reconciled with his God, can now say the proper prayers, and Dracula is once again friated. Unbeknownst to us in the audience, a merchant is standing close by to collect that dust so that lusty Lord Courtly can mix with a little blood to get *Taste the Blood of Dracula* (1970) started. In *Dracula Has Risen from the Grave* the boys finally learned the value of Christianity; popular culture got one of its most alluring theater posters—a sexually sated young beauty with two puncture marks just over her cleavage: "Dracula Has Risen from the Grave . . . obviously"; and Hammer Studios got the Queen's Award for Industry.

Clearly, the vampire, even the Hammer Dracula, has more going for him than just being the resident demon in Christian folklore. For the last few generations he has also served to explain the dynamics of human social and sexual behavior. And it is here, especially as a paradigm of suppressed inter-familial struggles, that the vampire has become a central figure in popular culture. He is no longer a figure of demonic terror; he has become an eidolon of sexual horror. How this transformation occurred is illustrative not only of the romantic imagination, but of the mythopoetic process in general, for it shows how certain myths continually re-magnetize themselves around the audience's changing lodestones.

The vampire was not a subject of artistic concern prior to the turn of the nineteenth century. Although mentioned in a few ballads like "Sweet William's Ghost," in travelogues (usually ones that detailed English adventures in Central Europe) or in histories, especially those of an ecclesiastical bent where the pre-Reformation church fathers carried the day against the "Sanguisugae" or blood-suckers, such references were always made in passing. I

Dracula Has Risen from the Grave: lobby poster, 1968 (Hammer Studios)

suppose a case could be made (and it has been) that the Beowulf monster, Grendel, is vampiric, or that Caliban is also, but such an interpretation usually mixes the vampire with his stronger mythic cousin, the incubus. Most pre-romantic blood-thirsty monsters are more informed by the incubus myth than by the vampire.

The fact is that the vampire was too raw, too uncouth, too predictable to be of much interest to any but the most gothic of imaginations. This may partially explain why he left the fireside of the folk and the parchment of church scholars to enter the slightly soiled world of late-eighteenth-century poetry and prose fiction. He started his migration in German gothicism, in Ossenfelder's "The Vampire" (1748) and Bürger's *Lenore* (1773), in which he played the part of a revenant come back from the dead to collect his living bride. By the time Goethe wrote his more allusive *The Bride of Corinth* (1797) it is clear that "collect the bride" was a code for "sexually molest." And what better image of gothic terror, of the master of the castle and the farmer's daughter, than this new vampire as lover, coming up out of the grave (later up from the cellar) to collect his tabooed bride, princess, queen.

The most important English translator of German shivers into English was Robert Southey. Southey was a poet more eager than most to be current, and he was more able than most to be inappropriate. In book eight of *Thalaba the Destroyer* (1797) Southey takes his chivalric hero, Thalaba, into a buried vault where he pays his respects to his one-time bride, Oneiza. She was taken from him on their wedding day by a demon. Now, rising from the mist like her Teutonic male counterpart, Oneiza beckons Thalaba to follow her beyond the grave. But Thalaba has a wise friend who has read all those German poems and warns the ephebic hero; the fiend is "lanced" and we're off to another adventure.

Southey realized his readers might have some problem here (it all happens in two stanzas) so he appended a prose commentary, which is really the first extended psychological explanation of the vampire in English. In retrospect Southey summed up what the French Benedictine scholar Dom Augustin Calmet had expounded in his most important *Traité sur les apparitions des espirits, et sur les vampires* ... (Paris, 1746). Southey's well-researched, five-page gloss introduced the vampire to the best of people, especially the Lake Poets, Wordsworth and Coleridge, and this is just the kind of entrée into literary society that no monster should be without.

Although the vampire's debut did not go unnoticed, it had stiff competition. There were many other new archetypes after the turn of the century who were also appealing: the reclusive poet, the melancholy man of feeling, the emotive child, the Promethean overreacher, to say nothing of Don Juan or the Wandering Jew. But the vampire was not neglected for long. His image can be seen lurking in the shadow of Schedoni in *The Italian*, or beside Ambrosio in *The Monk*, or stepping out in such characters as Geraldine in *Christabel*, the Ancient Mariner in *The Rime of the Ancient Mariner*, the leech gatherer in *Resolution and Independence*, Lamia and La Belle Dame Sans Merci in Keats' poems of the same names, or in the menacing protagonists of Byron's *Manfred* and Shelley's *The Cenci*.[4]

The poets especially understood that here in the vampire archetype was an apt mythologem that could be used to express some psychological truth. And the "truth" they were most fascinated by had to do with the interaction between artist and family, and art and audience. This fascination was carried from the romantic poets into such works as Poe's *The Oval Portrait*, where the artist "vamps" the sitter of a painting so that the subject on the canvas can "come alive," Wilde's *The Picture of Dorian Gray*, where this theme is reversed, and even into Henry James' experiments in *The Sacred Fount*, where the narrator enervates his characters in order to create both a work of art and a "theory of reality."[5]

The vampire who skulks about in romantic polite literature is certainly a far distant cousin of the vampire who was to strut around the backlot at Universal Studios and who now seems omnipresent on late night airwaves. The modern vampire, however, is related to the romantic-art vampire in one important way: the modern vampire is not only interested in blood, he is interested in the process of seduction and forbidden possession, in the transfer of energy, of life, from someone to himself. He is a psychosexual leech. Thanks in large part to his transformations in romantic art, he is no longer a facinorous beast snarling at all who come between him and his victim; instead, he has become almost an aesthete who seeks and "loves" particular victims. And what "evil" he does is strangely attractive to his victim. His actions are surely sexual, but without the confusions of the body. The vampire has become part of an elaborate cultural fantasy: he finds young females, he does something to them, and he leaves them. Now the problem is to determine what, exactly, he does and, more important, to whom.

To understand the complexity of the modern vampire and his victim, we need to trace his progress not through poetry, but through prose and drama. If the modern vampire is both a literal and a figurative lady-killer, then how appropriate that the first extended vampire story should have indirectly come from the pen of that arch-adolescent himself, George Gordon, Lord Byron. *The Vampyre*, the first English story, came to us by a most circuitous route, and although it has been retraced often enough before, let me briefly travel the route again if only because it leads to the Frankenstein myth as well.

In the early summer of 1816 a most unusual colony of English poets and poetasters convened around the Villa Diodati on the shores of Lake Geneva.

It was an unusual enough assemblage so that even the professionally blasé Swiss took to their telescopes to spy on the proceedings. The local people were excitedly outraged by stories of drugs, free sex, and general debauchery characterized by Robert Southey as a "league of incest." The central characters were already well known: Percy Shelley, recently separated from his wife and now squiring Mary Godwin, the seventeen-year-old daughter of William Godwin and Mary Wollstonecraft; and Lord Byron, at once the most famous and infamous person in Europe, and his young retinue which included (along with a veritable menagerie) a young Scotsman and Byron's traveling physician, Dr. John Polidori. The Shelley and Byron parties had not previously known each other, but they had much in common: both were organized around prestigious and aristocratic poets, both poets were in self-imposed exile (Byron for his supposed incest with his half-sister, Shelley for his adultery), and both poets were involved in varying sexual degrees with Mary Godwin's stepsister Claire Clairmont. Young Polidori was also attracted to Miss Clairmont and this inappropriate attraction—he was an irritable and melancholy young man as well as an employee—may well have had considerable bearing on how the first vampire story ever made it into print.

On a rainy night sometime between June 15 and 17, both groups made a friendly wager that was to influence the shape of modern horror profoundly. As they had all been reading gothic tales from German, it was only natural that they should try their hands at composing one. So they made a pact— each member of both groups should write a scary tale and they would then see whose was best. Percy Shelley wrote a scary tale which, if his early attempts at the genre are any indication, happily he destroyed; Claire Clairmont contributed something but probably not much, since she had more pressing interests elsewhere (she was at this time carrying Byron's child); Polidori wrote something which Mary Shelley reports as being "about a skull-headed lady" who saw something through a keyhole that drove her insane; and so only two contestants were left—the seventeen-year-old Mary Godwin and Lord Byron. Mary Godwin wrote the first draft of what we will learn in the next chapter was to be not just the most famous and popular early-nineteenth-century gothic novel, but the copy-text of one of the most stable archetypes of twentieth-century horror, *Frankenstein*. Lord Byron, meanwhile, wrote a series of notes in the back of his wife's account book about a mysterious man who, according to Polidori in his introduction to *Ernestus Brechtold* (1819), was traveling east with a young friend, died of some strange disease after extracting an oath from the friend to keep mum, then reappeared a year later in London to "make love to his former friend's sister."

Certainly, this is not much of a horror story, but Polidori, ever mindful of his patron's eminence, re-formed the tale; and after he was discharged from Byron's service for a cause Polidori did not consider just (Polidori was not just a whiner, he was paying too much attention to Claire), he wrote up the story himself and sold it to Henry Colburn, then the most notorious publisher and literary entrepreneur in London. In the April 1819 issue of Colburn's *New Monthly Magazine* a tale entitled *The Vampyre* appeared, written by a "Lord B." From the editorial introduction there was no doubt who this "Lord B." really was—he was a friend of "P.S." living at the Villa Diodati. When John Murray, Byron's London publisher, saw the story, he described to Byron

a copy of a thing called The Vampire, which Mr. Colburn had had the temerity to publish with your name as its author. It was first printed in the New Monthly Magazine, from which I have taken the copy which I now enclose. The Editor of that Journal has quarrelled with the publisher, and has called this morning to exculpate himself from the baseness of the transaction. He says that he received it from Dr. Polidori for a small sum, Polidori saying that the whole plan of it was yours, and that it was merely written out by him. The Editor inserted it with a short statement to this effect, but to his astonishment Colburn cancelled the leaf on the day previous to its publication, and contrary to, and in direct hostility to his positive order, fearing that this statement would prevent the sale of this work in a separate form, which was subsequently done. He informs me that Polidori, finding that the sale exceeded his expectation, and that he sold it too cheap, went to the Editor, and declared he would deny it. . . . (John Murray to Lord Byron, April 27, 1819)

To substantiate his non-authorship, Byron found his fragment and sent it off to Murray who was to attach it to the end of *Mazeppa* and later include it in Byron's *Complete Works*. It is a poorly crafted tale, not just incoherent but often nonsensical, and it is a testament to how much Byron disliked Polidori that he was willing to have it published at all. Colburn, who may have used the young doctor to capitalize on Byron's name, finally admitted the authorship; Polidori conceded the truth in public—the idea was Byron's but the actual prose was his. Polidori was so disgraced that a year later he committed suicide.

Polidori's story is not bad at all—in any case, certainly better than the one projected by Byron. It tells of Lord Ruthven, a heartless lady-killer in London society, who goes to the continent with a young neophyte named Aubrey. They have a series of adventures, the most important of which involves a young girl, Ianthe, who is cruelly murdered by a vampire. This vampire obligingly leaves his knife beside her body. Why the vampire should need a knife is unclear, but to quibble is quite beside the point: it is a *clue*. For when

Ruthven dies, he leaves a bejeweled sheath that just fits the knife. But before Ruthven dies, he extracts a pledge from Aubrey not to mention a word of his eccentric behavior for a year and, when Aubrey foolishly consents, he asks for just one more thing: Would Aubrey be kind enough to bury him on top of a nearby hill open to the rays of the moon? After all, Ruthven has been kind enough to show Aubrey European nightlife.

We all know the rest from here on—we've heard it often enough. Ruthven revives in moonlight, returns to England, enraptures Aubrey's sister (exactly as in the Byron outline reported by Polidori, but not in Byron's written fragment), and Aubrey can't say a thing because of the oath. Finally, a year and a day after the oath, and one day after Ruthven has married Miss Aubrey, he blurts out the truth. The authorities pursue the fiend and his bride, "but when they arrived, it was too late. Lord Ruthven had disappeared and Aubrey's sister had glutted the thirst of a VAMPYRE."

Goethe, at least, claimed this was the best thing Byron ever wrote, and had Byron really written it, it probably would have been his most influential piece of prose. In the history of popular culture it often makes no difference who actually does what; if a media hero is perceived to be connected with some new development in taste, let no reality intrude. And Byron was the first great character in popular culture; his name alone was sufficient to introduce this new image to the consumers of pulp.[6]

The vampire didn't need much introduction, for in just a few years he was already on stage. The first adaptation of Polidori's work was J. R. Planche's *The Vampire: Or the Bride of the Isles*, which was first performed August 9, 1820 complete with this explanatory playbill:

> This piece if founded on the various traditions concerning THE VAMPIRES, which assert that they are Spirits, deprived of all Hope of Futurity, by the Crimes committed in their Mortal State—but, that they are permitted to roam the Earth, in whatever Forms they please, *With Supernatural Powers of Fascination*—and, that they cannot be destroyed, so long as they sustain their dreadful Existence by imbibing the BLOOD OF FEMALE VICTIMS, whom they are first compelled to Marry.

Planche's vampire must have cut quite a figure, dressed in plaid kilt and sporran, and was such a success that some twenty other vampire plays, including an opera, "Der Vampyr," followed his lead. Two facts about the vampire melodrama for students of the arcane: (1) the trapdoor, complete with smoke-screen, was first used in these plays and still continues to be called by its original name, "the vampire trap," even in the most recent Broadway revival (1979) and (2) one of the first twin bills in the English theater was Planche's *The Vampyre* and R. B. Peake's *Presumption: Or the Fate of Frankenstein*.

This is probably the longest playing double feature in Western theatre—the vampire and the manmade monster are still very much together.

In one important way, however, Byron's presence in the introduction of the vampire into popular culture should not go unnoticed. Byron, no doubt inadvertently, first coupled the folklore nosferatu with his own magnificent creation—himself. The character of the Byronic hero, that lusty libertine in the open shirt that Byron made such a part of his verse dramas and life dramas, is simply the vampire with a pedigree. This figure is the eternal searcher for sexual happiness, even if he has to destroy women in the process. Before Bram Stoker finally transformed the barbaric nosferatu into the suave Dracula, Byron had already started the metamorphosis. Polidori may even have realized this, for he consciously patterned Ruthven (a name already coined by Lady Caroline Lamb to satirize Byron in her novel *Glenarvon*) on Byron in order to take a poke at his erstwhile employer. On one level *The Vampyre* is clearly a roman à clef with the innocent Aubrey being Polidori himself.

More important, for our purposes, is that later in the summer of 1816 Byron wrote *Manfred*, in which he created his most thoughtful and thought-provoking Byronic hero around the skeleton of the vampire. Manfred is a superhuman seeker of pleasure who now wants only death, but is condemned, fated, to live. Here is a man with extraordinary magical powers, yet who cannot extricate himself from the chains of memory. Here is a moody lover who has so transgressed the bounds of eroticism that he has destroyed those whom he loves in the process. Here is a man who, unlike the Hollywood Dracula, cannot even drink red wine for it reminds him of the blood he has already swallowed. And whose blood is that? It is the blood of a woman he should not have loved; it is blood of his blood, the blood of his sister Astarte (Byron's half-sister, Augusta Leigh).

I would not emphasize the connection between the implied vampirism and incest had Byron not already done so. Byron knew only too well what everyone else knew—he was himself now a pariah for breaching the most hallowed sexual taboo. Here in *Manfred* Byron begs the reader to commit the biographical fallacy, and he doesn't have to beg much.[7] What is interesting is that in portraying his incestuous hero, Byron uses the same archetype he had been discussing at the beginning of the summer, the same demon he had decided to write his scary story about, the vampire. And still more interesting is that Byron seemed to understand, albeit unconsciously, that the connection between incest and vampirism would become the mainstay of the myth, the prime generator of the horror.

It is not surprising, considering the events of the summer of 1816, that Shelley too should have been drawn to this new bogey, for he was more than passingly interested in the dynamics of forbidden love. But while vampirism is implied and tangential in Byron, it is quite actual and straightforward in Shelley. This is a little unexpected, for Shelley wrote his most gothic and macabre work, *The Cenci*, at the same time he was composing his most ethereal and glorious hosannahs in *Prometheus Unbound*. In fact, it seems at the end of Act III Shelley was so entangled in wisps and sprites and nixies and pixies that he almost had to reassert the world of blood and gore.

I suppose there is some preparation for this change of tenor, for at the end of Act III in *Prometheus Unbound* we are told that as the millenium approaches, "The wretch [who] crept a vampire among men,/Infecting all with his own hideous ill" (scene iv, 147–48) has been cast out. Perhaps this reference reminded Shelley of his earlier gothic endeavors, such as his boyhood novels; perhaps it reminded him of his pact to write a scary story; or perhaps he was just tired of "pinnacl[ing man] dim in the intense inane." Before he finally etherealized what was left of mankind in the last act of *Prometheus Unbound*, the work he chose to write was as gruesome a bit of the gothic as was ever produced in the nineteenth century.

Shelley's story is of the Cenci family, a family devoured from within by the fiendish appetites of a cruel father and then left to moulder by a paternalistic church and oppressive state. The family's story was already famous by the time Shelley retold it, except that the story was usually told as a piece of tabloid journalism—"Mad father tortures family, rapes daughter, destroys sons, and escapes on a legal technicality; daughter then takes law into her own hands, kills father, is caught and legally killed." Shelley, however, tells the story as an allegory of contagious evil, just as he was telling *Prometheus Unbound* as an allegory of contagious good. If the means for apocalyptic release is forgiveness, then the means for evil entrapment is incest. Evil for Shelley is a plague, a contagious virus that spreads outward from a specific violation of just order. It is a disease inseminated by a demonic parasite into an innocent and ignorant host.

No one who has ever read Shelley's *Cenci* has ever doubted that incest was the dominant motif; in fact, that is essentially why the play went unproduced until the 1920s. To make Count Cenci a credible carrier of the plague of evil, Shelley had to first make a credible virus, and this he found in the actual and metaphorical spermlike germ: blood. Blood is a botular poison in the play, and much of the initial action centers around how Cenci delivers his rot into others. As with Byron, it was almost inevitable that Shelley would use the emerging image of vampire-virgin, except that in Shelley's case the victim was not his protagonist's sister, but his daughter. *Manfred* was unactable, in part because of the supernatural machinery, but *The Cenci* was unproduceable because of the unsupportable and continual violation of mores.

Here, for instance, is Count Cenci, a half-century before Count Dracula, preparing for his Eucharist of evil:

> (Filling a bowl of wine, and lifting it up)
> *Oh, thou*
> *bright wine whose purple splendour leaps*
> *And bubbles gaily in this golden bowl*
> *Under the lamplight, as my spirits do,*
> *To hear the death of my accursed sons!*
> *Could I believe thou wert their mingled blood,*
> *Then would I taste thee like a sacrament,*
> *And pledge with thee the mighty Devil in Hell,*
> *Who, if a father's curses, as men say,*
> *Climb with swift wings after their children's souls,*
> *And drag them from the very throne of Heaven,*
> *Now triumphs in my triumph—But thou art*
> *Superfluous; I have drunken deep of joy,*
> *And I will taste no other wine to-night.*
> (Act I, scene iii, 76–80)

Although Cenci claims he will drink no more—that he is sated with evil for a while—this is not to be. Later that evening, after Beatrice has initiated a confrontation, he again returns to the communion wine:

> (Exeunt all but Cenci and Beatrice)
> *My brain is swimming round;*
> *Give me a bowl of wine!*
> (To Beatrice.)
> *Thou painted viper!*
> *Beast that thou art! Fair and yet terrible!*
> *I know a charm shall make thee meek and tame,*
> *Now get thee from my sight!*
> (Exit Beatrice.)
> *Here, Andrea,*
> *Fill up this goblet with Greek wine. I said*
> *I would not drink this evening, but I must;*
> *For, strange to say, I feel my spirits fail*
> *With thinking what I have decreed to do.*
> (Drinking the wine)
>
> *Be thou the resolution of quick youth*
> *Within my veins, and manhood's purpose stern,*
> *And age's firm, cold, subtle villainy;*
> *As if thou wert indeed my children's blood*
> *Which I did thirst to drink! The charm works well;*
> *It must be done; it shall be done, I swear!*
> (Act I, scene iii, 163–78)

Cenci spills more than wine that night: Beatrice, his daughter, is commanded to come to him "at midnight and alone," and she is inducted into the nightmare world of his evil. She wakes the next morning profoundly distressed:

> My God!
> The beautiful blue heaven is flecked with blood!
> The sunshine on the floor is black! The air
> Is changed to vapours such as the dead breathe
> In charnel pits! Pah! I am choked! There creeps
> A clinging, black, contaminating mist
> About me . . . .
>
> (Act III, scene i, 12–18)

It is here in Beatrice's transformation from innocence to experience, from virgin to vamp, from passive goodness to active evil, that Shelley attempts to picture the growth of embryonic evil. Her "pernicious mistake," as he called it, is that, in order to redress a wrong she now must act, must seek vengeance, and this willy-nilly leads to the casuistry that, for Shelley (at least in 1819), allows evil to breed elsewhere. Meeting evil with evil actions is evil, and to make sure he gets his heroine properly evil, Shelley depends on our knowing the doppelgänger transformation inherent in the vampire myth. Beatrice is virtuous only to the point at which she decides to destroy malignity with malevolence.

I mention Byron's Count Manfred and Shelley's Count Cenci not to comment on the artistic appropriateness of romantic vampirism, but to point out that here in these closet melodramas of the early 1800s the old menacer of young women—that staple first of Elizabethan drama and then of the gothic novel—is getting a bit long in the tooth. He is still a figure of some sympathy, but he is turning into a horror monster. Cenci is not happy—he is possessed. Manfred is not pleased—he is driven. They thirst for what is forbidden; they hunger for sexual knowledge that is tabooed. Incest has always been embedded in the vampire folklore; after all, the vampire (like the werewolf) is supposed to return to attack first those whom he most loved in life, but what the romantic poets did was to so exaggerate the family context that the vampire *only* attacks his female kin.

The vampire stays at home for the rest of the century unhappily feeding off family, lustily violating sexual taboos. When you look at later art treatments of this horror myth, say in Poe, you find the family relationship always implied, if not stated. With the famous triplets—*Berenice, Morella*, and *Ligeia*—Poe has a narrator attempt to explain away some strange sexual behavior with a "cousin" (whom he has "married") by encouraging us to believe that he was crazy or on drugs. But if you look carefully at these stories you will find the narrator is a psychological rapist; he is, in fact, a vampire. Finding this stated or implied vampirism in Poe is, as D. H. Lawrence first explained, an occupational hazard for the reader. Here in Lawrence's own coruscating prose:

> [The] secondary law of all organic life is that each organism only lives through contact with other matter, assimilation, and contact with other life, which means assimilation of new vibrations, non-material. Each individual organism is vivified by intimate contact with fellow organisms. . . . In spiritual love, the contact is purely nervous. The nerves in the lovers are set vibrating in unison like two instruments. The pitch can rise higher and higher. But carry this too far, and the nerves begin to break, to bleed, as it were, and a form of death sets in. . . . It is easy to see why each man kills the things he loves. To *know* a living thing is to kill it. You have to kill a thing to know it satisfactorily. For this reason, the desirous consciousness, the SPIRIT, is a vampire. ("Edgar Allan Poe," *Studies in Classic American Literature*)

For Poe, the family is always a hothouse of energy. Each human plant struggles for the life-energy of others. Family life is a battle for nourishment, and Poe shows us the extreme consequences of this struggle. So in *The Fall of the House of Usher*, the house actually tumbles down as the last of the survivors, Madeline and Roderick, finally collapse in each other's arms.[8] We will never know who was host and who was violator—all we know is that the "vibrations" between brother and sister have reached too high a pitch and now both partners are "bled" to death.

By no means do I mean to imply that the vampire was progressively more sophisticated in the nineteenth century, but only that certain aspects of the myth were being refined in art. In popular culture the vampire was still the night molester, the bedroom intruder, the fiend who kept coming in from the cold with hot-blooded rape on his mind. He is still a beast and his bestiality is still obvious in his animal transformations: he is lupine or batlike.[9] And one can see his feral qualities whenever he is visually reproduced. Regardless of how the artist may want him to appear, the folk want him monstrous—a fiend first, a family man second.

The greatest work in popular culture on the vampire theme before Bram Stoker's *Dracula* (1898) was a bloody pulp, *Varney the Vampyre, or the Feast of Blood*. *Varney* first came out as a penny throwaway in the late 1840s and was read until it was almost in shreds; then it was collected into book form and again was read almost into tatters. *Varney* guaranteed that no popular artist would ever allegorize this demon into respectability, for he kept returning month after month, always doing the same thing—only the necks

Georg Kininger, *The Dream of Eleanor*, c. 1795 (Albertina Museum, Vienna)

Cauchemar, c. 1830, after
Tony Johannot (Francis
Haskell Collection,
Oxford)

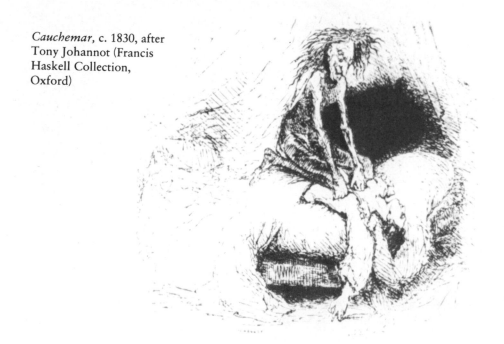

Tony Johannot, *Rêve*, c. 1830 (Bibliothèque Nationale, Paris)

Smarra, 1845, after Tony Johannot
(Bibliothèque Nationale, Paris)

Henry Anelay, *Varney the Vampire*, 1847

changed.[10] Published during the height of the sensational pulps, Varney was king of vampires. In 868 pages of double-columned, miniscule print, he wandered around London and England and the Continent doing what vampires always do best and doing it with admirable panache. It was Varney first, then Dracula, who was the people's vampire. He is as responsible for all the vampire costumes, fangs, capes, blood, and coffins in moonlight as is the Count. But as E. E. Bleiler has contended in his introduction to the Dover edition, *Varney the Vampire* "may well qualify as the most famous book that almost no one has read."

No wonder! Here is the plot: in the first hundred or so thousand words Varney attacks Miss Flora Bannerworth again and again and again, each time in different disguise, but with the same results—at the moment of success he is thwarted and must redouble his efforts. In Volume II he tries his hands, or rather his teeth, on other victims with varying success (he even travels to Italy where he attacks the daughter of Count Polidori), until finally exhausted, bored, and a little conscience-stricken, he jumps into Mount Vesuvius and is incinerated. The only other such self-effacing vampire who committed suicide was the cinematic Blacula, who in the early 1970s voluntarily submitted himself to the California sun rather than continue to live off the public blood.

Varney was written by many hands, including two of the most famous shiver-masters, James Malcolm Rymer and Thomas Pecket Prest, was spewed from the maw of the first steam presses in the House of Edward Lloyd, and might have been forgotten—like *Wagner the Wehr-Wolf*; *The Coral Island, or The Hereditary Curse*; *The Bronze Statue, or The Virgin's Curse*; *Pope Joan, or the Female Pontiff*; *The Greek Maiden, or The Banquet of Blood*; *Ada the Betrayed, or The Murder at the Old Smithy*; *The Child of Mystery, or The Cottager's Daughter*; *The Maniac Father, or The Victim of Seduction*; *Ernestine de Lacy, or The Robber's Foundling*; *Almira's Curse, or The Black Tower of Bransdorf*; *The Skeleton Clutch, or The Goblet of Gore*; *The Death Ship, or The Pirate's Bride and the Maniac of the Deep*; *Sawney Bean, The Man Eater of Bidlothian*—had not *Dracula* come along thirty years later to pick up the gauntlet. Bram Stoker had read *Varney*, as well as everything else about vampires in the British Museum. Thanks to *Varney*, most of the myth's major données—the moonlight revival motif, the Middle European ancestry, the courtly manner, the hunt by the mob, the quasi-medical explanation, and, most important, the theme of forbidden heroine initiated through contact with the vampire—were already in place for Stoker to assimilate.

And assimilate them he did, as well as so much else. With the exception of the Transylvanian accent, everything now included in the vampire myth was either stated or implied in *Dracula*. Stoker maintained both the tradition of the vampire as sexual oppressor (an interpretation that had grown still stronger as the century progressed, thanks to J. Sheridan Le Fanu's gem of a horror story *Carmilla*, 1871) as well as the episodic attack that had been the staple of the sensation novel. What is more, he introduced a historical basis for Dracula. There really had been a Middle European Dracula. His name was Vlad Tepes and he was an obscure Wallachian prince caught between opposing Christian and Moslem cultures, who happened to have a fondness for staking his victims—staking them in the stomach, in the heart, and in the groin. He even impaled the whole population of a town in concentric circles leading up a hill with the mayor, like a cherry, stuck at the top. For this, and many like exploits, he earned the nickname "tepes" or "the impaler," but this was not the name that stuck. His father had been a "Dracul," a member of a paramilitary sect, and since "a" is a Rumanian suffix meaning "son of," Vlad junior would be forever known as "Dracula."

Because *Dracula* has become the copy-text for the most pervasive horror myth, I will discuss the novel in some detail, emphasizing what I take to be its main contribution—namely, the projection of interfamilial sexual fantasies. This is not to imply that *Dracula* does not have many other important facets—for it does, as recent books like Leonard Wolf, *A Dream of Dracula: In Search of the Living Dead* (1972); Anthony Masters, *The Natural History of the Vampire* (1972); Raymond T. McNally and Radu Florescu, *In Search of Dracula* (1973); and Gabriel Ronay, *The Truth about Dracula* (1974) clearly attest. But there must be something special in this coding of the vampire story that is so potent that "Dracula" has become an eponym for "vampire."

Like *Frankenstein* and *Dr. Jekyll and Mr. Hyde*, *Dracula* was produced as one of the aftershocks of a nightmare. In contrast to the dreams of Mary Shelley and Robert Louis Stevenson, however, we know very little of Bram Stoker's nightmare other than that it came, so he said, as the result of eating too much dressed crab meat at London's famous Beefsteak Room. In the dream he reported seeing a huge crab king rising up from the plate and slowly approaching him with open pincers. This image is certainly not much to go on, even though a critic writing in *The American Imago* some years ago claimed that a crab, "viewed horoscopically," is the astrological sign of Bram's younger brother George, and so "eating the dressed crab meat meant unconsciously eating up and killing baby George."

There is a more tantalizing relationship between *Dracula* and what was actually going on in Bram Stoker's life at the time, of which this dream is only a symptom. During the 1880s and 1890s Stoker was the factotum of Henry Irving, an actor and impresario of great renown and a demanding employer. The suggestion has been occasionally made that Dracula is a caricature of Irving, and indeed the physical similarities are striking. Was Irving the crablike figure rising up to torment his aide? Equally tantalizing is the fact that Stoker in 1890 had met Arminius Vamberuy, a professor from the University of Budapest, who told him wondrous tales of the Transylvanian undead and encouraged the young man to look into the esoteric holdings at the British Museum. Stoker had already read *The Vampyre, Carmilla, Varney*, the pioneering *The Land Beyond the Forest* (i.e., Trans-sylvania) by Emily Gerard, and Sabine Baring-Gould's *The Book of Werewolves*, so when he found a cache of documents on the Viovode Drakula he must have realized that life was intruding into art. All three forces, the unconscious recreation of the dream, the biographical portrayal of "Father" Irving, and the conscious fictionalization of a historical character seem to be interwoven in the novel. Behind this fabric is yet another design that makes all the parts fit: the unfolding of the vampire myth as a fable of sexual initiation.

What sets *Dracula* apart from other gothic romances is that here somehow is a web of modern horror. Other works still are caught up in its patterns: this is the text that the others continually re-create; the anxiety of its influence is still felt. Yet, when you read it, it seems an unsubstantial and even feeble piece of prose. It is striking in its absolute lack not just of causality, but of probability. Nothing important is ever really completely explained, yet the text is full of explanations. Who is this King of the Vampires? Where is he from? How did he get so rich? Why haven't we heard of him before? Most important, why is he coming to England and why is he choosing these women, our women? This novel has the internal organization of a dream or a fairy tale. All we ever know for sure is that Dracula is a bloodsucker who comes out of the East to attack specific women. He is the uncanny personified. Even the Frankenstein monster and Mr. Hyde provide some sense of predictability in their choice of prey, but not Stoker's Dracula. He just *is*, that's all. The movies, of course, can't stand this indeterminacy and so have filled in all the blanks. "Is this your wife?" the cinematic Dracula now says to the requisite young man who has entered Transylvania. "My, what a lovely neck she has." But Stoker did no such thing. He packed his monster in special dirt, moved him to England, and then let him hunt a woman he supposedly never even heard of—Miss Lucy Westenra. (Stoker's names are well chosen, in this case the name meaning "Light in the West," and it is unfortunate that invariably retellers of Stoker's tale have first changed the names or coupled various names in order to not just get extraneous characters out, but to "make sense" of Dracula's appetites.)

The dreamlike pattern of the novel's causality has caused critics, as well as screen adapters, some consternation. *Dracula* really is, as one contemporary critic has put it, a "spoiled masterpiece," especially if you judge it by the standards of the conventional novel. Of course it's not a traditional novel; like *Dr. Jekyll* and *Frankenstein* it is a mess. In the first place, the story is told from a series of narrative points of view, which is fine, but then these points of view are delivered to us in the form of diaries, letters, stenographic transcriptions (one of the first instances of the dictaphonic mode in literature), all of which sound exactly alike. Bram Stoker is not Wilkie Collins; he has only one voice and whenever he tries to alter even the tone, as he does with van Helsing or Quincey Morris, it too often sounds silly. Second, the middle of the book—especially the Mina-Lucy correspondence—is tedious, even distracting. Third (maybe this is an asset), Stoker simply cannot delineate young male characters. Jonathan Harker, Arthur Holmwood, and John Seward all sound exactly alike. The fourth "boy," Quincey Morris, the Winchester-packing American, sounds as if his speeches were written by John Wayne.

If *Dracula*'s claim on our attention is not artistic, it must be psychological. Here is a gothic novel that has rarely appeared in classrooms, yet makes money for any publisher. Here is a book that has been condensed, mutilated, rewritten, revamped as a classic comic-book, yet, like the vampire itself, does not die. There is only one vampire text—nothing has displaced it. Here is a work, like *Dr. Jekyll and Mr. Hyde* and *Frankenstein*, that has simply left the literary world to be absorbed by popular culture. These works have left the medium of print, but have never gone out of print. The sense of uncomfortable admiration that we associate with liking what we are not supposed to like can be seen in the announcement by Oxford University Press that *Dracula* was to be the one-hundredth title in its acclaimed World Classic Series. The Press admitted that many of the authors in this series, which includes Thoreau, Dickens, Trollope, Henry James, and Tolstoy, would "no doubt turn over in their graves" if they knew what was going to be the one-hundredth World Classic.

Why did *Varney* perish and *Dracula* survive? What gives *Dracula* its endurance? Why has it become a classic, albeit a slightly embarrassing one? It must be that there is some other story enfolded within Stoker's endpapers—some story that we want to hear badly enough to put up with all the cardboard characters, dull asides, and desultory plotting—a story we *wish* to be horrified by; a story we want made classic.

There is, I think, this other story, and it is buried just below the surface of the printed text. This story is of incest, of the primal horde, and of the establishment of social and sexual taboos.[11] Essentially, the story between the covers of *Dracula* describes the struggle of a band of boys (Jonathan Harker, Quincey Morris, Arthur Holmwood, John Seward) against a foe of great strength and cunning. The foe is, of course, Dracula—a man of eternal retirement age, subtle intelligence, and social position, a man who already has his own castle, already has his own wealth and serfs, already has his own women. Dracula's women are, by the way, not old hags, but the stuff adolescent boys can only dream of, and so why Dracula should want to leave these women is of more than passing interest. Here are Dracula's women as perceived by a recumbent Jonathan Harker:

> In the moonlight opposite me were three young women, ladies by their dress and manner. I thought all the time that I must be dreaming when I saw them, for, though the moonlight was behind them, they threw no shadow on the floor. They came close to me, and looked at me for some time, and then whispered together. Two were dark and had high aquiline noses, like the Count, and great dark piercing eyes, that seemed to be almost red when contrasted with the pale yellow moon. The other was fair, as fair as can be, with great wavy masses of golden hair and eyes like pale sapphires. I seemed somehow to know her face, and to know it in connection with some dreamy fear, but I could not recollect at the moment how or where. All three had brilliant white teeth that shone like pearls against the ruby of their voluptuous lips. There was something about them that made me uneasy, some longing and at the same time some deadly fear. I felt in my heart a wicked, burning desire that they would kiss me with those red lips. It is not good to note this down, lest some day it should meet Mina's eyes and cause her pain; but it is the truth.

> •   •   •

> The fair girl advanced and bent over me till I could feel the movement of her breath upon me. Sweet it was in one sense, honey-sweet, and sent the same tingling through the nerves as her voice, but with a bitter underlying the sweet, a bitter offensiveness, as one smells in blood.

> I was afraid to raise my eyelids, but looked out and saw perfectly under the lashes. The girl went on her knees, and bent over me, simply gloating. There was a deliberate voluptuousness which was both thrilling and repulsive, and as she arched her neck she actually licked her lips like an animal, till I could see in the moonlight the moisture shining on the scarlet lips and on the red tongue as it lapped the white sharp teeth. Lower and lower went her head as the lips went below the range of my mouth and chin and seemed to fasten on my throat. Then she paused, and I could hear the churning sound of her tongue as it licked her teeth and lips, and I could feel the hot breath on my neck. Then the skin of my throat began to tingle as one's flesh does when the hand that is to tickle it approaches nearer—nearer. I could feel the soft, shivering touch of the lips on the super-sensitive skin of my throat, and the hard dents of two sharp teeth, just touching and pausing there. I closed my eyes in languorous ecstasy and waited— waited with beating heart. (pp. 45–47)[12]

Perhaps Dracula wants to leave these voluptuaries because he has already "loved" them; or maybe he is such a dog in the manger that he wants only

Vampire women moving toward Jonathan in *Dracula,* 1931 (Universal Studios)

the women the "boys" want. His first Western victim is exactly that; she is almost a mirage, and her name, "Lucy Westenra" (light in the West), tells it all. She has been courted by all the boys except Jonathan, who is already engaged, yes, but secretly lusting after those vampire princesses in Dracula's cellar. Lucy has entertained marriage proposals from Messrs. Seward, Holmwood, and Morris, and she has, as the action begins, just chosen Arthur Holmwood. Arthur's wealthy father now conveniently dies, thereby passing his title, Lord Godalming, on to his son. So whatever doubt we may have had about Arthur's appropriateness is over: he is quite simply the best of English, nay Western, manhood—noble, honest, robust, stalwart, just a little dim, and very rich.

Dracula would have the woman of the boys' dreams to add to his collection were it not for the intercession of wily Herr Professor, Doctor, Lawyer Abraham Van Helsing, "M.D., D.Ph., D.Lit., etc., etc." (How Van Helsing, whose English teacher seems to have been a New York cabbie, ever won a D.Lit., an Oxford-only degree for advanced studies, is anyone's guess.) Van Helsing is of Dracula's apparent age, position, and reputation, except that he has no women in his basement, only a wife who has recently been committed to an asylum. Yet, clearly, he would not be averse to joining the boys in their pursuit of Lucy if he thought he could get away with it. But he can't and so he represses his barely sublimated sexual drives to struggle instead for propriety and social justice. Into this struggle he brings all that Western culture has to offer: logic, science, reason, and an abiding faith in God and superstition.

The central action of this book, which really has little action, entails the boys joining forces with the wise father, Van Helsing, in order to pursue and destroy the evil patriarch, Count Dracula. They must get him before he gets their women. The metaphor to describe this "getting" process is the transfusion: who is going to get into whose blood. At the center of the vampire myth transfusion is always implied—the vampire sucks blood from the victim and somehow leaves some strain of himself, some evil germ that will transform the host. But in *Dracula* there is another series of transfusions that is far more revealing of the embedded psychosexuality of the myth.

After Lucy has been twice bled by Dracula, Van Helsing realizes she desperately needs replenishment. He realizes that she languishes by day because she is being "loved" by Dracula at night. Usual defensive measures are taken (garlic, cross, and so on) but to no avail, so Van Helsing takes John Seward aside and from his instrument bag (a motif that is almost always in the myth) removes "the ghastly paraphernalia of our beneficial trade"—not hammer and stake, but the needles and tubing necessary to connect John with his erstwhile inamorata, Lucy. He is going to let the life fluid pass from John to Lucy. Neither doctor worries about matching blood types, nor does Van Helsing do anything in the way of "prepping" donor or host; he simply plugs them together and shunts John's life elixir into Lucy's emaciated body. After all, she must be saved. Who should now appear but Arthur, Lord Godalming, the Jack who has won this Jill fair and square, and he is understandably bewildered at the sight of this hose connecting his boyfriend to his own fiancée. At once Van Helsing understands and explains:

> "Young miss is bad, very bad. She wants blood, and blood she must have or die. My friend John and I have consulted; and we are about to perform what we call transfusion of blood—to transfer from full veins of one to the empty veins which pine for him. John was to give his blood, as he is the more young and strong than me"—here Arthur took my hand and wrung it hard in silence—"but, now you are here, you are more good than us, old or young, who toil much in the world of thought. Our nerves are not so calm and our blood not so bright as yours!" (pp. 130–31)

Setting aside the "empty vein" and "bright blood" references, Van Helsing realizes Arthur is the only proper one for Lucy to draw from and so he pulls the tubes, reconnects them properly, and "performs the operation" once again. It is a direct body-to-body transfusion and, as C. F. Bentley first pointed out a decade ago, is clearly suggestive of coitus.

Arthur, alas, is soon called away on business, so Dracula returns to his and two days later Lucy is again in need of blood. This time Doctor Seward must finally perform the deed himself. Lucy is hazy and Van Helsing, afraid that she might wake and "that would make danger" (p. 136), gives her a dose of morphine. All hooked up to Lucy now, young John realizes he too can perform the task: "It was a feeling of personal pride that I could see a faint tinge of colour steal back into the pallid cheeks and lips. No man knows, till he experiences it, what it is to feel his own life-blood drawn away into the veins of the woman he loves" (pp. 136–37). Van Helsing warns his young colleague to stay quiet: "Mind, nothing must be said of this. If our young lover should turn up unexpected, as before, no word to him. It would at once frighten him and enjealous him, too" (p. 137). Lucy wakes, sees her pale donor, and remarks rather too perceptively:

> We owe you so much, Dr. Seward, for all you have done, but you really must take care not to overwork yourself. You are looking pale yourself. You want a wife to nurse and look after you a bit; that you do!" As she spoke, Lucy turned crimson, though it was only momentarily, for her poor wasted veins could not stand for such an unwonted drain to the head. The reaction came in excessive pallor as she turned imploring eyes on me. I smiled and nodded, and laid my finger on my lips; with a sigh, she sank back amid her pillows (p. 138).

This is Lucy's second transfusion, this one from her cast-off suitor, but she has other young gentleman friends, especially the straight-talking, straight-shooting Texan, Quincey Morris. A few days later Dracula makes yet another visit and Quincey is looked for, but can't be found. Van Helsing himself is pressed into service. It's over in a nonce—just a sentence: "As he [Van Helsing] spoke he took off his coat and rolled up his shirt sleeve. After the operation . . ." (p. 143). Then Lucy is attacked for the third time and no new donor can be found, even though there is a houseful of devoted and healthy female servants. Women, it seems, cannot perform this life-giving task. The donor must be a man, a young, well-born man—if not an English man, then maybe a virile American. Van Helsing explains: "A brave man's blood is the best thing on this earth when a woman is in trouble. You're a man and no mistake. Well, the devil may work against us for all he's worth, but God sends us men when we want them" (p. 157). Quincey has his turn.

During all this hubbub the young people's parents are removed from the text by death: Arthur loses his father, Lucy her mother, Jonathan his mentor, Mr. Hawkins; they are now all orphaned adolescents in the care of fatherly

Van Helsing. And soon they are even to lose the one character around whom the family has now re-formed: Dracula is about to get "sister" Lucy and make her his Queen. "Check to the King," Van Helsing unironically says, but still, one might add, not yet a "mate." They can never allow Him to get Her.

Just how important these transfusions were finally becomes apparent on the day of Lucy's burial. The disappointed young men are all gathered around when Arthur provides exactly the information Van Helsing wants kept secret. "Arthur was saying [reports Seward] that he felt then as if the two of them had really been married and that she was his wife in the sight of God" (pp. 180–81). The boys all blanch, knowing that if Arthur thinks the transfusion has married him to Lucy, then he has been cuckolded a number of times by his best friends. It is Van Helsing, however, who is most embarrassed, and he erupts into his confusing "King Laugh" hysterics. When the paroxysm is over he finally explains to his protégé, John Seward, why he was so upset. Van Helsing claims that at moments of intense anxiety one can either dissipate pressure through laughter or tears. He favors laughter. Seward sees nothing laughable:

> "Well, for the life of me, Professor," I said, "I can't see anything to laugh at in all that. Why, your explanation makes it a harder puzzle than before. But even if the burial service was comic, what about poor Art and his trouble? Why, his heart was simply breaking."
> "Just so. Said he not that the transfusion of his blood to her veins had made her truly his bride?"
> "Yes, and it was a sweet and comforting idea for him."
> "Quite so. But there was a difficulty, friend John. If so that, then what about the others? Ho, ho! Then this so sweet maid is a polyandrist, and me, with my poor wife dead to me, but alive by Church's law, though no wits, all gone—even I, who am faithful husband to this now-no-wife, am bigamist."
> "I don't see where the joke comes in there either!" I said; and I did not feel particularly pleased with him for saying such things. He laid his hand on my arm, and said:—
> "Friend John, forgive me if I pain. I showed not my feeling to others when it would wound, but only to you, my old friend, whom I can trust. If you could have looked into my very heart then when I want to laugh; if you could have done so when the laugh arrived; if you could do so now when King Laugh have pack up his crown, and all that is to him—for he go far, far away from me, and for a long, long time—maybe you would perhaps pity me the most of all."
> I was touched by the tenderness of his tone, and asked why.
> "Because I know!" (pp. 182–83)

Seward still sees nothing laughable, for if the transfusions were sexually conjunctive, coital, then Van Helsing, the superego himself, has transgressed one of the great sexual taboos. Van Helsing has been a bigamist, to be sure, but worse yet, he has been incestuous. For if the boys are his surrogate sons then, indeed, as he himself says, Lucy has been "almost a daughter" to him.

Certainly in the text of *Dracula* blood and semen are closely linked, even psychologically interchangeable. But is this relationship true outside the text? Yes, or at least so says Ernest Jones, the Freudian analyst. Here is Jones explaining this particular aspect of the vampire myth as it relates specifically to adolescent masturbatory fantasies:

> The explanation of these phantasies is surely not hard. A nightly visit from a beautiful or frightful being, who first exhausts the sleeper with passionate embraces and then withdraws from him a vital fluid; all this can point only to a natural and common process, namely to nocturnal emissions accompanied with dreams of a more or less erotic nature. In the unconscious mind blood is commonly an equivalent for semen. (*On the Nightmare*, 1931)

Jones is not alone in believing this; other analysts have concurred, if only because blood and semen are such observable plasmas of life that mixing them up or displacing them in dream life seems inevitable.

Although blood and semen are elixirs, they are most definitely not to be drunk. The vampire drinks blood and so signals his demonism; the sexual degenerate indulges in acts of fellatio and in so doing signals his perversion— at least to high Victorians. In this context we might recheck the other important scene of transfusion that occurs, not between the boys and their "sister" Lucy, but between Dracula and their "mother," Mina. Here is the scene set down by John Seward in his diary. He recalls how he burst into Mina's room to see exactly how Dracula was attacking his second victim:

> The moonlight was so bright that through the thick yellow blind the room was light enough to see. On the bed beside the window lay Jonathan Harker, his face flushed and breathing heavily as though in a stupor. Kneeling on the near edge of the bed facing outwards was the white-clad figure of his wife. By her side stood a tall, thin man, clad in black. His face was turned from us, but the instant we saw all recognized the Count—in every way, even to the scar on his forehead. With his left hand he held both Mrs. Harker's hands, keeping them away with her arms at full tension; his right hand gripped her by the back of the neck, forcing her face down on his bosom. Her white nightdress was smeared with blood, and a thin stream trickled down the man's bare breast which was shown by his torn-open dress. The attitude of the two had a terrible resemblance to a child forcing a kitten's nose into a saucer of milk to compel it to drink. (pp. 287– 88)

Seward's physiological response tells all: "What I saw appalled me. I felt my hair rise like bristles on the back of my neck and my heart seemed to stand still" (p. 287). He is literally horrified.

I do not want to go too far with the implied fellatio because it is an aspect of the vampire myth that has not really been assimilated into popular renditions. But things are fast changing in the myth. To the best of my recollection, it first appeared in a number of Hammer versions of the late 1960s, starting with *Dracula, Prince of Darkness*, in which Christopher Lee first slowly draws his razor-sharp finger talon across his breast, leaving a foot-long serration, and grabs his victim by the hair, forcing her to his chest in an unsubtle-enough way to titillate the audience and also get past the censor.[13] I suppose this scene was implied in the 1931 *Dracula* when Helen Chandler says, "He opened a vein in his arm and made me drink," but somehow it is not the same. The chest incision scene is so much a part of the myth now that when it appeared in the 1978 *Count Dracula* (with Louis Jourdan), the video-effects man went crazy with dissolves, fades, and all manner of computer-assisted design. And in the more recent Frank Langella versions on both Broadway and in film, the scene played as *the* central image of forbidden romance. In fact, in the movie the camera shoots through gauze and chest hair to make sure we understand the nether counterparts.

While it would be a mistake to force the blood/semen analogy, it may account for the myth's almost uncanny ability to reflect the audience's sexual excitements as well as sexual anxieties. In this context one should look at Mina's response to Dracula's advances, for it prefigures the "modern" view of the female victim of such assaults. Lucy, we recall, was a giddy child-woman whose naiveté and zest for sexual excitement made her easy prey for Dracula's appetites. She even thrives on the encounter, becoming far more ravishing in deathlessness than she ever was in life. She was raped by Dracula but, in street talk, she "was asking for it." In terms of the novel, as a result of "it" she becomes by turns "langorous," "voluptuous," "sensuous," and "wanton." Lucy becomes La Belle Dame Sans Merci. On the other hand, Mina is no "la belle dame" either before or after Dracula's attack. And what separates her from fluffy Lucy? Only this: she is respectable; she is married; she is within a family. Mina is the Victorian woman's idea of the "new" woman: helpmate, stenographer, all-night typist, bookkeeper, but most of all, wife. She has a woman's heart and a man's brain. So she should not, if literary history can be taken as prescriptive, have to deal with the advances of a Schedoni, Melmoth, Antonio, let alone a Dracula.

But she does; Dracula almost makes her his wife. "When I call, you will come," he says to Mina. "Together we will make a new world," he says to Lucy. From the perspective of the late twentieth century we might expect her response to him to be one of revulsion and, of course, to a considerable extent it is, but if you look again at this scene and its aftermath you will see a little of Lucy lingering in Mina. As Dracula bends to Mina's body, he whispers,

"You may as well be quiet; it is not the first time, or the second, that your veins have appeased my thirst"; and she later numbly explains, "I was bewildered, and, strangely enough, I did not want to hinder him" (p. 293). She colludes, just a bit. Why?

Is it part of the vampire curse that she should be so willingly unwilling on this his third invasion of her body, or is there something in the evil father's phallic bite that she secretly desires? Is there a craving under her revulsion, just as there was in her husband's terror at Castle Dracula, when he secretly sought the bite of, which was it, Dracula's daughters or wives? Lest we conclude that Mina's "desire with loathing strangely mix'd" is just a momentary feeling of guilt and should thus be treated as the confused rape victim's occasional confession that somehow she has encouraged the attack when indeed she hasn't, we should remember that Mina's self-acknowledged complicity lasts until the end. Months later, on the night before the intrepid band of vampire hunters has at last cornered the fiend in his native Transylvania, Mina has this strange confession:

> Oh, what will tomorrow bring to us? We go to seek the place where my poor darling suffered so much. God grant that we may be guided aright, and that He will deign to watch over my husband and those dear to us both, and who are in such deadly peril. As for me, I am not worthy in His sight. Alas! I am unclean to His eyes, and shall be until He may deign to let me stand forth in His sight as one of those who have not incurred His wrath. (p. 366–67)

Why does she, a good Christian woman, not consider herself redeemable unless she realizes that to some degree she has been a conscious participant in desired but forbidden acts?

The vampire "attack" on first Lucy and then on Mina constitutes the first half of the myth and is noticeable for its conspicuous lack of violence. I cannot think of another night molester who does such ghastly and horrible things in such a gentlemanly manner. Certainly, this is not the behavior of Dracula's forebearers—certainly not the nosferatu who ripped his victims apart in order to get at the blood. But as we have seen, Dracula is after more than blood; he is after a certain kind of sex. The sexual act he performs is, ostensibly at least, sucking. Could it be that on one level the most immature audience, say the pre-latency audience, interprets the "horror" as simply the result of violating what for them has been recently tabooed, namely nursing. To this still androgynous audience Dracula himself is orally cannibalistic and this, they know, simply will not do. This audience knows Dracula is a big bad boy and so must be punished and suffer. If you continue to look at the psychosexual dynamics of the myth, you realize that the victim, the woman, also enjoys it; as a matter of fact it gives them both sensual pleasure—but it is still wrong. And if she continues to receive his advances, she will have to suffer as well.

To the slightly older audience, however, the scenario becomes sexually more complex because, as the vampire takes blood, he inseminates his victim with the germ of his forbidden obsessions. He makes her, by turns, "langorous . . . sensual . . . wanton." The attack is an impure carnal defilement of family. Again, no mention of this in the text of *Dracula* is explicit, but both in the characters' responses and in the constellating mythography that has radiated from this novel we find evidence of the perverse effect of violation. The female victim now almost invariably wants what is forbidden, even after she knows what it will cost, and so she encourages her own defloration before it begins (as she had done in the pre-Dracula folklore) as well as after. Victim and violator both desire each other, and both know that this desire is horribly wrong.

Perhaps we can best understand this ambivalence by seeing the assault not only from the viewpoints of the participants, but from the vantage point of that adolescent audience. In this context the vampire story seems a playback of an already recorded program—the primal young male audience witnesses the older man defile the virgin (for indeed to this audience the mother is eternally virginal), while at the same time imagining himself to be that powerful man. Hence the audience response to the vampire is oxymoronic: on one hand, the vampire is bad, evil, sucking what he should not be sucking, being sexual where he should not be; yet it's all somehow very alluring. The vampire himself is powerful; he has all the night to himself, all the women he wants, especially this one. This ambivalence is played out in the affective response in which the audience seems to say: "The vampire, if he would play by the rules and not attack (my) woman/mother/sister, is wonderful, but if he mistakes and overreaches his limits, I'll have to fight with him." Hence the young male must abandon the old patriarch and join the youthful throng that seeks his overthrow.

From the young woman's point of view, feelings are also ambivalent. She may well sympathize with the victim for she too is virginal, she too hungers to satisfy those strange new appetites, and she too is anxious to cross that threshold into the presumed wonderland of adulthood—namely, genital sexuality. So what stops her? What stops her is what stops all of us—fear. Fear not just of the unknown, or of performance, but fear that an improper partner can make her pregnant and that pregnancy caused by the wrong man can result in her being cast out of the tribe. And so what does the vampire do but remove all fear. He comes in the dead of night; he knows exactly what to do; he will not make her pregnant (for vampires breed sideways from victim to victim); all she has to do is be a bit interested and he'll do the rest.[14]

But who is he to her? If (1) the vampire is a projection of self for the male and the victim is a projection of self for the female, and (2) if the victim for the male is maternal, then shouldn't the vampire for the female be paternal? Is he not, on one level, a surrogate father? For he is lord of the manor exercising the *droit du seigneur* and he is also the elder priest, the holy man who baptizes the unenlightened into the ways of his sensualism.[15] Along with the word "marriage" and all its attendant terms like "bride" and "wife," and along with the perversion of transubstantiation, the other Christian ceremony subverted in *Dracula* is "baptism." So Van Helsing, the wise but initially impotent father-priest, refers to Mina as "tainted . . . with that Vampire baptism" (p. 369), while she herself earlier has recognized, wiping her face clean of blood, that some perfidious sacrament has been performed.

Essentially, the horror that resides in the modern myth of the vampire, as translated through the text of *Dracula*, is not generated by the sexual act per se, but by the psychological and social undesirability of these particular participants. To both sexes in the adolescent audience, the myth articulates and upholds the taboo of incest. Break the code and invite a punishment worse than death. "There are," the cinematic Dracula keeps reminding us, "things far worse than death . . . to die, to be really dead—that would be wonderful." Still the young male audience is ambiguous: they want to do what the vampire does, but they now know the consequences. And the young female audience is also nonplussed: they want the "love" of the vampire, but they too now know the eventualities. The myth makes these ever so clear—female victims are condemned to become "bloofer" ladies, lamias, vamps, unable to be sexually reproductive or satisfied, while the vampire himself remains a prisoner of his unsatisfied desires, unable to know the relief of death.

Understanding the dynamics of vampire attack leads us into the second half of the myth, namely the destruction, or, in Van Helsing's more appropriate trope, "the sanitizing" of such a stain. Again, it is to the text of *Dracula* that we must turn, for Stoker unconsciously assimilated the folklore and then rearranged it into the pattern we now so easily recognize. The first victim/sinner is Lucy. Lucy is twice a victim of displaced incest: first, when she is attacked by Dracula, which causes her to start her metamorphosis, and second, when she is metaphorically "victimized" by Van Helsing (via the transfusions), which slows the doppelgänger process but is still a violation of sorts. The "evil" father, however, finally has his way and she is transformed, made vampiric. She must then be "destroyed" for her sins by Van Helsing and the young men. Van Helsing leads the prospective bridegroom, Lord Godalming, up to her charnel bed and places the phallic stake in his hands:

Arthur took the stake and the hammer, and when once his mind was set on action his hands never trembled nor even quivered. Van Helsing opened the missal and began to read, and Quincey and I followed as well as we could. Arthur placed the point over the heart, and as I looked I could see its dint in the white flesh. Then he struck with all his might.

The Thing in the coffin writhed; and a hideous, blood-curdling screech came from the opened red lips. The body shook and quivered and twisted in wild contortions; the sharp white teeth champed together till the lips were cut, and the mouth was smeared with a crimson foam. But Arthur never faltered. He looked like a figure of Thor as his untrembling arm rose and fell, driving deeper and deeper the mercy-bearing stake, whilst the blood from the pierced heart welled and spurted up around it. His face was set, and high duty seemed to shine through it; the sight of it gave us courage so that our voices seemed to ring through the little vault. (p. 222)

Lucy is culpable because she has been sexually careless. It is in the destruction of the male vampire that we are vouchsafed insight into what really generates the horror. In the young boy's pursuit of the old vampire we see what the English anthropologist Maurice Richardson first pointed out in "The Psychoanalysis of Ghost Stories" (1959)—an almost exact retelling of Freud's primal horde theory. Dracula, the fallen father, has attempted to withdraw two of the most important women from the breeding pool: Lucy, the about-to-wed, and Mina, the mother-to be. He will not let the boys, in a sense his sons, near them. Lucy is clearly the more sexually exciting, but Mina is more important to the tribe, and the fact that she is able not just to survive, but to reproduce, is as damaging to the foul patriarch as any stake through his heart. It is not coincidental, I think, that the novel ends not with Dracula's death, but with the birth of Mina's boy child—a lad appropriately named John Quincey Arthur (the order is not clear) Harker. For the boys have all participated in his creation, and his presence proves that they are able to reproduce now without fear. The adolescents are adults now; they have had to sacrifice Lucy and Quincey, but at last they are potent and free.

The retelling of the vampire myth buttresses the more modern explanation of the Oedipal desire in the male: namely, there is no specific desire to possess the mother (or sister), but rather such incest is tied to more fundamental social drives. The boys need women; they don't necessarily want them. To be sure, Mina does mother the boys; in fact, she speaks consolingly of Arthur after he has "staked" Lucy:

We women have something of the mother in us that makes us rise above smaller matters when the mother-spirit is invoked; I felt this big, sorrowing man's head resting on me, as though it were that of the baby that some day may lie on my bosom, and I stroked his hair as though he were my own child. I never thought at the time how strange it all was. (p. 236)

It would be a mistake to see Mina as the primary love object of the boys, for they clearly most want what Dracula most wants—the virgin, Miss Lucy.

It is in this context that Van Helsing's role is so enlightening. The boys can undergo supervised transfusions with Lucy, but the older men must not approach so close. Van Helsing and Dracula do, and their reactions show exactly what the deed entails. Dracula has an easy victim; Van Helsing a nervous breakdown. Note that Van Helsing never suggests transfusing the boys' blood into Mina, even though with Lucy this was prescribed. Van Helsing has sexually desired Lucy, repressed the urge, then found an opportunity to express it. And what does "it" do to him? It summons up "King Laugh," an irrational return of the repressed desires, signaling a momentary lapse of superego control. Dracula, on the other hand, follows the same desire seemingly without deflection and thereby commits a horror so potent that it calls forth the combined wrath of the civilized world. He must now contend with the wrath of Harker a lawyer, Seward a doctor, Lord Godalming an aristocrat, and Morris a New World colonist. And who is the leader of this British Empire? None other than the new Urizen from the Old World, Van Helsing. In spite of his momentary transgression, Van Helsing has, in Blakean terms, learned to "suppress desire"; in Freudian terms, to sublimate libido; and so it is he who leads the posse of the primal horde to destroy his tyrannical double, Dracula.

The vampire myth, like all horror stories, is conservative. The superego finally contains the id. This mythic parable continually articulates the need for repression, a lesson we will see again in the adventures of Frankenstein, of the werewolf, and of Dr. Jekyll/Mr. Hyde. They are the morality plays of our time. Their moral is biological efficiency, repression in the service of protecting established reproductive patterns. Such sagas articulate the best way to ensure the generative safety, not so much of the individual but of society. From such stories adolescents learn what is sexually permissible and what is sexually damaging, again not damaging to the specific person, but to the species. The horror of Dracula is not that he sleeps in the dirt, or doesn't brush after meals, or can grimace and growl, or can be lupine or batlike, or even that he preys on young virgins. The horror of Dracula is that within his infantile desires, within his misdirected libido, is the promise of profound interfamilial strife, and hence nonproductive sexual behavior. And this is the fear that has generated the taboos that have produced the institution of the family and, as Lévi-Strauss argued, culture as well. In our early teenage years we learn that Dracula must be driven out, even though what he promises is so attractive. We know he is so rich, so much a man of the evening, so sexually knowledgeable, so suave; and yet we must learn that he is so awful.

We now pass this message along to the next generation, as eager and receptive as we were, through what has become the most effective medium, the film. It is no happenstance that, of all movie subjects in the West, the vampire story is the favorite. Nothing comes close—not the Western nor the detective nor the musical offerings. And of all the vampire stories, Dracula is preeminent; in fact, as a screen character in a story film, only Sherlock Holmes has appeared more often.[16] When the vampire is in vogue, as he seems to be every twenty years or so, each generation can fashion a contemporary image, his worldwide reincarnations can be prodigious: David Pirie, in *The Vampire Cinema* (1977), counts more than two hundred movies of this ilk produced between 1955 and 1970, chiefly in the United States, England, Spain, Mexico, France, and the Philippines (p. 6).

If we look carefully at the vampire myth in this century, we will find it has been returned to folklore. The vampire moved from mythos to logos, as it were, in romanticism, and now he's moved back to mythos. That is not to say he is no longer a character in prose fiction; he is, as many modern works will attest.[17] But if you want to find both mythic continuity and psychological insight, you will more likely find it at the movie theater in the mall than in books in the library.

For the time being I have no interest in the art manipulation of the vampire myth, other than to mention that it has been used by such luminaries in the literary cosmos as James Joyce, G. B. Shaw, D. H. Lawrence, H. G. Wells, Henry James, Edward Bulwer-Lytton, Walter de la Mare, Rudyard Kipling, Virginia Woolf, and F. Scott Fitzgerald. I am interested in the unaffected and artless return of the vampire back into popular culture. We see this most clearly in film, but the vampire has also infested comics (two complete Marvel series and reams of others), the radio (Orson Welles' *Dracula* for "The Mercury Theater" is still a classic), television (there was an entire soap opera, "Dark Shadows," back in the 1960s, a sitcom, "The Munsters," and hundreds of made-for-TV movies, one of which, *The Night Stalker*, 1971, was the highest-rated feature film ever made for television), cartoons (the vampire has been on almost every animated series almost from the first), and wax museums, coloring books, breakfast cereals, figurines, masks, bath mittens, erasers, stamps and decals, plastic model kits, wallets, bubble bath, bracelets, paint-by-number kits, costumes, kites, play money, candy, pencil sharpeners, Mon-Stirs swizzle sticks, muppets, popcorn, and lunch boxes. If a twelve-year-old can use it, the vampire has been on it.

Since film has been the dominant medium of the vampire's return to the folk, let me briefly graph Dracula's family tree, emphasizing his Anglo-American descendants. Actually, since he progenerates laterally, for his "children" are those he has loved, not fathered, a family "shrub" might be a better image. In any case, we can consider the most important family branches.

I should also mention the distaff side of the vampire family shrub which descends first from the classical myth of Lamia through J. Sheridan Le Fanu's *Carmilla* (itself a stepchild of Coleridge's *Christabel*) and Elizabeth Bathory (the sixteenth-century "blood countess"). Again, the diagram is pruned by my own prejudices.

The destructive woman is one of humankind's oldest images of terror, but she first became vampiric in romanticism. In English poetry she was Coleridge's Geraldine and Keats' "La Belle Dame Sans Merci" or his Lamia; in American prose she was Poe's Morella or Ligeia, but it has been in the movies that she has really come of age.[18] One can start to see her visual powers exploited in a late-nineteenth-century series of devouring females by Edvard Munch. In time she will become one of the clichés of popular culture: the Hollywood vamp, the modern version of the man-eating female.

Before discussing a few vampire and lamia films, let me explain what I am not interested in. I am not interested in any of the "important" films, such as Murnau's *Nosferatu*, Dreyer's *Vampir*, Browning's *Dracula*, or Vadim's *Blood and Roses* because, instead of advancing the myth, they promulgate one particularly self-conscious version. Art renditions tend to make the saga socially relevant, allegorical, or atmospheric, rather than just letting it play itself out. Artists like Murnau, Dreyer, Vadim, and even Browning, usually try to turn the myth away from the one thing it most assuredly is in popular culture—namely, a fairy tale. Artists are cultural architects—they don't want to just restack the blocks of myth, they want to rearrange them, create something of their own, something interesting.

I have tried to pick instances where the vampire myth was retold not for art, but for money—where it was simply exploited, where those camp counselors simply told the story to get us off to bed as quickly and as frightened as possible. For the most part, these films resulted from instances where the CPAs in the "front office" saw a hole in the production schedule and plugged it with "another vampire movie." Most of these films were written by hacks, filmed by technicians, and advertised by artists, and most of them made just enough money so that the CPAs in "front offices" of the competing studios started murmuring about "another vampire movie."

When you now look at these films from the point of view of a myth critic, you see in them the unaffected and unconscious retelling of a fairy tale, a fabulous yarn full of sexual information that is being unraveled again for each new adolescent audience. To dislodge that fairy tale, let me turn to a few artistically unimportant, but mythically resonant, renditions from each

A PREJUDICIAL VAMPIRE FAMILY TREE

BRAM STOKER, *Dracula,* book published 1897

*Murnau, *Nosferatu* (1922) [Max Schreck]
Herzog, *Nosferatu* (1979) [Klaus Kinski]
King/Hooper, *'Salem's Lot* (1980)
  (the best TV movie yet of the nosferatu)

UNIVERSAL DRACULAS
*Browning
  Dracula (1931) [Bela Lugosi]
  Dracula's Daughter (1936) [Gloria
  Holden]
  Son of Dracula (1943) [Lon Chaney, Jr.]
  House of Frankenstein (1944)
  [John Carradine]
  House of Dracula (1945) [Carradine]

PARODY
* *Abbott and Costello Meet
  Frankenstein* (1948) [Lugosi]
*Old Mother Riley Meets the
  Vampire* (1948) [Lugosi]
* *Polanski, The Fearless Vampire
  Killers* (1967) [Ferdy Mayne]
Andy Warhol's Dracula (1974)
  [Udo Kier]
Old Dracula (1974) [David Niven]
Love at First Bite (1979)
  [George Hamilton]

AMERICAN
(a) Standard low-quality 1945 to 1975 like *The
    Return of Dracula* (1957), *Grave of the
    Vampire* (1972), and vampire cowboys
    like *Curse of the Undead* (1959) and *Billy
    the Kid vs. Dracula* (1965)
(b) Vampire as minority; homosexual:
    Does Dracula Really Suck? (1969), *The Mad
    Love Life of a Hot Vampire* (1971) and black:
    Blacula (1972) and *Scream Blacula Scream* (1973)
    [William Marshall] and from outerspace: *The
    Thing from Another World* (1951) [James
    Arness], *Plan Nine from Outer Space* (1956)
    [Lugosi], *It! The Vampire from Beyond Space*
    (1958) and for deaf: *Deafula* (1975)
(c) Count Yorga series, interesting for the amount of
    money it made and its unresolved endings:
    Count Yorga, Vampire (1970), *The Return of
    Count Yorga* (1971) [Robert Quarry]
(d) Vampire on television:
    "Dark Shadows" (soap opera, 1968–1971),
    The Night Stalker (1972), * *Dracula* (1973) [Jack
    Palance]
(e) The most recent U.S. productions:
    * *Martin* (1977), *Dracula* (1978) [Frank Langella]

LAMIA—From Classical Myth and Greek Folklore

Coleridge, *Christabel* (1797–1801)

Le Fanu, *Carmilla* (1871)

*Dreyer, *Vampir* (1932)
  Dracula's Daughter (1936) [Gloria Holden]
*Vadim, *Blood and Roses* (1960) [Annette Vadim]
Miller, *Terror in the Crypt* (1963)

Hammer Studios

The Vampire Lovers (1970)
Lust for a Vampire (1971)
Twins of Evil (1972)

Recent American Versions

Velvet Vampire (1971)
The Hunger (1983)

Elizabeth Bathory (d. 1614)

Daughters of Darkness (1970)
Countess Dracula (1971)
[Ingrid Pitt]

ENGLISH

Hammer Studios

Horror of Dracula (1958) [Christopher Lee]
Bride of Dracula (1960) [David Peel]
Dracula, Prince of Darkness (1966) [Lee]
Dracula Has Risen from the Grave (1968) [Lee]
Taste the Blood of Dracula (1969) [Lee]
Scars of Dracula (1970) [Lee]
Dracula A.D. 1972 (1972) [Lee]
The Satanic Rites of Dracula (1973) [Lee]

Amicus Studios: anthology tales

The House That Dripped Blood (1971)
Vault of Horror (1973)
BBC television's *Dracula* (1978)
  [Louis Jourdan]

FOREIGN

German

Jonathan, Vampire Sterben Nicht

Mexican

Santo and Nostradamus series

Italian & Spanish

Many low-budget vampire films by directors like Jess Franko, Paul Naschy, and most important, Mario Bava

Note: Important versions are starred, dates are in parentheses, and important vampire actors are in brackets.

Edvard Munch, *Vampire*, 1895 (Kommunes Kunstsamlinger, Oslo)

of the above categories: (1) *Son of Dracula* (1943), from the Universal series; (2) *Return of Dracula* (1957), made at the nadir of American efforts at the same time Hammer Studios was producing its first and, to many, its best, *Horror of Dracula*; (3) *Brides of Dracula* (1960), a typical Hammer potboiler; (4) *Countess Dracula* (1970), an example of the female vampire à la Hammer; (5) *Grave of the Vampire* (1972), an American exploitation effort made with the unconscious skill of people who just wanted to jar the audience; and finally, (6) a few parodies, like *Andy Warhol's Dracula* (1974) and *Old Dracula* (1974), which once again show that caricature and burlesque are often more insightful than straight renditions. As movies, they all deserve their occasional berths on midnight television, but as artless returns to the family romance, they deserve a little comment.

The most important information to be gleaned from *Son of Dracula* (1943) is that Lon Chaney, Jr., simply could not play the title role. His father could have; in fact, the elder Chaney was first choice for the role in Browning's *Dracula* (1931). The son couldn't. This is not because Junior could not act, but because he didn't look right. In the 1940s no one yet realized what the "look" was, but in *Son of Dracula* they learned what it was not. Lon Chaney, Jr., looked like the perpetual son, and he could act like one in his Wolfman roles, but Dracula is anything but a child—he is only a parent, more specif-

Lon Chaney, Jr., as *Son of Dracula,* 1943 (Universal Studios)

ically, only the father. Bela Lugosi was right for the part because he could *only* act like a father speaking in that ponderous diction with that threatening finger and using that look from above.

This is more than a casual observation of the now obvious psychodynamics of the myth. Although you can make *I Was a Teenage Werewolf* or *I Was a Teenage Frankenstein*, you really cannot make *I Was a Teenage Dracula* (although George Romero came close in *Martin*). When Universal made *Son of Dracula* it seemed a natural enough extension of the myth: they had made *Dracula* père in 1931 and *Dracula's Daughter* in 1936; it was only natural to add the third, the son. After all, *Son of Frankenstein* kept the monster and only changed the doctor; *Son of Dracula* tried to change the monster and keep the victim.

Here is the story in brief. Count Alucard (spell it backward) has run short of European blood and so has come to America. Appropriately, he goes to the one place in our society where blood still means something—the South. There in Louisiana, at Dark Oaks Plantation under the Spanish moss, he observes the Cauldwell family awaiting his preannounced arrival. He does not appear and, as they disband, Alucard transforms himself into a bat and flaps up to Colonel Cauldwell's bedroom where he unexpectedly dispatches the old father.[19] The Colonel's daughter, Catherine, inherits the property and she has the requisite fiancé to manage the estate. Frank, in turn, has the requisite medical friend, Dr. Brewster. What makes this version so interesting (Curt Siodmak, who wrote *The Wolf Man*, scripted it; his brother Robert directed) is that Catherine is not seduced by Alucard. This is not because Lon Chaney, Jr., would have credibility problems, but because this movie clearly attempts to skirt the sexual dynamics of incest. Catherine, already motherless and with her father now dead, is drawn to Alucard; she wants his attention, his nurturing, and she especially wants to experience his—in the movie's terms—"forbidden life." So she willingly goes off with him to the Justice of the Peace, not as victim, but as co-conspirator. Marriage is not what the vampire has on his mind; it's on Catherine's mind. When Frank, the fiancé, finds out what has happened, he is understandably upset, fights with the Count, and shoots at what he considers the Count's substantial body, only to see the bullet whiz through the Count and kill his Catherine. Frank tells Dr. Brewster what has happened; Dr. B. now checks with the older Dr. Laslo (the Van Helsing figure) and the diagnosis is almost made—Dr. Laslo can spell backward. Dr. L. now comes from far away to make a house call and helps the young boys plan the disposal of the foul patriarch. It's not so easy because Catherine (who has come back from the dead) is continually trying to get Frank to leave her alone, but Frank will have none of it. She relents, thanks to his insistent love, and tells him how to find and sterilize the vampire's lair, which he does. Alucard is caught in the rays of the sun. Then Frank does something rather interesting—he burns the body of Catherine, his inamorata. That's not how things are supposed to end; she's supposed to be liberated by the vampire's death and made fresh again. But it's clear; Catherine was not seduced, she volunteered, and that is unacceptable, especially to Southern gentility. She has wanted what she should not want, done what she should not have done, and so is done for.

The incest motif in *Son of Dracula* is as unsophisticated as the lesbianism in *Dracula's Daughter*. There is nothing contrived about it, no attempt to explain, let alone exploit. When a moviemaker of horror has an ax to grind, he usually shows you the whetstone in every possible frame. When Dracula is allegorized as a capitalist, fascist, minority, or even cowboy, the metaphor is clearly there. But in *Son of Dracula* the Siodmaks just let the myth unravel and followed it along. It would have been interesting had they gone farther, but Universal had other ideas after the disappointment of *Son of Dracula*, and most of their ideas involved conventions of from three to five monsters at *House of Dracula*, or *House of Frankenstein*, or in *The Monsters Meet Abbott and Costello.*[20]

Dracula had made a number of return trips to the States after Alucard, but the one I'd like to single out was one made in the same generation that the vampire was strapping on his spurs in *Curse of the Undead* or riding around in flying piepans in *Plan Nine from Outer Space*. In 1957 United Artists made *The Return of Dracula* (also known as *The Curse of Dracula* and, for some reason, *The Kiss of the Ghost*), a throwaway film notable for what characterized so many UA films of this decade—an utter lack of pretense. It is in a sense a "Grandson of Dracula," for once again the moody malefactor has had his Transylvanian well run dry and has had to migrate to the New World. This time, however, he has pushed his luck, for he is pursued by dedicated vampire hunters from Interpol to the U.S. Immigration Service. In the days of Senator Joe McCarthy, even Comrade Dracula should have known he'd be a goner from the start.

Under the guise of Bellac Gordal (don't bother with a translation; it's Calleb Ladrog, and it's doubtful the screenwriter, Pat Fielder, ever heard of William Godwin), the vampire makes his way to Carlton, California, and presents himself as the Middle European cousin of the widow lady, Cora, who has the beautiful daughter, Rachel, who has the requisite girlfriend, Jenny, and the boyfriend, Tim. "Would it be all right if I move in with you for a while?" queries Cousin Bellac. "It will only be for a short time." "Please do," says the widow Cora. "You know there's room upstairs." Bellac makes himself at home, encouraging Rachel to pursue a career in fashion design and discouraging her from pursuing a career with Tim—all this in a fatherly-enough way. Things go well in Carlton, California, until Mr. MacBryant comes from Washington to "check the papers" of our visiting friend, is suspicious, surreptitiously photographs Bellac with his government-issue trick Minolta lighter-camera, and—well, Bellac doesn't photograph well; in fact, not at all. So the hunt is on: Bellac first attacks blind Jenny, giving her night vision, dispatches MacBryant, and is moving fast on Rachel. Unknown to Bellac, however, is Meyerman, professional vampire tracker, who has also trailed Bellac to his lair in Southern California. Rachel is losing ground fast: Bellac's fatherly concern and transcendental talk ("I promise you life . . . real life") is affecting her. All that comes between them is her crucifix and soon even that slips off.

Bellac is finally cornered, of course, but not before he has "corrupted" Rachel. Meyerman, in a truly ecumenical move, joins forces with the local priest who, in turn, is helped by Tim. While the older vampire hunters relieve poor Jenny with a stake, Tim closes in on Bellac. Rachel tries to help; Bellac trips, falls into a pit of conveniently upturned stakes, and vanishes into dust. His spell is broken; Rachel is free; and she returns to Tim almost as virginal as she had once been. She is now ready to marry Tim—she has learned the lessons of the tribe. What is interesting about this film is that, once again, there is an absolute innocence in dealing with daughter and surrogate father. There is no attempt to disguise the incest motif or to make it titillating; it is just there, accepted as a donnée.

At the same time *Return of Dracula* was being shown, Hammer Studios was making *Horror of Dracula*, the first major break in cinematic renditions since the Universal films of the 1930s. Jimmy Sangster, who wrote many of the Hammer screenplays, and Terence Fisher, who did the important directing, simply made the implicit obvious: (1) They made everything about Dracula lush and opulent and everything about his victims Victorian and repressed. Dracula always chose the bosomy girlfriend/daughter after first dispatching her older duenna or father and intimidating her bourgeois boyfriend. (2) They filmed all Dracula's elegance in vibrant color. The spectrum was always keyed to blood-red; Christopher Lee even wore red contact lenses. (3) They returned Dracula to his role as Byronic hero, and so had to make his victims worthy of conquest and his acts worthy of condemnation. Needless to say, the family romance was always portrayed from the most Freudian of viewpoints. She was the co-conspirator; he the overreaching patriarch. Hammer's major helpmates in this endeavor were never the critics, who were uniformly hostile, but the censors. Hammer not only accepted an "X" rating (in 1951 the British censor changed from "H" for horror to "X" for sex; the over-eighteen age limit now acknowledged more than just nasty monsters, but monsters doing nasty things); they made certain that their films got the lowest possible ratings. Hammer would shoot three versions of the sex scenes, then try to get the middle one past the British censor, keeping the "lewd" one for the Japanese and the "tame" one for the Americans. (4) Even more important than sex and color was Hammer's luck in casting Christopher Lee as Dracula. Lee became a most hesitant vampire who, after saying "I'll never play another Dracula," usually, like Byron's Dona Julia, "consented." He was perfect: arrogant, athletic, and, when outfitted in his cape, incisors, and lenses, he could be very snarly. Lee also had just the right amount of "come hither, my child" to snare Barbara Shelley, Veronica Carlson, Jenny Hanley, Stephanie Beacham, Joanna Lumley—everyone except the femme fatale of horror films, Barbara Steele.

The real sensation of Hammer—and no one has really appreciated it, not even the Cahier du Cinema critics—was that the Hammer scriptwriters, especially Jimmy Sangster and Anthony Hinds (listed on credits as John

Christopher Lee as Dracula in *Taste the Blood of Dracula,* 1970 (Hammer Studios)

Elder), always knew where the horror of Dracula was, and returned to it like bankers to the vault. Any number of movies in the 1960s offered the adolescent male the opportunity to ogle big breasts—even Russ Meyer dabbled in ersatz horror motifs with *Kiss Me Quick* (1963), in which a mad doctor creates a vampire and a couple of big-breasted girls, and *Beyond the Valley of the Dolls* (1970) where "Count Dracula" molests the same—but Hammer always did more, and did it better. Almost invariably Hammer structured their plots around the sexual violation and then the rapid demise of the family caused by the intrusion of the paternal fiend. Hammer may not have publicly acknowledged it, although Sangster has almost coyly admitted as much in interviews, but they were clearly conscious that horror was indeed a family affair. They discovered the formula early and exploited it without mercy for two decades. Let me illustrate with two examples, rarely mentioned in criticism in part because they were so derivative, one from Hammer's male vampire line, *The Brides of Dracula*, and the other from the female, *Countess Dracula*.

Hammer made *The Brides of Dracula* (1960) after the astonishing success of *Horror of Dracula* (1958) and before they learned what they had in Christopher Lee. Almost as a casual oversight, they allowed a much less dynamic, almost effeminate, David Peele to play the role. Here is the tale—clearly a Sangster special, just reversing the roles a bit. A buxom young school marm, Marianne, is stranded en route to her new job at a Transylvanian finishing school for young ladies, and is invited to spend the night with Baroness Meinster at her castle. There is no Baron; he presumably is dead. Once at the castle, Marianne finds that the affable Baroness keeps her son in chains. The young man has a mental disease, the Baroness explains, but later that night he seems normal enough to Marianne when he claims that mother keeps him in chains in order to get his inheritance. Marianne unlocks the junior Baron and, of course, he is a vampire. Strangely enough the Baron does not attack the plump young schoolteacher; he goes quickly off camera to his mother. He is not interested in Marianne; he is not a patriarch yet.

Marianne learns from the requisite demented housekeeper that the mother has spoiled the boy from the first and now has taken to bringing him young morsels like Marianne to keep him out of trouble. That's enough for Marianne; she skedaddles off and just happens to run into Van Helsing, who just happens to be in the neighborhood checking the vampire population. The good father first gets her to the finishing school (full of more nubiles and a lecherous headmaster, the displaced evil father), slips on his gloves, picks up his suitcase of destruction tools, joins forces with the parish priest, and heads for the castle.

He is met at the clanking castle door by the Baroness who, thanks to her son's off-camera attack, is a little worse for wear. She coyly tries to cover her mouth while talking, but Van Helsing cannot be deceived. He sees her nascent fangs. The mother has been made a vampire by the son! Van Helsing says it out loud: "The Baron has taken the blood of his own mother!" The Baroness, acknowledging her guilt—after all, she indulged the boy from the beginning—now consents to being staked. She's done wrong; she knows it. Van Helsing takes off his gloves, the organ music booms, and he obliges.

The Baron, meanwhile, is off at the finishing school trying to capture Marianne. He'll marry her if necessary. Finally, just as he's all set to seduce/bite her, Van Helsing arrives, pursues the fiend to a windmill (shades of the Universal *Frankenstein*), they fight it out, and the vampire Baron takes a nip out of Van Helsing's arm. That is unique in vampire lore, but the good doctor gamely cauterizes the wound with a red-hot poker and then maneuvers the bad Baron into the cross-like shadow formed by the vanes of the windmill. That does it; the vampire is a goner. Marianne is safe.

In *The Brides of Dracula* for the first time Hammer was not just unabashedly Oedipal, but unavoidably so; after all, there was only one "bride" of Dracula. Ten years and more than fifty horror films later they were still at it, the same psychological content, implied if not overtly stated. Hammer made all the old stories into one: *The Two Faces of Dr. Jekyll, The Phantom of the Opera, Maniac, The Evil of Frankenstein, The Curse of the Mummy's Tomb, The Plague of the Zombies, Dracula, Prince of Darkness, Frankenstein Created Woman, Dracula Has Risen from the Grave, Frankenstein Must Be Destroyed, Taste the Blood of Dracula,* and *Horror of Frankenstein* are just a few of their efforts at family romance in the 1960s. But let us look at *Countess Dracula* (1971) because it breaks Hammer's mold of father-aggressor. Here the "mother" is active and the "son" passive, but incest still inspires the horror.

Countess Dracula was made soon after Hammer had produced its lesbian, *Carmilla*-inspired duo, *The Vampire Lovers* (1970) and *Lust for a Vampire* (1971). The figure of a vampiric femme fatale convinced the studio that they had found yet another nerve to tingle. They took the Countess Bathory story (the sixteenth-century "blood countess" who supposedly bathed in the blood of virgins), added the name "Dracula," peddled it under such misleading blurbs as "the more she drinks, the better she looks," and planned to sit back and grow richer. To protect their investment, Hammer signed Ingrid Pitt, the sensational star of *The Vampire Lovers* (1970), to do the job Barbara Steele had done in Mario Bava's surprisingly successful *Black Sunday* (1960). But the movie didn't work.

The horror was simply not there. In the first reel the aging Countess learns that blood will indeed reverse the aging process. But what's sexy about bathing in hemoglobin? So to give the story some pizzazz, Alexander Paal and Peter Sasdy contructed a family for the Countess. It develops that the Countess must compete with her long-lost-daughter-now-recently-found for the affection of a young gentleman friend. The mother would have won the lad if she could have stopped transforming herself into an old crone just when things were going her way. On every romantic occasion the Countess must rush off for more blood. The young Hussar, named Imre Toth, soon tires of her inappropriate exits and turns his attentions toward the daughter. Finally, Imre asks the old crone for the hand of the daughter and, although she tries to be nice, calling him "my son, my son," it is clear her feelings are anything but motherly. After he's started to suspect that the Countess is not getting better, only temporarily younger, she clutches him to her breast and moans "my son, my darling son."

The people of Transylvania are getting restless, for the Countess has decimated the supply of local virgins to restore her youth. The only virgin left is her daughter, whom she now taps in order to make one last play for Imre

Ingrid Pitt and recent victim in *Countess Dracula,* 1971 (Hammer Studios)

her daughter, whom she now taps in order to make one last play for Imre Toth. Could any contrivance be more self-consciously Oedipal; she lives off the daughter in order to experience the son. When the wedding day of the Countess and young Toth arrives, the enervated daughter wanders into the ceremony; the ceremony is stopped and the Countess, now aging fast, lunges at her daughter and is stabbed by the phallic knife of the groom. He realizes his mistake, grabs the girl, and rushes away. As the Countess now becomes literally prune-faced in front of all, the crowd is heard mumbling "Countess Dracula, devil woman."

The theme of the blood-countess was being almost simultaneously resuscitated by the Belgians in *Daughters of Darkness* (1971), and the continental version shows how unimaginative and formulaic Hammer had become. Especially in retrospect, *Daughters* seems so much more risqué and interesting. On the French Riviera, Countess Bathory conspires with an unhappy English bride to be first lovers and later drinkers of the chauvinistic husband's blood. If only Hammer could have kept things so simple! They had followed the Freudian route so often that they finally thought it was the only way to reach the audience. At the end, in the late 1970s, Hammer was making movies interesting now only for postmortem commentary. As had Universal in the 1940s, Hammer thought that established iconography alone could carry the horror, but the audience wanted something new. They had had enough of the heaving breasts, extended incisors, bats, velvet curtains, stakes and snarls, all that syrupy blood, and plots built just to facilitate images.

Examine *Taste the Blood of Dracula* (1970), for instance. The incest theme is triplicated when Dracula seduces three daughters of three pompous, high-Victorian fathers and then directs the daughters to kill their fathers in order to be "adopted" by Dracula. It's more complicated than this, of course, but that is the gist. Or next in *Dracula Today* (a.k.a. *Dracula A.D. 1972* or, still worse, *Dracula Chases the Mini-Girls*), Dracula hangs around with a gang of dope-smoking, pseudo-hip Teddy Boys while Hammer gets a chance to "showcase" some of the acid rock music of the teenyboppers. At the end Van Helsing, Jr., pushes Dracula into a pit of conveniently upturned stakes. *Dracula A.D. 1972* was a TV movie, nothing more.

The worst was yet to come. In *The Satanic Rites of Dracula* (1973) (a.k.a. *Dracula Is Dead and Well and Living in London*), Dracula is revived in the form of a latter-day Howard Hughes, as a reclusive billionaire and real-estate magnate. Making money (bleeding the people dry) has proved as dull as blood-sucking, so Dracula wants death. But how can a vampire die? Someone should have told scriptwriter Don Houghton that even Varney the Vampire had the grace to jump into Mount Vesuvius. In this travesty, Dracula turns into a James Bond villain who plans to infect the world with a new plague, killing everyone, thereby starving himself to death. Instead, Dracula is lured by Van Helsing, Jr., into a hawthorn bush and impales himself on a thousand tiny stakes. Hammer finally shipped Dracula off to the Hong Kong Shaw brothers for a little Kung Fu in *The Seven Brothers Meet Dracula* (1973). (I have not seen this movie—even Christopher Lee would have none of it.) The once-exciting Hammer series had finally degenerated into pure exploitation. When Dracula has to befriend Bruce Lee you know things are in trouble.

Money was still to be squeezed from the myth, however, and I will mention two recent films notable for their insightful crassness: the American *Grave of the Vampire* (1972) and the English potboiler *Old Dracula* (1975). When they appeared they were justly excoriated in reviews, but I think they may still be remembered by mythographers, each for different reasons. In *The Grave of the Vampire* a vampire attacks a young teenage couple smooching in a car, kills the boy, and kisses/rapes the girl, who nine months later gives birth to the fiend's issue. This boy-child is one of the first child monsters born in the 1970s. The babe soon sprouts incisors, which makes nursing a bit difficult. To make things even worse, he soon spurns breast milk for blood, making his mother puncture her breast to feed him. She dies after prolonged torment and he sets out after his "father," who is teaching night classes at a nearby college. Father and son battle it out, son wins, and now, just as we are finding ourselves sympathetic to the boy's plight as unwanted child, he turns to kiss his girlfriend. Once we see the teeth, we realize that the cycle is going to start all over again: Rosemary's baby once more. What is interesting about *Grave of the Vampire* is that the Oedipal/incestual theme is so closely and consciously linked to the theme of the demonic child. This seemingly new convention is appearing again and again in contemporary shockers: *Eraserhead, Omen I, II, III, It's Alive, It Lives Again, The Beast Within, Possession*, among many others, where the hideous child wreaks havoc on the incautious parents.

The other movie, *Old Dracula*, will be remembered because it shows how unabashedly accretive horror schlock can be. Old Dracula (the late David Niven) has imported a bevy of Playboy bunnies into his Transylvanian Hefner hutch because he needs blood for his wife, "Vampira" (this was the movie's working title, a play on the successful comic book "Vampirella," changed after the success of Mel Brooks' *Young Frankenstein*), who has been feeling out of sorts, thanks to her inappropriate bite of an anemic peasant. She has difficult blood to match, and so Old Dracula has to "sample all the bunnies" and transfer their blood to Vampira. Because of a mix-up in the transfusion process, as Vampira revives her complexion turns steadily darker. She starts talking jive talk, sashaying about, snapping her fingers, and turns into none other than Teresa Graves of "Laugh-In" fame. Alas, the bunnies have all jetted back to their London warren, and since the debonair Dracula is not so sure that black really is beautiful, he takes off after them with Vampira. He'll have to get some of the offending blood so he can recombine it to return his spouse to proper paleness.

So it's off to London. Old Dracula is sure he can reverse the cultural damage if he can recheck the bunnies. He's too old to do it alone, so he inducts (bites) a nice young man and makes him his helper. The young man goes to gather samples in his hollow vampire fangs and then, like a good son, returns them to Daddy. The lad finally ends up at the Playboy Club discotheque where all the bunnies are hopping about, and you can guess the rest. After the antidotal blood is prepared, Vampira gives Old Dracula a love-peck on the neck just for luck. The now-detoxified blood is pumped back into her, but wait! What is happening? Why is Old Dracula blushing? We abruptly cut away. The boy, the "son" who has been released from the vampire's toils after his successful retrieval work, goes to the police, but Mr. and Mrs. Dracula escape. We now cut to the seating section of an airborne jet. Winging their way back to Transylvania is Teresa Graves, still black, and we slowly pan to her husband. There he is, an embarassed David Niven in blackface.

Old Dracula seizes upon everything in the 1970s: black consciousness (not just the *Shaft* movies, but the black vampire subgenre, including *Blacula* and *Scream, Blacula, Scream*), the Playboy mode of voyeurism (Old Dracula looks at the centerfolds for "nice veins"), the disco and Chelsea scene, and then, for good measure, a dollop of incest. What a nice touch to have the young boy bring home the blood elixir that the father is "too tired" to find, the blood elixir that will restore the "mother," ironically, to the father. Had Mel Brooks' *Young Frankenstein* not come out in 1973, this movie would not have been renamed, and it would probably have stayed forever where it belonged—on the distributor's shelf.

As with the Universal Draculas of the late 1930s, the Hammer Draculas of the 1970s were followed by either parody or excess. Andy Warhol had a shot at Dracula in *Blood for Dracula* (1974), which had two scenes of high camp. First, since Dracula is dying of anemia because of the paucity of virgins ("vvergins," he calls them), he journeys over to Italy, hoping that a Catholic country will have a greater supply. But there he is beaten to the last virgin by a preposterous woodcutter (played by Joe De Dallesandro complete with Brooklyn accent), who announces as he throws the last virgin to the ground, "There is only one way to save you." By the time Dracula finds her she is no longer a virgin and he is reduced to licking her hymenal blood from the floor. Rivaling this scene in raucous bad taste is the second venture into the ludicrous. The woodcutter takes off after the enfeebled "vampiyah," lopping off his limbs one by one, until the poor fiend is totally limbless.

Roman Polanski doubtless enjoyed his bit part in the Warhol film as one of the heavies in the requisite country-pub scene, for a decade earlier he had made his own send-up, *Dance of the Vampires*. Polanski's film deserves some comment because, even though he was dissatisfied with the way it was cut, *Dance* is still provocative. What else could be expected from the maker of two of the most important horror films of the 1960s and 1970s: *Repulsion* and *Rosemary's Baby*.

Polanski's film is entertaining, for he knew what Hammer had wrought with the myth: *Dance* had returned the vampire back to folklore, more specifically to the fairy tale, but kept the Hammer *mise-en-scène*. Polanski's movie, unfortunately renamed *The Fearless Vampire Killers or Pardon Me,*

But Your Teeth Are in My Neck, complete with cartoon credits and Swingle Singers soundtrack, gives the story over to Mel Brooks and Walt Disney—in a sense, the modern Brothers Grimm. *Dance of the Vampires* is an insightful movie because, in aping all the best Hammer claptrap and in reducing the plot to the minimum, Polanski could celebrate the story as it really is—an adolescent dream vision.

Once upon a time in Transylvania a boy-crazy girl is sent to her room by her father. Dracula (appropriately played by Ferdy Mayne) happens by, sees her in her bath, is interested, dispatches the father, kidnaps her, and is pursued by her boyfriend, Alfred (inappropriately played by Polanski himself). Alfred is aided by the wise professor who, like all professional wise men, is partly a fool. The forces of the good but foolish finally catch up with the forces of the wise but evil. On the way, there are some sexual slurs (Dracula's gay son pursues Alfred while Alfred pursues Dracula who pursues the girl—played, incidentally, by Sharon Tate), parodies of scholarship (Van Helsing is more interested in plundering Dracula's bookshelves than in plundering vampires), lots of Abbott and Costello double-takes, and, best of all, a Dracula who presides over his vampire flock like the chairman of GM in a poor year. Like all Juvenalian satire, *Dance of the Vampires* ends up celebrating the wild improbabilities and exaggerations of the myth with genuinely affectionate concern.

It becomes clear when we look at these offerings of Warhol and Polanski that the vampire myth is really just an overgrown fairy tale. Essentially, the last hundred years of the Dracula myth in print and on celluloid have made it legendary. Here is what it now entails: a boy and girl in their late teens are in love. Very often she has a father who objects. The young lovers are either contemplating marriage or are even on their honeymoon when the girl is whisked off by Dracula. He takes her away from the boy to make her his "bride" and she is not totally unwilling. The boy, now separated from his love, is desperate and luckily is helped by an older wise man who happens by. Together they track down the outlaw kidnapper; then the boy, who has been instructed by the shaman in the ways of eradicating the monster, stakes the fiend and so liberates his true love. At the end the young couple are to live happily ever after. There are variations on this ending that seem to depend on how willingly unwilling the damsel was about the earlier seduction. If she was too compliant she may have to be staked, and the boy find another mate. If she has resisted, however, the staking of the vampire will set her free. In Polanski's *Dance of the Vampires* and in the *Count Yorga* movies, the girl is so vampiric at the end that after the boy has destroyed the evil father, she turns on him and we are left with the final frisson that the story has no ending. She will initiate him and he will become the next . . . Dracula!

Now listen to another fairy tale—we already know this one by heart. We have heard it over and over, years before we ever knew about vampires. One morning Little Red Riding Hood sets off from her mother's house to take her grandmother some cakes and wine. When she gets to the woods she meets a wolf who asks where she's going and she tells him. She is not frightened by the wolf, in fact, at most maybe a little uncomfortable. The wolf tells her to linger awhile and pick some flowers for grandmother and, even though she had been told earlier by her mother not to dally, she does. Meanwhile the wolf has gone to granny's, has swallowed her whole, and waits between the sheets for the next morsel—the granddaughter. She comes; they perform the famous litany about large ears, eyes, hands, and mouth, and Red Riding Hood is soon swallowed up. Just happening by is the woodsman; he finds the wolf in a postprandial snooze, slits open the wolf's tumescent tummy, and out pops LRRH and her grandmother. They then fill the wolf's tummy up with stones, and when he wakes, he falls over and dies.

Bruno Bettelheim in *The Uses of Enchantment* (1975) argues that this tale has lasted through generations because it addresses the problems of a young girl's (and by extension, a young boy's) sexual initiation. The fact that the girl-child must travel from mother's house (there is no mention of father) past a wolf to whom she is attracted (surely his questions belabor the obvious, for he knows the way to grandmother's house and if he had only wanted to eat her he could consume her now) until she comes to her destination ("grand" mother's bed, complete with that wolf). Note, says Bettelheim, that the wolf is not the seducer; true, he eats her, but she is profoundly implicated. Remember, she gives the wolf directions, then dallies sufficiently for him to be abed before she arrives, and certainly she can't be that ingenuous about grandmother's lupine appearance. The implied moral, unknown even to the teller of the tale, is that she had best be careful not to lose "her little red cap" to the first man she meets, because we all know who that first man will be. She should work together with her (grand)mother to make sure this particular wolf is kept from the door.

But in the story, mother and daughter don't work together. In fact, it is important that the wolf dispatch the surrogate mother before the (grand)daughter can be his. Both parties unconsciously collude, and so it is left for a third party, the woodsman, the good father, as it were, who has hitherto been missing from the family, to intercede. Rife with associations of pregnancy and birth, the wolf's stomach is cut open and mother and child are reborn. Then, as if to make sure the wolf will not stir again, the woods-

Gustave Doré, *Little Red Riding Hood*

man fills the belly with rocks. In some renditions, especially those "collected" (i.e., sanitized) by Perrault in the seventeenth century for the court of Versailles, the story ends without this return to normalcy. There is no woodsman. The little girl has been bad and she must be punished. But the good woodsman belongs in the tale, for he reminds us that what LRRH has done may be wrong, yes, but not immoral or even unexpected. LRRH has followed bad advice. She will not let such careless seduction happen again.

Bettelheim considers LRRH "a pubertal encounter with Oedipal attachments" and indeed makes a convincing case.[21] I contend that the Dracula story is in this same mythic constellation, addressing the temptation of seduction not to a pubescent, but to a latency audience. All that really separates these two "fables of identity" is the presence of the young man, the girl's suitor. His inclusion completes the full family context for the adolescent. The girl must now choose not between mother and wolf-father/woodcutter-father, but between boyfriend and Dracula-father. I wonder if it is coincidence that the vampire's lycanthropy parallels the sexual connotations of the folkloric wolf. He is a wolfman, a werewolf. In the Dracula myth the girl is literally swept away by the bad father, and so the boyfriend must seek out the good father in the person of Van Helsing, who comes to the aid of the youngsters.

Things are not so clear in the male version of the story, in which the boy is victimized by the older femme fatale. What is clear is that this version of the vampire story is seldom told; in fact, in the most recent rendition, *The Hunger* (1983), the lamia and her victim were, at least visually, contemporaries. Could this version be rare because mother-son incest is exceptionally uncommon? When it is told, however, it is more possible for the young man to dally with the lamia, the older woman, the Countess Dracula, and survive, than it is for the girl to withstand the onslaught of Dracula. Is this because we realize that the male's Oedipal liaisons are less important, less consequential, because the older woman has no reproductive position in culture and hence raises no family problems to be solved? Or is it simply because there is not much audience out there interested in this version; certainly, there is less of an adolescent female audience. The lamia story usually ends as a male induction into sexuality story or more probably degenerates into a voyeuristic peek at lesbian encounters. In *The Hunger* this is exactly what happens. Either way, as Hammer first found out, there is not much interest at the box office.

The vampire still persists, educating the young in spite of themselves and their parents. The autocrat of evil has died a thousand deaths, but as long as he can lift the hair on the nape of the nubile neck, he will continue to be revived on stage, screen, television, toys, cereal boxes . . . and in print. Within his cursed life is one of society's most sacred truths, and as long as that truth seems important enough to preserve, and as long as the elders cannot articulate it to the young, the vampire will return to us night after night for the generations to come.

4

Frankenstein and Sons

"Your father was Frankenstein, but your mother was the light-e-ning."
Ygor in *The Ghost of Frankenstein*
and *Frankenstein Meets the Wolfman*

If the horror of Dracula lies in inappropriate seduction, then the horror of Frankenstein lies in unnatural creation. In fact, in contemporary folklore the Frankenstein story focuses on the generative scene in which a slightly deranged, white-frocked doctor animates a humanoid and then shrieks, "It's alive, oh, my God, it's alive, it's *really* alive!" We see from the hulk's eyelid flutter and finger twitch that the medico is right: it is alive. From about the age of four we know exactly what the "thing" looks like. The story, from here on really anticlimactic, explains how this creature grows up monstrous, how it turns on its creator, how it often molests his girlfriend, and how it is finally destroyed in such a way as to make a sequel impossibly possible.

Now why should this story, along with that of the vampire, be one of the great horror sagas of our time? And why should these two monsters have been for the last century and a half almost mythic bedfellows? I say "almost" because the vampire story explains whom not to get into bed with, while the man-created-monster fable details what results when, instead of a wrong partner, there is none. Together the stories form a diptych of the everlasting sexual concerns of youth and are often even linked together as parts of the same twin bill. Since that infamous night at the Villa Diodati, these two monsters have shuffled through the nights and across the stages of Western man, profoundly influencing not just popular culture but the arts as well. Here, for instance, is the 1826 account of what the peripatetic Prince Hermann von Pückler-Muskau found playing at London's Lyceum Theatre (the Lyceum was also known as the "English Opera House" and it was doubtless this misnomer that enticed the continental dilettante through its ornate portals):

> There was no opera, however; instead, we had terrible melodramas. First *Frankenstein*, where a human being is made by magic, without female help—a manufacture that answers very ill; and then the Vampire, after the well-known tale falsely attributed to Lord Byron. The principal part in both was acted by Mr. Cooke, who is distinguished for a very handsome person, skillful acting, and a remarkably dignified, noble deportment. The acting was, indeed, admirable throughout, but the pieces so stupid and monstrous that it was impossible to sit out the performance. (*Tour in England*, pp. 26–27)

The *Frankenstein* that the Prince refers to is one of the many early adaptations of Mary Shelley's novel (there were at least nine done in her lifetime) entitled *Presumption, or the Fate of Frankenstein* and was heartily approved by the author herself, although clearly not by the Prince. We know the myth today not by this transformation, but by others re-formed almost a century later by Peggy Webling, then by Robert Florey, and, recently, by Jimmy Sangster. For a number of years Peggy Webling's *Frankenstein* was, with Hamilton Deane's *Dracula*, a sure-fire evening of horror, and they are still parts of a double bill at the summer drive-in. Not only did Dracula and Frankenstein travel together in dramatic form, but just as Pückler-Muskau reports that Mr. Cooke played the vampire and the monster, so too did Hamilton Deane play Van Helsing and the monster, and so too today it is not uncommon for actors to play in both sagas. (Incidentally, Cooke was known in the playbill as "_____!" while Karloff was announced as " ? " in the credits of the first Frankenstein at Universal.) This crossover of actors is one of the most illuminating aspects of these myths because it shows that the audience is not disturbed when the fictive characters, as well as the players, intermingle. Since the texts interpenetrate, why shouldn't they exchange players? This is the reason why Lugosi can play Dracula in one film, the Frankenstein monster a few years later, and then play Ygor, the mad doctor's assistant, elsewhere. Likewise, Christopher Lee is the first Hammer Frankenstein monster as well as its premier Dracula. And so today on television James Mason is the Nosferatu's mentor in *Salem's Lot* and mad Dr. Polidori in *Frankenstein: The True Story*. This reciprocation even extends to the mirror roles: Dwight Frye was Fritz in Whale's *Frankenstein*, then Karl in *The Bride of Frankenstein* and Renfield in Browning's *Dracula*. But for that matter, what

Boris Karloff as the monster in *Frankenstein,* 1931 (Universal Studios)

Frankenstein/Dracula double bill, 1939 (Forrest J Ackerman collection)

about Edward Van Sloan as Van Helsing in the early *Dracula* and then as Dr. Waldman in *Frankenstein*; or John Carradine as Count Dracula in *House of Frankenstein*, but as the monster hunter in *The Bride of Frankenstein*; or Karloff as the most important early Frankenstein monster, then turning up as the mad doctor himself in *House of Frankenstein*; or Lon Chaney, Jr., as the monster in *Ghost of Frankenstein*, Dracula in *Son of Dracula*, as well as being the Wolfman everywhere else?

Horror actors can migrate between similar parts and the audience is not distracted, because they know the parts are interchangeable anyway. Even more curious is the fact that adolescents really don't seem to care if the myth is blatantly confused with reality; hence a 1949 *Abbott and Costello Meet the Killer, Boris Karloff* was followed by *Abbott and Costello Meet Dr. Jekyll and Mr. Hyde*, in which Karloff was first a bogeyman, then both Jekyll and Hyde, while the audience knew full well that he was really the Frankenstein monster. Critics in the 1940s often complained about Universal's "monster mash" movies like *House of Frankenstein* or *House of Dracula*, saying that the monsters should be kept apart, but this only shows a misplaced concept of horror categories—a concept that respects genres, not image clusters and sequences. The inappropriateness of *Billy the Kid vs. Dracula* or *Jesse James Meets Frankenstein's Daughter* never bothered their audiences' sensibilities; it more probably simply bored them; and so too no one was upset that a cowboy actor, Glen Strange, became the Frankenstein monster for a while in the late forties. The only way such seemingly inappropriate interweaving can occur is if there is only one story being told. It is always the same family romance, all that changes is where to start and who is going to play which part.[1]

Another way to understand the interconnections between these monsters is to realize that however different they may seem, they all share the same victim. In horror stories that have currency, not just during one generation, but between generations, the victims are invariably the same—young and innocent and curious. Most often in horror myths a monster interrupts the courtship of a boy and a girl; the girl is attacked and the boy must avenge. Assuredly, matters often become more complex, but to understand what is going on we need to forget the victim's plight for a moment and just watch the monster. For what we will find is that while humans make mistakes, monsters never do. The vampire is never confused about whom to seduce; the Wolfman never gets lost; Mr. Hyde never clubs bystanders. Even though their actions may appear random, monsters are never capricious. So too the Frankenstein monster, stupid as he may seem, is always smart enough to hurt only those who "deserve" it—at least from the point of view of his creator, the monster-maker. Only transitory mutants, stalk-and-slashers, zombies, aliens from outer space, or creatures from the deep are indiscriminate. Every creature from the mythic black lagoon who wants to survive in retellings keeps his eye on only a few victims, a well-chosen few, a few chosen by the martyr who is supposed to suffer most.

With this in mind, we turn to the infancy of the most important "incredible hulk" in our folklore—the Frankenstein monster. First, he has not always been so inarticulate as he now appears; in fact, before Hollywood lobotomized him, he was far and away the most erudite monster in all Christendom. He was a precocious monster from the hand of a precocious novelist. But what makes him even more extraordinary is that he was birthed not from an earlier myth, such as the Jewish legend of the Golem, but in a specific work, a gothic novel.

The Frankenstein myth is unique in that we actually have a generating "text" (Mary Shelley's 1818 novel; revised in 1832), but as with the other modern horror stories, most of what we know about the story comes from non-print media. The novel itself tells a confusing tale of a young man who creates a larger-than-life humanoid that then destroys much of the creator's family before presumably destroying himself. What distinguishes this myth through its many renditions is an overwhelming amount of confusion. For instance, who is Frankenstein? If you ask your local preteenager he will tell you it is the monster. It is not, of course; it is the protagonist. Although this confusion was already in place by the turn of the century, it was compounded by the Universal series. Universal added to the confusion by having the son called Wolf Frankenstein in *Son of Frankenstein* (the third Universal retelling) complain that even he can't keep all the names straight. En route to Village Frankenstein from America, Wolf complains to his bride: "Why, nine out of ten people call that misshapen creature of my father's experiments_____." At that moment the conductor interrupts with "Frankenstein," announcing that the train has arrived at its destination. The father, the son, the monster, and the town are all deliberately confused. If you ask a youngster about this Wolf (or Victor or Henry) Frankenstein, you will probably be told he is an older man, a doctor, a mad scientist. He is not: in the novel and in most early films he is a callow youth. If you then ask how the audience feels about the "monster," you will probably learn a very important fact. You will learn that this creature, far more than the other horror monster, Dracula, is really sympathetic. While it would seem logical to return to the text to resolve these ambiguities, the reverse will happen. What we will see, however, is where the "horror" comes from, how it got embedded into the text, and how it continues to excite regardless of the medium of transmission.

Frankenstein is, as George Levine has written in a recent collection of criticism appropriately entitled *The Endurance of "Frankenstein"* (1979), "one of the great freaks of English literature." Outside the text is the fascinating question of authorial gender, which has recently been raised by feminist critics who see the novel as a "woman's book." Those who assert the impersonality of texts have countered that *Frankenstein* was published anonymously and that reviewers like Walter Scott in *Blackwood's Edinburgh Magazine* and John Wilson Croker in the *Quarterly Review* were convinced it was not only written by a man, but that the man was Percy Bysshe Shelley. Inside the text we find an awkwardly written, inconsistently plotted narrative, peopled with a host of seemingly superfluous cipher-characters, and full of the kind of inappropriate longueurs that characterize artistic insecurity. A young man, Robert Walton, writes to his sister a verbatim account of what a young scientist, Victor Frankenstein, has accomplished in creating a "monster" who, in turn, has given young Frankenstein a verbatim account of what has happened to him during four years of the eighteenth century in Europe. This narrative china-box is a characteristic device of the early novel, especially the gothic, as it safely cocoons "meaning" inside a double layer of stories.

Yet, in spite of all the obscuring effects of these buried narratives and the ironic juxtapositions of narrators, there is not enough authorial control to save the tales from some incredible silliness. Students of absurdities have a field day wondering how Victor could create a being eight feet tall from the body parts of ordinary men (to say nothing of the fact that Victor might well have started creating life first on a less sophisticated level); how this creature could become fluent in English and French in less than a year (we are told he just happens to find the books—Milton, Plutarch, Goethe); why Victor did not create a female partner without reproductive apparatus to quiet the monster; exactly how the monster finds Victor's journal or a regular-sized cloak that just happens to fit someone of his prodigious size; and this is to completely overlook the implausibilities (nay, impossibilities) of some of the time sequences and the wild coincidences of serendipitous meetings.

In this story coincidence, so much a staple of the gothic anyway, is extended, I think deliberately, beyond the limits of credulity. In fact, it is taken into the levels of dream life where, after all, Mary Shelley says the story was first enacted. However, hidden under the ludicrous coincidences is a subtext of compelling interest that has nothing coincidental about it at all; in fact, it is ruthlessly predetermined. A young man creates a being larger than life, then spurns this creation, making it monstrous, and "it" turns on him and his family. In the text, much is made of the fact that this love deprivation has transformed prelapsarian Adam into Satan. "Remember that I am thy creature," says the monster. "I ought to be thy Adam, but I am rather the fallen angel, whom thou drivest from joy for no misdeed" (p. 95).[2] In his role as satanic scourge the monster (1) removes Clerval, Victor's only male friend and adviser, (2) throttles Victor's brother William and frames Justine, a family friend, (3) harasses Victor for more than a year, (4) strangles Elizabeth, Victor's new bride, on their wedding night, and (5) leads Victor off on a continental chase finally ending up on the arctic wastes where Victor expires and the monster finally (supposedly) immolates himself.

The novel is about the birthing of a creature who enacts a systematic ravaging of the Frankenstein family by the calculated destruction of particular people. But what is so interesting about that or, more particularly, why should the story have held our impassioned interest for so many generations? As I mentioned in an earlier chapter, for a horror story to endure, it must not only be adaptable into different media, it must also be appealing to either sex, especially during adolescence. Masculine horror (say, Maturin's *Melmoth the Wanderer*) will be as soon neglected in popular culture as feminine horror (for instance, Ann Radcliffe's *The Mysteries of Udolpho*), if only because the young audience, the primary audience of horror art from the eighteenth century onward, is uninterested in specific sexual roles. College professors, who read these gothic novels for reasons best known only to themselves, are the only contemporary audience for these old *Schauerromans*. I will try to demonstrate how the implied androgyny of Frankenstein keeps the myth alive; and let me proceed by first interpreting the saga from first the male and then the female point of view. For I intend to show that the sublimated sexual aspects of the novel are the key to its potency even though the novel seems—like *Dracula* and *The Strange Case of Dr. Jekyll and Mr. Hyde*—to be singularly devoid of any tabooed sexual, let alone specifically incestuous, references.

The male part of the myth is clearly embedded in the second half of Shelley's novel; what the monster does, rather than how he was created. In fact, the whole creation scene is condensed into a few sentences at the beginning of chapter five:

> I had worked hard for nearly two years, for the sole purpose of infusing life into an inanimate body. For this I had deprived myself of rest and health. I had desired it with an ardour that far exceeded moderation; but now that I had finished, the beauty of the dream had vanished, and breathless horror and disgust filled my heart. Unable to endure the aspect of the being I had created, I rushed out of the room. . . . (p. 56)

Victor abandons his creation ostensibly because it is unaesthetic, because it has "watery eyes, that seemed almost of the same colour as the dun-white sockets in which they were set, [a] shrivelled complexion and straight black lips" (p. 56). Very rarely does Victor think what he has done is presumptuous or Faustian or sacrilegious. It is more usually the adaptors and critics who feel that way. In fact, Victor really doesn't know why he made this creature in the first place, other than it was the result of "my obsession." Initially, he doesn't even think the creature monstrous and so repeatedly calls him a "daemon," a word which originally meant a neutral spirit before being appropriated by the Christian fathers to mean evil spirit, as in "demon."[3]

Once "born," however, the creature must be "educated," and his schooling occurs in the awkward episodes in which the eight-foot daemon is literally hidden behind the De Lacey household where he passively participates in a surrogate family. This is more than a convenient narrative device to resolve such problems as language and socialization; this is a way to mature him to Victor's level so that by the time he leaves, or rather is ejected from, the bosom of the family, he is Victor's coeval, perhaps ready to fulfill Victor's secret wishes. The metamorphosis from noble savage to adolescent (almost separated from the family) takes only a few months in his sped-up life, but he is now fully ready to do what every teenager wants to do—he can at last "get even" with those who have suppressed him.

But who is "getting even" with whom? Is it the daemon with Victor or Victor (via the creature) with his family? What the monster does is in no way capricious; from Victor's point of view, it is clearly the fulfillment of desire. The monster's first victim is Victor's baby brother William. Admittedly, the monster is in a bad mood (he has been abandoned by his creator and recently wounded while helping a little girl) when he happens on young William. William certainly does not make him feel any better by telling the creature to leave him alone; in fact, William even tells him that his father is Monsieur Frankenstein, municipal magistrate. That is enough for the monster; it is all over for William and he is strangled. Any brother of Victor's is no friend of Victor's son (i.e., creation); there is nothing avuncular here. In the monster's words: "I grasped his [William's] throat to silence him, and in a moment he lay dead at my feet. I gazed on my victim and my heart swelled with exultation and hellish triumph . . . " (p. 136). By wild happenstance, around the child's neck is a locket with a picture of Mrs. Frankenstein (Victor and William's mother), and the monster grasps it and gazes in rapt attention:

> I took it; it was a portrait of a most lovely woman. In spite of my malignity, it softened and attracted me. For a few moments I gazed with delight on her dark eyes, fringed by deep lashes, and her lovely lips; but presently my rage returned; I remembered that I was forever deprived of the delights that such beautiful creatures could bestow and that she whose resemblance I contemplated would, in regarding me, have changed that air of divine benignity to one expressive of disgust and affright. (p. 136)

Just the sight of Victor's mother is sufficient to melt the monster's rage. Justine then happens to pass by; she is Victor's surrogate sister who has been cared for by the Frankenstein family. She stops for a short early morning nap (it takes all of a minute) in a nearby shed, and the daemon "places the portrait securely in one of the folds of her dress" (p. 137). It is a propitious act, for Justine, as we are to learn, will be tried and convicted of William's murder. Much later, Victor finally admits responsibility; sick with a fever (repressed guilt?), Victor learns that in his ravings he has "called myself the murderer of William, of Justine . . ." (p. 169). Precisely what he means we still don't know, but we already have a hint that the monster is fulfilling the desires of his creator.

We are now given a short reprieve during which Victor receives a most peculiar letter from home. His father writes:

> I confess, my son, that I have always looked forward to your marriage with ["your cousin" in the 1818 text] our dear Elizabeth as the tie of our domestic comfort and the stay of my declining years. You were attached to each other

from your earliest infancy; you studied together, and appeared, in dispositions and tastes, entirely suited to one another. But so blind is the experience of man that what I conceived to be the best assistants to my plan may have entirely destroyed it. You, perhaps, regard her as your sister, without any wish that she might become your wife. Nay, you may have met with another whom you may love; and considering yourself as bound in honour to Elizabeth, this struggle may occasion that poignant misery which you appear to feel. (p. 144)

Admittedly in the 1831 edition Mary Shelley has struck the word "cousin," but the damage, so to speak, has been done: a glimmer of truth has shown through. Elizabeth is somehow a member of the family, but what member? Young Frankenstein's father implies sisterhood, but to substantiate this we need to know about Victor's previous relations with Elizabeth. Here, for instance, is her induction into the "family circle":

On the evening previous to her being brought to my home, my mother had said playfully, "I have a pretty present for my Victor—tomorrow he shall have it." And when, on the morrow, she presented Elizabeth to me as her promised gift, I, with childish seriousness, interpreted her words literally and looked upon Elizabeth as mine—mine to protect, love, and cherish. All praises bestowed on her I received as made to a possession of my own. We called each other familiarly by the name of cousin. No word, no expression could body forth the kind of relation in which she stood to me—my more than sister, since till death she was to be mine only. (p. 35)

So it is with good reason that Victor responds to his father's suggestion of marriage "with horror and dismay" (p. 145), for Elizabeth seems more than a cousin, rather like a sister.

Victor has more pressing problems before he can consider a wife—the daemon has first demanded a mate of his own. Consistent with his problem-solving behavior, Victor first swoons at the news and then embarks on a leisurely trip that for some unexplained reason (probably Percy Shelley's suggestion) takes him across the continent to England and then up to the Orkney Islands. Here in splendid isolation he again engages in the "filthy process of creation" (p. 156), this time to make the companion for the monster, the female who will become in a much later cinematic operation (thanks to popular confusion of the proper name) the eponymic "Bride of Frankenstein."

Victor typically has second thoughts and recants his promise. His love-sick daemon is distraught and first implores, then threatens, but to no avail; Victor will not be swayed. Victor will not allow his creation, his double, to mate. Finally, as the creature turns on his heel to go, he makes one last promise to his creator: "I will go; but remember, I shall be with you on your wedding night" (p. 161). This is a powerfully ambiguous threat; surely, the monster is promising vengeance, but on whom—Victor or Victor's bride? Since Victor has doomed his progeny to sexual frustration, is the creature promising to repay in kind? Or will the monster return to destroy, not Victor's wife, but Victor himself? As we soon see, Victor, ever the egotist, pretends the intended victim will be himself, but he acts as if it were to be his wife. We should know better: if the monster wanted to destroy Victor he could dispatch him at any time. Instead, the monster wants the bride and Victor subconsciously knows it, maybe even wants it.

After this threat Victor falls into the requisite "deep sleep" and the plot is driven through some conventional gothic territory rather the way the Polar Spirit moves the ancient mariner into place for his next confrontation. The monster kills Victor's best friend, Henry Clerval, and frames Victor, who is freed thanks to the good offices of his father, and Victor makes the usual half-hearted attempts at suicide. Victor is at last prepared for his most important scene. Elizabeth writes to him to think again about the unthinkable:

> You well know, Victor, that our union had been the favourite plan of your parents ever since our infancy. We were told this when young, and taught to look forward to it as an event that would certainly take place. We were affectionate playfellows during childhood, and, I believe, dear and valued friends to one another as we grew older. But as brother and sister often entertain a lively affection towards each other without desiring a more intimate union, may not such also be our case? Tell me, dearest Victor. Answer me, I conjure you, by our mutual happiness, with simple truth—Do you not love another? (p. 178)

Although Victor knows that the monster has always been true to his Delphic threats, he writes back to Elizabeth of his willingness, but warns her:

> I have one secret, Elizabeth, a dreadful one; when revealed to you, it will chill your frame with horror, and then, far from being surprised at my misery, you will only wonder that I survive what I have endured. I will confide this tale of misery and terror to you the day after our marriage shall take place, for, my sweet cousin, there must be perfect confidence between us. (p. 180)

Just whom is he trying to protect—himself or her?

The wedding day arrives and with it, of course, Victor's anhedonic dread. Surely, such dread is occasioned by incest—the references to brother/sister, Victor/Elizabeth have been an unmistakable motif even though we have often had to look beneath the *pentimento* of the 1831 revisions. Simply put, the monster has cleared a way for Victor to anticipate a level of sexuality that has been tabooed, while at the same time promising to appear on the nuptial night to make sure the literal marriage is not consummated. We are getting our fillip of horror not only from sibling incest, but also from hints of an Oedipal relationship as well. We know this cannot be, for we have been assured that Victor's real mother has died from a disease carried into the family by Elizabeth, her "present" for her son, and that her dying wish was that her son marry this very girl. A mother would never allow anything horrible to happen; even Christabel's mother was there to protect her from Geraldine.[4]

To find out how Victor really perceives Elizabeth, rather than how his mother wants him to, we need to recall the dream he had during his post-monster creation swoon. Here is the dream, complete with the daemon's cameo appearance:

> I was disturbed by the wildest dreams. I thought I saw Elizabeth, in the bloom of health, walking in the streets of Ingolstadt. Delighted and surprised, I embraced her, but as I imprinted the first kiss on her lips, they became livid with the hue of death; her features appeared to change, and I thought that I held the corpse of my dead mother in my arms; a shroud enveloped her form, and I saw the grave-worms crawling in the folds of her flannel. I started from my sleep with horror; a cold dew covered my forehead, my teeth chattered, and every limb became convulsed; when, by the dim and yellow light of the moon, as it forced its way through the window shutters, I beheld the wretch—the miserable monster whom I had created. He held up the curtain of the bed; and his eyes, if eyes they may be called, were fixed on me. His jaws opened, and he muttered some inarticulate sounds, while a grin wrinkled his cheeks. He might have spoken, but I did not hear; one hand was stretched out, seemingly to detain me, but I escaped and rushed downstairs. (p. 57)

Events may at last fall into place, for if Elizabeth is the displaced mother, then Victor will not be able to consummate the "marriage" without utter psychological disintegration. Recall the comment made by Henry Clerval after young William's death because it is not just consoling but prescriptive: "Dear lovely child, he *now* sleeps with his angel mother" (p. 71; emphasis added). But Victor is still curious and he wants, as does the dreamer, to get as close as possible to the forbidden event in this world. Ironically, the monster will protect Victor just as he had earlier befriended him in Victor's Elizabeth/dead mother dream: "I beheld the wretch . . . he held up the curtain of the bed . . . he might have spoken, but I did not hear; one hand was stretched out, seemingly to detain me . . ." (p. 57). All along the daemon has acted out Victor's wishes: he has systematically destroyed family and friends, clearing the way for this central encounter of Victor's fantasy. Now here on his wedding night Victor is so close to the sexually forbidden that he is understandably hebephrenic. Elizabeth inquires, "What is it that agitates you, my dear Victor?" Her husband can only reply, "this night is dreadful, very dreadful" (p. 185). He now leaves her, ostensibly to look for the monster; the monster conveniently takes his cue and throttles Elizabeth; Victor returns, swoons at the sight of his dearly departed, then covers her face with a hand-kerchief, and for the first time in their relationship embraces her "with ardour" (p. 186). Unlike brother William, who had to die to lie with his mother, Victor is still alive, so, of course, it must be the sister/mother figure who must go. However, there is guilt as well as horror to deal with.

The scene trembles with, as Coleridge said of his own incest dreams, "desire with loathing strangely mix'd." Victor knew what the monster had promised, yet went ahead with the marriage. Victor knew the monster would be there on his wedding night, yet Victor did not stay in the room to protect his bride. Like the little boy who has been told not to stand too close to the fire, Victor's first response was to inch closer. No wonder he was burned. He has had more sexual excitement than he can withstand and so once again he dissembles.

If we had any doubts about the doppelgänger relationship between Victor and the monster, the last quarter of the book resolves them.[5] For from now on Victor pursues the monster to set things right, just as earlier the monster had dogged Victor for what he felt was just. First the shadow chases the man, then the man chases the shadow. Victor's repressed desires have broken the surface and he must now struggle to bury them again. It is almost as if Victor's ego, having liberated his monstrous but still protective id, now feels compelled to return to some psychological stasis, even if it means insanity. But his superego will have none of it now and so unity, even lunacy, is denied. Victor monomaniacally pursues his "devil" (p. 149; the "daemon" has now become "demon") to the ends of the civilized world, "more as a task enjoined by heaven," he explains, "as a mechanical impulse of some power of which I was unconscious, than as the ardent desire of my soul" (p. 195). He knows what he is doing but he can't stop.

Here appropriately Victor's narrative ends and we are returned to Robert Walton's epistolary frame. Victor is rescued from the icy wasteland of insanity just long enough to warn Walton, another curious seeker after forbidden knowledge, to turn back.[6] Victor expires, but the monster lingers on to let us know that even now he is not satisfied. He tells the ephebic Walton:

> You, who call Frankenstein your friend, seem to have a knowledge of my crimes and his misfortunes. But in the detail which he gave you of them he could not sum up the hours and months of misery which I endured wasting in impotent passions. For while I destroyed his hopes, I did not satisfy my own desires. They were forever ardent and craving; still I desired love and fellowship, and I was still spurned. Was there no injustice in this? Am I to be thought only criminal, when all humankind has sinned against me? (p. 210)

But now separated from his other half, his substance, the shadow wanders off, presumably to immolate himself.

When the pieces are put together we may see a buried design in the novel that explains such peculiarities as why the monster reacts to the locket-picture of Frankenstein's mother, why Elizabeth is displaced from "mother" to "sister" to "cousin" to "foundling," why the monster reappears on the wedding night, and why the final symbiosis of monster and man is so fantastic, even dreamlike. It also explains why the story should appeal to the young male, for it is clear that this audience too is concerned about the choice of following curiosity without caution. Do we follow the path which will lead to knowledge and horror (Victor), or should we be restrained and careful, which will turn us away from the hyperborean Eden (forbidden sexual knowledge), but promise safety (Robert Walton). Once Victor's fictive journey is over, once his rite of initiation is finished, it should be clear to us from the text which path we ought to follow (Walton's), and equally clear to us which path we are still tempted to pursue (Frankenstein's). We are finally left lingering between the two in the limbo of adolescence. If we are going to be "mature," however, we are going to have to learn from Victor Frankenstein to follow Robert Walton.

The story is equally exciting and sexually implosive from the female point of view. Although it might be presumptuous to present a "feminine" reading of the novel, let me condense a few points that have become almost données in recent Shelley criticism.[7] First, although one risks committing biographical and intentional fallacies, it is tempting to extrapolate from child-bearing events in Mary Shelley's life to the daemon-bearing events of Victor's. And, second, this single event, parturition, and all that entails, seems to be a condensed analogue to what happens both in and around the text. Here is a novel given birth by an artist almost morbidly obsessed by the psychological pains and complexities of labor and delivery. In a sense, *Frankenstein* is Mary Shelley's primal scream—bibliogenesis.

And well it should be, for her life at the time of composition centered around the paradox of birth. Her own initiation into this world was powerfully ambiguous: she was born five months after her illustrious parents, Mary Wollstonecraft and William Godwin, were married. Clearly, although they married for her, her birth divorced them forever. After a particularly difficult labor, Mary Wollstonecraft had difficulty expelling the placenta, infection set in, and, eleven days after her daughter's birth, she died. If there is one thing the "posthumous child" soon learned, it was that coming into being is intertwined with departure. It was not a lesson later lost; in fact, Mary Godwin (soon to be Mary Shelley) relearned it again and again. She herself had just become pregnant in July 1814, when she ran off to the continent with Percy Bysshe Shelley, and she would continue to be pregnant off and on for the next five years. Also pregnant at this time was Shelley's wife, Harriet, who was to give healthy birth in November. Mary was not so fortunate: in February 1815 she gave birth, or rather in a macabre sense gave death, to a sickly and illegitimate daughter. She notes in her *Journal* only: "Find my baby dead, a miserable day" and a few weeks later (March 19, 1815) continues, "Dream that my little baby came to life again; that it had only been cold, and that we rubbed it before the fire, and it lived. Awake and find no baby. I think about the little thing all day. Not in good spirits." She was pregnant again in April. As she carried this child, she was doubtless full of dread and guilt, but this time pregnancy was a success. In January 1816 a son, William, was born.[8]

When the famous pact was made in June 1816 at the Villa Diodati—a pact as important to the creation of modern horror as the decision by Wordsworth and Coleridge to collaborate on the *Lyrical Ballads* has been to modern poetry—one might have guessed what Mary would have chosen to write about. One does not have to delve very far below the surface to see that even in her 1831 "Introduction to the Third Edition" she is still working out her own mothering anxieties: "I shall . . . give a general answer to the question so very frequently asked of me—how I, then a young girl, came to think of and to dilate upon so very hideous an idea [as the creation of a monster]" (p. vii). What she did not realize, at least not consciously, was that her procreative act, what she had to dilate, efface, and present, was the opus of art, *Frankenstein*. The idea may have come to her in a "dream":

> My imagination, unbidden, possessed and guided me, gifting the successive images that arose in my mind with a vividness far beyond the usual bounds of reverie. I saw—with shut eyes, but acute mental vision—I saw the pale student of unhallowed arts kneeling beside the thing he had put together. I saw the hideous phantasm of a man stretched out, and then, on the working of some powerful engine, show signs of life and stir with an uneasy, half-vital motion. . . . His success would terrify the artist; he would rush away from his odious handiwork, horror-stricken. He would hope that, left to itself, the slight spark of life which he had communicated would fade, that this thing which had received such imperfect animation would subside into dead matter, and he might sleep in the belief that the silence of the grave would quench forever the transient existence of the hideous corpse which he had looked upon as the cradle of life. (pp. x-xi)

However, the actuality—the text—is the compulsive abreaction of anxiety. Little wonder that Mary, now thirty-two, concluded the introduction to her work at seventeen by bidding "my hideous progeny to go forth and prosper. I have an affection for it, for it was the offspring of happier days . . ." (p. xii).

Ellen Moers, the first critic to interpret *Frankenstein* as a study of female anxieties, has called the work "a horror story of teenage motherhood," but it would also be correct to say that *Frankenstein* is a study in sexual ontology, for it details how life is conceived and brought forth. This subject causes anxiety in the adolescent female just as incest seems to excite shivers in the young man. In other words, Mary Shelley did not write a gothic story in which we have, say, a young heroine pursued by an evil, glowering man à la Mrs. Radcliffe; she was not interested in terror. She knew horror was something else, and she knew firsthand what that was; it was somehow connected with what she experienced sexually as a woman—all the dread, fear, guilt, depression, and excitement of birthing. The marvel of her story is not that she successfully articulated her feelings, but that she captured the shared anxieties of her sex without even mentioning copulation, let alone reproduction.

Psychiatrist Marc Rubenstein has asserted in "'My Accursed Origin': The Search for the Mother in *Frankenstein*" that, for all "its exclusion of women, *Frankenstein* is really about motherhood" (p. 165), and I think he, too, is correct, especially with respect to the female audience. Young Frankenstein's progeny becomes a monster not because he violates the demands of death like the vampire, but rather because he has not been "mothered" properly. What makes him monstrous to the female audience is not his lust for revenge or his appetite for violence, which seem to play out the male romance, but instead that he has been made hideous by his creator's unwillingness to nurture. Again and again we are told in the text, especially by the monster, that if someone would just take a little time to attend to his needs, everything would be just fine. Thus the pubescent female can witness this tale of initiation into the anxieties of motherhood with as rapt an attention as her male counterpart, for she wonders if she will be willing to attend to her own biological production. Much of this mothering content has been excised in the movie versions, but to substantiate it let us again return to the text.

Recall that after his own mother has died, Victor left home to pursue his arcane studies at the University of Ingolstadt. There, although "in my education my father had taken the greatest precautions that my mind should be impressed with no supernatural horrors" (p. 50), Victor starts to tinker with the processes of creating life. "In a solitary chamber, or rather a cell, at the top of the house, and separated from all the other apartments by a gallery and staircase, I kept my workshop of filthy creations ... " (p. 53). Here we are told he spends his days and nights at work—"winter, spring and summer passed away during my labours" (p. 54)—until finally in November new life issues forth.

The manufacture of a baby is precisely what is occurring in that womblike room at the top of the stairs. The "labour in that filthy workshop of creation" is the unconscious gestation of new life, and so we should not be surprised when Victor's creation bears an uncanny resemblance to a human child:

> His limbs were in proportion, and I had selected his features as beautiful. Beautiful! Great God! His yellow skin scarcely covered the work of muscles and arteries beneath ... but these luxuriances only formed a more horrid contrast with his watery eyes, that seemed almost of the same colour as the dun-white sockets in which they were set, his shrivelled complexion and straight black lips. (p. 56)

Of course this cannot be, not because it is sacrilegious or immoral, but because it is so sexually implosive. Life is being made without a partner, without copulation, without sex.[9] It is certainly easier to give birth this way, but it is not right, just as it is not right for Victor to act on the feelings he has for Elizabeth. And lest we forget that this child-making is not being done properly, we are respectfully told the child is wildly inappropriate: this baby is eight feet tall! Little wonder that Victor's response to his newborn should be to fall into a deep postpartum sleep.

Outside of the text, Mary Shelley recalls the phantasmagoric image of the creature who came to her in a dream and, indeed, it still has almost the ooze of dream-life about it. As is typical in dreams, the one thing this creature cannot be is the one thing it is: Victor's child. In horror tales, as in dreams, it is common enough to have a central figure perform actions that mock all common sense, almost as if the reasoning powers of the superego must be short-circuited before the id is allowed out. How could Victor create a being eight feet tall from normal human parts found in nearby charnel houses and boneyards? Well, what is King Kong doing fondling the hand-sized Fay Wray—this can't be sexual, not because he is an ape, but because he is so big. Or why hasn't the vampire overpopulated himself into starvation, since his species grows in geometric progression? Why does the Wolfman first take off his clothes before transforming, yet then appear in shirt and pants? Why does Mr. Hyde never touch Dr. Jekyll's fiancée, yet invariably brutalize her father? The list of such contradictions is as long as the number of horror myths. In horror stories as in dreams, we try to pass by these rational objections because, if we can get past them, we can find what we really want— namely, a forbidden text of sexuality. If we ever stop to think about it, Van Helsing's "King Laugh" will soon take over. So in each enduring monster story there is some obstreperous contradiction of reality that must be circumvented, and the Frankenstein story is no exception.

The creation scene ends on a simply ludicrous note with Victor waking to see his progeny peering at him from "behind the curtain of the bed" (p. 57). He exclaims: "Oh! No mortal could support the terror of that countenance.

Frontispiece illustration of Mary Shelley's *Frankenstein*, 1831 (Harry Ransom
Humanities Research Center: The University of Texas-Austin)

A mummy again endued with animation could not be so hideous as that
wretch" (p. 57). It is tempting to suppose that we are getting a continuation
of the rebus-like dream puns with the word-image "mummy," as we earlier
had with "conception," "incredible labour," "dilate," "workshop of filthy
creation," "instruments of life," and "effacement." I suspect so, if only
because the train of associations, initially so helter-skelter, really does lead
directly here to the central actor of creation: mother ... "mummy."

When the two "selves" of this extraordinary protagonist, Victor Frankenstein, are disassembled, we get an almost clinical description of the anxieties
of latency, for he/she deals with the great biological and psychological
dilemma of adolescence: sexuality and its consequences. How do we pro-

create, how is "it" done, with whom, when, what happens next, and what are we going to do about what we produce? I don't think Mary Shelley at eighteen, or at thirty, quite understood the sexual dynamics of her protagonist, but perhaps intuitively she did, for she entitled her novel *Frankenstein: Or, the Modern Prometheus*. In the summer of 1816, Mary Shelley certainly was exposed to the myth, for she was not only reading Ovid's treatment of Prometheus in Book I of the *Metamorphosis*, but also doubtless listening to Byron and Percy Shelley discuss their own renditions ("Prometheus" and *Prometheus Unbound*). In classical myth Prometheus was both creator of man, the *Prometheus plasticator*, and the giver of fire, the *Prometheus pyphoros*. These functions, of course, have sexual correlations: the female is the molder of life; the male is the heroic rebel. Her *Frankenstein* articulates through its buried and unconscious allegory both the male impulses and anxieties about incest as well as the female impulses and anxieties about parturition. It is a horror novel not because there is a huge, violent, mindless, destructive monster lumbering about the countryside, but because human desire, our desire, has made this protoplasm and is strangely motivating it to play out roles in the family romance.

I hope that this sense of embedded androgyny in some way explains why such a clumsy novel by such a "green" artist could have achieved such a compelling influence on the popular imagination. In the retelling of the tale most of the superfluities of the printed text (tedious travelogues, digressions on contemporary science, descriptions of Alpine sublimities, extraneous characters) have been sloughed off in favor of the central acts of creation and sexual quest. If one doubts that *Frankenstein* is a central saga of initiation into adulthood, one need only drop in at the local cinema showcase and "see it with your own eyes." The movie is the ideal form of this saga's transmission, for it much more nearly approximates the dream context: we sit quietly in the dark, giving ourselves up to a fantasy supposedly beyond our control. The tensions and fears of our conscious mind are muted; superego censors are stilled because it is, after all, "only a movie" ("only a dream").

Victor and his monster had considerable success on the nineteenth-century stage, often as a double bill with a vampire play adapted from Polidori's novella. However, it is on celluloid that they have really prospered.[10] Not only was this one of the first stories filmed (in 1910 Thomas A. Edison made a "liberal adaptation of Mrs. Shelley's famous story," starring the frantic Charles Ogle, who looks as if he has electrified Brillo for hair), it has also been one of the most enduring. In general, one need say little more about the filmic adventures of Frankenstein other than that they have been ridiculous, sublime, silly, profound, ludicrous, and unusually profitable; in fact, they have pretty much paralleled the fortunes of Count Dracula.

Charles Ogle as the first filmic Frankenstein monster, 1910 (Edison Studio)

What I should like to concentrate on are not just the various renditions of the story line, but the mutations of the character of Frankenstein. For he had been cast—I suspect quite unconsciously, until recently, at least—as bisexual. I hope to show that, when we look at what has happened to the myth as it has evolved on film, what we see is that the buried sexual content is being progressively made manifest. So it should come as no surprise that in the most successful remake on both stage and screen, *The Rocky Horror (Picture) Show*, the role of Victor is played precisely for what had previously only been implied—namely, androgyny—and that the creature, Rocky, is also bisexual. But before discussing this extraordinary rendition, let me briefly review its important predecessors so we can see how the changes have unfolded.

Although there is only one great cinematic monster (Karloff), there are two dominant Frankensteins: Colin Clive of the Universal series in the thirties and Peter Cushing of the Hammer series in the sixties. Interestingly enough, the moral tones of their characterizations vary greatly. Clive plays the young scientist as upright, neurasthenic, and good, although too curious and careless, while Cushing plays him as haughty, misogynistic, and, especially in the last version (*Frankenstein and the Monster from Hell*, 1972), as downright demonic. However, the sexual, or rather asexual, nature of his character has been changeless. He is a neuter, sublimating his erotic energies into the mechanical creation of life. In fact, in all the *Frankenstein*s both at Universal and at Hammer, the creation scene is always played very close to a scene of sexual arousal. The music, the lighting, the responses, are blatantly lifted from their usual matrix, and with good reason. After a great deal of tantalizing foreplay with electrically charged, sparking instruments, the scene centers around "Doctor" "Baron" "Professor" Frankenstein's discovery that "There, you see, it moves, it's alive; I've made life!" The scene is so visual that we pass by the obvious sexuality to watch the pyrotechnics.[11]

James Whale, the virtuoso screenwriter and director at Universal in the early 1930s, made the scene first and his (and Kenneth Strickfaden's) imagery has stuck. Here in Whale's words is the importance of that birthing scene:

> I consider the creation of the Monster to be the high spot of the film, because if the audience did not believe the thing had been really made, they would not be bothered with what it was supposed to do afterward .... By this time the audience must at least believe something is going to happen; it might be disaster, but at least they will settle down to see the show. Frankenstein puts the spectators in their positions, he gives final orders to Fritz, he turns the levers and sends the diabolic machine soaring upward to the roof, into the storm. He is now in a state of feverish excitement .... The lightning flashes. The Monster begins to move. Frankenstein merely has to believe what he sees, which is all we ask the audience to do. (*New York Times*, December 20, 1931, p. 4X)

But Whale was clearly buffeted by his intuitive knowledge that Victor's (or "Henry's" as he was called for some unknown reason) sexuality was frighteningly onanistic, and by the demands of the "front office" that every Jack must have his Jill. So, to make the creation scene presentable, Whale set out to rearrange the relationship of Frankenstein and Elizabeth in a way that both he and the studio could accept. Of the many things that were added to the saga because of Whale's genius—such as Fritz, the evil hunchback who delivers the damaged brain, clearly marked "Abnormal Brain," the "doctor," the watchtower laboratory, the crucifixion scene, the windmill ending— none has been more important than what was done with the monster and Elizabeth. Whale's monster was a long way from Mary Shelley's creature: it was essentially a huge child, sensitive but ignorant. It was the Golem of Paul Wegener's *Der Golem* (1920) all over again; in fact, Lugosi, who first tested

Paul Wegener as the living creature in *The Golem*, 1920 (UFA-Germany)

for the part, was supposedly made up to look just like the Golem. The monster was energy without intelligence, and that is why Whale was right, and Karloff wrong, in not wanting the scene cut in which the monster throws little Maria into the pond like a flower petal.[12] In addition, if the monster was made a child, then Elizabeth was in a sense made the mother—the proper but spurned mother. In the 1931 *Frankenstein* she was heroic. She was the one who twice led the posse (Victor Moritz and Professor Waldman) to the lab to rescue her fiancé from the perversion of single-sex baby building. She was spurned, of course ("You must leave me alone! You'll ruin everything!" Frankenstein blabbers), while he retires to create life on the operating table. But she will not be easily pushed aside and continually calls for caution. Though Henry assures her, as the phallic lift hoists the lifeless hulk skyward, that "there is nothing to fear," he is a fool and she knows it. He may say, as he does four times, that he has created life "with my own hands," but she knows this is not the proper manner. So when he later grandly announces, "In the Name of God, now I know what it feels like to be God," Elizabeth seems to realize that the word he wants is not "God" but "mother."[13]

It is interesting to speculate on the rapprochement that develops between Elizabeth and the monster, for in a sense both of them are left out and exiled by the menfolk. Perhaps this is why the creature does not kill her (as in the novel), but simply appears on the wedding night to give her a good scare and then hustles off. This "hands off" policy is also because no monster could touch a Hollywood heroine in 1931 and get away with it. It may also be the result—as we will clearly see in Whale's *Bride of Frankenstein* (1935)—of a bond, albeit unspoken, developing between them.

The creature is finally destroyed in a burning windmill, but only after he heaves Henry over the side. Frankenstein's death (he hits one of the turning vanes on the way down) was to be the end of the movie, but once again Universal insisted that no hero of theirs was going to be so short-lived, and so Whale had Henry revived and returned to his father. The movie thus ends with the promise of impending matrimony and a toast to the future issue of the young couple. This ending was certainly the triumph of bookkeepers over moviemakers, for in no way has Henry been deserving of such salvation. When Whale's *Frankenstein* was re-released a few years later with his *Bride of Frankenstein*, the final scene of the convalescing Henry was removed, as well as the epilogue to *The Bride* (in which Byron and the Shelleys discuss the famous pact to write horror stories), so that the two stories have no break between them. The end of *Frankenstein* is really a tribute to giddy nonsense, for the Baron, Henry's pompous father, has the last word giggling and drinking with the servant girls. Clearly, young Frankenstein has not learned his lesson.

Universal Studios didn't care; they made about $10 million on the movie, and so three years later it was time to ring up the cash registers again. This time it was *The Bride of Frankenstein*, and this time it was one of the few Hollywood sequels better than the original. Once again, I'm especially interested in the role of Elizabeth, for it is she who continually explains what Henry is after. But first, just who is the "Bride" of Frankenstein? In the movie there are two of them: (1) Elizabeth, now played by the brunette Valerie Hobson rather than the blond Mae Clarke of the first version, and (2) the monster's intended, the seven-foot Queen Nefertiti with the famous lightning bolt in her hair, played by Elsa Lanchester. For literary purists, of course, there can only be one "bride" of Frankenstein and that is Henry's wife, but for movie buffs Frankenstein is the monster and it is his bride that the title describes. The confusion is not without intention, for Whale had planned something quite extraordinary: in *The Bride* Whale attempted to sever the evil aspect from his protagonist and introduce a mad scientist, Dr. Pretorius, who would do all the genetic tampering. This meant Henry could remain the curious but decent scout while Pretorius did all the nasty things. And the nasty thing Pretorius originally had in mind was to transplant Elizabeth's heart into the body of the female creature. Unfortunately, this bizarre plot never really made it into the finished film, although it came close, and we can still see that Whale almost had his way. If you remember the film, one of the most unsettling scenes is when the monster is grandly presented with his "bride," who recoils from him as if he were a pimply blind date. We are still amazed that she could so immediately detest him; her first response is a mad swan hiss. What happened is that this scene was shot before the producers vetoed the heart transplant idea and Whale could not re-do the laboratory scenes because the sets had been destroyed. Little wonder the bride with Elizabeth's heart recoils in horror, for she realizes that she is to be "mated" to her husband's progeny, the monster, by extension the proper issue of her own body! In other words, the same "horror of incest" that permeates the text of Mary Shelley's novel also energizes the James Whale movie, except that here it inheres in a mother/son rather than a brother/ sister relationship.

In the first cut version of the film, in the famous explosion scene in which the monster pulls the Destruct Lever (all laboratories in the 1930s were equipped with such a well-marked lever), Henry is included among those destroyed. Since Elizabeth had been spared her vivisection by the Universal panjandrums (Karl, Dr. Pretorius' demented lackey who will develop into Ygor in the sequels, kills an unidentified village girl instead for the "bride's" heart), Henry must also be saved. Whale had already shot the explosion scene with Henry, and so rather than reconstruct the set he simply tried to excise

Henry Frankenstein (Colin Clive) and Dr. Pretorious (Ernest Thesiger) with their new creation—the bride (Elsa Lanchester) in *The Bride of Frankenstein,* 1935 (Universal Studios)

Henry in the cutting room. Whale didn't entirely succeed; you can still see Henry getting blown up along with the other mischief-makers. Whale also added an ending in which Henry and Elizabeth escape and are last seen silhouetted against the burning tower, Henry promising never to meddle again in the act of creation. Now, presumably, they will go home and make babies the right way.

But they don't. Naturally enough in this genre they continue to be unnatural. In the next rendering, *Son of Frankenstein* (1939), the young man, now known as Baron Wolf von Frankenstein, has finally had a son the respectable way, but it doesn't take long for the old habits to return. Wolf's onanistic behavior must be phylogenetically activated, for no sooner is he back in Castle Frankenstein, having lived as an American professor for a number of years, than he is tempted to fiddle around with "the source of life" just like his father. Once again his wife—Elizabeth is now known as Elsa—is kept out. Even their beds have been arranged so that normal procreation is out of the question: they are placed at an angle so that only the headboards touch. The maid introduces Elsa to the master bedroom, saying, "When the house is filled with dread, place the beds at head to head." And head to head they remain. Clearly, Wolf prefers to spend his productive time in his father's broken-down "lab across the ravine," which is all that is left of the old watchtower since the explosion.

To his credit, Frankenstein père has warned his son of the dangers. He has left a letter for Wolf saying that "If you, like me, burn with the irresistible desire to penetrate the unknown, carry on. Even though the path is cruel and tortuous, carry on. . . . You have inherited the fortune of the Frankensteins. I trust you will not inherit their fate." Wolf makes a beeline for the lab, led by the demented retainer, Ygor, doubtless himself a descendant of Karl, Dr. Pretorius' aide-de-camp. Ygor (Bela Lugosi) has his own reasons for wanting the creature revived. He wants vengeance on the town fathers for sentencing him to death. En route to the inner sanctum Ygor and Wolf pass the tomb of the elder Frankenstein, complete with this graffiti scratched by some dim villager: "Maker of Monsters." Wolf pauses momentarily, carefully reads the epithet, and is then led still farther into the laboratory, right up to the slab where the enfeebled monster now lies. "Will you help revive your brother?" asks Ygor. "My brother!" gasps Wolf, looking at the Frankenstein monster. The truth slowly settles on Wolf as Ygor cocks his head: sons of the same father are brothers. Finally, in the name of science, Wolf consents. As they leave the lab Wolf scratches out the word "Monster" from his father's tomb and heroically writes with a fiery torch, "Maker of MEN."

From here on, the problem with Rowland V. Lee's exposition of the saga is that it is so predictable. Ygor is bad, Wolf is good but misdirected, and the monster well-meaning but unsympathetic. What is noteworthy is that poor Elizabeth/Elsa is once again prevented from partaking in life-delivering processes. It is still men's work in the Frankenstein family. Inspector Krogh (Lionel Atwill) comes to call with his prosthetic arm, and it is poor Elsa who must stand in that cold Caligariesque castle making small talk with a man who can speak thus of his amputation: "One does not easily forget an arm torn out by the roots." So she must play a menial role, caressing her infant son Peter, while her husband is in the back room nursing his monster with volts. It is especially hard to be concerned about Wolf's "baby" because, once on his feet, the monster is in the service of Ygor, who is using him as a bravo to settle grudges. Had Ygor's relationship with the monster been less exploitive, or had Wolf's been less clinical, or had Wolf's natural son been more a friend to the monster, this movie might well have made sense. But as it is, *Son of Frankenstein* looks great but adds little to the saga.

Universal's next four attempts add nothing but confusion: they are *Ghost of Frankenstein* (1942), *Frankenstein Meets the Wolf Man* (1943), *House of Frankenstein* (1944), and *House of Dracula* (1945). In *Ghost* Sir Cedric Hardwicke does the honors as Dr. Ludwig Frankenstein by introducing a new twist that is still tangled up in the myth. Since the monster's problem is his bad brain, why not give him a new one, a sensible one? In 1941 *Black Friday* made plenty of money with the nasty transplant idea, so it must have been appealing to its producers. But whose brain? While the monster has his heart set on the brain of a neighborhood girl, Cloestine, Dr. Frankenstein wants to use the brain of a good scientist, Dr. Kettering. Ygor has a better idea. Why not use his own brain? While the little girl's brain would have made the movie fascinating, as Hammer Studios was to show in *Frankenstein Created Woman* (1966), it was Ygor who carried the day at Universal. Thanks, however, to problems with incompatible blood types, the operation succeeded but the patient died. The addlepated monster stumbles into some strategically located combustible chemicals and the lab explodes.

Universal missed the point in *Ghost*: the monster must be sympathetic for the story to work. In *Frankenstein Meets the Wolf Man* (1943) the monster doesn't even have a chance to be sympathetic as he is shoved aside by the melancholy Wolfman. It is the Wolfman's show from the first reel, and really the monster is there only to battle him at the end. Still, the monster revival scene is interesting. A Dr. Mannering has taken over Victor's role and while this doctor is "pumping the juice" into the creature, Baroness Elsa Frankenstein, Victor's granddaughter who has kept his "Secrets of Life and Death," rushes into the lab. "You're making him strong again!" she shouts as she lunges for the Destruct Lever. The good doctor retorts, "I can't destroy Frankenstein's creature. I've got to see it at full power." Needless to say, the monster at full power gets loose and lunges at Elsa. Her grandfather should have told her to steer clear of boys in the lab. The Wolfman saves her. As always, the townspeople have the last word; they dynamite the dam upstream, which inundates the lab, drowning the monsters.[14]

Frankenstein Meets the Wolf Man made so much money that the studio executives would have gladly used mouth-to-mouth resuscitation to bring them back to life. As it was, the Frankenstein monster was barely able to shuffle through two more appearances, both of them little more than cameos in the monster reunion movies of the mid–1940s. After all, if two monsters could turn a profit of almost $4 million in 1943, think of the possibilities of three or even four monsters. So *House of Frankenstein* (1944) is really just a menagerie of monsters, each doing its predictable thing—the vampire is vamping, the Wolfman moping, the mad doctor conniving, and the Frankenstein monster mostly just defrosting. It seems that he and the Wolfman had been stuck in huge ice chunks since their watery demise in *Frankenstein Meets the Wolf Man*. Once again, there is a lot of mumbo-jumbo in *House of Frankenstein* about transplanting a new brain into the monster's skull, and again the mad doctor "just wants to see the creature at full power." He gives the hulk 100,000 megawatts of power and the monster comes alive, beats up the bad guys, grabs the doctor who re-created him—in a sense his surrogate father—and stiffly trudges into a convenient bog of quicksand.

There must have been a trap door below the quicksand ooze because in *House of Dracula* (1945) the monster, with the skeleton of the first mad doctor in his arms, is found by yet another doctor. The new doctor, Dr. Franz Edelmann, really wants to help, but because the vampire has infected his blood with a parasite, he can't be trusted at night. Thanks to Dracula's bad blood, Dr. Franz becomes a nocturnal Mr. Hyde by moonlight. As might be expected, his Mr. Hyde self decides to give the monster a new lease on life: "I'll make you strong . . . stronger than ever before!" "No, no!" cries the requisite nurse who has taken over Mrs. Frankenstein's role. "Remember your promise not to," and the doctor glowers at her, "You're spying on me . . . you shouldn't have come here . . . I don't like people who see what they're not supposed to see." His warnings are too late; she sees, she screams, the townspeople hear, and once again they descend on the castle. The monster

House of Dracula: lobby poster, 1945 (Universal Studios)

bumps into those strategically placed chemicals and perishes in the towering inferno.

Although the *New York Times* quipped that "Frankenstein's little boy doesn't die easily, and unfortunately neither does this type of cinematic nightmare" (December 22, 1945), this time they were wrong. The Universal saga was over; the Destruct Lever had been pulled. Karloff was no longer playing the creature, leaving it to Chaney, Lugosi, and Glen Strange, the cowboy heavy. Frankenstein himself had all but disappeared. Somehow all the sincerity had gone out of the productions. Perhaps World War II horrors were proving too competitive, but more probably it was because on October 1, 1946 Universal merged with International Pictures to become Universal-International, and this new unit had publicly pledged itself to only "high-quality pictures." First to go was what Universal did best: horror films were over.

Looking back to the 1930s and the 1940s one sees the Universal deluge of horror movies coming in two waves: in the first, the individual film makers experimented with motifs, situations, and characters, and in the second, the studio executives sought to consolidate their gains by working the same sequences over and over. In the first surge (*Frankenstein, Bride of . . . , Son of . . .*) Frankenstein is young and confused, the creation is central, and the monster is inarticulate but oddly sympathetic. In the second wash (*Ghost of . . . , Frankenstein Meets . . . , House of . . .*) the creator is older, a Baron or a doctor, the creation scene is partially displaced by the transplant motif, and the monster is a tool used by either Ygor or some madman to further some nefarious end. Along with these transformations Elizabeth changes from being a cast-aside wife to being an unimportant, unmarried nurse or a Frankenstein descendant. Clearly, it is the first wave that still surges through popular culture. Yet, as we will see, Hammer Studios, too, thought they could make something out of the transplant motif, but their real success came only by returning the protagonist to his earlier ephebic self, which they did by providing the scientist with a wide-eyed young assis tant.

Before we look at Hammer's inundation in the 1960s we should pause to look at one of the more intriguing aspects of horror films—the parody that is better than the original. Clearly what happens is that the parody maker, remembering his youth, reconstructs the plot with greater affection and knowledge than was ever lavished on the original work. After all, he remembers exactly what it was that was so frightening. Assuming that parody does indeed unfold what lies along the seam of its subject, it is especially instructive to look at Mel Brooks' *Young Frankenstein* (1975). *Young Frankenstein* simply continues the argument begun with *Frankenstein, Bride of . . .* and

Son of . . ., but wisely neglects the inadvertent parodies of Universal's second wave.[15]

The first half of *Young Frankenstein* opens by extending the standard introductory scenes by exaggeration, but then the plot, which has been mimicking Rowland V. Lee's *Son of Frankenstein*, takes a rush forward, a rush beyond the usual narrative. For, while the mob is out chasing the monster, he is, in fact, being seduced by Elizabeth. In the novel the monster murders Elizabeth and in Whale's *Frankenstein* he simply terrifies her, but in Brooks' version the monster has everything he could want, and more. If my understanding of the buried psychology of the saga is correct, this has been the monster's function all along. He is indeed a projection of the young male and he is finally—safely protected by parody—getting what he wants. In parody nothing stops him, because no one bothers to take him seriously.

In a sense the monster at last is "young Frankenstein" acting out the libi-

Young Frankenstein (Gene Wilder) and his best friend (Peter Boyle) in *Young Frankenstein*, 1974 (20th Century Fox)

dinous desires of his maker. The earthy humor here is that, because of his prodigious size, a size that extends to all members of his body, he is able to satisfy Elizabeth as she has never been satisfied before. It is in this broad humor that one clearly sees the implied adolescent fantasies being played out. For not only is the id-monster the first to sleep with the tabooed partner, he is successful beyond his wildest dreams. In a real tour de force—because the story simply can't end here (for what would become of the pallid Franken-stein?)—there is a transfusion of parts between the neurasthenic young doc-tor and the prepotent monster. Because the transfusion machine is shut off too soon, young Frankenstein ends up the possessor of the monster's repro-ductive organ. The movie concludes with Frankenstein's female assistant asking Victor as they start to make love, "The monster got part of your won-derful brain [in the exchange], but what did you get from him?" As the lights fade she finds out. The last thing we hear is her shriek of joy.

The Americans relinquished the Frankenstein saga in the 1950s to the English. It was just as well, for nothing new was being added to the story except more werewolves, more mad doctors, more transplants, and more nonsense. With the exception of *I Was a Teenage Frankenstein* (1957), in which the teenage monster "son" kills the father-creator (an Oedipal layer of the story strangely enough not exploited before), it was a dull time indeed for this kind of horror story. But Hammer Studios, then just a small inde-pendent producer and distributor, decided to remake Frankenstein in its own image. It was certainly not going to use Universal's image, for Universal's lawyers had copyrighted the money-making mise-en-scène, from Jack Pierce's makeup for Karloff to Kenneth Strickfaden's rendition of Franken-stein's laboratory, and Universal was loath to deal with this upstart English studio. So Hammer did it on its own. In the fifteen years from 1957 to 1972 they made seven full-length features and each, until the end, made a substan-tial profit. The titles reveal Hammer's bias: *The Curse of Frankenstein* (1957), *The Revenge of Frankenstein* (1958), *The Evil of Frankenstein* (1964), *Fran-kenstein Created Woman* (1967), *Frankenstein Must Be Destroyed* (1969), *Horror of Frankenstein* (1970)—the only one without Peter Cushing, and the worst—and finally, supposedly Hammer's last, *Frankenstein and the Monster from Hell* (1974). Having seen them all recently, I was amazed at how well most of them have held up while so many other horror movies of this time are so "dated" by comparison. Think only of the countless outerspace mon-sters and mutants, let alone killer tarantulas, snakes, rats, even tomatoes, which are not even good enough, or bad enough, to reappear on middle-of-the-night TV, and one realizes the staying power of Hammer's efforts. These Hammer movies are still playing almost every weekend on television chan-nels across the country.[16]

This "staying power" is, I think, the same that has led audiences to the Mary Shelley novel and the James Whale films. The plot is kept simple, some would say simplistic, the anchor scenes, like the creation, are played to the hilt, and the implied sexuality is always there. There are, however, three major shifts in the saga according to Hammer. First, Frankenstein is no longer the adolescent over-reacher, but is now a controlled master scientist. To a considerable degree this shift was mandated by the choice of Peter Cushing, for he is so urbane and suave that one imagines he couldn't lose control even if he tried. He never says, "It's alive! My God, it's alive!" Universal had already been moving the saga in this direction with their older mad doctors. And, second, the saga is no longer about creating life, but about transplanting life. In the days of Christiaan Barnard this was nothing if not relevant, and now that cloning is in the news, doubtless the next Frankensteins will be tampering with strands of DNA. In the most recent of the English "Frankensteins," *Frankenstein and the Monster from Hell*, the doctor is actually transplanting whole brains and even "souls," so one can well imagine that the possibilities for horror (i.e., tabooed sexuality) are vastly increased. These two shifts mandated a third—the doctor is given an assistant who acts the role of the "green" protagonist who traditionally had driven the plot by drawing back the curtains of forbidden sexual knowledge. Thanks to the genius of Jimmy Sangster, Hammer's screenwriter for the first movies, this role was not given to an Ygor or Fritz, but to a young, wide-eyed, sexless, lisping helper who stands by the doctor/father and asks the appropriate questions: "Should we be doing this?" "Can you teach me to create life?" "Here, let me try." In other words, this young man is the traditional Frankenstein, except that he is totally guiltless because he is, after all, "just helping the doctor."

So in the Hammer version the adolescent has it both ways; he sees how life is generated by aberration, and he learns by extension how to be cautious and respectful and genital. To practice this method properly he is paired with a buxom, technicolored, nubile girlfriend whom he initially spurns when working with the master, but later embraces after he sees how Frankenstein has botched it. Interestingly, in many of the Hammer *Frankenstein*s the monster comes back to destroy (not really, because there must always be a sequel) the father-figure, for this Oedipal level of the story could only occur when Frankenstein, the father-creator, was divorced from Frankenstein, the adolescent son.

Of all the Hammer efforts, the most psychologically interesting is the 1967 *Frankenstein Created Woman*. The plot, so simple and bizarre, shows how close these latency sagas are to the fairy tales of childhood. Here is how it goes: Teenaged Hans is orphaned when his ne'er-do-well father is guillotined

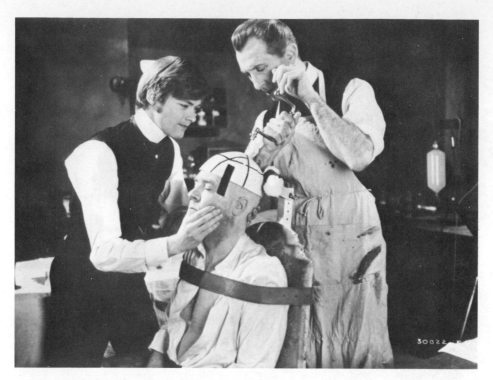

Simon Ward as helper and Peter Cushing as doctor operating in *Frankenstein Must Be Destroyed,* 1970 (Hammer Studios)

by the town mob. He is "adopted" by the kind Dr. Frankenstein, who is in the midst of experimenting with the cryogenic preservation of his own body. The doctor is amazed that in this frozen state of suspended animation nothing leaves his body, no soul, no spirit, nothing. "Dead for an hour, yet my soul did not leave my body. Now why?" the doctor queries after defrosting. He is too kind to experiment on other people—at least yet.

On a more mundane level, Hans has become friends with Christina, the local innkeeper's daughter. She is stunning: full-breasted but, alas, painfully shy. Not only does she limp, she also suffers the embarassment of her teenage complexion, for one side of her face is blemished. She and Hans fall in love, but are separated by her father who, knowing of Hans' father, does not consider him "of the proper type." Now into the inn come three bully-boys, complete with top hats, whiny voices, and atrocious manners. These dandies want Christina to serve them some wine, but she is mortified to appear in public and they mock and taunt her. When Hans protects her, they give him a good thrashing and escape in the melee, stealing his overcoat.

Meanwhile, back at the laboratory, Dr. Frankenstein is working in his Hammer-equipped version of the Universal workshop. There is the inevitable huge water tank that resembles a bathtub-sized aquarium in which bits of human anatomy usually float (a visual donnée in the Hammer creation scene, just as the elevating table had been for Universal). There is also the requisite electrical apparatus—wire, sparks, and levers (no "self-destruct" ones, however; these English are too cagey). The scene is all in lush, rich color, an effect contemplated, but never used, by Universal. The Doctor/Baron, who knows Nietzsche, has finally discovered that no "soul" leaves the body after death because there is a biological life-force: "You see the energy ... the force trapped in the cells." The Baron hopes to use this energy to repair the feeble bodies of the unfortunate, but, alas, he will have no such opportunity, for his altruistic world is soon overtaken by stark reality.

The three dandies who stole Hans' coat return to the inn later that night to steal wine, are discovered by the innkeeper (Christina's father), whom they kill, and then flee into the night, leaving Hans' coat. They are successful in framing Hans for the police find the coat, and although the Baron testifies as a character witness, it is not enough: Hans is to be, like his father, guillotined. When Christina finds out it is too late, for justice here in Ingolstadt is swift. Hans is decapitated. She is despondent, jumps into the river and drowns. The Baron loses no time and dutifully collects the two bodies. The operations can now begin.

Since Hans has been decapitated, his life-force is transferred by the Baron into Christina's revived body. After the operations are completed, one by one the bandages are removed from her body. As the last bandage is unwrapped, the camera keeps us from seeing the results. We see only the face of Frankenstein as the creature asks, "Please, please, who am I?" The best the doctor can answer is, "You are a nice lady." She now becomes, as David Pirie has written in his history of English horror films, A *Heritage of Horror* (1973), "an utterly sensual, hermaphroditic and polymorphous perverse rejuvenation" (p. 77). She also becomes stunning to look at, because it seems the doctor, something of a dermatologist, has taken off her blemish and, as a bonus, repaired her limp. You see, he is not at all evil. Christina, inspired now by the male life-force of Hans, sets about seducing and then decapitating the bully-boys who killed her father and framed her boyfriend.

In all of this the Baron is a willing co-conspirator, but not directly involved. Hans is using Christina's corpus to further his bloody revenge and the doctor goes along, realizing that some restitution of order must be made, yet clearly knowing that things are all wrong. Those Russian bullies were nasty, but Hans goes too far by having Christina write his name in blood after he/she has decapitated, à la guillotine, one of the rascals with a meat cleaver. The townfolk believe Frankenstein must be up to mischief, and so they dig up Hans' body. They find his body, all right, but his head is missing. The head, we now learn, is resting on the post of Christina's bed, and it is

Peter Cushing as the Baron unwrapping the body of Christina (Susan Denberg) with the soul of Hans in *Frankenstein Created Woman*, 1967 (Hammer Studios)

only a matter of time before the mob pays Baron Frankenstein its time-honored visit.

The Baron, fearful for his life, goes off to hunt down Christina to remove Hans' life-force ("call it a soul if you still want to," he says) from her body, yet knows something horrible has happened. It is too late; Christina has lured the last of the scoundrels into an almost surrealistic picnic ground, and to this pastoral glen she first entices, then decapitates, her last victim. As Frankenstein happens onto the scene, she is speaking with Hans' voice to Hans' head, which she is cradling between her hands just as Keats' Isabella did with her Lorenzo. Amazingly, the head replies in *her* own voice, thereby mixing forever spiritual, corporeal, and sexual identities. We have had the doppelgänger motif, always extant in the saga regardless of the rendition, carried about as far as it can go. Poor Christina/Hans ends it all, finally, by jumping again into the river and receiving, once and for all, the blessed baptism into the world beyond. The Baron flees from the mob so he can reappear two years later in *Frankenstein Must Be Destroyed*.

In the context of family romance run amok, *Frankenstein Created Woman* is a natural enough, although startling, continuation of the saga narrative. The Frankenstein archetype has again been split in two, leaving Hans to play the Victor role of "young" Frankenstein and the Baron to play the Dr. Pretorius role of conniving parent: in a sense the boy-child and his view of his father. As he grows up, the child becomes curious about a young girl who is denied by another father, the innkeeper, but once that father is removed the path is clear. Both youngsters, already motherless and now with only one surrogate father, do indeed become as one. But their union is all wrong; it is not at all what they intended; it is instead the result of the "father's" manipulation. There is no joy in this "marriage" (that word is never used but it is clearly implied by the officiating Baron), only utter despondency. Hence we are as relieved as they when matters end with the joint suicide and the banishment of the "father."

Two other revivals are worthy of note. In 1974 Paul Morrissey made a 3-D version which exploited his mentor's name in the title, *Andy Warhol's Frankenstein*. Although this film lacks the droll humor of *Andy Warhol's Dracula*, preferring instead to dangle as many parts of human anatomy as possible under our noses and then to pour countless buckets of blood into our laps, it is the first film to portray Baron Frankenstein as aggressively and unremittingly androgynous. Frankenstein commits incest with his sister and, after they are both killed, their children—born of this incest—go on to populate yet another generation of Frankensteins. Far more interesting, however, is a television extension of the transplant motif written by Christopher Isherwood and Don Bachardy modestly titled *Frankenstein: The True Story* (1974). In viewing this "true story" it is hard to ignore Mr. Isherwood's sexual preferences, for it tells of how Victor leaves his Elizabeth to join Henry Clerval in creating "life." These two boys are going to do it together and, after Henry banishes Elizabeth from Victor's presence, they succeed. Lurking in the background, however, is the evil presence of Dr. Polidori (James Mason), who has no hands and thus needs the help of these brilliant young surgeons. To condense the four-hour drama: the boys succeed in creating an effeminately handsome creature (Michael Sarrazin), Henry is killed in an accident, Victor puts Henry's still-living brain into the creature, and Victor and his creature become like mother and child. The creature even wears diapers and is led around to be introduced to the wonders of life. They play games and hug each other, and Victor plays dress-up with his monster, saying such things as, "And now you will be the grandest dandy in town." However, the life process is reversing and the creature is starting not to mature but decay. Victor is shocked and spurns his huge child. Despondent, he yields to social pressure and marries Elizabeth, and who should appear at the reception but Dr. Polidori, complete with the now-ugly monster in tow. It seems that Dr. P. wants to make a girl monster of his own and needs Victor's technical skills. Victor is blackmailed and together, again almost father and son, they fabricate the full-grown woman, "Prima." When Prima takes off to court Elizabeth, the undertones of *Carmilla* are too obvious to miss, but Elizabeth is neither available nor amused. The boys have the boys; the girls almost have the girls. Elizabeth is not alone in being startled by this extraordinary course of events; so too is the Frankenstein monster. In fact, he is so upset that he literally pulls off Prima's head. Victor and Elizabeth flee to America on a chartered ship, but en route the monster and Polidori reappear; the monster kills Polidori and Elizabeth, turns the ship northward to the Pole, and the story ends with Victor and his monster embracing as an avalanche is about to bury them eternally in snow and ice.

These variations show the malleable qualities of the myth, but in each version sexual aberrancy is the trigger for horror. To see real insights into the psychodynamics, we must look to see not where the myth is not overturned, but rather to where it is first imitated and then extended. If imitation is the sincerest form of flattery, then parody is the sincerest form of imitation. For in parody you must first recognize the essential nature of the subject as well as its effects, and then you must turn the subject in on itself so that you achieve not the opposite effect, but a logical continuation. As we have seen in the *Young Frankenstein*, parody in the visual arts usually is most easily achieved through caricature of specific scenes or image clusters. The later Hammer movies, especially *The Horror of Frankenstein* (1970) and *Frankenstein and the Monster from Hell* (1974), are actually poor parodies of the more vibrant work of Terence Fisher's *Curse of Frankenstein* (1957) and *Revenge of Frankenstein* (1958). Although recent Hammer attempts to retell the saga often degenerate into desultory and febrile campiness, this does not mean that the story has been overtold, but only that this version, with its blood and bosoms and aquariums, has run out of interest. *Andy Warhol's Frankenstein* and *Frankenstein: The True Story* show this: they turn to their subject with ridicule because they have nothing new to say. The same thing happened at Universal in the forties.

Just as *Young Frankenstein* pokes fun at the Universal "Frankensteins" in what is really an affectionate tribute to the American horror films of the thirties, *The Rocky Horror Picture Show* is a frantic and admiring burlesque of the Hammer versions as well as the English heritage of slightly skewed horror. Not only was *Rocky Horror* filmed at Bray Studios where the first Hammer "epics" were made, it also uses parts of the sets of such classics as *The Curse of Frankenstein* and *The Horror of Dracula*. If Brooks' *Young Frankenstein* is quintessentially American in its broad vulgarity and visual puns, then *RHPS* is almost a caricature of English schoolboy humor: it is a horror movie playacted with Monty Python verve. Its very Englishness may account for the fact that the stage musical, *The Rocky Horror Show*, was a smash hit at London's King's Road Theatre, but a flop on Broadway. The same thing almost happened to the movie, but the movie allowed something the theater never could—audience participation.[17]

The movie, *The Rocky Horror Picture Show*, is finally something quite different from any other parody; it is almost *sui generis*. *RHPS* has become the largest audience participation film in history (admittedly not much competition in this category), drawing enthusiastic fans back week after week to reenact what has become almost a religious ritual. Literally from coast to coast, each weekend before midnight (Twentieth Century Fox has wisely forbidden any other kind of showing than this Friday/Saturday midnight show), thousands of adolescents line up in costume and makeup to replay and mime this mythic rite of initiation. Fans also have their own newsletter, *The Transylvanian*, their own books, *The Rocky Horror Picture Show Book*, *Rocky Horror Official Poster Book*, and, since 1977, their own yearly convention. The film audience, calling themselves "veterans," invariably know how many performances they have attended and are increasingly joined by their elders who go more to reminisce than to participate. For *RHPS* is not just an entertaining movie: it is one of the most artful condensations of the anxieties and excitements of puberty. It does for this generation what the print and celluloid *Frankenstein*s have been doing for the last five generations: it provides a text, quite literally a recitative reading, of the do's and don't's of sexuality. Little wonder, then, that first-time viewers are referred to as "virgins" by the cognoscenti who have "seen the show" and are so introduced to the crowd before the film rolls.

The plot, what there is of it that can be discerned, is a bit more complex than usual. Brad and Janet, a well-scrubbed couple from the Midwest, drive off after a friend's wedding to consult their high school teacher, Dr. Scott, about matrimony, and well they should, since Janet has caught the bridal bouquet and Brad has taken the cue and proposed. En route they are caught in a storm, have a tire blow-out, and take refuge in a remote castle that has a sign out front—"Frankenstein Place." The castle has a rather eerie look to it—"Enter at your own risk" the sign outside also says—but it is too late to turn back. The door creaks open and we are met by a Nosferatuesque butler, Riff-Raff. Along with Brad and Janet, we are led by this menacing Ygor through more doors, over yet more thresholds, until we enter the grand ballroom filled with a giddy assortment of guests in penguin-like spats and sun-glasses dancing the "Time Warp." It is clearly a sexual dance ("But it's the pelvic thrust that really drives you insane," the revelers sing), and Brad and Janet are understandably hesitant to join the throng.

Lowered by elevator into this melee is a caped, white-faced, lipsticked, eyeshadowed, sultry dynamo, Dr. Frank N. Furter. It is certainly a shock to our sexual stereotypes in horror films when he sings, "I'm just a sweet trans-vestite from Transsexual Transylvania," and, as he does, bumps and grinds his way out from beneath his cape. He is wearing black fish-net stockings and a corset. It's Frederick's of Hollywood at Fire Island, yet what makes it so startling is that it is alluring. The mise-en-scène is all Hammer Grand Guignol, but this central character definitely is not. Peter Cushing had been effete, but Tim Curry plays the role with so much sexual gusto and reckless-ness that it can only be called lust. He is so gleefully transsexual, so raucously alive, so husky beneath the sequins, that it's hard not to be swept along.[18]

After crossing the "Time Warp" we are all led upstairs to Dr. Frank N. Furter's laboratory. But wait—it's the Hammer laboratory, complete with that aquarium and all the electrical gear, yet the Hammer monster is nowhere in sight. And when Frank N. Furter unwraps his creation it is no deformed creature, but instead a hulk of beefcake in jockey shorts named Rocky Horror. With clear reference to Hammer's transfusion epics, Rocky's life-force has been drained from Eddie, a "normal" delivery boy (played by the corpulent Meatloaf, a rock star in his own right) who has strayed from his normal deliveries and is now being held in cryogenic suspension in a nearby food locker. Suddenly, Eddie breaks loose from his freezer and causes mayhem by accelerating around the lab on his motorcycle. Frank N. Furter brutally bludgeons Eddie to death. It is shockingly violent, but strangely not out of character, for Frank N. Furter has always hidden his Mr. Hyde side under an overabundance of kinetic energy. Here, for a moment, we see vio-lence without repression, and it is awful, even horrible.

We are now prepared for the third shock: this modern Frankenstein seduces first Janet, then Brad. Janet is upset: "You're to blame! I was saving myself," she moans. While Brad complains: "You're to blame—I thought it was the *real* thing!"; but it is clear that both enjoy forgetting, not who they are, but what they are. After these two brittle virgins give in, when these examples of middle-class repression fall, there is not much left to debauch. But as the music and dance continually tell us, it is only good fun and will only last for a night. There is no longer any "normal" sexual identity, so nothing can be wrong. As a dour narrator intones, "It was a night out they would remember for a very long time," and, one might add, "never repeat."

Tim Curry as Frank N. Furter, Peter Hinwood as Rocky Horror, and Little Nell (Laura Campbell) as Columbia in *The Rocky Horror Picture Show,* 1975 (20th Century Fox)

On the most obvious level this movie seems to say that it is okay to be sexually confused; it is okay for boys to run around in corsets and garters, to prance and flaunt and dance and sing; it is okay for girls to be naughty and dirty, to be sexual, bisexual, transsexual—you name it as long as you enjoy it. Or perhaps, to be more accurate, it says it is acceptable to *pretend* to be this way, as long as it doesn't last. Horror sagas generally have such a level of "let's pretend" that long ago in another part of the world there were people who did act out, not so much our buried desires, as our curiosities. This version just does it with music and dances. Yet, in the tradition of the *Schaeurroman,* there is an intimation embedded in the text that reminds us of what happens if pretending becomes reality. There is always that image of Eddie axed to death for staying too long under the spell; for taking things literally. But even that is clothed in irony, for we are continually assured that what we see on the screen is all an elaborate trompe d'oeil, a make-believe. A fatherly narrator often intrudes, book in hand, assuring us that he is telling this story from a big book just as our own fathers once did. We are again being "read" into Fairyland. Below this ambiguous level, however, we get the far more serious retelling of the Frankenstein story with all its attendant mythology and psychodynamics and horror.

Paradoxically, for all its sportiveness, this movie celebrates the end of make-believe; it is the last of make-believe; it is the last Frankenstein story. *RHPS* is almost the exit ceremony from adolescence, the saying good-bye to polymorphous perversity.[19] It is, in a sense, a modern saturnalia. In "Rose Tint My World" Rocky sings this passage:

> *And somebody should be told*
> *My libido hasn't been controlled*
> *Now the only thing I've come to trust*
> *Is an orgasmic rush of lust*
> *Rose tints my world, keeps me*
> *Safe from my trouble and pain.*

Tim Curry as Frank N. Furter in *The Rocky Horror Picture Show*, 1975 (20th Century Fox)

to which Brad adds:

> *It's beyond me.*
> *Help me, Mommy.*
> *I'll be good, you'll see.*
> *Take this dream away*
> *What's this, let's see*
>
> *I feel sexy*
> *What's come over me. Whoa—*
> *Here it comes again.*

Janet continues:

> *Oh I—I feel released*
> *Bad times deceased*
> *My confidence has increased*
> *Reality is here*
> *The game has been disbanded*
> *My mind has been expanded*
> *It's a gas that Frankie's landed*
> *His lust is so sincere.*

And Frank N. Furter concludes:

> *Whatever happened to Fay Wray?*
> *That delicate, satin-draped frame.*
> *As it clung to her thigh*
> *How I started to cry*
> *'Cause I wanted to be dressed just the same.*
> *Give yourself over to absolute pleasure*
> *Swim the warm waters of sins of the flesh.*
> *Erotic nightmares beyond any measure*
> *And sensual daydreams to treasure forever—*
> *Don't dream it. Be it.*
> *Don't dream it. Be it.*
> *Don't dream it. Be it.*
> *Don't dream it. Be it.**

That such sexual exuberance should be tied to the saga-lines of the Franken-stein story is not inappropriate. For Victor Frankenstein, asexual producer of a life turned monstrous, is simply the converse of Frank N. Furter, mon-ster producer of a life turned bisexual. The allure of the myth is the same:

*Lyrics written by Richard O'Brien, copyright © by Druidcrest Music. All rights for the United States and Canada are controlled by Hollenbeck Music (BMI), Los Ange-les, California. All rights reserved.

we celebrate without real consequence the libidinous dreams of non-role, non-specific sexuality. Since we do not have to accept the rigors of sex-role behavior, incest has become possible.

And that, of course, is why there must be horror; society cannot exist without procreation, and procreation depends on these distinct sexual roles. The result of what happens if one stays too long under the spell of Frank is Eddie. We have earlier seen Frank brutally ax Eddie to death, and with the unexpected appearance of the partly paralyzed Dr. Scott (the mentor whom Brad and Janet were seeking to explain marriage to them) this part of the story now becomes clearer. For Eddie, Dr. Scott explains to all, was a rebellious child whose only concerns were rock-and-roll music, motorcycles, drugs, and sex. He presumably made a "delivery" to Frank and was entranced. However, by the time he wants to leave the "Frankenstein Place" it is too late; he stayed too long; he has been used by Frank in the creation of the androgynous Rocky and discarded. We now see what has happened to Eddie, for his butchered body is stored under Frank's glass-topped dining table. After dinner Frank pulls off the table cloth to show his guests what they have been eating—Meatloaf. It is a gross scene: Eddie's guts spill out of his breached stomach, his head cracked and chopped. This image finally spoils our fun; it goes too far—we want relief.

It is the bizarre Riff-Raff who puts Frank N. Furter back in his proper place. Although Riff appears to be only a "handyman hunchback," he and his sister Magenta are in reality the masters of the place, custodians of the social norms they themselves subvert. "It's all over," they tell Frank. "Your mission is a failure ... your lifestyle's too extreme." And so at the end his theme song, "Don't Dream It—Be It," reverts to its sublimated text, "Don't Be It—Dream It." When Brad asks Riff-Raff what Frank has done wrong, it is Dr. Scott, the "good father" who has repressed his own bisexuality, as we see from his black net stockings, who answers: "Society must be protected." Riff-Raff and Magenta agree. In a finale worthy of Busby Berkeley, the Marx Brothers, Esther Williams, and King Kong, Riff-Raff and Magenta disintegrate Rocky with ray guns and levitate the "Frankenstein Place" and all its inhabitants back to the planet of Transsexual in the galaxy of Transylvania. Brad and Janet are cast out of the land of puberty, now to follow their crippled but steadfast mentor, Dr. Scott, into the prescribed sexual world of men and women. We are returned to the avuncular narrator; he closes the book; the house lights come up.

There will be many more renditions of the Frankenstein saga, but I doubt if there will soon be any as perceptive and artistic: *Rocky Horror* is a celebration of a meridian crossing, the last stage of latency, the acceptance of procreative sexual roles. As such, it recapitulates the whole history of the saga. In its narrative muddle it makes clear sense of the psychological import of the myth, the attraction and the repulsion that have always been involved in Frankenstein's act of creation, the excitement and the horror of sexuality. When we juxtapose this saga with that of the vampire, we see an almost complete code of adolescent sexual behavior. Both myths tell us precisely whom to avoid as reproductive partners. In the next modern horror myth, that of the transformation monster, we will see the extent to which individual and social repression make certain that this code is not broken. And we will see the extent to which some people are willing to go to break it, and the extent to which they must suffer if they do.

5

Dr. Jekyll and
Mr. Wolfman

Let me turn wolf, be whole, and state, for once,—
Wallow in what is now a wolfishness
Coerced too much by the humanity
That's half of me as well! Grow out of man,
Into the man again, be man indeed
And all man? Do I ring the changes right?
Deformed, transformed, reformed, informed, conformed!
The honest instinct, pent and crossed through life,
Let surge by death into a visible flow
Of rapture. . . .
>   Count Guido Franceschini in Robert Browning's *The*
>   *Ring and the Book* (11, 2049–2054)

Like so many clichés in intellectual and cultural history, the current interpretation of the late nineteenth century as marking the onset of modern
schizophrenia is not without basis. The breakdown of the belief in a uniform
consciousness, with the subsequent acknowledgment of the divided self were,
however, a long time coming. Superficially, we can chart the dissociation of
sensibilities from the Cartesian assertion that a soul/flesh division was natural through the Neoclassical observation that absolute mind/body unity
was impossible anyway, because we were only "touched" by God, to the
romantic acceptance, gleeful at times, of our animal nature, to the disinter-
ested but clearly frightful Victorian observation that man was indeed perpetually trapped between the beast and the angel. Now, thanks to developments in psychology, we not only accept multiple personalities or roles, but
many analysts like R. D. Laing even contend such schizophrenia is the basis
of normalcy. In retrospect, we can see by the innovations in the doppelgänger motif that this move toward diversity of selves was well under way before

the rise of modern horror. What is interesting is not that Victorian man was divided, but that he was so passionately divided against himself. Matthew Arnold had contended that modern man was caught between worlds, "one dead and the other powerless to be born." Robert Louis Stevenson knew better: there was a "war," he contended, "among the members," hostilities *within* the self. So what we often see in the doubles of *fin-de-siècle* fiction are monsters, not as externally independent projections of repression, like the vampire or the Frankenstein monster, but as internally unfolded aberrations like Dorian Gray or Mr. Hyde. These new secret sharers come from within and never even pretend independence from their parental host.

There was a precedent for this kind of fiend in folklore, not in English lore but in ancient Irish and continental legends of the werewolf. For the werewolf literally turns his skin inside out as the transformation from man to wolf is effected. This beast is a "versipellis," literally a skin changer, a pagan turncoat who did for generations of Europeans what Mr. Hyde does for us: he provided first the frisson of a metamorphosis gone awry, and then the shock of ensuing bestial aggression. To understand how these two horror archetypes are related, and to explain why they have both been so successful in this century, we need first to find out where they came from.

There are three man-wolves in Western mythology, only two of which interest us here: (1) the werewolf, a four-legged wolf by night who is a man by day; (2) the Wolfman, a recent cinematic adaptation who has two legs, a lot of yak hair, and is terribly confused about his sex life; and (3) the lycanthrope who is a human psychotic suffering from the delusion that he is indeed a wolf. The last creature need not concern us, since his "lycorexia," or ravenous hunger for raw meat, does not, thankfully, have to include human flesh. Still, we should be aware of this aberration if only because his lupine delusions have provided the basis for the myth and may even have animated such modern maniacs as Adolf Hitler (at least according to Robert Eisler in *Man into Wolf*, ca. 1951). The extremely popular woodcut by the sixteenth-century German artist Lucas Cranach gives us some idea of the creature.

Oddly enough, one of the most perceptive diagnoses of this derangement was proposed by James I of England, who considered lycanthropes "victims of delusion induced by a natural superabundance of melancholy" (*Daemonologie*, 1645), thereby reiterating the conclusion made by the master of melancholy, Robert Burton, who referred to this delusion as pure and simple madness (*Anatomy of Melancholy*, 1621). In either case, thanks to the widespread eradication of a once large wolf population (England was wolfless by 1530, Wales by 1576, Scotland by about 1740; Ireland still had need of its

Sixteenth-century woodcut by Lucus Cranach of lycanthrope carrying off baby after ravaging family (Bibliothèque Nationale, Paris)

Lon Chaney, Jr., and Evelyn Ankers in *The Wolf Man*, 1941 (Universal)

Eighteenth-century engraving of
werewolf carrying off young woman—
seemingly unperturbed by her rosary
(Mansell Collection)

Werewolf imaged in *The Howling*,
1981 (Avco Embassy)

wolfhounds well into the nineteenth century), lupine delusions were extremely rare in Victorian times.

We have, however, not lost our interest in the werewolf or his modern cousin, the Wolfman: these two creatures continue to fascinate us.[1] We all know the junior Lon Chaney's eternally bewildered Wolfman who looks as Carlos Clarens has said in *An Illustrated History of the Horror Film*—like "a hirsute Cossack." The werewolf, on the other hand, never had much success on the silver screen until very recently, and true to form when he appeared he came in a pack: *The Howling* (1980), *Wolfen* (1981), and *An American Werewolf in London* (1981) and *A Company of Wolves* (1985). Since the werewolf surpasses the Wolfman in both age and beauty, let me first describe his lineage and habits before tracing his progeny from the wolves into such human forms as Mr. Hyde and a host of "stalk-and-slashers," from the fictionalized Jack the Ripper to the modern midnight molesters.

The werewolf is every bit as old as the vampire; in fact, he seems related, if not by blood, then by behavior. Not only are they both quiescent by day and molesters by night, and not only are they both excited by the moon and incited by women, they also transmit their obsession by biting. In some Middle European countries where both monsters are still rampant, they even have the same name: in Serbia, for example, "vulkodlak" means both werewolf and vampire. Typically, the werewolf can be created by certain specific acts like drinking water out of a werewolf footprint or eating meat killed by a wolf, but also, like the vampire, quasi-ecclesiastical sins will suffice: being cursed by a witch, dying excommunicated, and so on. However, the one attribute that separates the werewolf from other monsters is that a werewolf is created out of a man who *wants* to be possessed. Whereas the vampire's victim may unconsciously desire the transformation, usually in order to attack women without guilt, the human about to become a werewolf consciously participates—at least initially—in the process. The most important shift in the werewolf myth as it becomes that of the Wolfman is that the Wolfman *never* wishes to metamorphose. So, in terms of volition, the werewolf is rather like Dr. Jekyll while the Wolfman resembles the Frankenstein creature.

The werewolf of folklore, just like the vampire, is mandated to attack first those he loved most in life—usually members of his human family. This mandate is a key to understanding the psychodynamics of the myth, for it is clear the wolf acts out the once-repressed familial aggression, now safely protected by his furry disguise. The werewolf is, in a sense, a sheep in wolf's clothing. The myth makes no mention of any sexual molestation—it seems to only rage and devour, grab and smash, but knowing how the vampire acts, it seems the werewolf is only a cruder version. For this coarseness the werewolf might have been cast onto the slag heap of worn-out myths; certainly, he never had as much luck as an allegorical monster as did the vampire. The werewolf seems all too firmly based on aggression without grace, profligate snarling about, and carelessness in choosing specific victims. So it is interesting that when a werewolf is improperly killed, or incorrectly exorcised, he occasionally becomes a vampire. As a vampire, of course, he performs exactly the same kind of outrages, except now he speaks, wears nice clothes, and is discriminating. The migration from bestial werewolf to atavistic vampire may occur because the vampire is a "living dead" human, while the werewolf is always "just an animal." The vampire is the husk of a sinner animated by the devil, while the werewolf is a living man transformed into a brute.

When the werewolf is returned to human form at daylight he still bears many lupine stigmata. His eyebrows meet on the bridge of his nose, he has an extra-long third finger, he has bristles under his tongue, and he has lots of hair. (It may well be that hypertrichosis or extreme hairiness encouraged the belief that such wolfmen existed in various stages of transformation.) But the stigmata are not all one-sided; as a wolf he is a misfit too—he is the only tailless wolf in the pack. One of the most intriguing characteristics of his transformation from human to wolf is that he first carefully takes off all his clothes and leaves them neatly in a pile. The Wolfman, however, thanks to Hollywood's more delicate sensibilities, always performs his nocturnal chores completely dressed in long pants and sleeved shirt. Regardless of attire, when a werewolf is wounded he returns to his human state with the wound intact, and this, as one might imagine, is one of the recurring motifs in werewolf literature from Petronius' *Satyricon* to Kipling's *The Mark of the Beast*.

Every culture has its own man-beasts. In Africa it is the were-hyena and were-leopard, in India it is the were-tiger, and doubtless among the central Australians it is the were-kangaroo. Of all the were-animals, however, the werewolf is not only the best developed as a myth, it is also the most sensible. Lest that sound like cultural jingoism, we should remember that the wolf has resided in almost every corner of the world where man has tilled the soil, and that he is related to one of the few animals man has ever succeeded in domesticating: the dog. It is not by happenstance that wherever man has shepherded flocks the werewolf has mythically come alive. It may well be that the rabid wolf which bit the shepherd's dog, which then bit the shepherd, who then started to foam at the mouth, rant and rave, become thirsty yet unable to drink, and writhe in agony, was the genesis of this myth. Predictably, one finds the strongest werewolf beliefs in those countries that have developed their own breed of dog to combat the "predator"—the Irish wolfhound, Russian wolfhound, among others. The virus of *rabies canina*, transferred from wild wolf to tame dog to man, almost duplicates the same causality that informs the vampire/plague connection: from flea to rat to man. Pre-modern man, not understanding the transmission of bacterial toxins, made a natural enough leap from symptom to cause.

This analysis of the werewolf belief becomes especially interesting when we realize that the great werewolf epidemics occurred at approximately the same time as the vampire scares. In the hundred or so years from 1520 to 1630, thirty thousand cases of wolf transformations were reported in France alone. Surely, this mythic irruption was not because of an outbreak of porphyria or a resurgence of the line of Romulus and Remus (as was long ago suggested). There must have been an actual, observable occurrence that caused so many people to be convinced that such creatures really existed.

And of course there was: the Plague. Little wonder that in the panics that surged across Europe during the seventeenth century the Church was close by with the explanation. Once again, the demons had gotten into human forms and were maneuvering them against the forces of God. After all, there was some precedent for this in the Bible. The Holy Word is full of caveats against wolves, just as it is rife with condemnations of blood-sucking. Are we not warned to "Beware of false prophets, who come to you in the clothing of sheep, but inwardly they are ravening wolves" (Matthew VII:15), and are we not told by St. Paul that Christ himself promised that "after my departure, ravening wolves will enter among you, not sparing the flock" (Acts XX:29)? If we accept the image of the "good shepherd," there is little hope for compassion for the wolf. During the Inquisition churchmen went one step further, providing legal proof that the speculations of St. Augustine and Albertus Magnus about the devil's ability to travel in lupine forms were substantive. Animals could not be trusted; the snake in the Garden was the first of many examples. After all, the whole ontological basis of witchcraft rested on the assumption that shape-changing is demonic subterfuge, and what other beast is so directly the result of such shifting than the folkloric werewolf? But demonic transformations were never exact; God would never allow such blasphemous plagiarism. Hence the werewolf went forever tailless and had to return to his human corpus at daybreak.

The folk werewolf never had as much success in literature as he did in ecclesiastical affairs, though he was revived from time to time by some extraordinary talents. I suspect that this is because the werewolf is not sufficiently anthropocentric to arouse much more than stark terror; there is too much wolf and not enough "were." So the werewolf is frightening, yes, but not horrifying. The Wolfman, as we will see, is a different story, for he is really "one of us" and can act out clearly human behavior. But the werewolf is always "one of them," and animals, even the fiercest, seem too distant from modern man to be able to trigger particularly deep responses. They are the stuff of childhood; they live in the Land of the Wild Things; they only maim and kill. In adolescence we seem to lose our fear of physical attack and supplant it with new fears of sexual violation. So it is interesting to find in antiquity the classical myth of Lycaon, King of Arcadia, for here we have one of the earliest wolf transformations, enacted by the gods on a king who mocked Zeus by sacrificing children. Not much seems to happen to Lycaon; in fact, after nine years of eating fruits and vegetables he was offered safe passage back into human form. Even Ovid didn't know quite what to do with this disappointing metamorphosis; he just told the story quickly almost to have done with it.

There are other such stories in antiquity, of which the most famous, and certainly the most arresting, is retold by Petronius Arbiter in *The Satyricon*. Here it is, complete, as jauntily narrated by the slave Niceros:

When I was still a slave, we used to live in a narrow little street about where Gavilla's house stands now. There the gods decreed that I should fall in love with the wife of the tavernkeeper Terentius. You remember Melissa, don't you? Came from Tarentum and a buxom little package, if ever I saw one. But, you know, I loved her more for her moral character than her body. Whatever I wanted, she gladly supplied, and we always went halves. I gave her everything I had, and she'd stow it all safely away. What's more, she never cheated.

Well, one day, down at the villa, her husband died. Needless to say, I moved heaven and earth to get to her, for a friend in need is a friend indeed. By a stroke of real luck my master had gone off to Capua to do some odds and ends of business. So I grabbed my chance and persuaded one of our guests to go with me as far as the fifth milestone. He was a soldier and strong as the devil. Well, we stumbled off at cockcrow with the moon shining down as though it were high noon. But where the road leads down between the graves, my man went off among the tombstones to do his business, while I sat by the road mumbling a song to keep my courage up and counting the graves. After a while I started looking around for him and suddenly I caught sight of him standing stark naked with all his clothes piled up on the side of the road. Well, you can imagine: I stood frozen, stiff as a corpse, my heart in my mouth. The next thing I knew he was pissing around his clothes and then, presto! he changed into a wolf. Don't think I'm making this up. I wouldn't kid you for anything. But like I was saying, he turned into a wolf, then started to howl and loped off for the woods. At first I couldn't remember where I was. Then I went to get his clothes and discovered they'd been changed into stones. By now, let me tell you, I was *scared*. But I pulled out my sword and slashed away at the shadows all the way to my girlfriend's house. I arrived white as a ghost, almost at the last gasp, with the sweat pouring down my crotch and my eyes bugging out like a corpse. I don't know how I ever recovered. Melissa, of course, was surprised to see me at such an hour and said, 'If only you'd come a little earlier, you could have lent us a hand. A wolf got into the grounds and attacked the sheep. The place looked like a butchershop, blood all over. He got away in the end, but we had the last laugh. One of the slaves nicked him in the throat with a spear.'

That finished me. I couldn't sleep a wink the rest of the night and as soon as it was light, I went tearing back home like a landlord chasing the tenants. When I reached the spot where my friend's clothing had been turned into stones, there was nothing to be seen but blood. But when I got home, I found the soldier stretched out in the bed like a poleaxed bull and the doctor inspecting his neck. By now, of course, I knew he was a werewolf and you couldn't have made me eat a meal with him to save my own life. You're welcome to think what you like of my story, but may the gods strike me dead if I'm feeding you a lie.

(as translated by William Arrowsmith)

What is particularly interesting here is that the werewolf seems to have no interest at all in the pretty maiden. It's just a tall tale—quite probably a schoolboy tale of Milesian origin. The transformation may startle, but as long as the werewolf then proceeds, not to the farmhouse, but to the barnyard, there is not much prospect of horror. Even the wolf in Little Red Riding Hood knows that.

Perhaps the reason that the werewolf himself has transformed into the modern Wolfman was that by the Middle Ages he was too inhuman to be taken seriously, yet still too real to be fictionalized. Vladimir Nabokov used to theorize that

> Literature was born *not* on the day when a boy crying "Wolf! Wolf!" came running out of the Neanderthal valley with a big gray wolf at his heels; literature was born on the day when a boy cried "Wolf! Wolf!" and there was no wolf behind him. That the poor little fellow because he lied too often was finally eaten by a real beast is quite incidental. But here is what is important. Between the wolf in the tall grass and the wolf in the story there is a shimmering go-between that is the art of literature. (*Lectures on Literature*, p. 5)

What has happened, in a sense, is that this "go-between" has shifted along with our cultural fears, from wolf to werewolf to Wolfman. However, the excitement of the fiction remains intact; only the imagery has changed. So although the little boy told a wolf tale, and although such ancient worthies as Lucian and Apuleius told werewolf fables, and although medieval clerics recorded wolf histories, it was not until the nineteenth century that the beast was finally domesticated in popular fiction. The little boy was replaced by the little girl and the wolf wore pants.

Like the vampire, the werewolf entered English prose fiction by the back door, as it were, being used first as a descriptive device in the late gothic novel before dropping on all fours to roam the midcentury "bloody pulps."[2] So there is a lupine snarler in Charles Maturin's *The Albigenes* (1824) and a passing reference to a doglike shape-shifter in "Monk" Lewis' *Journal of a West India Proprieter* (published posthumously in 1834), but such allusions are really like Charlotte Brontë's characterization of Bertha Rochester: stock snarling and grimacing that is only incidentally wolfish. Such narrative color is invariably used only to tint transitory characters that populate the attics and cellars of the gothic. This kind of shading simply can't flesh out a full-bodied character—at least not yet.

Even when such delineation is sustained as in, say, G. W. M. Reynolds' *Wagner, The Wehr-Wolf* (1857), it so soon lapses into such hyperbolic melodrama that it can only be read in short stretches. That is why the shilling shocker, the episodic soap opera of the Victorian bourgeoisie, was the initial modern lair for the fictional werewolf. That is also why Dan Curtis' daytime gothic serial on television, *Dark Shadows*, was so successful doing something so ludicrous—a daily monster soap opera! Both Wagner and Chris Jenning were relegated to occasional cameo flashbacks and visual asides, never appearing long enough to be scrutinized. The problem with reading *Wagner the Wehr-Wolf* (Dover Publications reprinted all the serial parts from *Reynolds's Miscellany* in book form in 1975) is that Wagner was no Varney the Vampire. He has no independent personality with which to sympathize. Not only is the werewolf foreign to English readers (almost all the action in the novel takes place around the Mediterranean), but the plot device (Wagner's Faustian pact with the devil, exchanging wolfishness once a month for wealth) soon becomes tiresome and simply cannot sustain Wagner's behavior. We can get a good look at him as drawn by the staff illustrator at *Reynolds'*, Henry Anelay. The image does justice to the prose description and inadvertently exposes the problem: how can you empathize with a wolf unless the wolf is more than a berserker, more than a beast? We can't, and that is essentially why Wagner never captured anything but the most ephemeral of audiences, the bulk consumers of pulp.

Clearly, one of the reasons why the werewolf comes of age at the end of the nineteenth century is that, although *Wagner* may have proved excessive, it did show that prose fiction was a suitable medium, especially in serial publication. Werewolf stories, because of their single-minded drive toward transformation, have to be short, yet must reach an audience sophisticated enough to appreciate that such transformation needs what Aristotle called "extension." In the usual werewolf story, at least in English, the author does not so much create a double as attempt to set the scene necessary to dissolve his

Wagner as illustrated by Henry Anelay, *Wagner the Wehr-Wolf*, 1846–7

protagonist into a more atavistic form. The center of consciousness must somehow shift from human to wolf without losing the audience's willing suspension of disbelief. For this reason most werewolf stories after *Wagner* are told by a narrator repeating a second-hand story. The problem really is, what do you do then? What do you do once he is down on his paws, for the werewolf does not have mandated behavior like the vampire. The transformation scene is not only important, but tricky to continue. It is at the middle of the myth but at the end of the story.

So when the Victorian werewolf story succeeds, as it does in Clemence Houseman's *The Were-Wolf* or Rudyard Kipling's *The Mark of the Beast* or Saki's (H. H. Munro) *Gabriel-Ernest*, it is because the author always distances us, makes us accept the word of his storyteller and never tampers with the "far, far away and long, long ago," and, in a sense, finesses the ending. The price paid is that, while the stories make good reading, they have only anticlimaxes and thus are not very scary.[3] As long as the werewolf retains his relatively benign (i.e., nonsexual) post-alteration demeanor there does not seem much hope for him in popular folklore. He will continually be upstaged by his anthropocentric cousin, the Wolfman.

One of the best werewolf stories ever written was a story by Bram Stoker. The story, now called "Dracula's Guest," has a curious history. Initially intended to be the first chapter of *Dracula*, it is Jonathan Harker's description of an adventure that occurred between Munich and Bistritz. Briefly, what happens is that en route to Dracula's castle Jonathan is stranded in the countryside by a superstitious coachman who is unwilling to venture further on *Walpurgis Nacht*. Now on his own, Jonathan makes his way through a gloomy cluster of cypress trees into a cemetery where he takes refuge from the stormy night in a dank mausoleum. He reads the inscription: "Here lies the body of a Countess Dolingen of Gratz who sought and found death." While Jonathan is recalling the local superstition that suicides become vampires on *Walpurgis Nacht*, up from the tomb comes "a beautiful woman with rounded cheeks and red lips." But before she reaches him Jonathan is thrown suddenly to the ground "as if by the hand of a giant," and later wakes to find himself warmed, not by the passionate embraces of the femme fatale, but by

> the low panting as of some animal close to me. I felt a warm rasping at my throat, then came a consciousness of the awful truth, which chilled me to the heart and sent the blood surging up through my brain. Some great animal was lying on me and now licking my throat. I feared to stir, for some instinct of prudence bade me lie still; but the brute seemed to realize that there was now some change in me, for it raised its head. Through my eyelashes I saw above me the two great flaming eyes of a gigantic wolf. Its sharp white teeth gleamed in the gaping red mouth, and I could feel its hot breath fierce and acrid upon me.

The wolf is soon scared away by the propitious oncoming of "a troop of horsemen"; and later it becomes clear that the wolf intended no harm; instead, it seems to have protected him. For the wolf not only yelped to alert the horsemen, it had spent the night, as one of the horsemen reports "lying on him [Jonathan] and keeping his blood warm." Who was this wolf who saved Jonathan, and why should it want to keep his blood warm? It was none other than the only other person, aside from Mina Harker, who is really concerned about Jonathan's blood—it was Count Dracula. It was he who in wolf form blanketed our hero from the night cold, and now we learn it was he who had written to the local gendarmerie requesting that they "be careful of my guest—his safety is most precious to me."

It is a poignant touch to have the Count protecting his future victim, but Stoker wisely decided to remove it. Did he excise it, as is sometimes suggested, because the first chapter was already too long, or because he wanted to get Jonathan to Castle Dracula sooner, or even because his publisher supposedly complained that the manuscript needed trimming and this was the easiest place to start? Probably all three, but Stoker also must have realized that the Count lost more than he gained by his association with the wolf. As it is, Dracula's wolf transformations in the zoological gardens or in disembarking from the *Demeter* have never proved particularly important in later renditions. Dracula is, after all, noble, and the werewolf is, well, only a wolf.

It is because the wolf is so irredeemably a beast that there are so few straight werewolf movies. In fact, in spite of such alluring titles as *Werewolf of London* or *Curse of the Werewolf* or *I Was a Teenage Werewolf*, which are all misleading, there have been very few folkloric werewolves on celluloid. Appropriately, perhaps, both the oldest and the most recent of the Hollywood wolf transformations are the genuine article—that is, werewolves; the others are all Wolfmen. In both *The Werewolf* (1913) and *The White Wolf* (1914) we see by a simple dissolve the transformation of man into wolf—in both cases a Navajo Indian becomes a timber wolf. By the time Universal came to make *Werewolf of London* (1935) it was clear that the wolf as wolf was not going to be very scary. What was needed was something that (1) could get close to the camera and (2) could create the horror. Something more human was needed. So Jack Pierce, who was responsible for the other Universal monsters, gave Henry Hull a face that almost looked like Frederick March's Mr. Hyde. However, while March's upper teeth extended outward, Hull had two nether incisors that extended upward rather like the vampire's in reverse. Even though there are some stock wolf shots (a big German shepherd) at the beginning and later at the zoo, *Werewolf of London* showed, at least at the box office, that the Wolfman, not the werewolf, was going to attract the audience.[4] And that the Wolfman did until very recently.

In the Year of the Wolf—1980–81—three American wolf movies were either made or distributed: *Wolfen, The Howling,* and *An American Werewolf in London. Wolfen* is noteworthy because it attempts to take the wolf's point of view (thanks to computerized "alienvision," which highlights certain foreground figures against a whitewashed background). The other two movies may prove more important because, for the first time in half a century, they returned the werewolf to its folkloric iconography. Once again, the afflicted human drops down on all fours and goes berserk.

It would be nice to think that this "new" image, as it was advertised, was the result of filmmakers' passion for authenticity or even of Universal's copyright restrictions, or, better yet, represented some new awareness of our common repressed bestiality, but in truth it was because makeup artist Rick Baker had devised a set of pneumatically operated masks that eliminated the

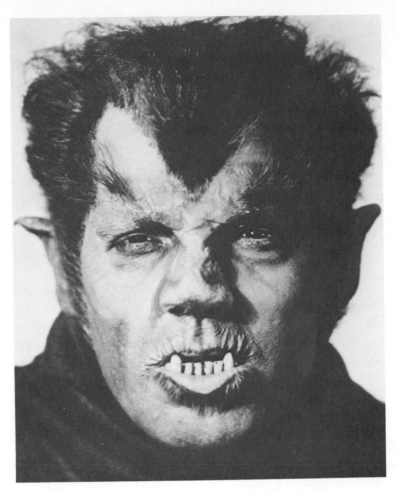

Henry Hull in *Werewolf of London*, 1935 (Universal Studios)

need for stop-action filming or, more usually, the slow dissolve. What we see in both *The Howling* and *An American Werewolf in London* is what appears to be an uninterrupted progression from recognizable man into recognizable wolf. And this seamless metamorphosis happens with no break-away before our unbelieving eyes, almost as if the wolf is unfolding outward *through* the skin of a man.[5]

Once the wolf has popped out of the human husk (complete with the same knuckle-cracking sound effects first used in the remake of *Invasion of the Body Snatchers*), the makers of these modern werewolves lose interest. They know the wolf is not interesting as wolf; only the transformation is. So in *The Howling* Joe Dante ends up not following a plot, but playing with visual puns (cans of "Wolf" brand chili in the kitchen, Allen Ginsburg's *Howl* on the reading table, Disney's *Three Little Pigs* on the TV) or entertaining horror film fans with cameo appearances by Roger Corman, Forrest Ackerman, Kevin McCarthy, Ken Tobey, John Carradine, and Barbara Steele, making gross jokes about giving someone "a piece of my mind" while the werewolf digs out some of his own brainstuff, and generally just letting John Sayle's screenplay develop in the time-honored B-movie mode—scares in the service of a whodunit. Ironically, buried beneath all the contrivances is a perceptive commentary on the influence of television (we have become a nation of voyeurs) and the touch-me therapy of the 1970s (getting "in touch" means turning on the TV). *The Howling*'s denouement seems almost predictable: the deranged psychiatrist is a brainwasher who contends that "getting in touch with yourself" means "tuning to your werewolf channel."

The plot is again in the service of special effects in John Landis' *An American Werewolf in London*, except that there is no John Sayles fable, only a feeble mishmash of Landis' *Animal House* and *The Blues Brothers* scenario. But who cares? For once again the movie has no interest in horror or werewolves or even in plot. It has instead some of the most technically superb skin-erupting scenes ever on film. Rick Baker's special effects surpass Rob Bottin's: not only can he make a fascinorious wolf pop out of David Naughton (all the more shocking since Naughton is better known to the pop-drinking audience for his good-humored Dr. Pepper commercials), but he also shows the horrid transformations of Naughton's confrere who was killed in the initial werewolf attack and does not die but literally rots before our eyes.[6] As is so often the case in modern films, the audience applauds each new shape-altering mechanism where a generation ago it would have gasped. It is of more than passing importance that when these werewolf films premiered around the country the real stars were Bottin and Baker, not those whose names were on the marquee. Bottin even made the publicity tour to promote the film in lieu of the "stars" and reviewers concentrated on the stiletto fingernail trick or the "Change O' Head" routine. For his efforts Baker won an Oscar, the first ever given for "makeup."

The reason these werewolf movies don't horrify is that the werewolf is only a terror-monster. He has no family connections, no sex interest, no claim to any desire other than revenge and hunger. He is just there to say "boo!" and be gone. If the monster is going to drop down on all fours, as, say, Val Lewton implied in *Cat People* (1942), the audience must be sufficiently confused as to the reality of its existence to make the beast ambiguous. Does Irena become that stalking panther or not? We will never know. Paul Shrader resolved the ambiguities almost too well in his rendition (hardly a remake) of *Cat People* (1982). The transformation scenes were so complete, the incest motif so blatant, and the voodoo so ritualistic, that there was not enough obscurity. One way to resolve the werewolf problem may be seen in the Wolfman: the beast walks on two legs, still can't talk, but once we see him in pants and shirt we know exactly who he is and what he wants. Our language has already encoded this wolf: think only of the sexual connotations of "wolf whistle," "lone wolf," even "hungry as a wolf," to say nothing of what happens when "wolf" and "man" are conjoined into "Wolfman." "Wolfman Jack," the omnipresent, syndicated midnight DJ, is still speaking to adolescents with the kind of forbidden knowledge that one gets by being out late at night. But the werewolf, even if he could talk, knows nothing we want to hear.

One reason Michael Jackson's "Thriller" video (1984) proved so successful is that Landis and Baker were able to tie the wolf transformation to a clearly sexual scenario. In the video Mr. Jackson is on a date with a beautiful young girl, drives her to an isolated spot in dark woods, proposes a serious relationship with a ring, and then, after warning her that not all is as it seems, literally shifts from being a polite and thoughtful young man into a growling and fanged wolf. But he is not a complete wolf, just his face—the rest of him can still dance. He is a wolf*man*. After a number of such transformations and wonderfully choreographed strut numbers with zombies and ghouls, as well as a "rap" spoken by Vincent Price, the young lovers promise fidelity. Michael has convinced her that his "good" side is in control. Then, just as they are set to leave hand-in-hand, he spins to face the camera and we see from his yellowing eyes that he is still having those problems. Although the video began with a disclaimer asserting that Michael Jackson does not believe in the occult, and although the Jehovah's Witnesses chastized their most famous member ("The Watchtower," October 15, 1983) for implying monsters really exist, the youthful audience will later learn that this kind of midnight madness is all too real.

The only modern horror myth to have succeeeded with a beast as beast is King Kong. Still, it is clear that beneath all his ape hair and chest-pounding Kong is really just human sexual hyperbole. Thanks to the assimilation of Darwin in popular culture, Kong is the simian exception. One can see the more usual shifting of monsters from terror to horror, from beast to man, developing in the high Victorian novella. The sons of Caliban—that dormant race of modern monsters—reassert themselves in H. G. Wells' *The Island of Dr. Moreau* (1896), where the physical conjunction of man and various animals is the scariest when the humanness is most prominent. Clearly, this continues to fascinate us in our own film versions of the Dr. Moreau story, as well as in the incredible success of the *Planet of the Apes* movies (*Beneath* . . . , *Escape from* . . . , *Conquest of the* . . . , *Battle for the* . . .). This anthropocentric change had to happen to the werewolf if his mythic line was to survive. The wolf is a fright image in such modern pastorals as *The Jungle Book*, but to make him a carrier of horror he must endure the same unhappy irreconciliation of opposites we observed with the vampire and the Frankenstein monster. He must be made part human.

In this sense, what the folklore nosferatu is to the modern vampire, the ancient werewolf is to the modern Wolfman. Both mythic archetypes had to be domesticated, personalized, elevated from lore to art, and then returned in new form to lore. They have changed their manners, been humanized, and this evolution has really only happened since the mid-nineteenth century, thanks in large measure to the imagination of one artist. For what Bram Stoker did for the vampire, Curt Siodmak did for the werewolf. Like Stoker, Siodmak intuitively realized the necessary changes that had to be made to the old form, and, again like Stoker, was willing to make major changes in the received myth in order to get the beast out and the man in. Could there be a more lasting and unconscious testament to Darwin than the fact that, since the 1860s, we have done to animal monsters what evolutionary forces have done to us?

Siodmak knew from Henry Hull's success in *Werewolf of London* that the form must be human first, wolf second, and he knew from the recent success of all the filmic versions of *Dr. Jekyll and Mr. Hyde* that Hyde only does what Jekyll wants. Siodmak's unsung contribution is that, for the first time, he made his protagonist an unwilling, nay, downright pathetic, participant in the horrors, not just of transformation, but of a family romance as well. You may not like Dr. Frankenstein or Count Dracula or Dr. Jekyll, but little (actually huge, but he always seemed so small) Larry, the Wolfman, is everyone's friend. Still, we see just enough of the voluntary, yet suppressed, desire to make us realize that Larry has the same animal passions that we all pretend don't exist. The only difference between Larry and us is that his erotic passions somehow get revealed and drive him in a clearly predictable pattern.

Although the Wolfman has now been superseded by the more articulate Mr. Hyde (it was not entirely by accident that Victor Fleming's *Dr. Jekyll* was released just after *The Wolf Man*), he still deserves a second look if only because in the early 1940s he was more popular than Dracula and almost as popular as the Frankenstein monster. The Wolfman is also interesting because he is the only major monster not to have been continually revived. Why he has been relatively neglected for the last thirty years is not clear, but certainly one reason is that he is bereft of a generating literary text. The only template we have is the visually superb, but dated, Universal movie. (Guy Endore's fascinating case history, *The Werewolf of Paris*, 1933, was the basis of only one movie, Hammer Studio's *Curse of the Werewolf*, 1961.) In addition, *The Wolf Man* is worth looking at again because it is remarkably propitious in its manipulation of character, image, and narrative.

Here is how the story goes: Young "Master" Larry Talbot is returning home to his father's estates in Wales after eighteen years of fortune-seeking in America. Larry has no mother—no mention is ever made of her—and his father, Sir John, is the only family left. Larry's older brother, clearly his father's favorite, has died. In fact, Larry is returning home to be groomed for adult responsibilities; he is all that's left of the Talbots. Manhood won't come easily, for Larry is ungainly, a little dim, able to "work," he says, "only with my hands"—in short, hardly suited for a life of managing monies and property. He seems an almost perpetually awkward adolescent. For instance, one of his first acts at home is to shuffle up to the observatory to tinker with Dad's telescope. He points it not at the stars but over at what he is more interested in observing—girls. He swings the lens toward town and, drop-jawed, views Gwen, a local beauty who lives with her father (again, the motherless motif) above their antique shop. Larry is already exhibiting just a touch of the old wolf; for the first time he is excited.

The next day Larry bumbles about in the antique shop, hoping to bump into Gwen. He happens on a walking stick capped with a huge wolf's head carved in a five-sided silver star. This pentagram, Gwen patiently explains, is the "sign of the werewolf." Since Larry seems confused she explains the beast in a way Larry can understand, as a nursery rhyme:

> *Even a man who's pure at heart*
> *And says his prayers at night*
> *May become a wolf when the wolfbane blooms*
> *And the autumn moon is bright.*

She even explains the pentagram. It seems the werewolf can see the five-pointed star in the hand of his next victim. Larry, now at a loss to explain what he is looking for in the antique shop, buys the cane and the werewolf myth (none of it is in folklore; still, it's astonishing how many commentators consider the quatrain and pentagram authentic lore), and for his troubles finally gets a date with Gwen for the gypsy fair.

As R. H. W. Dillard has argued in his chapter on *The Wolf Man* in *Horror Films* (1976), Larry is pure Adam, Gwen pure Eve—well, almost pure, for she is engaged to Frank, the Talbot's gamekeeper. All we now need is to have the Devil appear and induct Larry into the complexities of manhood. This happens that night when he escorts Gwen and Jennie, her friend, to the gypsy fair. At the camp the fortune teller, Bela (Lugosi, of course—subtlety with names is not important here; after all, by 1941 it's no use pretending that art more usually imitates art than life) predicts Jennie's future. Bela sees the feared pentagram in her hand and warns her to escape. She doesn't. The werewolf (now in the form of Chaney's German shepherd) attacks her. Larry tries to help by beating the "wolf" to death with his silver-tipped cane and is bitten. We all know the rest: Larry has been bitten by Fate not because of some flaw, but because he was just trying to help a damsel in distress, a damsel who had been well forewarned. Larry must fall, and this fall has precise sexual overtones.

The next morning he wakes with the mark of his initiation, the mark of the beast, the pentagram, on his chest. He worries about this nocturnal emission of sin, but his father says it's unimportant and almost incidentally adds that Bela's body has been found with Larry's cane nearby. "But I killed a *wolf* with my cane," protests Larry. "Nonsense," says Sir John, knowing full well that as a Talbot it makes little difference if it was a gypsy or a wolf—the local constable will understand. Here a Marxist critic might make much of the Talbot hauteur, but the movie does not. Larry suffers in isolation and misunderstanding. He can't sit still in church, he can't talk things out with his dad, he can't even shoot straight at the fair—the target is a wolf. Even the psychiatrist is stymied. Here he is, the boy who has everything, but lacks an understanding of the world. Larry is an alien in this sealed-off Welsh world, isolated by birth, deed, and happenstance. So in true horror film fashion, he must accept superstition and visit the old gypsy lady to find out what's happening.

The scene with the gypsy, Queen Malvena, has been overlooked by the few interpretive critics of *The Wolf Man* because it seems to add only more confusion to the plot. Of course it does—Malvena (played by Madame Maria Ouspenskaya of the Moscow Arts Theatre) tells Larry he has been bitten by a werewolf and that the bite means he too will transform. She gives him a countermanding charm, a pendant with the sign of the pentagram, which Larry ironically, but again nobly and stupidly, gives to Gwen. Under all this gypsy magic we see the dim outline of a family romance again being drawn. Remember that Larry has returned to Talbot Castle because his older brother has recently died, and remember also that he is motherless. Two important figures are missing from Larry's family—mother and brother—because they are, in a sense, over at the gypsy camp. Malvena, who is sought out by Larry for information about the world, is Bela's mother. Bela is the werewolf whose bite has caused Larry to be inducted into the fraternity of werebeasts, and now it is Malvena, Queen of the Gypsies, who tries to protect Prince Larry, heir to Sir John's throne. It is no accident that she tries to protect her new son from the world of sexual experience even though he has killed her other son with a stick. She tries to explain the horrors that lie ahead, but it is clear that Larry must find out for himself.[7] She "knows that whoever is bitten by a werewolf becomes a werewolf," and so she bids him a melancholy goodbye, saying: "The way you walk is thorny through no fault of your own, but as the rain enters the soil, the river enters the sea, so tears run to a pre-destined end. Find peace for a moment, my son."

Returning now to his father's house with his "mother's" knowledge, Larry is about to embark on the uncharted waters of adolescence. He will set sail, as always, alone and at night in dreams. He prepares for bed; off come the shoes, off comes the shirt, and we see through a quick series of breakaway dissolves what he is only barely conscious of: he is becoming hairier. Then with a whoosh and a whoop he disappears off into the night.

But is he a werewolf? Bela certainly was supposed to be. But no, Larry is a *Wolfman*. Even though he supposedly has taken off his clothes and should at least be in pajamas, here he is now before us, complete in long pants and matching shirt. Only pedants could care that Larry is now in all-brown cloth-ing where earlier the colors were different, but these would be the same "close readers" who would complain that Bela's werewolf had a nice long tail. And is he ever down on all fours the way Bela was? No, never! He walks like a teenager who has not yet caught up with his size ten feet. His walk is "thorny," indeed. Larry now has a face full of yak hair, a set of lower jaw fangs, long fingernails, and an "appliance" lupine nose. He is all set for a night of wolfish adventure.

When Larry awakes the next morning from a night of uneasy dreams, he learns that wolfprints have been located leading from the castle to the body of a gravedigger and back to his bed. The next night the same thing, except that this time Larry is leg-trapped by the police and is saved by the maternal Malvena, who just happens to be passing by in her buckboard. To make mat-ters worse for Larry, he visits Gwen and sees the pentagram in the palm of her hand. It is clear that Gwen is not really attracted to Larry, but he cer-tainly is fated to be attracted to her. Some awful climax is surely at hand. We might recall the first werewolf attack made by Bela, for the mythic symme-tries are still in place. Jennie, Gwen's friend, went to the fortune teller and asked whom she was going to marry. When Bela saw the pentagram in her palm he knew what he was to do. Now Larry, in love with Gwen, sees in her palm what Bela found in Jennie's. Bela did not want to hurt Jennie—he told her to flee—and Larry certainly does not want to hurt Gwen—he has even given her the protective talisman, but what can he do? There are forces in the world that even the Wolfman can't control.

Larry will make a heroic effort. He begs his father to tie him up, to lock him into the bedroom, and although Sir John refuses, at least he tries to help. Larry entreats his father to take away the walking stick with the strange wolf

Father Talbot with cane and son with girl in *The Wolf Man,* 1941 (Universal Studios)

head—the phallic instrument, if you will—that caused all the trouble in the first place, and again the father consents. Sir John is then off to help the posse locate the wolf. Meanwhile, Gwen, who has been warned by Malvena to stay away from Larry and keep close to home, is also inexplicably out in the woods.

The central scene is set: the fog crew at Universal does its best to lay down a blanket of lather. This fog seems to seep upward from the moist earth like wet, thick steam. Sir John is there with the wolf stick. Gwen is there. All we need is Master Larry and Malvena. Here comes the Wolfman, almost pushing his way through the fog. He sees Gwen; he clearly doesn't want to approach, but he is drawn to her. He rushes to embrace her with the grip that will kill, but wait! Here is Sir John. Their encounter is bloody. Sir John first cracks the Wolfman over the head and then brutally clubs him to death. Just like the then-recent Mr. Hydes in the thirties and forties, Larry's human features are reasserted in death. Sir John is as startled as we by his violence and moves back into the white fog soup. But again wait, who is this moving through the miasma? It's Malvena, who cradles Larry's head in her lap and delivers the eulogy: "Your suffering is over . . . you will find peace, my son." Gwen steps back into the waiting arms of her manly fiancé, Frank, and Larry is at last at peace. The police inspector (Ralph Bellamy) views the final scene and delivers the public judgment: Larry was killed by the wolf while coming to rescue the damsel in distress, and the past is fogged over and forgotten.

But Gwen knows better; her last words are a startled "Larry!" as she sees that it was no wolf at all, but a "wolf" in wolf's clothing. And Sir John also knows better; he is dumbstruck and must be led numbly away. After all, he has just bludgeoned his son to death.[8] The question we are left with is simply, why should Larry have had to undergo the wolf transformation in the first place? If my understanding of transformation monsters is correct, the alteration always just precedes the act of wish fulfillment. Thus the "victim" must transform into the vampire before he attacks certain tabooed women, or Frankenstein must act out his ambivalence about Elizabeth in the safe form of a huger-than-human creature, or Dr. Jekyll, as we will see, must depend on his libidinous double Mr. Hyde to cross forbidden boundaries. So what is the boundary that Larry Talbot can't cross but the Wolfman can?

Clearly, the question of taboo involves Gwen. Just who is she? All we know about her is that she is engaged to Frank and that she is the object of Larry's unexpressed passion. We also know that, like Larry, she is without a mother. This is not much to base an opinion on, and so we may be forced to ascribe more meaning to insignificant acts, such as the fact that Malvena attempts to protect Gwen from Larry just as the old gypsy has sought to protect Larry from the curse of his new desires. Again I suppose a Marxist might attribute the young people's inhibitions to social class distinctions: Larry is privileged, Gwen is common, and the oppressive moral articulated in *The Wolf Man* demands that she stay with the gamekeeper and force Larry to search elsewhere. The social injunction of the State operating through the oppressive father causes Larry to rebel (i.e., transform) if he is to get what he wants. After all, the violation of class distinctions is operative in other horror sagas like the vampire or man-created monster; it is *Count* Dracula and *Baron* Frankenstein, and for that matter it is Jekyll's social position and prestige that keep him from the street woman. Here in the Wolfman saga it is Sir Larry Junior. But once again, I don't think this view is totally supported by the text. Larry may be to the manor born, but he is certainly not to the manor bred. He is just a big American chump, a nice enough guy who has spent a lot of time playing pinball, and chewing gum, and tinkering with radios and not much time thinking about girls.

It would be convenient for critics if, in the Universal Wolfman series that followed (in which Chaney always played the part—the case with no other monster), Larry's relationship with his victims had been clarified. But not so; in fact, just the opposite: the victims become progressively less distinct. It is clear that when Universal made *The Wolf Man* in 1941 they had no idea of its potential; it was dismissed by both the critics and the front office, and the studio seems to have made it primarily because they knew Jack Pierce's transformation scenes would be sensational. After it proved Universal's biggest money-maker of the season, they went back to Siodmak and asked for more of the same. The sequels were clearly hurry-up jobs played for the thrills and scares of introducing more and yet more monsters to each movie. These movies represent no real continuation of the story; they are just a proliferation of stock sequences. Still, they are worth looking at if only to establish Larry's extended family.

In *Frankenstein Meets the Wolf Man* (1943) Larry is rather fond of Elsa, daughter of Dr. Frankenstein Junior, but he is much more interested in being cured of his affliction and in tussling with the monster than in playing with the girls. His relationship with Malvena, however, becomes clearer. Her motherly "I will take care of you as if you were my own son" should have caused Larry some concern, in view of what has happened to her own son (incidentally, Bela plays the Frankenstein monster in this picture), but they are very tender with each other. Malvena even takes Larry on her ubiquitous buckboard to see the doctor for help. In *House of Frankenstein* (1944) Larry plays a somewhat minor role. Dracula, the Frankenstein monster, and the hunchback lackey are also involved, but young Talbot has time to fall for Iloka, a gypsy girl who introduces some new information. The Wolfman, she says, can be killed "by a silver bullet fired from a gun in the hand of a woman who loves him." Iloka is that woman. Again in *House of Dracula* (1945) the Wolfman plays a minor role, for this time we have all the five Universal monsters. Now at last we learn that Larry's problem is caused by pressure on the brain (completely forgetting Bela's bite in the gypsy camp— Siodmak did not write this screenplay!), because Larry's brain is too big for his head. The about-to-be-mad doctor performs his last sane act by surgically letting the pressure escape from the brain, and Larry is dumbfounded to learn that he is no longer a moon-child. Suffering no ill effects, he embraces the doctor's nurse and presumably will live happily ever after. The other monsters are not so lucky for they are all burned up in an explosion of the doctor's lab. In *Abbott and Costello Meet Frankenstein* (1948) Larry is once again pressed into service, this time to help Bud and Lou stop a mad Dracula from more transplant hocus-pocus—Dracula wants to put Lou's brain into the Frankenstein monster's body. Larry, the hero, saves the day by clutching bat-shaped Dracula and leaping off a cliff with him to certain death below.

In the Wolfman's subsequent reincarnations of the fifties and sixties his family relations are still unsettled; in fact, he even loses what little family he has while turning into the stalk-and-slash sociopathic killer of the late seventies. There were, however, two notable exceptions: one made by AIP, *I*

Was a Teenage Werewolf, and the other by Hammer Studios, *Curse of the Werewolf*. *I Was a Teenage Werewolf* (1957) is noteworthy because here at last the werewolf's age and social status finally duplicate the audience's. Tony, the change-over candidate, is a bumbling adolescent, confused, awkward, insecure, and sexually confused, just like "Master" Larry Talbot. He visits a psychiatrist for help with his antisocial school behavior, but the well-meaning doctor is of the hand-wringing, mad lab variety and so gives him a drug that "destroys the superego." Tony, now with no superego, is pure wolf, werewolf, and the fact that Tony only changes when a pretty girl walks by only reinforces the obvious.

Subtlety was never AIP's strong point. Finally, the high school janitor from Bulgaria makes the diagnosis and tells the police, who gun down Tony as the inspector remarks, "It's not for man to interfere with the ways of God." What makes *I Was a Teenage Werewolf* interesting is that in its artless exploitation it dispenses with all the full moon and silver bullet motifs and concentrates on the libidinous excitement of the bestial.

Hammer Studio's entry into the werewolf market took the opposite approach. They made *Curse of the Werewolf* (1961) to complete their Dracula, Frankenstein, Mummy, and Dr. Jekyll entourage, and for once they elevated rather than debased the tradition. *Curse* is intriguing because it is the only werewolf film to be adapted from a serious literary text, Guy Endore's *Werewolf of Paris* (1933), and the only one to explain the affliction in familial terms. The protagonist, Leon, is the bastard son of a deaf-mute servant girl who was raped by a foamy-mouthed beggar (Richard Wordsworth, great-great-grandson of William). In this casebook chronicle of the life and times of a werewolf we follow Leon through adolescence as he attempts first to neglect, then to fight off, and finally to accept the curse of his bestiality. While out marauding in the countryside he is caught, and, in an extraordinary gesture, begs his stepfather to kill him with a "silver bullet moulded from a crucifix." Once again, the father figure kills the son to prevent the young man from attacking innocent victims, namely, young women. Both *I Was a Teenage Werewolf* and *Curse of the Werewolf* will probably be remembered not for their mythic acuity, but because their stars—Michael Landon and Oliver Reed—went on to greater things.

To find any complexity in the werewolf myth after the 1940s, one must jump the mythic tracks and follow the narrative progress of a similar saga, *Dr. Jekyll and Mr. Hyde*. For the werewolf, usually in the guise of the Wolfman, degenerated into such spoofs as *The Werewolf of Washington*, in which a Nixon-like president is bitten, presumably explaining the travesties of Watergate, or *Werewolf in a Girls' Dormitory* (1961) and *Nympho Werewolf* (1970), which exploit the obvious, or *Werewolf on Wheels* (1971), a

Michael Landon in *I Was a Teenage Werewolf*, 1957 (American-International Pictures)

rowdy adolescent two-wheeler action flick, *The Beast Must Die* (1974), a whodunit, and a lot of out-and-out schlock, like *Legend of the Werewolf* (1974), *Scream of the Wolf* (1975), *Werewolf of Woodstock*, which really don't even belong on midnight television, but are.

Essentially, the Dr. Jekyll/Mr. Hyde saga has reversed the mythic dispersion of the Wolfman by refocusing attention on the family. In so doing, Jekyll/Hyde has become one of the central horror sequences of our time, itself fostering such variants as the Jekyllesque doctor of *The Invisible Ray* (1933), the out-of-Hyding slasher of *Silent Scream* (1980), and the amusing and morbid tale of Duane and his nasty sidekick Belial in *Basket Case* (1982). If you ask a teenager to tell you the "whole" Jekyll/Hyde story he will usually start by attributing a werewolfesque causality into Jekyll's behavior. Dr. Jekyll is not cursed like the vampire, but instead initially *wants* to transform and then, once transformed into Hyde, he is powerless to re-create Jekyll. As Hyde, Jekyll now disturbs women, usually at least two women, one of whom he supposedly loves. Your adolescent informer may also tell you that Hyde kills the father of Jekyll's intended bride, that Hyde is finally caught, killed, and that the story ends with Jekyll's visage once again asserting itself through Hyde's hide.

This story begins to answer questions raised by the werewolf-Wolfman scenario. For instance, who is Jekyll, the candidate for transformation into beast? As the story now goes, Jekyll is a good but fussy scientist who concocts

Oliver Reed annoying Yvonne Romain in *The Curse of the Werewolf*, 1961 (Hammer Studios)

a potion that allows him safe passage into the atavistic Mr. Hyde. But why Jekyll should want this brew in the first place has to be explained to the modern audience; it is not enough to just want to be a werewolf. Often Jekyll is a good man who wants to help mankind; he wants to separate the evil animal part and cast it out. He wants natural goodness to prevail. Rarely, if ever, is he just curious about evil—his acts are always tinged with brittle altruism. And so is his medical sub-specialty: sometimes he is a charity doctor, sometimes a psychiatrist, sometimes a social worker, sometimes a professor of medical science; always his initial desires are for the improvement of us all.

Along with his altruism he is very sensitive. When he is handed any setback he literally falls apart, and the setback in the saga occurs when the woman he intends to marry is temporarily kept from him by her father. The "mother" in this story is rarely seen and never does anything important. Jekyll always (that I know of) drinks the brew right after the marriage ceremony is postponed. Jekyll is "beside himself" with anxiety, goes into the backroom lab, gulps down the id-emetic, and part of him comes loose. Hyde is not a monster yet, but it is clear *he* is not going to waste any time moping over Jekyll's lost love. Hyde is off for a night on the town. Let Jekyll still love the young lady; Hyde knows where the excitement is, and is soon courting a young wench. Could there be a more Victorian solution to a more Victorian problem: the double standard is taken literally.

In our modern version, culled from hundreds of movies and television shows, things initially go well. But then Hyde turns nasty; he brutalizes the "other woman." In fact, he is a Wolfman to her. It is no accident that Hyde is actually pictured as lupine in such movies as *Daughter of Dr. Jekyll* (1957), *Abbott and Costello Meet Dr. Jekyll and Mr. Hyde* (1953), or, better yet, the Spanish *Dr. Jekyll and the Werewolf* (1971), in which Hyde is clearly portrayed as a Wolfman. Interestingly, in the first major werewolf/Wolfman movie, *Werewolf of London* (1935), Henry Hull is pure Dr. Jekyll and his wolf pure Mr. Hyde. But what separates the young man/wolf and Jekyll/ Hyde is that, by the time Jekyll's inamorata is finally allowed to marry him, it is too late: Hyde has taken control and is brutalizing the street woman just for the fun of it. Jekyll's "wolf," now in control, goes to the house of the forbidden lady and kills, not her, but her father. He is then pursued until death by the police and changes, too late, back into Jekyll. Is he unhappy in death? No, rather like the vampire, he has probably had a better life as a monster than he would have had as a man. But he has to die for it.

There have been many renditions of this story, all of which exaggerate various aspects: the altruism of Jekyll, the prohibited love, the transformation, the "other woman," the sadism of Hyde, the pursuit and destruction.

But the one aspect that has made them all interesting to students of modern horror is that they have not just strayed from the printed text, they have positively overturned it. When we look at Robert Louis Stevenson's *The Strange Case of Dr. Jekyll and Mr. Hyde* (1886), we find not two women, but one little eight-year-old girl. We see no father-in-law but a doddering old Sir Danvers Carew, whose only link with Jekyll is that they have the same lawyer, and we follow no linear development of narrative but are cocooned inside pockets of narratives so that we are often getting the tale third-hand. What we find in the printed text is "a strange case," indeed a case more in keeping with the detective story than with a gothic horror story. But a gothic horror story is surely what it has become; one genre has cannibalized the story line of another.

To understand how and why Jekyll/Hyde has joined the ranks of Dracula and Frankenstein we return momentarily to the Victorian context. Carlyle, who understood so well the achievement of the early nineteenth century, said that what made romanticism so revolutionary was the acknowledgment of states of consciousness. The romantics, moreover, were interested not in consciousness per se but in its extremes: in transcendent consciousness, the sublime, on one hand, and the subverbal, the dream, on the other. To the nineteenth-century artist man was still, as Pope had said in *An Essay on Man*, in a middle state: "With too much knowledge for the Sceptic side,/ With too much weakness for the Stoic's pride,/ He hangs between; in doubt to act, or rest;/ In doubt to deem himself a God, or Beast" (Epistle II, 5–8). Man was divided within the self as well: there was the urge to soar and the urge to sink, the urge to multiply and the urge to divide; as Blake said, the urge of the Prolific and the urge of the Devourer. Christianity had initially tried to separate consciousness in order to glorify the transcendent, the "good thoughts," the Prolific, but the romantics realized that the bestial, the Devourer, could not only not be discharged, but that it was instead a source of tremendous natural energy. One need only look at animal paintings early in the century, paintings by Goya, Delacroix, Géricault, Stubbs, and Blake, to see the new enthusiasm for the beast.

In a sense, a simple awareness of consciousness itself implies division. For to be aware of the self means that there are at least two parties, the observed and the observing. The dispassionate observer may well condemn the erotic and passionate self as brutish, but without this self the "higher" self is barren. This ironic observation of the self in which the thinking ego comments on the feeling ego represents a logical development of one aspect of romanticism—what has been called "negative romanticism"—and is at the epistemological heart of so much of modern horror. Indeed, it is the basis of late gothic, the Victorian horrors.

What the neoclassicist attempted to reconcile and the romantic acknowledged, the mid-Victorian tried to repress and the late Victorian delighted in, or at least pretended to. In this sense modern horror can be said to begin with the late eighteenth century rediscovery of Milton's Satan, the feral double of Christ, for clearly at the beginning of *Paradise Lost* Milton is more than willing to give the devil his due. The beast is there and it is trite but true to say that he is more interesting than his ariel counterparts. This is a development not lost in the gothic novel, for one finds the same doubling, or in reverse, the same splitting, in the protagonist/antagonist in *Castle of Otranto, Vathek, Caleb Williams, The Italian, The Monk, Melmoth the Wanderer*, and many others. In each, a case can be made for the fatal attraction of the satanic second self. So it should come as no surprise that James Hogg's *Confessions of a Justified Sinner* was Robert Louis Stevenson's confessed model for *The Strange Case of Dr. Jekyll and Mr. Hyde*, nor is it any wonder that Hyde *in print* is a strangely sympathetic figure.

What characterizes Victorian schizophrenia is not that the nasty shadow gets loose—the Victorians all acknowledge that is almost inevitable—but that, once outside, the second self is often rather appealing. Far more unattractive is the attempt to repress the split. Tennyson's Ulysses sublimates with conquest, Arnold's Merman with denial, Browning's Lippi with artifice, but somehow the beasts manage to get out: in *Maud*, in *The Buried Life*, in *The Ring and the Book*. It is splendid for Carlyle to say "Work" or Newman to say "Study" or Arnold to say "Search"; in the dark night of the soul the creatures will have out, and, as Thompson, Rossetti, and Pater found out, nothing can contain them.

Had *Dracula* been written in 1810 it would be now hailed as a great romantic novel, but had *Dr. Jekyll and Mr. Hyde* also appeared then it would have been forgotten. *Dr. Jekyll and Mr. Hyde* was a stunning success in the 1890s precisely because of what had happened in the 1860s and 1870s. Although no one would compare it to *Jude the Obscure* or *Our Mutual Friend* or even *The Picture of Dorian Gray*, which are in many ways rather similar, its influence, especially in popular culture, is far more profound. Masao Miyoshi makes the case in *The Divided Self: A Perspective on the Literature of the Victorians* (1969) that *Jekyll and Hyde* was at the epicenter of the literature of the 1890s—in fact, the masterpiece of the gothic revival. John Fowles, in *The French Lieutenant's Woman* (1969), goes even further:

> This—the fact that every Victorian had two minds—is the one piece of equipment we must always take with us in our travels back into the nineteenth century. It is a schizophrenia seen at its clearest, its most notorious, in the poets . . . Tennyson, Clough, Arnold, Hardy; but scarcely less clearly in the extraordinary

political veerings from Right to Left and back again of men like the younger Mill and Gladstone; in the ubiquitous neuroses and psychosomatic illnesses of intellectuals otherwise as different as Charles Kingsley and Darwin, in the execration at first poured on the Pre-Raphaelites, who tried—or seemed to be trying—to be one-minded about both art and life; in the endless tug-of-war between Liberty and Restraint, Excess and Moderation, Propriety and Conviction, between the principled man's cry for Universal Education and his terror of Universal Suffrage; transparent also in the mania for editing and revising, so that if we want to know the real Mill or the real Hardy we can learn far more from the deletions and alterations of their autobiographies than from the published versions—more from correspondences that somehow escaped burning, from private diaries, from the petty detritus of the concealment operation. Never was the record so completely confused, never a public facade so successfully passed off as the truth on a gullible posterity; and this, I think, makes the best guidebook to the age very possibly *Dr. Jekyll and Mr. Hyde*. Behind its latterday Gothic lies a very profound and epoch-revealing truth. (p. 169)

I also think one of the reasons for this short work's long influence has to do with the refreshing surprise of modern schizophrenia. For buried under all the blankets of narrative is a figure of forbidden attractiveness, a figure who has since become one of the central archetypes of modern horror—Mr. Hyde. Hyde is part of us all and reminds us what we have repressed or grown out of, namely, early adolescence. Far more than the vampire or the Frankenstein monster, Hyde is the monster of latency.

That is the Hyde of the literary text; the Hyde we now know, thanks to film, is remarkably different. Once again, as with Dracula and Frankenstein, Jekyll and Hyde were profoundly changed as they leapt from medium to medium. What Peggy Webling did for *Frankenstein* and John Balderston did for *Dracula*, Thomas Sullivan did for *Dr. Jekyll and Mr. Hyde*. The stage play made the story part of popular culture; it straightened out the plot, it provided causality, it made sexual interactions clear, it excised all narrative sophistication, and it profoundly transformed the monster. By the time these adaptations of Victorian horror in prose had made it to film, the stage plays had already made them myths. To understand how this transformation took place with *Jekyll and Hyde*, let us go back to the text.

According to academic lore (no scholar has been able to document the whole of this story) the idea of Jekyll/Hyde came to Stevenson in a dream. As in the works of Mary Shelley and Bram Stoker, a specific, recorded nightmare seems to lie at the heart of their stories as well. In 1885 Stevenson was living on the coast at Bournemouth without money, without much hope of success, with a wife about whom he felt sexually ill at ease, and with a mother who was still a dominant force. He was sick, suffering the initial onslaught of tuberculosis, and he was taking narcotic painkillers. Stevenson's dream, so he reported, was brought to him by his "little helpers, the brownies"—the muse—but it may have been helped on by drugs. It was a brief dream as he reported:

> For two days I went about racking my brains for a plot of any sort, and on the second night I dreamed the scene at the window, and a scene afterwards split in two, in which Hyde, pursued for some crime, took the powder and underwent the change in the presence of his pursuers. All the rest was made awake, and consciously, although I can trace in much of it the manner of my Brownies. The meaning of the tale is therefore mine, and had long pre-existed in my garden of Adonis, and tried one body after another in vain; indeed, I do most of the morality, worse luck! and my Brownies have not a rudiment of what we call a conscience. Mine, too, is the setting, mine the characters. All that was given me was the matter of the three scenes, and the central idea of a voluntary change becoming involuntary. (*On Dreams*)

This is not much dream-stuff to analyze (although this scene appears as the "Incident at the Window" in the text), but we know it made him so uneasy that he screamed. Stevenson was awakened by Fanny, his wife, for he was, she said, shrieking. Stevenson knew the dream was ripe with unexplored excitement—he was, remember, "racking [his] brains for a plot of any sort" and complained to Fanny that she had disturbed "a fine bogey tale." In retrospect, however, she may have done him a service, for at least the images did not slip away unrecovered. During the next three days Stevenson tried to re-create the scene in prose, but succeeded in writing only a tale of supernatural terror—his wife called it a "crawler, a shilling shocker." Fanny said the story should be written as an allegory. In a fit of bravado, the kind loved by compilers of literary anecdotes, Stevenson threw the first draft of some forty thousand words into the fire, turned on his heel, and stomped upstairs. Four weeks later he had the text ready for publication.

This story, doubtless exaggerated in many respects, does more than buttress the romantic myth of inspirational composition. It shows instead that Stevenson was finally forming a context for a subject that had been of continuing interest: "doubling" as a literary theme and device. In the years before the composition of *Jekyll* he had collaborated with William Ernest Henley on *Deacon Brodie; or, The Double Life*, a play about a mild-mannered carpenter by day, a violent burglar by night, as well as finishing *Markheim*, which dealt with the transformation of selves. Whether it was this dream that gave Stevenson the inspiration for the doubling motif, or the fact that he himself was taking powerful drugs, quite possibly opiates, we will never know. But the personality-splitting draft was a stroke of original genius—a fact now obscured because it has become such a donnée of modern renditions that it is never omitted. While Henry James found it "too explicit and explanatory," we still, thanks no doubt to our own pharmacological culture, find the device necessary.

However, the real excitement in the story is not so much the potation or the transposition of selves, but the fact that the double is not an animal like the werewolf, but in fact another human, an antagonist who is physically, mentally, and spiritually of the same protoplasmic stuff as Jekyll. We may have some trouble believing this because all but the most recent films have made Hyde, not metaphorically, but actually, bestial. Hyde is a tarantula in the Barrymore version, an ape in the March version, and a wolf in numerous other ones. While we may find much to criticize in the Spencer Tracy version (namely, the acting of Spencer Tracy), at least the truth of the printed text comes through: Hyde is Jekyll first and a beast second. As G. K. Chesterton observed long ago in *Robert Louis Stevenson* (1928),

> The real stab of the story is not in the discovery that the one man is two men; but in the discovery that the two men are one man. After all the diverse wandering and warring of those two incompatible beings, there was still one man born and only one man buried. . . . The point of the story is not that a man *can* cut himself off from his conscience, but that he cannot. The surgical operation is fatal in the story. It is an amputation of which both the parts die. (p. 54)

Stevenson clearly had technical troubles with this transformation that was not literally a clean split. Metamorphosis, from classical myth to German fairy tale to English lore, has involved significant shape-shifting. From Ovid to Kafka the human structure usually had to be regressive, but Stevenson shoved it—at least initially—sideways. In the printed text Hyde is apish, to be sure, or better yet troglodytic, but he is always sentient and fully conscious and, until the very end, very human. In fact, the irony is that he may well be far more sentient and conscious than Jekyll. Hyde is not all glands and Jekyll all mind. This is not originally a "blow the lid off the id" tale or a Manichean tale, even though it has often been told in those ways.

To observe Hyde's humanity we may have to burrow back into the text. And "burrow" is not an inappropriate trope, for Stevenson has delivered the story with so much narrative complexity that we find ourselves led from one cul-de-sac into another. This is, of course, exactly how *Frankenstein* and *Dracula* were constructed. We are continually distanced from the horror until, too late, we find ourselves at the top of the stairs and the attic door is opening before us. We must be taken level by level to the monster, from Walton to Frankenstein to the creature, from Harker to Seward to Van Helsing to Count Dracula, or in this case from Utterson to Enfield to Layton to Jekyll to Hyde.

As with the other modern horror stories, *The Strange Case* is told to us by the kindest of gentlemen: in this case two doctors, one lawyer, and a "man about town." Each takes a little different narrative stance, and we pass by two first-person points of view, then an impersonal report, followed by a third-person narration based on first-and second-hand information. The printed text of *Dr. Jekyll* is thus a tilted house of mirrors, each interdependent and all concealing/revealing the central lore, the explosive shock, those brief appearances of Hyde. Since this shock is so well disguised, we might do well to see how each of the gentlemen reacts to Hyde, for if such controlled men of reason cannot stanch the horror, how can we expect to survive?

The first man to actually observe the monster is Mr. Richard Enfield, a jovial, fun-loving bon vivant. He sees Hyde knock down and run over a young girl. "It was like some damned Juggernaut," he initially reports (p. 3), and later adds yet more obfuscation to this already dim image:

> He is not easy to describe. There is something wrong with his appearance, something displeasing, something down-right detestable. I never saw a man I so disliked, and yet I scarce know why. He must be deformed somewhere; he gives a strong feeling of deformity, although I couldn't possibly specify the point. He's an extraordinary looking man, and yet I really can name nothing out of the way. No, sir; I can make no hand of it; I can't describe him. And it's not want of memory; for I declare I can see him this moment. (pp. 8–9)[9]

The next person to describe Hyde is Gabriel John Utterson, a witness who needs some introduction. Although "Gabriel John" is the center of the narrative consciousness, and although his first two names are biblical terms for "justice" and "mercy" and his surname "Utterson" implies that his utterances are to believed (after all, with names like Hyde, "hide" in both the sense of "out of sight" and integument, and Jekyll, the French "I" and "kill," it is hard for the reader not to make puns on all the names), we may well conclude that he is going to be an accurate observer. He is, in addition, a lawyer, a man of acute powers of observation. But from the very first page there are hints that work against his credibility. We may well suspect his brittleness; in fact, we may well conclude that he is really a Jekyll manqué. We are told on the first page by an omniscient narrator: "[Mr. Utterson] was austere with himself; drank gin when he was alone, to mortify a taste for vintages; and though he enjoyed the theater, had not crossed the doors of one for twenty years" (p. 1). The good lawyer may well be incubating his own repressed demon. Utterson's response to Hyde is first excitement ("If he be Mr. Hyde ... I shall be Mr. Seek"; p. 15) and then nausea. He is horribly nauseated when he sees the "faceless" monster. But if both Enfield and Utterson are repulsed by Hyde, observe the reaction of Hastie Lanyon, a Scottish doctor like Jekyll who is also morally fussy. After seeing Hyde,

> The rosy man had grown pale; his flesh had fallen away; he was visibly balder and older and yet it was not so much these tokens of a swift physical decay that arrested the lawyer's notice, as a look in the eye and quality of manner that seemed to testify to some deep-seated terror of the mind. (p. 41)

Lanyon dies from the awful sight of the Jekyll-Hyde transformation. In his own words now,

> My life is shaken to its roots; sleep has left me; the deadliest terror sits by me at all hours of the day and night; and I feel that my days are numbered, and that I must die; and yet I shall die incredulous. As for the moral turpitude that man unveiled to me, even with tears of penitence, I cannot, even in memory, dwell on it without a start of horror. I will say one thing, Utterson, and that (if you can bring your mind to credit it) will be more than enough. The creature who crept into my house that night was, on Jekyll's own confession, known by the name of Hyde . . . . (p. 77)

What can be so bad, so horrible, that it causes one grown man to be unable to describe it, another to vomit, and a third to die? First, let us see what Hyde really looks like and then what he actually does. We all think we know what he looks like—his face is on the cover of every paperback edition of the text. He looks like Fredric March in Rouben Mamoulian's 1931 film version. He is a buck-toothed Neanderthal. This image is not quite true to the text. Certainly it is truer than a spider or a wolf, and certainly it is more literal than our current folk images of Dracula and the Frankenstein monster, but it is not interpretatively helpful. March's Hyde is too old and too big, much too old and much too big. As we will see, this makes a difference in how we have come to understand Jekyll/Hyde, for the price of having the filmic story become a "star vehicle" is that Hyde is forever physically the same as Jekyll. In the text this is initially not so: Hyde is played off against Jekyll. Jekyll is fiftyish, suave, well-dressed, and large, while Hyde is twentyish, apelike, feral, and small. One of the few common characteristics of eyewitness accounts is that Dr. Jekyll's clothes are far too big for Hyde and that Hyde moves not like a juggernaut, but like an ape. He is a dwarfish Jekyll, a miniature, yet, as Utterson reminds us, with something "troglodytic" about him.

In a crucial sense, a sense long since absent in our current renditions, Hyde is almost Jekyll as a teenager, the "Jekyll" that Dr. Jekyll has had to repress in order to become, like Utterson, a man of property, a man of means. Utterson keeps his "Hyde" hidden when he abstains from "vintages" or stays away from the theater. Perhaps this is why Utterson makes the proper diagnosis:

Fredric March and Miriam Hopkins in *Dr. Jekyll and Mr. Hyde,* 1931 (Paramount Studios)

> [Jekyll] was wild when he was young; a long while ago to be sure; but in the law of God, there is no statute of limitations. Ay, it must be that; the ghost of some old sin, the cancer of some concealed disgrace: punishment coming, *pede claudo,* years after memory has forgotten and self-love condoned the fault. (p. 20)

He concludes this line of thought by suggesting that Hyde might even be Jekyll's illegitimate son come back to torture him. This conclusion may be wrong, but not inappropriate. Just look at the youthful vigor of Hyde as he comes bounding forth after Jekyll's first encounter with the forbidden vintages. In Jekyll's words,

> The most racking pangs succeeded: a grinding in the bones, deadly nausea, and a horror of the spirit that cannot be exceeded at the hour of birth or death. Then these agonies began swiftly to subside, and I came to myself as if out of a great sickness. There was something strange in my sensations, something indescribably new and, from its very novelty, incredibly sweet. I felt younger, lighter, happier in body; within I was conscious of a heady recklessness, a current of disordered sensual images running like a millrace in my fancy, a solution of the bonds of

obligation, an unknown but not an innocent freedom of the soul. I knew myself at the first breath of this new life, to be more wicked, tenfold more wicked, sold a slave to my original evil; and the thought, in that moment, braced and delighted me like wine. I stretched out my hands, exulting in the freshness of these sensations; and in the act, I was suddenly aware that I had lost in stature. (p. 82)

A loss of stature, yes, but what exaltation of sensation, what a return to youth! Jekyll's fascination continues:

And yet when I looked upon that ugly idol in the glass, I was conscious of no repugnance, rather of a leap of welcome. This, too, was myself. It seemed natural and human. In my eyes it bore a livelier image of the spirit, it seemed more express and single, than the imperfect and divided countenance I had been hitherto accustomed to call mine. And in so far I was doubtless right. I have observed that when I wore the semblance of Edward Hyde, none could come near to me at first without a visible misgiving of the flesh. (pp. 83–84)

Yet, Hyde becomes evil to Jekyll; evil in the way the vampire is evil to his victim, in the way the Frankenstein monster is evil to his creator. It is a malevolence emanating from "desire with loathing strangely mix'd." Hyde is evil not because he attacks Jekyll, but because he acts out Jekyll's own base desires and gets away with it. Jekyll knows he is supposed to abominate his savage Hyde, but he secretly is fond of him, at least until it is too late. Jekyll rationalizes:

Men have before hired bravos to transact their crimes, while their own person and reputation sat under shelter. I was the first that ever did so for his pleasures. I was the first that could plod in the public eye with a load of genial respectability, and in a moment like a schoolboy, strip off these lendings and spring headlong into the sea of liberty. But for me, in my impenetrable mantle, the safety was complete.

.   .   .

When I would come back from these excursions, I was often plunged into a kind of wonder at my vicarious depravity. This familiar that I called out of my own soul, and sent forth alone to do his good pleasure, was a being inherently malign and villainous; his every act and thought centered on self; drinking pleasure with bestial avidity from any degree of torture to another; relentless like a man of stone. Henry Jekyll stood at times aghast before the acts of Edward Hyde; but the situation was apart from ordinary laws, and insidiously relaxed the grasp of conscience. It was Hyde, after all, and Hyde alone, that was guilty. Jekyll was no worse; he woke again to his good qualities seemingly unimpaired. . . . (pp. 86–87)

Consider what this adolescent Hyde does for his mentor, look at what this son, so to speak, does for his father. First, he wantonly runs down a young

girl, "tramples" her, Utterson says, and demands that the paternal Jekyll pay
the damages. Next, he carouses in Soho and thrashes what seems a supernumerary on the London scene, Sir Danvers Carew (who will become the
father-in-law figure in the film versions), just for the lusty thrill of killing.
All we ever know about Carew is that he was Jekyll's elder by a good many
years, that he was a pillar of established society, and that Hyde pummeled
him mercilessly.

What we begin to see is that Hyde is not so much Jekyll's double, his id,
but instead, as the transactional analysts would say, his repressed "child."
Hyde is the "child" that Jekyll, the single and celibate parent, has had to push
aside. As long as these two aspects are in conflict, Jekyll will never be simply
"adult." Jekyll almost says as much in his concluding "Full Statement": "[I]
had more than a father's interest; Hyde had more than a son's indifference"
(p. 91). He then proceeds to condense his own family history:

> I saw my life as a whole: I followed it up from the days of childhood, when I
> had walked with my father's hand, and through the self-denying toils of my
> professional life, to arrive again and again, with the same sense of unreality, at
> the damned horrors of the evening. (p. 94)

Toward the end Hyde has become such an obstreperous child that he threatens to destroy the parental Jekyll. So Jekyll abstains from the brew for two
months, but to no avail. While resting in Regent's Park, Hyde bursts forth
without pharmacological help, and, although Jekyll tries desperately to
repress him, Hyde clearly now is in control. And what does Hyde do to torment his parental host? He makes still bigger messes. Jekyll reports:

> Hence the ape-like tricks that he would play me, scrawling in my own hand
> blasphemies on the pages of my books, burning the letters and destroying the
> portrait of my father; and indeed, had it not been for his fear of death, he would
> long ago have ruined himself in order to involve me in the ruin. But his love of
> life is wonderful; I go further: I, who sicken and freeze at the mere thought of
> him, when I recall the abjection and passion of this attachment, and when I know
> how he fears my power to cut him off by suicide, I find it in my heart to pity
> him. (p. 101)

Surely, it is important that Hyde's enemies are Jekyll's books (Utterson had
been reported earlier as being "amazed" to find Hyde's "blasphemous anno-
tations" in one of Jekyll's "pious" works; p. 64) and this, along with the
destruction of the image of Jekyll's father, is tantalizing to speculate about.
Hyde is, after all, like the Frankenstein monster, going to clear a path for
Jekyll, a path Jekyll could only dream of clearing for himself. Hyde is Jekyll's

self-confessed "bravo." Yet, one of Jekyll's utterances says more of Hyde: "He, I say—I cannot say, I" (p. 98). But Hyde will clear Jekyll a path to where, to what? The answer is that this is simply not in the printed text, or, if it is there, it is only by exclusion. Women are the one important element so prevalent in the movie and stage and television versions of *Dr. Jekyll and Mr. Hyde*, yet are almost totally missing in the novella. There are really no women characters in Stevenson's text, only a maid, a match girl, and that nameless waif who is out late at night, that little girl whom Hyde tramples.[10]

Stevenson's "bogey tale" has been made one of the central horror myths of our time not because of literary or artistic merit, but because it was clearly telling the werewolf story right—or almost right. Let Protestant ministers like Joseph Jacobs claim that *"Dr. Jekyll and Mr. Hyde* stands beside *Pilgrim's Progress* and *Gulliver's Travels* as one of the three great allegories in English" (*Literary Studies*, p. 179); anyone who has read the first two might do well to pass it by. The attraction of Dr. Jekyll is not that it is a cautionary tale lauding Calvinist repression, but that it is a sensational playing-out of buried desire. It is an allegory, yes, or rather it has been made allegorical in the manner of pornography—it projects repressed desire *not* to censure it, but to experience it. The censure comes later, and has been softened by the contritional death scene.

The achievement of Thomas R. Sullivan's stage adaptation is that it started to exploit all the excitement and cast away the narrative slag, that is to say, the "art." The most obvious "art" to be deleted (and this invariably troubles literary critics who mourn the "coarsening" of almost any work when it changes medium) is the china-box structure. Here, for instance, is Professor Edwin M. Eigner in *Robert Louis Stevenson and Romantic Tradition* (1966): "After Sullivan's play, there were three successful movie versions ... each one did its bit to coarsen Stevenson's ideas" (p. 149). Eigner's response is typical, but in the transition from print to celluloid certain changes are inevitable, and certainly the most important is how the story can be told. Sophisticated shifts in point of view as with Enfield to Utterson to Lanyon to Jekyll simply cannot be achieved on the stage or on film. The novel can *enfold*, but the stage play and movie are most efficient when *unfolding*, when they essentially unreel before our eyes. Sullivan's 1887 adaptation does just that. It starts at the beginning, goes to the middle, and ends where it ought to, with the death of Hyde. In the third act Hyde transforms into Jekyll; in the last act Jekyll transforms into Hyde.[11]

In retrospect, Sullivan's most important contribution was not the untangling of narrative sequences, but the provision of family connections for Jekyll. Here they are as developed through the plot. Sir Danvers Carew, a widower, has a daughter Agnes who is being courted by the eligible Dr. Jekyll.

As the play opens Danvers is entertaining friends, Utterson and Lanyon, and the subject of Hyde comes up. A nasty man if ever there was one, all agree, just as pale Jekyll comes on the scene. Carew is fond of Jekyll and the subject changes to Jekyll's experiments or, in Carew's words, Jekyll's "scientific balderdash." If only the young doctor would abstain, things would improve and maybe Carew would soften. But Jekyll is committed and we overhear him telling Agnes that he is about to discover the "duplicity of man." Alas, however, just as he is expounding on the Janus-like nature of man, he feels a change coming on and must abruptly leave. "My God! I feel the change approaching. I must go at once to my cabinet." A skulking malevolent next appears at the window and asks Sir Danvers to fetch his daughter, and when the old man refuses, he is choked to death by the shadowy thing.

No sophistication here: boy loves girl, intended father-in-law disapproves, boy turns bestial and kills older man. The die is cast; Jekyll may struggle against Hyde, but in vain. We next see Hyde in his Soho apartment perversely toasting the ghost of Sir Danvers. It is a scene straight out of Elizabethan blood-and-thunder drama. Hyde is an evil and conniving marplot gloating over his victory: the damsel will soon be his! But wait, here come the police, so first a quick change—back into Jekyll. As Jekyll he soon beseeches Lanyon to bring Agnes to his window so he may explain all. Lanyon does; Jekyll confesses, but halfway through his plaint the change overcomes him. Heroically, Jekyll poisons Hyde before he can attack Agnes. Jekyll succeeds; he dies. The curtain falls.

Sullivan's play found the audience for *Dr. Jekyll*, an audience that is still very much in place: it is not a literary or sophisticated audience; it is an audience eager to be thrilled. Sullivan was not without imitators; in fact, at least two other full-length dramas were performed that season, as a result of improper copyright protection, but Sullivan's version prevailed. It had the pièce de résistance: Richard Mansfield. Mansfield's virtuosity in the dual role set the standard for all future performances—the actor who plays Jekyll must be a master of the art, for he has to unlock Hyde in full audience view. Ironically, Mansfield, aptly referred to as "jack of all trades, master of one," perfected the transformation that has done the original text the most damage. Thanks to Mansfield's on-stage virtuosity, Jekyll and Hyde will continue to be played by the same actor, and this almost mandates what we see in the photograph: Jekyll saintly and Hyde demonic. Hyde will never be small enough and young enough to do justice to the text, and Jekyll will always be too saintly and heaven-searching. It would now be almost impossible to play the parts with two actors because the audience has been conditioned to expect a dramatic triumph of one actor. So, from the very first, *Jekyll and Hyde* has been a "star vehicle," and most of the movie versions are known

Richard Mansfield playacting both "Dr. Jekyll and Mr. Hyde," 1887

not for the playwright or screenwriter but for the actor. So it was first the "Mansfield *Jekyll*," then the "Barrymore," then "Tracy," "Palance," "Michael Rennie," "Kirk Douglas," "Oliver Reed," and, most recently, the "David Hemmings *Jekyll*." The only exception to this rule is that the Fredric March rendition (ironically the best acted, at least according to the Academy of Motion Picture Sciences, which awarded March the only Oscar ever for a horror performance) is usually referred to as the "Mamoulian *Jekyll*," a tribute to Rouben Mamoulian's important contribution, not just to the story, but to filmmaking in general.

Dr. Jekyll has provided an almost countless number of renditions; arguably, the "divided personality" has provided the most popular subject of horror movies, maybe of all movies. From the 1908 Selig Polyscope Company's *The Modern Dr. Jekyll* to the Ken Russell/Arthur Penn/Paddy Chayefsky *Altered States* (1980), the idea has proved the basis of modern man's favorite stories. I am not so much interested in what this myth may say about the schizophrenic quality of modern life as I am in how the filmic versions have built, often unconsciously, on each other to produce a saga so prevalent that it is known to us before we enter the movie house. We get to know this story early, about the same time that we learn about Dracula and Frankenstein, and we never forget it. In addition, many of us know the movie versions even though we have never seen them flickering before our eyes. S. S. Prawer perceptively claimed in *Caligari's Children: The Film as Tale of Terror* (1980) that this adventure was almost made for film; that there is an almost perspicacious relationship between print and celluloid renditions already embedded in the novella. He reminds us that the "cinematic image existed well before the cinema" by citing this revealing passage from the text:

> Six o'clock struck on the bells of the church that was so conveniently near to Mr. Utterson's dwelling, and still he was digging at the problem. Hitherto it had touched him on the intellectual side alone; but now his imagination also was engaged, or rather enslaved; and as he lay and tossed in the gross darkness of the night and the curtained room, Mr. Enfield's tale went by before his mind *in a scroll of lighted pictures* [Prawer's italics]. He would be aware of the great field of lamps of a nocturnal city; then of the figure of a man walking swiftly; then of a child running from the doctor's; and then these met, and that human Juggernaut trod the child down and passed on regardless of her screams. Or else he would see a room in a rich house, where his friend lay asleep, dreaming and smiling at his dreams; and then the door of that room would be opened, the curtains of the bed plucked apart, the sleeper recalled, and lo! there would stand by his side a figure to whom power was given, and even at that dead hour, he must rise and do its bidding. The figure in these two phases haunted the lawyer all night; and if at any time he dozed over, it was but to see it glide more stealthily through sleeping houses, or move the more swiftly and still the more swiftly, even to dizziness, through wider labyrinths of lamplighted city, and at every street corner crush a child and leave her screaming. And still the figure had no face by which he might know it; even in his dreams, it had no face, or one that baffled him and melted before his eyes; and thus it was that there sprang up and grew apace in the lawyer's mind a singularly strong, almost an inordinate, curiosity to behold the features of the real Mr. Hyde. (pp. 13–14)

Prawer is correct, of course. This description *is* cinematic, not because Stevenson was anticipating film, but because film takes its inspiration from the same source as the horror story—dream-life. Movies are indeed, as the surrealists loved to say, "dreaming with the eyes open," the cinéma vérité of the unconscious. We may not need Suzanne Langer to remind us what everyone since Georges Méliès has known, but it helps to be reminded: films are dreams.

I would like to concentrate on the major productions of this version of the ancient werewolf fable by starting with the American versions: Barrymore, March, and Tracy, and concluding with the English versions made by Hammer in the 1960s. A few general points can be noted at the outset. First, Jekyll/Hyde is a werewolf, not a Wolfman transformation, which is to say that Jekyll always initially desires the change. Second, the woman introduced in the Sullivan stage play remains, but is joined by another woman who becomes Hyde's ostensible counterpart. Third, the father-in-law remains a constant motif and is usually pummeled to death with Jekyll's walking stick which, as we have seen in the Wolfman saga, has a rather precise sexual meaning. Fourth, there is little experimentation with the central action other than the attribution of motivation to Jekyll, motivation that usually entails altruism. And finally, at the end, Hyde is usually transformed à la the Wolfman back into Jekyll.

After Colonel William Selig's one-reeler, *The Modern Dr. Jekyll* (1908), in which the stage play was condensed and filmed complete with rising and falling curtain all in fifteen minutes, there were a number of lesser versions, the most influential being King Baggot's Universal production of 1913. A year earlier there had been a version interesting primarily because it is the only major version to use two actors for the double parts: James Cruz as Jekyll and Henry Benham as Hyde. The Cruz/Benham version was moderately successful; the Baggot version was Universal's biggest hit of 1913. The lesson was not soon forgotten; from then on one actor would play both parts. The retelling that all horror film buffs would love to see, however, is F. W. Murnau's *The Head of Janus* (1920, *Der Januskoph*), but this film is apparently lost, which is not surprising considering Murnau's legendary carelessness. As with *Nosferatu*, Murnau reportedly took the Stevenson story—protected by the copyright—changed the names of Jekyll and Hyde to Dr. Warren and Mr. O'Conner, altered the plot a bit, and filmed it. Only luck and greed saved the print of *Nosferatu*, and so who knows, maybe this print will show up. Conrad Veidt's metamorphosis is supposedly stunning, and since Bela Lugosi played the part of Poole, the butler, it would be wonderful to see.

We are left with ten or so films adapting the basic story prior to 1920. So by the time Adolph Zukor signed John Barrymore in 1920 for Paramount's *Dr. Jekyll and Mr. Hyde*, the concept was already well established. Still, the director, John Robertson, took few, but important, chances with it. One

John Barrymore as Hyde, 1920 (Paramount Studios)

chance he took was having Sir George, the intended father-in-law, attempt to debauch Jekyll by introducing the brittle doctor to London low-life. And another chance was in having Barrymore portray Hyde as a giant tarantula with pointy head, long black locks, stooping walk, and talons. Hyde looks rather like an albino coconut with dark bangs. We even see a whole dream sequence in which the huge tarantula with Hyde's head comes crawling onto a sleeping Jekyll, but these changes did not take hold. The father-in-law should not be a Lord Henry to Jekyll's Dorian Gray, and the spider is a most inappropriate image to convey Hyde's virility. Robertson succeeded elsewhere. First, at the end, after Jekyll has done in Hyde by drinking poison (from a poison ring—another motif soon dropped in later versions), we see, thanks to stop-action photography, the transformation *back* to Jekyll. Of course, this plays havoc with Stevenson's supposed theme of Calvinist irredemption, but it made Barrymore fans happy to know that the Great Profile received a proper Hollywood ending after all. The other major change was more important. Stevenson's eight-year-old girl who was run over by the Hyde "juggernaut" and was then made into Jekyll's fiancée in the Sullivan play is here split in two: the love object, Carew's daughter, and the lust object, a sultry Italian dancer. This splitting of the female role at last allows us to see what was lurking in Stevenson's text; Hyde's aggression is sexual and its object is displaced from Jekyll's porcelain madonna to the fleshy tramp. The rest of this movie simply re-creates the Sullivan play, but the important changes had been wrought and the story would always be the stronger for it.

Yet whoever mentions John B. Robinson as the director of this film? No one, but within a year of this rendition the stage director Rouben Mamoulian remade the story almost perfectly.[12] After Mamoulian, *Jekyll and Hyde* would never return to the stage—it was forevermore a movie. Everything that is stuffed into those slack terms beloved by moviemakers and press agents, "state of the art" and "production values," is here as of 1931: subjective camera, voice-over dialogue, 360-degree pans, split screen, dissolves, horizontal and diagonal wipes, contrast shots, montage, superimposition, arresting angles, jump cuts, and, best of all, the transformation scenes.[13] This is one of the few movies for which the frame-by-frame reproduction by the Film Classic Library (ed. Richard J. Anobile) truly reveals the director's art. But director's art is not what I am interested in here; what makes this version so interesting in terms of horror is that it is the first of the self-consciously Freudian versions. In fact, Jekyll states his interest in "psychoanalysis" (the word is actually used) right from the start. He wants to separate the feral part of the self and neutralize it; he wants to separate the id from the ego in hopes that the superego will prevail. Almost as important is the fact that, whether we like it or not, we are forced to sympathize, even empathize, with the protagonist. We become Jekyll, thanks to the justly famous opening shots in which we merge, via the subjective camera, into his consciousness; we link our fate to his. We move with him as he pounds the Bach fugue from his organ; those are our hands; we rise and travel to the lecture room. Then the camera pans 360-degrees and now, for the first time, we are outside and we see him straightaway. Again and again we hear his heartbeat (actually Mamoulian's), see with his eyes, and, thanks to the most artful use of a central image in all the Jekyll/Hyde movies, watch in the mirror as the self—ourself, in a sense— comes apart.

To the best of my knowledge this is the first Hollywood film in which we in the audience are forced to become stalk-and-slasher. For after Jekyll has raised the effervescing potion to our lips, the room whirls around us, we look in the mirror, and there Hyde is coming out of us. And what does Jekyll do now that he has been transformed? Almost immediately he starts to chase women. This is such a cliché now since the rip-'em-ups of the 1970s, but it was dramatically powerful in the thirties. The love/lust situation is the same as in the Barrymore version: Jekyll is caught between Muriel Carew, pale daughter of the dotty General Carew, and "Champagne" Ivy Pierson, the colorful girl from the bawdy house. The General considers Jekyll's marriage proposal untimely, "positively indecent," and wants the young couple to wait for the anniversary of his own marriage eight months hence. His repressive, even capricious, officiousness releases Jekyll from guilt over letting his libidinous part come loose. After all, this movie seems to imply, a man has urges beyond his control. Desire must be served. So it is the General's sexual quarantine of his daughter that makes Jekyll's future actions vaguely heroic because Jekyll will preserve Miriam's virginity by allowing his Hyde to visit Ivy. In the terms of this movie Jekyll willingly transforms lest his fiancée be stained: civilization has its own discontents and this is one of them.

Ironically, the price of this civilization is displaced savagery. Hyde is aboriginal, a Neanderthal, not quite a King Kong, but certainly moving back in that simian direction. Hyde exults in animal-like enthusiasm (his first act is to run out hatless into the rain—something Jekyll would never do), but he is also profoundly human. As he becomes more sure of himself he wants more than to indulge the impulses of his own flesh; he must control the flesh of others. His own sexual satisfaction soon depends on torture. He mutilates Ivy, beats her, bites her, whips her, and menaces her. The March Hyde lives out the implications of the Barrymore Hyde. This Hyde is so nasty that it even helped bring about the Production Code censorship in 1934. I suppose one might argue that, after the successes of Universal's *Dracula* and *Frankenstein*, violence was becoming acceptable, but in 1931 *Dr. Jekyll and Mr. Hyde* must have been shocking to see. Today, of course, Hyde would be wielding a yard-long phallic knife instead of his cane and doing all his quartering and dicing in slow motion. Even so, Mamoulian's direction still jolts, because by the time Hyde is out of Jekyll, we have come to sympathize with him. We don't need the subjective camera any longer. Jekyll is so brittle and simpering, so much the plaster saint, that we almost feel relieved to see Hyde. Jekyll too seems almost relieved with Hyde. So when Muriel finally persuades her stuffy father to relent, Jekyll turns his back on her, goes back to his organ, and there plays a joyous but masturbatory hallelujah by himself. His secret desires will be entertained.

Jekyll, like Victor Frankenstein, wants what he knows he should not have. Only his Hyde, his remote-control "bravo," can get it while at the same time protecting Jekyll, who is supposedly protecting Muriel. Remember, Jekyll ostensibly lets Hyde go in order to save Muriel. So, appropriately en route to publicly announce his engagement, Jekyll pauses in Regent's Park, sees a cat strangle an innocent bird (this, a too contrived but nonetheless an effective scene, has been cut from the current print; Mamoulian claims it was not censored but was stolen by a collector), and for the first time he transforms into Hyde without any pharmacological help. Hyde simply pushes out through Jekyll. Although as Jekyll he has given his word to Ivy that Hyde would nevermore molest her, now Hyde, loose at last, makes straightaway for Soho. He is more bestial than ever before—the fun is over for both victim and voyeur.

Hyde is capriciously cruel. He mimics Jekyll's voice and repeats to Ivy what only Jekyll could have known: Jekyll's pledge of protection. Hyde makes sure Ivy knows who Jekyll really is. It is a wretched scene. After he physically and psychologically subdues her, he spreads her body out on the bed, saying, "There, there, my sweet, there, my dove, there, my little bride." Suddenly all the images coalesce—he is the cat, she the bird; he the groom, she his chosen bride. He will have her at last, just as the Frankenstein monster had Elizabeth and Dracula had Lucy. Hyde drops below the camera eye and we hear the screams—first of rape, then strangulation. From here the plot is predictable: the scene with Lanyon, the retransformation, Jekyll's promise not to stray again ("I have trespassed on God's domain"), and then the straying back to Hyde. Finally, Jekyll returns to sexless Miriam. Heroically, at least for Jekyll, he promises to give her up—he is, after all, a sinner—and even though she forgives him, he will renounce her forever. Once again, one has the lingering feeling that this is not as difficult as Jekyll makes it out to be. He then transforms back into Hyde, who makes a desultory pass at her just as her father enters. Hyde clubs the father to death with Jekyll's walking stick. Then there is the quick trip back to the lab pursued by the mob and at last Hyde's death at the hands of the police with his return to Jekyll à la Barrymore and Chaney. This denouement is one of the fastest ever filmed. It is, after all, straight anticlimax, and the audience knows it.

There is no hint of incest in either the Barrymore or March versions. There is no hint of incest in the Mansfield/Sullivan play and certainly none whatsoever in the Stevenson novella. As of 1932 the story had been expanded, yes, but only to provide causality and verisimilitude. Jekyll "loves" a woman whom some stuffy, tyrannical father-figure denies to him. "You won't get close to this woman, at least not while I'm around," the father says, and the younger man is so frustrated that he transforms in order to get what he wants. In his transformed personage he is indeed sexual, nay, carnal, with a woman, but she is not the woman he supposedly wants. As a matter of fact, Hyde never tries to touch the woman Jekyll professes to love. Instead, he concentrates his wrath on street women and on Jekyll's future father-in-law. In all the adaptations of Stevenson's novella the Sir/General Danvers Carew character plays the part of the intended father-in-law, and in all versions he is brutally clubbed to death with Jekyll's cane. Could it be that what is developing here is yet another rendition of the Ur-horror story—the story of the family romance, and beneath that, of the primal horde? Except that here the horde is composed of just two: Jekyll the instigator and Hyde the perpetrator, brothers under the skin. Boy wants girl, patriarch denies, boy initially sublimates aggression which leads to transformation, which in turn "frees" one part of his personality to act the repression out. And who is the object of violence? It is the hoarding father. The Hyde persona overthrows the patriarch not so much to get the forbidden daughter as to express the biological demands of youth. Ironically, Hyde is pure "child" brought forth from Jekyll because Jekyll is unwilling to be "parented" any longer. What has made *Dr. Jekyll and Mr. Hyde* a modern horror is exactly what has made the vampire and the man-created monster into vehicles for the shivers: the fiend performs the tabooed acts that the public, polite protagonist could only dream of. And monsters, we would do well to recall, never make mistakes.

I mention this now because the most intriguing version of the saga is Victor Fleming's 1941 *Dr. Jekyll and Mr. Hyde* starring Spencer Tracy. I think everyone has been surprised at how good this rendition is, if only because here is a horror film produced under the auspices of a man, Louis B. Mayer, who knew better than anyone how to make ladies' pictures. And Mayer chose a ladies' director, Victor Fleming, who chose an actor from ladies' movies, Spencer Tracy. This movie is an extraordinary triumph: a ladies' horror movie. The core of this film is that the women are switched: the "bad"— i.e., sexual—woman is played by a lady, Ingrid Bergman, while the "lady" is played by a woman with a screen history elsewhere, Lana Turner. This casting against the grain was supposedly made by the stars themselves, which makes a nice story, but ignores the fact that Mayer always made it his business to decide how much skin could be shown, and whose. In any case the switch was a stroke of genius and luck: it worked. It worked because in a psychosexual sense the women are interchangeable. They are, after all, just like Jekyll and Hyde, parts of the same human. When Hyde attacks Ivy, a part of Jekyll is really attacking Miriam.

The other arresting aspect of the Tracy version is that Jekyll is nearly adopted into the surrogate family of the Carews, here called the Emerys. Again there is no mother figure and the father, Sir Charles, is a crusty fellow who stands in the way of the young lovers' happiness, that is to say— although it never is—their sexual union. All along it is clear that Sir Charles is fond of his future son-in-law, even addressing Jekyll: "Harry, I've always wanted a son; now you're going to be that," but before "Harry" can wed Beatrix (no longer Alice or Miriam), the father intercedes in the name of social decorum and, as we know, "forces" poor Harry to retreat into his lab.

Tracy's Jekyll is much more wry and self-deprecating than March's or Barrymore's, and his Ivy (Bergman) is much more the country girl than previous

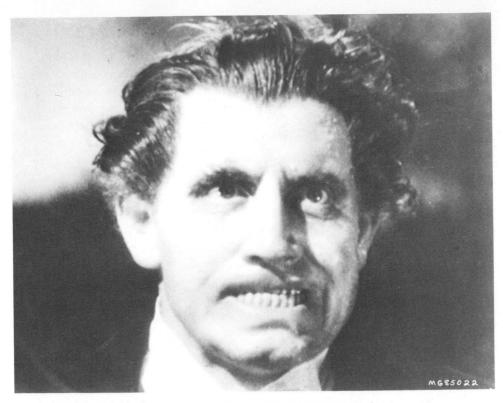

Spencer Tracy as Hyde, 1941 (M-G-M Studios)

ones. She is so much the farmer's daughter that we don't expect her to be pouring champagne, but milk. She is so fresh and good that we have the distinct impression that Jekyll and Ivy could be happy together but, again, the other woman's father makes this impossible. Finding that his willful Beatrix has gone unchaperoned to Jekyll's house in the evening, Sir Charles cancels the wedding and takes his daughter where M-G-M fathers always go to keep the boys away—to the Continent. What is a potent young man to do? Jekyll knows. He goes back up to his room and, as in the masturbatory adolescent fantasy, he solves the problem by transforming into a stronger and more manly figure; he becomes Hyde.

Here the film turns inward to portray Jekyll's dream-life. We see a series of Freudian montages contrived to make sure we don't miss the point. Ivy pulls the cork out of Jekyll's bottle; Jekyll is in a chariot driving horses which turn into the nude figures of Beatrix and Ivy, the two women sinking now into seminal mud—everything but trains going into tunnels and waves crashing on the shore. It is a sign of changing times, however, that while critics of the forties usually thought the montage work of Peter Ballbush detracted from the story line, critics of *Altered States*, the most recent update of Jekyll/

Hyde, usually forgot the plot to praise the optical effects. Perhaps this is the result of our concentration on technique over story line, or it may simply be that the exciting content of Jekyll and Hyde has been expropriated by the stalk-and-slash genre, and hence all that the story now carries is the visual metamorphosis. After all, we now all know exactly how the story goes before we enter the theater.

In any case, the transformation episode in the Tracy version is what might be expected from Victor Fleming fresh from his *Gone with the Wind* triumph. M-G-M, perhaps knowing that they would not be able to surpass the Mamoulian version in tension, and perhaps also to protect themselves from charges of blatant plagiarism, bought up all the Paramount prints and stored them away. Comparisons were inevitable, however, if only because Tracy had decided to use no makeup but instead get Hyde out on his own. Tracy's Jekyll is certainly more interesting than earlier ones, but, alas, his Hyde is too much the avuncular Chicago gangster. This Hyde suffers only from terminal bad manners. It may well be that the only way to get Hyde properly foul is to first make Jekyll officiously priggish.

After Sir Charles relents and the nuptial date is set, Jekyll pledges to Ivy that Hyde will nevermore molest her—"on my honor as an English gentleman, I give you my word." Here follows the now-obligatory transformation scene in the park, the cloak and walking-stick sequence, the Ivy beatings between spits of cherry pits, the missed wedding announcement party which Hyde "saves" Jekyll from having to attend, the Lanyon scene, complete with backward transformation, and then finally the family destruction. In this version Jekyll goes to Beatrix to tell her that he won't marry her because he has changed in the park without drinking the nostrum and that now he can't be trusted. In a clever inversion of Hollywood melodrama he goes to the woman he "loves" as Jekyll, but becomes a Hyde in her presence. Beauty does not tame the beast; it releases it. Once the monster has broken loose, Beatrix faints, Hyde kills Sir Charles with Jekyll's cane, returns home to be recognized by Lanyon, who shoots him, and once again, like the Wolfman in death, Hyde returns to Jekyll. And, like the vampire in death, Jekyll is now at last happy.

Considering the films that followed this version, it might have been better to let poor Jekyll be as he was here, in final peace. Unfortunately, the price of success in popular culture is eternal life, and Jekyll was soon resurrected to wreak more havoc on the family. Of his many subsequent incarnations little need be said other than that they were, by and large, much more innovative than the resuscitations of the vampire, the manmade monster, the mummy, and other feature creatures, but less coherent. What seems to have happened is that certain aspects of the Jekyll/Hyde myth have been abstracted and performed independently so that, for instance, the stalk-and-slash motif and the computer-generated video transformation have become full-length cinema subjects on their own. Look back twenty years to such third-generation Jekylls as *Son of Dr. Jekyll* (1951) or *Daughter of Dr. Jekyll* (1957) and it is clear that the myth was already starting to unravel. Yet, as we have seen before, when mindless exploitation happens, startling innovations often occur. Once again it was Hammer Studios, ever anxious to add yet another monster to their steadily expanding chamber of horrors, that made Jekyll/Hyde over in their own image—namely, they made Hyde overtly and irredeemably, and even attractively, sexual. By so doing they showed us clearly what had always lurked below the murky waters of Stevenson's "crawler."

In *The Two Faces of Dr. Jekyll* (1960) Terence Fisher did the obvious: he told the story like an unreconstructed Freudian, and he almost succeeded. Fisher made Jekyll modern, for he is played as a simpering pedant while Hyde comes across as a fun-loving dilettante. In the battle between superego and id, the id will always be more interesting; Milton had certainly shown us that. But it would not be a Hammer film without a touch of sadism, and in this case the touch is more like a wallop. Hyde insists on debauching, even raping, Jekyll's wife. First, Hyde bankrolls the sexual onslaught of Mrs. Jekyll (played by the most un-wife-like Dawn Addams) by using a lecherous womanizer, but this turns sour when libertine and wife fall in love. Hyde then cuckolds Jekyll: he seduces, with bribes, the "better half" of his better half. And, of course, Mrs. Jekyll really loves it. This is the lewd stuff of dirty jokes which even eighteen-year-olds found dull, if not offensive, and *The Two Faces of Dr. Jekyll* failed at the box office. Things end in absolute pandemonium as Hyde frames Jekyll for some killings, engineers what seems to be Jekyll's death by fire, but is then caught in a hurry-up finale as he transforms into Jekyll, just as Hyde is exonerated by the law and is shot by the police. Terence Fisher was willing to accept what the audience did not want to be told: Hyde is not irredeemable. Mrs. Jekyll's rape scene is lifted straight from Hammer's stock footage of Dracula: moonlight, evening cape, unhasping the window, initial female gasp, slow-motion attack as molester bows to victim, cut! And the next scene, the at-last satisfied sexual look of contentment on her face. In the vampire movie such illicit pleasure must not go unpunished, but in *The Two Faces of Dr. Jekyll* there is no one able to play the avenger. As Fisher himself confessed,

> There was not one redeeming character in *The Two Faces of Dr. Jekyll*. Only one person had any semblance of good in him and that was Jekyll's friend who said, for God's sake be careful about what you're doing. And he didn't do much stopping. They were basically a shoddy lot, weren't they? Jekyll, who allowed himself to become shoddy. Chris Lee [who played the voluptuary], was shoddy. A wife

who was no good anyway. God—raped by her reconstructed husband! It was an exercise, rightly or wrongly, badly done or well done, in evil. You didn't have a single character in that story who was worth tuppence ha'penny. ("Interview with Harry Ringel," pp. 24, 26.)

Hammer's next attempt is a different story altogether.[14] *Dr. Jekyll and Sister Hyde* (1971) is, for me, the most interesting version yet told, in large part because it is so unashamedly exploitive. It wants everybody: Jack the Ripper, Burke and Hare, the mad doctor, Christine Jorgensen, the Frankenstein monster—you name them, they're here. And while spreading fuses all over, Roy Ward Baker at last detonates the charge that has always rumbled within the myth. He explains just exactly who that little girl in Stevenson's story was, how she developed through the Barrymore/March/Tracy renditions, and why she is so central to the eruption of horror. For the one question that we must always ask of a transformation monster like Hyde is not why is he doing all these awful things, but why they are supposed to be (but are not) so awful to the protagonist. Or, from a different point of view, why should the standard movie version in which the father-in-law denies the young doctor a female mate produce such catastrophic results: to wit, the transformation, the sexual sadism inflicted on the "other woman," the killing of the father-in-law, and the eventual self-destruction? Admittedly this almost ritualistic behavior shows what happens when a potent young man is separated from his biological destiny, but perhaps things are more complex. Perhaps the myth is telling us that biological destiny depends as much on staying away from certain mates as it does on choosing the proper ones. Perhaps the forbidden girl is not just any girl, but the daughter of a man who shares a special family relationship with the young man. It is when we examine the characters surrounding the fated lovers that we may indeed find reasons to prohibit the advances of this particular young man toward this particular young woman.

In *Dr. Jekyll and Sister Hyde* Dr. Jekyll (Ralph Bates) is a young man, complete with a Prince Valiant hairdo and dimple, who has rented a laboratory-apartment next to the Spencers—a mother and two children, Howard and Susan. Jekyll is the protégé of Professor Robinson, a fatherly mentor who stops by from time to time to check on the young man's experiments. Jekyll goes through the usual limp-wristed altruistic rigamarole about setting up his lab just right, trying to solve the problem of mortality, brewing up the elixir, and generally overstepping the bounds of science "to delve into knowledge best unknown." Along the way he finds that the "pick-me-up" potion does not let a monster out of hiding, but rather liberates "the opposite sex we have within." So having practiced on fruit flies, he takes some of the

Ralph Bates and Martine Beswick as *Dr. Jekyll and Sister Hyde,* 1971 (Hammer Studios)

drug himself and what should appear as he stands nonplussed before his full-length mirror but his female double (Martine Beswick), complete with Prince Valiant hairdo and dimple.

If Hammer had played this out for the frisson of androgyny, as an assertion of enduring polymorphous perversity, that would have been one thing, but there's no lasting horror in that; just shock. Hammer was not above exploiting the obvious; they gleefully advertised the movie with the words: "WARNING! The sexual transformation of a man into a woman will actually take place before your eyes." But the tremors of Jekyll looking down to see his swelling cleavage simply could not sustain the picture. The outcome of the story is that Sister Hyde falls in love with Howard Spencer, while Brother Jekyll pairs up with Howard's sister, Susan. Susan and Howard think that Jekyll and his unnamed female companion (his female transformation) are brother and sister. One can imagine the sexual taboos that almost get violated—I say "almost" because Hammer was always wise enough not to do what was implied. So just as "brother" Howard is about to seduce (be seduced by) Sister Hyde, she discreetly goes to "powder her nose" and returns as Brother Jekyll, who explains to the priapic Howard that his "sister" has been detained.

Soon Sister Hyde turns nasty and threatens to take over her brother's body. It seems she is too interested in Howard. To prevent her from taking control, Jekyll now has to kill women for the transforming chemicals (partly manufactured from the secretions of mysterious unnamed female glands); hence he becomes Jack the Ripper after his lackeys, Burke and Hare, have been caught. This movie spares nothing. Professor Robinson, the fatherly mentor, is suspicious about Jekyll's nocturnal wanderings and so Sister Hyde is sent to silence the venerable elder. In a scene dripping with seduction motifs she first sexually tempts the professor and then brutally stabs him to death. By now she is so powerful that Jekyll is desperate; for instance, just when he is all ready to escort Susan to the theater, Sister Hyde commandeers his body and rushes to the waiting arms of Howard. This battle of the sexes simply cannot continue. Jekyll needs one last draft of the elixir and then he will end it all. But after he has slashed his last victim to get the precious secretions, he is pursued by the police, is chased across the rooftops, slips, and is literally hanging by his fingernails. Here we cut to a close-up of those strong, hairy hands; we watch them elongate and become hairless. Sister Hyde is demanding to get out! She succeeds, but being of the weaker sex, she can't hang on and falls into the waiting arms of the police.

This is pretty heady stuff: brother/sister incest, father/daughter incest, bisexuality, androgyny; it must have been only the result of great restraint that Brian Clemens, author of the screenplay, did not write Brother Jekyll into the arms of Mrs. Spencer. After all, Sister Hyde had made it into the waiting arms of Professor Robinson. Hammer wasn't exaggerating when it warned: "Parents, be sure your children are sufficiently mature to witness the intimate details of this frank and revealing film." Naturally, however, the studio was delighted when this, the "Adult Version of Jekyll and Hyde," was awarded a PG rating.

Ironically, the two central aspects of the myth have become so potent that they can no longer be played out together. On the one hand, the transformation scene has become so much an actor's event that whole movies, such as Boris Karloff's *Abbott and Costello Meet Dr. Jekyll and Mr. Hyde* and Jerry Lewis' *The Nutty Professor* (1962), have been constructed only to offer it up in parody. Meanwhile, actors like Jack Palance, Kirk Douglas, Michael Rennie, and, most recently, David Hemmings have played it straight, but this retelling seems now to be reserved for television specials. There seems to be no current film audience for this version, or at least no major studios think so. However, reports of Hyde's demise have been exaggerated. What seems to have happened is that the werewolf myth has subsumed its own Jekyll/

Hyde variant and is now being told for its bestial misogyny. I think a clear case can be made that the "horror-of-personality" subgenre, coined by Charles Derry in *Dark Dreams: A Psychological History of Modern Horror Film* (1977), evolved from this werewolf/Wolfman, Jekyll/Hyde strain: a beastly self gets loose from its docile host and savagely attacks very specific women. Starting after the *films noir* of the forties, there has been a continual succession of dual-personality monsters along the line of brittle Jekyll and feral Hyde. One should note the number of sister victims even when the attacker is herself female, albeit a mannish female. Here are just a few films featuring schizophrenia from the 1960s and early 1970s: *Psycho* (1960), *Peeping Tom* (1962), *Whatever Happened to Baby Jane?* (1962), *Maniac* (1963), *Dementia 13* (1963), *Hush, Hush, Sweet Charlotte* (1964), *Repulsion* (1965), *Targets* (1968), *Pretty Poison* (1968), *Play Misty for Me* (1971), *What's the Matter with Helen?* (1971), *Images* (1972), and *Sisters* (1973). Now clearly these are vastly different films, many simply Grand Guignol, but they show our continuing interest in what may happen when the forces of repression are weaker than the potency of the beast within.

Then around the mid–1970s even this, the psychopathic schizophrenic, took yet another turn. Causality was dispensed with and the beast springs forth with no explanation. "It" just is, and it just wants to be malicious. Doubling was shoved aside by demonism. Think only of the purely destructive sociopaths in *Friday the 13th*, *Halloween*, *When a Stranger Calls*, *He Knows You're Alone*, and you have the picture; in fact, almost a decade of such pictures. As with all other mindless vignettes of terror, this one too will pass as it bores the audience away with repetition. We currently are witnessing the motif of the monstrous malignancy which literally emerges from the host-body in a mess of blood and gore, as in *Alien*, *The Beast Within*, or *Parasite*, but here I am getting ahead of myself. Before we examine the contemporary mutations of Dr. Jekyll/Mr. Wolfman, let me survey the "contemporary scene" to establish the necessary context by tracing the routes of other less successful emissaries of fright.

6

A Modern Bestiary

"Forgive me, I forget how ugly I am. I am your friend, so don't look at me . . . ."
The Beast/Phantom/Hunchback/Creature to his Beauty

The vampire, the hulk-with-no-name, and the transformation monster have all slithered up from the myth pool to become staple images on the dry land of popular culture because we want, and need, them around. We don't have to dream them anymore; veritable industries have been built to tell their stories. The minute we see the incisors, or the neck bolt, or the hirsute visage we immediately know what is to follow. No one needs to explain them: they are drawn all over the walls of the modern cave. Omnipresent during parts of early adolescence, these shapes may have become vulgar and trivial to us now, but that is only because we have outgrown our need for them. What were once insights become clichés after we have seen them too many times. When our children eat "Count Chocula" and "Frankenberry" for breakfast, they are ingesting more than cereal, and when they suddenly lose their taste for this sugary goo, it is because they have developed new appetites that must be satisfied. What I would like to do now is wade back into the brackish pool of modern horror myths and examine some of the monsters who are still trapped in the mire. For very often, when horror narratives do not work properly, we can see how minor shifts in sequence, victims, and imagery can produce major changes in our response.

To do this I would like to retrace the three paths we have already followed: the trails of Dracula, Frankenstein, and Dr. Jekyll/Mr. Wolfman, except that this time I would like to look briefly at some of the mutants that either died aborning or became stranded along the way. On the sides of the veritable thoroughfare of the vampire we can see others who have also cheated death, like the mummy and zombie, as well as those who are the devil incarnate. The beaten track of the Frankenstein monster seems to divide in this century into the tale of the mad doctor who is "tampering with the secrets of nature" and into a different, and often totally independent, story of a brute who may very well be sympathetic. Dr. Phibes, Dr. Moreau, Dr. Cyclops, The Invisible Man are all examples of the Faustian scientist, while the "incredible hulk" has been reincarnated in this century, first as the up-dated Golem, then King Kong and all the little Kongs, then the Creature from Below (Black Lagoon, 20,000 Fathoms), and today as a lot of rather stupid monsters along the genetic lines of the Japanese Godzilla, Mothra, and Rodan.[1] The transformation monster has come into his own, thanks to our continuing interest in schizophrenia, becoming by turns Norman Bates in *Psycho* and Mark Lewis in *Peeping Tom* (both 1960) and most recently reincarnated as the endless stalk-and-slashers operating out of most every cellar and attic in the neighborhood. But as I suggested earlier, since these psychopaths affect us with fear and rarely dread, I consider them more terror molesters than horror monsters. They frighten us until we understand them; then they have a tendency to become dull and predictable. What is truly terrible in the story of the transformation monster is incomplete transformation, as in *The Fly* cycle, in *Alligator People*, or in *The Island of Dr. Moreau*. The poor creatures we know as the Hunchback (especially of Notre Dame), the Phantom of the Opera, and the mad master of the waxworks are also mid-transformation monsters, or, rather, transfigured creatures who have not been able to fit into human categories. They are descendants of the Beast from the "Beauty and the Beast" fairy tales who produce additional shivers by threatening to violate sexual conventions.

Finally, in this chapter, I would like to pay some attention to a rather curious phenomenon of the last twenty years, a development which Detroit would probably call the "downsizing" of the monster product: children and childlike forms have become the compact vehicles for traditional acts of horror. We will follow the rather narrow pathway for pint-sized vampires, starting with *Grave of the Undead* and including *'Salem's Lot*, the nasty darling of the *The Bad Seed*, mini-zombies in *The Children*, telekinetic teens in *Carrie* and *The Changeling*, demonettes in *The Omen* and *The Exorcist*, and especially, since the implications of *Rosemary's Baby*, a nursery full of baby cannibals from *Eraserhead, Inseminoid, The Brood, It's Alive*, and maybe even *Alien*.

I think the reason that the mummy and the zombie never had the success of their cousin, the vampire, is because they are essentially orphans; they have no family and less prospect of developing one. Unless there is a family circle to breach, there is little hope for long-lasting shivers. True, life beyond the grave is terrible, but is it horrible? The mummy, who is hopelessly bogged down in a complicated story that involves capturing his reincarnated girl-princess and returning with her to the world of the dead, lumbered his way through about ten films on both sides of the Atlantic without developing a coherent text, let alone a family. What is really under all that gauze and why can't he articulate his desires? He can talk all right, but no one knows what it is he has to say. As Russell Baker once mused, the mummy is the only monster who seems to have memorized Amy Vanderbilt. When asked to dinner by the English archeologist who has desecrated his tomb, the man of bandages declines, saying only, "I regret I am currently too occupied to accept invitations." He is such a perfect gentleman that we never know exactly what it is that he is "occupied" by. Clearly, this confusion is purposeful in the short run, but has denied the mummy an enduring audience.

The initial *Mummy* (1932) is a veritable remake of *Dracula*, which is not surprising, considering it was written by the same adaptor, John L. Balderson.[2] Essentially, the story line tells us how the mummy has been revived by some English archeologists who have discovered a sacred scroll that, when read, brings the dead back to life. Centuries ago, the mummy himself had used the scroll to resuscitate his dearly beloved, but forbidden, princess. Now, accidentally revived by the archeologists, he attempts to revive his ancient love, but must settle for her spirit reincarnated in Helen Grosvenor, the young ward of Dr. Muller (played by Edward Van Sloan, the Van Helsing of *Dracula*). This father/surrogate-daughter relationship is developed but never exploited. The relationship is especially tantalizing to speculate about because Muller is the leader of the young boys who try to destroy the mummy. The plot is very confusing: it seems that Helen is none other than the virgin princess whom the mummy had loved unwisely in life and for whom he was buried alive by the ancient priests of Isis. She is the princess; he the trusted guardian who has violated her sanctity with his passion. Instead of intensifying this aspect, the moviemakers, especially Karl Freund, concentrated on a lot of rigamarole about the Scroll of Toth, the transformation of the mummy from Im-ho-tep to Ardath Bey, the spirit transfer of princess to Helen, and in so doing condemned their monster to eternal bluster.

Although the 1932 plot has more wrinkles than the protagonist, this film is much better than what followed. In later renditions, with titles like *The Mummy's Hand, . . . Tomb, . . . Ghost, . . . Shroud, . . . Curse*, there is still more hoopla made about tana leaves, primordial swamps, Kharis, fez-topped Egyptians, and such inappropriate shifts as moving the modern story into a small New England town or a London townhouse. As the story is now being told, the monster has all but disappeared and only the metempsychosis non-sense remains. Until the smoldering sexual relationships are made explicitly incestuous or forbidden (as they are in the adaptations of Stoker's *The Jewel of the Seven Stars*), the Bandaged One will probably molder for a few thousand more years.

While the mummy has been mired in plot complexities, the most important of which is our confusion about the relationship between events in the distant past and what is now occurring between the restored corpse and his reincarnated love, the zombie myth seems flawed by its lack of complexity. The zombie is really a mummy in street clothes with no love life and a big appetite. Both are automatons; neither is cunning nor heroic. They simply lumber about (Karloff called it "my little walk"), shuffling their feet like date-less high school students before the prom. As opposed to the vampire, who is crafty, circumspect, and erotic, these two cousins are subhuman slugs.

So why should the zombie be currently so popular and the mummy still dormant? After Hammer Studios' four mummy films, in which they lifted the Universal apparatus (in exchange for distribution rights), added color and cleavage, and then replayed the myth to a whole new generation, there seemed to be no more audience interest. Oddly enough, while the first impetus for the Universal saga was the 1931 discovery of the tomb of Tutankhamen, the elaborate traveling show of King Tut's riches a few years ago was sufficient to inspire huge museum lines, but no cinematic revival. Meanwhile, the zombie has been doing a land-office business eating up all in sight. This is not really the result of electronic arcade games, which give the zombie an appropriate milieu, but the result of a low-budget horror film made in 1967 by George Romero. For here in *Night of the Living Dead* the zombie was at last provided with a little family to work with.

Before Romero's thriller the zombie had only a sporadic career. I suppose a claim could be made that the first important zombie in horror films was Cesare, the "somnambulist," in *The Cabinet of Dr. Caligari* (1920), because here is a mindless creature who is controlled by a "master," but Cesare is not a cipher. Instead, he has powerful feelings that cause him not to throttle Jane, the damsel in distress, as he had been commanded, but to abscond with her. The zombie's claim on our imagination is precisely the opposite: he has no emotions at all, let alone erotic ones, and hence can venture into the land of

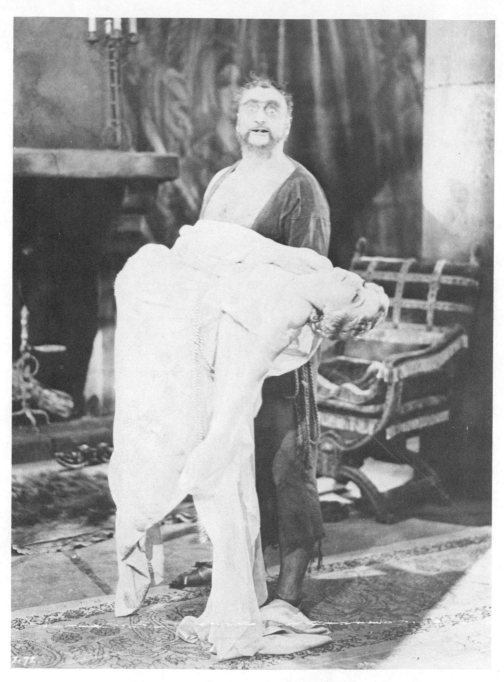

Zombie carrying Madge Bellamy in *White Zombie*, 1932 (Amusement Securities)

Mummy carrying Peggy Moran in *The Mummy's Hand*, 1940 (Universal Studios)

forbidden fruit (very often human flesh) and eat at his leisure. He is essentially a Western ghoul, except that no provision is made for his daytime rest. Like the mummy, the zombie entered popular culture not through a literary text, but through anthropological studies: investigations into voodoo cults in the Caribbean, especially Haiti. The journalists of the yellow-press tabloids soon made this academic research common knowledge, and William Seabrook's sensational *Magic Island*, published in 1929, made a film version almost inevitable.

The zombie myth can be culturally complex, as the anthropologist Francis Huxley has shown in *The Invisibles* (1966), but as simplified by Hollywood it involves the resurrection of the dead and their control by the sympathetic manipulation of a "devil doll." Unlike the vampire, who is animated by the devil within the body, the zombie is controlled from without by a sorcerer. The zombie is thus the archetypical slave, and it is certainly not happenstance that the myth developed as the beyond-death fantasies of African slaves. What has fascinated anthropologists is whether the myth developed before or after the slaves left Africa, and how close the American voodoo tradition is to that of the Caribbean. In other words, Is the zombie myth a cultural condensation of life under white rule from the black point of view?[3]

When the Halpern brothers made *White Zombie* in 1932, the economic allegory almost subsumed the horrors of life beyond the grave. In fact, the film provides the Marxist a casebook in which to view the horrors of Adam Smith; here capitalism literally grinds up the lives of the workers. The zombie proletariat is a scary lot as they first come parading over a hilltop, or as they are working in the mill, mindlessly munching one of their own who has fallen into the vat. They finally fall to their doom as they march like lemmings over a cliff, following their greedy white bourgeois employer. Their patron is one "Murder" Legendre (Bela Lugosi), and ostensibly the plot traces how he falls in love with a New York ingenue and tries to make her his own by turning her plantation-owning boyfriend into a zombie. It is the vampire story all over again, with blood replaced by property, and everything possible is done (including a cape and the slit lighting of Lugosi's eyes) to make sure that we do not miss the similarity. There is a core of real horror in *White Zombie* as the older man attempts to wrest the young girl from her boyfriend, who then goes to a wise island mentor for help in understanding voodoo; but bathos finally carries the horror away as the young plantation owner has an eleventh-hour revival of will power and tricks the evil sorcerer over a cliff. Behind their employer the other zombies obediently march to a domino downfall. The sets are pure *Dracula*, complete with gothic castle (on Haiti!) and circular staircasing, but the relationship between Madeline (the girl—her name and pale visage clearly lifted from *The House of Usher*) and

Legendre is never developed, let alone explained. Does he want her as a sexual object to violate, or as a way to extend his plantation empire? These ends are not mutually exclusive, but they do need some explanation that the film never offers.

Regardless of the narrative difficulties, the zombie scenes of men and women with blank, unseeing eyes, wind-up doll movements, utterly emotionless affect, and bloodless, yet still strangely human, behavior are some of the most concussive images in all moviedom. These are not mummies, vampires, or werewolves; there is little make-up and no masking. These monsters are like us, but just over the edge of life in a will-less, emotionless world of form without content, bodies without minds. If the audience of the Depression thought the blank stares of the bread-liners were unsettling, these images make them seem tame. It is not death that is macabre; it is living death.

Any image that is so exciting (and so easy and inexpensive to construct) was certain to be copied, and copied it was in the *Revolt of* . . . , *King of* . . . , *Return of* . . . , *Son of* . . . , *Revenge of* . . . , until Jacques Tourneur made *I Walked with a Zombie* in 1943. This is as close as any zombie movie ever came to having a literary text, so we should look at it for more than iconography. Val Lewton, the producer, called this his "Jane Eyre in the East Indies," and it is probably as faithful to the spirit of Charlotte Brontë's semi-gothic novel as any of the usual cinematic renditions of life at Thornfield Hall have ever been. In the novel Jane is a young lady who enters the world of an older man, Mr. Rochester, in order to care for his children. Mysterious employer and young tutor fall in love and would live happily ever after were it not for Rochester's first wife, Bertha, who lives in the attic. Exactly what Bertha Rochester is we are never told, but Charlotte Brontë certainly wants us to entertain the idea that she might be a vampire. She certainly is a monster of some sort and, in the sense that she possesses Rochester, Bertha *is* a vampire to Jane. Here is Jane's frenzied description and Rochester's undercutting responses:

> "O, sir, I never saw a face like it! It was a savage face. I wish I could forget the roll of the red eyes and the fearful blackened inflation of the lineaments!"
> "Ghosts are usually pale, Jane."
> "This, sir, was purple; the lips were swelled and dark; the brow furrowed; the black eye-brows wildly raised over the bloodshot eyes. Shall I tell you of what it reminded me?"
> "You may."
> "Of the foul German spectre—the Vampire." (Chapter 25)

Now what is a thing like that doing in a polite Victorian attic? It seems that Bertha is not a native Englishwoman, but is instead from the Caribbean. She is a Creole witchwoman, yet ironically her presence protects Jane until Rochester has been sufficiently weakened both physically and mentally so that Jane is no longer a "daughter" to him, but a helpmate.

Clearly, Ardel Wray and Curt Siodmak, who wrote the screenplay, had read *Jane Eyre*, but in their film, Elizabeth, a young Canadian nurse, is employed by a Jamaican planter, Mr. Paul Holland, to care not for his child, but for his sick, catatonic wife, Jessica. Bertha has come down from the attic, so to speak. Elizabeth soon falls in love with her employer and would marry him were it not for the spectral wife who sleeps by day and wanders about by night. What can they do? They try shock therapy, medication, and kindness, but nothing works. In desperation they seek help from Mr. Holland's mother, who happens to be the infirmary doctor. It seems that Jessica wants to leave the island, but that she has been made a zombie by the mother-in-law who wants her son to stay nearby. One night Paul and Elizabeth decide to let Jessica loose and in a wonderfully eerie scene, replete with the kind of atmospheric music that has become, especially since the pulsating scores of Bernard Herrmann, standard for night scenes, we follow as Jessica sleepwalks through the neck-high sugarcane, past other zombies, and straight into a voodoo ceremony. As it turns out, the mother-in-law is the chief priestess, and when confronted by her son, she relents and Jessica is finally allowed to experience real death as her waxen image is destroyed. A sepulchral voice tells us that Jessica really was evil and it is right that she should at last die. Nurse and plantation owner at last find peace together while the island full of zombies presumably settles down to read *Das Kapital*.

I Walked with a Zombie is a typical Tourneur film—everything misty, low-keyed, and muted. Nothing is really explained; nothing jells; no zombie jumps out at us in the cane fields; the whole tone is somewhat like Lewis Allen's *The Uninvited*—disquieting, perplexing, and spiritual. I mention this because the very mindlessness of the zombie, the insupportable boredom of his personality, tends to mitigate any conflict that could exist between monster and victim. The zombie is an utter cretin, a vampire with a lobotomy, and this is what has tended to make later films like *Voodoo Man* (1944), *Teenage Zombies* (1958), *Voodoo Island* (1959), *Plague of the Zombies* (1966), *Zombie Flesh Eaters* (1979), and the most recent *Zombie II* (1980), *Dead and Buried* (1981), and *The Evil Dead* (1983) little more than vehicles of graphic violence, full of people (usually men) poking other people and then occasionally eating them. The zombie is so shallow that with only a few exceptions, such as *The Cat and the Canary* remakes, he has not been a subject of parody. Even Abbott and Costello refused to meet with him.

There have been two variations on the zombie theme, however, that have already started to generate progeny: the first is Don Siegel's *Invasion of the*

Body Snatchers (1956) and its continuation in Philip Kaufman's 1978 film of the same title, and the other is George Romero's *Night of the Living Dead* (1968) and its continuation, the second part of a projected trilogy, *Dawn of the Dead* (1978). These movies brought the zombie home, took him out of the voodoo jungle, and put him next door to us in a California city, or near Pittsburgh, or, worse still, in a New York suburban shopping mall. They have also inspired a veritable zombie-cannibal industry which now promises Dan O'Bannon's *Return of the Living Dead* (1985), Romero's concluding *Day of the Dead* (1985), and enough potential copyright litigation to feed lawyers for years.

By far the most important of these films is Romero's *Night of the Living Dead*. Much has been made of its grainy texture (the Walter Reade organization, which distributed the film, made an extremely poor print), its shoestring budget ($114,000), its political overtones (Vietnam and Korean hordes coming after us in human waves or, better yet, ghouls as "the silent majority"), its science fiction causality (radiation brought back to earth by a Venus probe), its cinematic antecedents (such as the *I Am Legend* series or *Night on Bald Mountain*), racial overtones (Ben, the black man, is the "hero"), the acting (only two professionals, but with zombies not much finesse is needed), inconsistencies (what about the zombie upstairs?), and the bleak ending (à la the *Count Yorga* and *House of Dark Shadows* movies). But for me the most important development is what Romero did to the monster; he bred the zombie with the vampire, and what he got was the hybrid vigor of a ghoulish plague monster. For the monsters of *Night of the Living Dead* repopulate themselves by transforming victims into zombies—no more sympathetic wax figure nonsense. Romero's monsters are rather like those in the *Invasion of the Body Snatchers* in that they are common, everyday folk, except that these zombies have a mindless craving for human flesh and their victims will be reanimated after death into a new generation. Romero's other innovation is that, while he made his zombies into vampires, he subtracted, rather than added to, their physical power, so that they are now pathetic weaklings able to be destroyed by bashing their heads. Like insects, so familiar to fans of the 1960s terror films, they are powerful only when massed into living waves. *Night of the Living Dead* is the "Bolero" of horror films; taking one convention, the slow but persistent attack, and working it into a frenzy.

For all its innovations, both conscious and unconscious, none of these characteristics really explains why this *Night of the Living Dead* has such power. I don't believe that life beyond death, or unending living death, or cannibalism, or subverting fairy-tale motifs (courage is to no avail; goodness is annihilated), or even the racial reversals inspire the frisson here. Instead, once again, to pinpoint the horror one must ignore the monster and watch the transformations wrought on the victims, especially the family members.

In this movie there are three families. The first we meet are brother and sister, Barbara and Johnny, whose visit to their father's grave signals that they are now alone in the world with no parental guidance, no one to enforce familial bonds and taboos. Johnny, who is initially quite cynical about death, is the first victim of the zombies. Rather unexpectedly at the cemetery he heroically struggles with a mindless fiend, allowing his sister time to escape and find temporary sanctuary in the solitary farmhouse, the sanctuary of the American family. There she soon welcomes Ben, a black man with no family, a man who has only himself, yet who volunteers to protect others. The "others" are in two groups: a full-fledged American family, Harry, Helen, and their only child, Karen; and a young couple, Tom and Judy, who are about to be married and start a family. Tom and Judy are of little concern in the movie; they are in love and are kind and are killed by the zombies. The tension is between Harry, the family man, and Ben, the black man with no family. Harry, the father, is cowardly, snively, and correct—he wants to go to the cellar and hide until the plague passes—while Ben, the alien, wants to stand and fight. Ironically, "doing battle" only exposes all to the blight of the intruders.

If only as an analogy with the vampire, let's assume the zombie confrontation has buried sexual meanings. It would then be significant that the return of Johnny, now a full-fledged catatonic zombie, to his sister provides one of the first real shocks. We see in his cannibalistic embrace, and in her desire for affection even though it means death, that the boundaries we have been programmed to respect are slipping away. As Stuart Samuels has argued, this "hint of incest" adds to our growing sense that all family ties are becoming hopelessly knotted (p. 71). However, the real shock is to come. For the daughter, Karen, has been nipped by a zombie and her parents, unwilling to believe that she will share the destiny of the other victims, take her down to the cellar, the only isolated place in the house. There she proceeds to feed on her wounded father and kill her still-protective mother. Any idea we may have of the stability of the nuclear family is not just assaulted in this film; it is mauled. The jolt is not that Johnny, the brother, or Karen, the daughter, become zombies, but that, true to the demands of vampire and werewolf folklore, their first victims are those whom they loved most in life. In other words, safely protected as monsters, they proceed to do what they could never do in real life, and their "victims," instead of reacting with inhibition and trepidation, allow the unthinkable to occur. We voyeurs in the audience, we witnesses who have knowledge of the importance of family relationships, are the ones who are horrified.

Harry, Helen, and Karen—one of the families in *Night of the Living Dead*, 1968
(Libra Production)

In *Martin* (1977), made after *Night of the Living Dead* and before *Dawn
of the Dead*, Romero proceeds once again to rearrange the jigsaw pieces of
the fractured family puzzle. Again, it is the ineffectual child, now a teenage
boy, who, thanks to his undeniable madness, enacts the family romance with
his (grand)father, appropriately named "Cuda," and his displaced sister,
Christina. In the end, the "father" fatally stabs Martin on the erroneous
assumption that he has murdered a housewife, who ironically enough had
once "mothered" him and helped him overcome his fear of sex. If there is
anything to be concluded from this movie it is that without prohibitions *and*
compassion families will drive themselves crazy, making zombies of each
other, turning vampiric on one another. And they will do this not when they
repress, but when they believe themselves free to violate these taboos. The
grandfather makes Martin a bloodsucker by incessantly telling him that he
is a leech, so that when Martin does violate taboos he is simply doing what
Karen was doing at the end of *Night of the Living Dead*: he is acting precisely
the way his monster is supposed to act.

The threat to family well-being, to say nothing of the threat to personal
security, usually implies that the horror-carrier will attack from outside, that
he will come at us by climbing over the walls. Martin is the exception. This

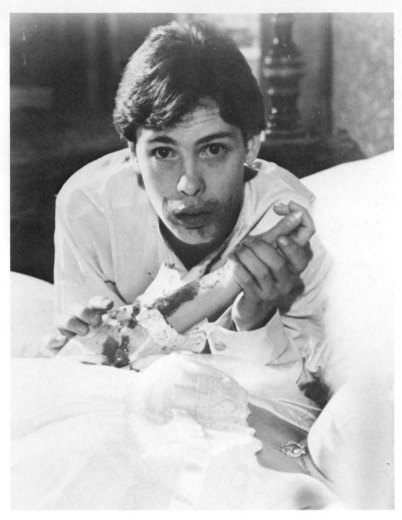

Martin with girl's bloody arm in *Martin*, 1976 (Libra Films)

is the Beast from Within, and the film derives its tingle, in part, by reversing our expectations. We do not expect, nor do we consciously want, ever to sympathize with the intruder. The simple xenophobia that seems to trigger our more complex fears of familial degeneration are obvious in the traditional horror myths: the vampire is from Transylvania, the mummy from Egypt, the ghoul from the Middle East, and the zombie from the Caribbean. As with *The Thing from Another World* (1951) and its hi-tech remake, *The Thing* (1982), the "Thing" is always outside trying to get in. Even in *Invasion of the Body Snatchers* or *Night of the Living Dead*, we are told that the "pods" or the "radiation" is from outer space. But in *Martin*, as in so much of the horror of the late 1960s and 1970s, the menace is inside the nuclear family.[4] In this context it might be a fitting conclusion to this discussion of the vampire/zombie/mummy to discuss a recent film that combines our fears of the Thing from Without with our fears of eruption from within.

Alien (1979) expresses its approach in the title, and were it not for the startling manipulation of a vampiric embryo, it might be dismissed as Lovecraftian outer-space fantasy. If ever there was a movie that showed how intellectually simple the surface of horror motifs is, *Alien* is it. Essentially, we follow a spaceship crew as it battles an intruder whose protean forms elude specific categories and whose ability to incubate inside the human form makes it impossible to draw boundaries between us and it. This organism is attacking us both from within and without, is as apt to burst through our belly as through any shield we can erect outside us. The Alien is the ultimate zombie: mindless, hungry, and anamorphic. This is a parasite straight out of *Fiend Without a Face*, or almost, for when we do catch sight of it we notice that the Alien has been fabricated (by the Swiss artist H. R. Giger) to resemble a vampiric phallus.

Were it not for this startling image, the temptation might be to pass *Alien* off as simply a late bloomer of the 1950s sci-fi weird genre. The plot of a spaceship picking up something repugnant in space has been the stuff of forgettables like *It! the Terror from Beyond Space* and *20 Million Miles to Earth*, but this little bit of repugnancy is different: it has all the graphic coding of a most particular form of the monster-on-the-loose. As a matter of fact, although the producers deny any conscious influence, *Alien* is almost a remake of Mario Bava's *Planet of the Vampires*, but with new technical virtuosity.

Critics have rightly praised *Alien* for its semi-documentary detachment and its crudity of texture (a development that is especially common since the success of Tobe Hooper's *Texas Chainsaw Massacre* and Romero's *Night of the Living Dead*, and illustrates again how unimportant context is if the images are correct), its fantastic effects (especially in the egg chamber where the Alien has incubated), the ensemble acting (mumbling carried to art), as well as its literary allusions (Melville and Conrad) and its folkloric undertones (especially Sleeping Beauty). And critics have been right to complain about the one-dimensional, comic-book plot: monster chases seven humans the length of one spaceship. But once again, the tingles and shivers have also to do with the violation of family, in this case a family of siblings. It is clear from the first reel that the family roles are all in place: the ship's computer is repeatedly referred to as "mother" and her wishes are carried out by the "father," the ship's chief technician, Ash, who is later shown to be a robot when his head explodes before our eyes and his "software" splatters about. The sibling crew steer clear of each other in kibbutz fashion, but not the

Monster in *Alien,* 1979 (20th Century Fox)

Alien. It infects everyone except our heroine, Sigourney Weaver, who escapes insemination and finally blasts the intruder to smithereens in the ship's rear thrusters.

I will not deny the visceral jolts associated with claustrophobia, the squirming monster, or exploding heads and bursting stomachs, but I do think that much of the emotional turmoil we experience may be because we have associated the crew not with technicians, but with family. We see them having breakfast together, wearing civilian clothes, complaining about "mother," being obedient to the paternalistic Ash, having mumbling conferences about food and chores, and so it is a shock to our arranged expectations when the Alien, which looks by turns like a fetus, a crab and a phallus with teeth, starts to literally intrude into first one, then another. By the time it finally confronts our heroine it has assumed arms and legs. The phallus has grown up to be a man and this man, we soon realize, is none other than the vampire in a latex suit of slime with a metal jaw and chrome teeth. This family relationship is unclear, but his sexual designs are not.

While the vampire has exploded outward into these new visual forms, the major figures in the Frankenstein myth seem to have contracted and split. On one hand, there is the mad doctor, no longer an inquiring youth as in Mary Shelley's novel, but now an older man with a Middle European accent who is violating the privacy of Man and Nature, and on the other, the sympathetic monster, no longer the articulate polyglot of the novel but now a hulk with the mind of a child. These characters are no longer in the same story; in fact, it is rare to find any interaction between quizzical youth and his monster. Only the various remakes of the Golem story, with the rabbi playing the scientist role, come close. So from Rotwang in *Metropolis* to Dr. Griffin of *The Invisible Man* series to Dr. Strangelove, we have separated the mad scientist from the curious youth and made him a calculating sadist. Even in the modern Frankenstein myth, ever since James Whale allowed Fritz to substitute that "abnormal brain" into the head of the creature, the scientist has created nothing but trouble. This motif stabilized in the Hammer Frankensteins, where as Peter Cushing got older and older, he got madder and madder, until finally his young assistant had to be introduced to play his previous role of curious observer. Doctors in horror films are indeed a sorry lot: think only of Dr. Moreau, Dr. X, Dr. Cyclops, Dr. Blood, Dr. Caligari, Dr. Death, Dr. Renault, the doctor in *Eyes Without a Face*, or the medico in *Scream and Scream Again*. The physician is both idolized and abhorred, reflecting our modern fear that the other side of healing is the exploitation of biology in the service of personal aggrandizement. Even in *The Invisible Man*, in which there is no horror, just good special effects, the very medical advance—the "monocane"—that produces Dr. Griffin's invisibility also stimulates his desire to dominate. In other words, the price of knowledge leads not to increased responsibility, as it did in the very early "Frankensteins," but instead to the compulsion to control.

So where do we go to find the sympathetic hulk, the Karloffian monster without the deranged criminal brain? We seem to have turned to freaks: on one hand, to actual freaks, such as those in Browning's infamous 1932 movie of the same title, and to Rondo Hatton, the famous "creeper," or, on the other hand, to human/animal mutations such as the Alligator Men, Leech Women, Mole, and Mushroom People.[5] Very often when we reverse the intellectual process that produces the scientist and returns man to the primitive, or even the bestial, we find a creature of considerable sympathy. In all the gorilla-at-large movies from *King Kong* and the Kong "knock-offs" like *Son of Kong* and *Mighty Joe Young*, through the endless Godzillas, and including the silly Dino de Laurentiis 1976 travesty, the ape has played out our childhood fantasies of what we could get away with if only we didn't have to think about it. The big ungainly, stupid hulk does get the girl, at least for a while, but then really doesn't know what he wants to do with her. As Carl Denham, the entrepreneur-explorer in *King Kong* said, "Kong was a king and a god," and indeed he was as long as he stayed on Skull Island. The *Planet of the Apes* cycle doesn't fit this paradigm in that these simian creatures are not just more emotionally stable than their human counterparts; they are far more intellectually balanced as well. Still they pay a price. They have absolutely no sex life.

Since Darwin, non-simian transformations have not fared well. Cat people (*Cat Girl, Catman of Paris*, even the recent *Cat People*) have real psychological problems, but nothing compared to fish-men, be they from 20,000 fathoms or just from any black lagoon. The creatures on *The Island of Lost Souls* are a pitiful, albeit strangely sympathetic, lot. And certainly woe be to him who ever gets caught halfway between man and insect, for, as we saw in *The Fly, Return of . . .* and *Son of . . .* , the only thing worse than animal transformation is partial transformation. After all, it is in the void between animal and man that Mr. Hyde and Dr. Jekyll wage their eternal war of atavism versus repression.

Here in *la zone*, beside the vampire and between the Frankenstein characters and Dr. Jekyll/Mr. Hyde, we might pause to observe the interactions of Beauty and the Beast. Admittedly, this confrontation is not a horror sequence per se, yet important versions of the major myths are informed by it: say, in the scenes of the modern vampire and the virgin, the Frankenstein monster and the girl beside the pond, Mr. Hyde and the little match girl. This nursery tale has elements of horror buried within it, for the Beast is a sympathetic monster (like the Frankenstein creature) whose dynamic love of the forbidden girl (like the vampire) involves a crucial transformation (like Jekyll/Hyde). But for all its internal and external similarities with the modern horror myths, Beauty and the Beast is not a latency horror story; it has little appeal to teenagers. So it is not surprising that aside from a few art versions like Cocteau's *La Belle et la Bête* (1946) or pornographic ones like Borowczyk's *The Beast* (1978) and Alfred Sole's *Tanya's Island* (1980), or recurrent television adaptations, the story has rarely appeared on film. It is neglected primarily because it is a fairy tale and not a horror saga, but as we will see, horror sagas have evolved from it by shifting emphasis.

Here is the unfolding of the standard Beauty and the Beast tale.[6] A rich man with many children, usually three boys and three girls, has fallen on hard times. The girls are like Cinderella's step-sisters, whining about their need for jewels and dresses, except for the youngest, called "the little

Beauty," who is sympathetic with her father's plight. As he prepares to go off to find another fortune, he asks what he may bring home as gifts and the older girls ask for expensive dresses and baubles, but Beauty asks only for a rose. Months pass and the father prepares to return empty-handed. A short distance from home he happens on a palace in the deep woods, and when he enters he finds everything seemingly prepared for his arrival. There is food prepared and a bed freshly made. He spends the night and the next morning he sees a rose in the garden. Remembering his promise, he picks it for his Beauty. This act alone calls forth a hideous beast (he is never described in the fairy tale) who, after a little intimidating banter, agrees to let the father go in exchange for one of his daughters three months hence. The Beast even gives the old man a chest full of gold to seal the bargain.

The father never intends to sacrifice a daughter; instead he plans to return to the Beast himself after providing for his family. But when he tells his children of his plans, his boys want to seek out and destroy the beast while his girls tell him to quit worrying and spend the gold—that is, all except one, and the adolescent knows who she is, and we all know what she does. Beauty goes to the Beast of her own free will as an act of selfless love for her father. The Beast accepts her. He does not molest her; rather, he tends her and only occasionally asks that she be his wife. She politely refuses and, again, he seems to understand and accept this. All he wants is that she stay near him and she promises to do so.

But soon she learns that her father is ill and she asks the Beast if she may go to visit him. "Promise you will come back to me in a week," the Beast says. "I will," she promises, and she would have, had her jealous sisters not detained her. On the tenth night Beauty dreams of her Beast; she misses him, remembers his tenderness, and she now realizes his happiness is more important to her than his looks. Quick as a wink, she is magically transported to his side where she tells him of her newly understood affection and how she now realizes she wants to marry him. At this very moment she looks into his ugly face only to see that he is no longer a beast but a handsome prince. The sick father recovers and comes to live with them, as do the rest of the family. The evil sisters, however, are turned into statues and will remain this way until they do penance for their hatefulness.

Bruno Bettelheim points out in *The Uses of Enchantment* that the barely concealed symbolism tells another tale. The father's love is symbolized by the immaculate rose; yet beastliness would occur if that image were violated. The father must love his daughter in a special way; hence they must separate during a crucial part of her maturation. The Beast takes over with tenderness and distance until the father is weakened. When the girl's willingness to leave her father and transfer that love to the Beast shows that she is strong enough, her father returns to her side. For only when both parties are stable and secure, when the father is old and the daughter mature, can the Beast finally transform into the prince. Only then is the sexual danger over. At last there is reunion and joy. As Bettelheim remarks, "Beauty and the Beast"

> foreshadows by centuries the Freudian view that sex must be experienced by the child as disgusting as long as sexual longings are attached to [the] parent, because only through such a negative attitude toward sex can the incest taboo, and with it the stability of the human family, remain secure. But once detached from the parent and directed to a partner of more suitable age, in normal development, sexual longings no longer seem beastly—to the contrary, they are experienced as beautiful. (p. 308)

And indeed I think this is the case, but note two important aspects of this tale: (1) it is told from Beauty's point of view and (2) there is absolutely no attempt to make the Beast horrible. The fairy tale illustrates what Bettelheim calls "the positive aspect of the Oedipal attachment"; it is not a horror story because the young audience is not mature enough to desire what is prohibited. There is only a need to prepare. All through the story Beauty moves of her own free will, and when she finally reaches the point where she can appreciate the Beast for what he is, she is at last ready to be inducted into mature sexuality. In other words, she is now ready for some real horror myths. At the end Beauty need not choose between her father and the Beast; she must only choose particular kinds of affection—both are loving, but one is sexual, the other Platonic.

How does this fable ever get to be a horror tale? As we have seen before, what has to happen is that the monstrous sexual love, the Beast, has to intrude on the protective love of the father. If this happens, the fairy tale ending is impossible; only destruction will result. Allow Beauty to yield to the Beast too soon, or let the Beast become too aggressive, especially while the father is foremost in her life, and the imagery of horror will intrude. The Beast will become a vampire, a stalker, a Mr. Hyde.

Two major Beauty and the Beast myths are now in circulation. Both had an initial anchor in a literary text, and both have broken loose to be retold as the audience prefers—as stories of the macabre. The two tales are of the Hunchback of Notre Dame and the Phantom of the Opera. Since the Phantom is far and away the more interesting as a quasi-horror story, let me first make a few remarks about the Hunchback.

In Hugo's 1831 novel, Quasimodo, a gargoyle come alive, initially serves a lecherous priest, Frollo, who has raised him from infancy like a son. Like Blake's priests in "Holy Thursday," Frollo has been kind to the hunchback only because he thinks he will be rewarded in the afterlife. Since Quasimodo

Charles Laughton and Maureen O'Hara in *The Hunchback of Notre Dame,* 1939 (RKO Radio)

Although there were numerous stage plays and even some silent movies, the first "classic" film adaptation was Universal's, starring Lon Chaney. No one has ever seriously claimed that this 1923 version was a horror story; in fact, Universal designed it as a spectacular, and it still is. It is an "epic" featuring the staples of this Hollywood genre—Quasimodo's rope slide, his molten-metal pour and his huge-rock throw. The plot is pure Hollywood as well. The malfeasor is the evil archdeacon's brother, Jehan, and Quasimodo is a big-hearted beast who is led around like a trained pooch. Esmeralda's Prince Charming, Phoebus, is waiting in the wings, and in the end beast and malfeasor cancel each other out while Phoebus gets the girl.

In 1939 the most impressive version was made, this one starring Charles Laughton which made the rope-swinging scene somewhat hard to believe, but no matter. It is the narrative I want to follow, and here RKO really did the impossible: both Esmeralda and Quasimodo survive, although to do it the Beauty-Beast confrontation had to be sacrificed. In the more daring 1950s, Quasimodo finally does have his way: this rendition ends with Anthony

Jean Marais and Josette Day in Jean Cocteau's *Beauty and the Beast*, 1945 (André Paulve Production)

proves both strong and obedient, when Frollo wishes to seduce the gypsy girl, Esmeralda, he dispatches his misshapen ward to kidnap her. Although Quasimodo is initially a tool used by the priest, when the hunchback learns of his patron's nefarious plans, and after Esmeralda has shown him compassion, he rebels. Quasimodo finally heaves the conniving "Father" over the balustrade of Notre Dame. But he still doesn't get the girl. Nor does the girl ever get her boyfriend, the callous Phoebus, who heartlessly has refused earlier to save her from death. The novel ends true to the expectations of gothic melodrama: years later two embracing skeletons are found in the Vault of Montfaucon, one a woman and the other a man whose spine was crooked and one leg shorter than the other. Like Heathcliff and Catherine, they can be together only in death.

The Hunchback of Notre Dame is remarkably close to the traditional gothic, not only in imagery (the cathedral as baronial manse), and in character (Quasimodo is literally a monster, a quasi-human, while Frollo is satanic), and in theme (fated destinies mandate tragedy), but also in motivation; each protagonist is driven by an *idée fixe*: Frollo's is lust, Esmeralda's is purity, and Quasimodo's is devotion. This is the stuff not only of the gothic but of melodrama as well.

Quinn entering the burial vault of his dead Esmeralda as the camera slowly retreats. Then in 1982 Hallmark Hall of Fame produced a surprisingly good television version in which Anthony Hopkins played the Hunchback looking like a singer in the "Sex Pistols," but that only worked with an Esmeralda who looked like Farrah Fawcett and a Frollo who resembled a priapic page. In this version the poet-minstrel gets the girl and Frollo is killed by Quasimodo, who falls from the tower as the camera comes in for a close-up. His last words, "Why ... why?" are maudlin enough for the housewife's tears, but, nevertheless, this was a valiant attempt to return to the text.

I mention these renditions because the Hunchback story as it is now being told is not a horror story at all. From the looks of it, especially in the Chaney and Laughton versions, it might have been, but instead the Hunchback is finally played for melodrama. Girl helps deformed man, who later saves her life for someone else. There are certainly sexual overtones, but never ones of violation. Pathos is the intended result, not horror: tears, no shivers.

To find horror, not compassion, we need to turn to the conscious recasting of the Hunchback narrative in Gaston Leroux's *The Phantom of the Opera* (1908). Here again a Caliban worships his Ariel from afar, and here again the frisson is achieved as he inches closer and closer. In fact, the central scene in all the Phantom renditions is when they are close enough so that she can, and does, peel off his protective mask. There is no prince under the facade, nor is there a tender heart. This phantom really is a beast. This unmasking scene is of such force that the whole waxworks genre is also based on it. It is never clear in the Phantom myth exactly why this Beast should want this particular Beauty. Is the attraction, as it was in *The Hunchback*, because the Beast had been befriended by the Beauty (whipped by the mob, Quasimodo utters a Christ-like "I thirst" and Esmeralda gives him water), or is it more like the fairy tale in which the Beast seems to have a different thirst to be quenched?

To find out, we might trace the adventures of the Phantom as he journeys from print to celluloid. In the novel there is no clear relationship established between the Beast, the Phantom (or Erik, as he is known), and the Beauty, a youthful singer named Christine. Like Quasimodo, Erik was born monstrous, not misshapen as much as shapeless: he was born skeletal, bones only, no flesh. From the epilogue, clearly Leroux's almost desperate attempt to account for the unaccountable, we learn that Erik is rather old, about retirement age, for he has spent his working life as a construction engineer erecting buildings in Europe and Asia. Presumably, his overalls have disguised his ill-made body. In any case, Erik came to Paris to construct the foundation of the Paris Opera House and decided to retire beneath it. When the novel begins he has already made his permanent home in the subterranean labyrinth.

Enter Christine, the young singer, and the Phantom becomes her voice coach. But why should Christine be interested in taking lessons from a "voice behind the walls?" Isn't she at all suspicious? The novel explains what most of the movies neglect. It seems that her father, a violinist, had been her original instructor, but that at his death he decreed that she should study under "the angel of music" who just happened to hold classes behind the walls of the Paris Opera. Of course, she doesn't know that the angel is none other than the mysterious Phantom who is becoming a nuisance to the new owners of the Opera House. She only knows that her father's last desire was that she study under this man.

As time passes she falls in love with the dashing Raoul and, although the "angel of music" has helped her career by eliminating her competition by dropping first poison and then a chandelier on Carlotta, the prima donna, Christine is smitten with her full-bodied suitor. The no-bodied Phantom cannot prevail on her to break off the affair. Once she learns that the "angel" is really the Phantom, she is still more eager to leave, but the older man insists and she promises to stay with him a short while. Initially, Christine studied with Erik because it was her father's will. Now she stays with him out of fear.

As with the Beauty and the Beast tale, she grows more trusting and even though all he asks is that she not remove his mask, naturally she does. The unmasking scene shows us that the Phantom is nothing but bone shanks: black holes for eyes, no mouth, no nose, just a skeleton. Although we are told in the epilogue that Erik has been this way since birth, we associate such a bare-boned creature with death, or, more precisely, the human body long *after* death. For two weeks Christine stays with this narrow being, and true to folkloric convention she overcomes her revulsion. In fact, she is almost ready to accept life with this very thin man and he, knowing this, allows her to leave his nether world if she promises to return.

She promises, but like Orpheus and Eurydice, once back in the presence of the relatively plump Raoul she has second thoughts. Now it is the Phantom who comes up to eavesdrop on her, and he learns that she is not intending to keep her promise. So that evening during her performance the house lights are mysteriously extinguished and when they come up again Christine is nowhere to be found. Raoul knows what has happened and, in pursuing the Phantom, is captured.

The Beast gives his Beauty a choice: marriage to him or death to them all. He has loaded the cellar with gunpowder and promises to blow everything to bits. It takes Christine only a moment, albeit an agonizing one; she

Lon Chaney starring in *The Phantom of the Opera*, 1925 (Universal Studios)

chooses the Beast and now it seems he is not such a bad fellow because he lets her and everyone else go. He simply cannot go through with the marriage, however, once he knows that she is willing to be his. In a postscript we learn that the Phantom freed Christine because she really did love Raoul. Although she continued to let the Phantom kiss and hug her, he knew it was only because she now felt sorry for him. The Phantom and Christine commiserated together; she holding one of his chilly hands, he resting his lantern jaw on her ripe bosom. But not all is lost. She promises to return to bury him when he dies. A few pages later he does, and she does, and the story really is over. Well, almost. A few years later some excavators find one skeleton, buried in a vault below the Opera House, alone. The Hunchback finally got his Esmeralda, Heathcliff got his Catherine, but the Phantom does not get his Christine. Nor should he after what he has done. He has been lecherous in thought and deed, and even death cannot forgive these sins.

When Universal Studios made the first important film of the Phantom, the only sequence they changed, except for casting a more robust protagonist, was to have the Paris mob stone the Phantom to death. As we have seen elsewhere in the 1930s, this was the standard demise of most monsters, and certainly was a favorite of Universal's. *The Phantom of the Opera* (1925) was not intended as a horror film, but as an attempt to exploit the same audience that had been unearthed a year earlier with *The Hunchback*. The film was made as a spectacle first, a vehicle for Chaney second (still to this day in criticism one finds an exorbitant concern with counting the number of hours Chaney spent in makeup and detailing the grueling pain he endured, almost as if this was an act of heroism), and only finally a cohesive narrative. Carl Laemmle did not build a facsimile of the Paris Opera House for the kiddies, just as he didn't erect the facades of Notre Dame for teenagers. This is an adult movie that has many horror motifs, but is essentially a showcase of movie craft. So, although the film abounds in Dracula motifs—Phantom's cape and cowl, his coffin bed, the trapdoors to his catacombs, his pounding-out "Don Juan Triumphant" on the organ when Christine is finally within reach, his promising to "secrete my venom" should she not stay with him—these allusions are never exploited. This *Phantom* is like the *Hunchback*: something to watch in wonderous admiration, not to stagger away from in fear.

I do not mean to detract from Chaney's masterful performance, but only to point out that this is a movie of display. Those wonderful subterranean sets in the Doré style are still magnificent, but we always know exactly where they lead. In this context it is understandable why Universal was so keen to insert the two color sequences during the masked ball where the Phantom parades about like Poe's Red Death in his hand-tinted red cloak. This is a technician's movie, a patchwork of virtuoso effects, and the fact that the Phantom should be stoned to death in front of the Cathedral of Notre Dame (the earlier set had not yet been struck) seems more a tribute to what could be fabricated by a studio with a million dollars to spend on thrills than a film made to unsettle the audience.

Subsequent *Phantom*s continued this interest. With the advent of sound the plot became a vehicle to carry the operatic strains of first Suzanna Foster (1943), then Heather Sears (1962), and most recently the rock-and-roll pastiche of Paul Williams (1974). Of all these versions I am most interested in the narrative by Erich Taylor and Samuel Hoffenstein for the Universal remake. By 1943 the studio had the good sense to use almost all the old sets of the Chaney original, but the bad sense to cast Nelson Eddy as Raoul. They did, however, refurbish the plot and in doing so unconsciously replayed the Beauty and the Beast scenario. Interestingly, this is one of the few Hollywood remakes in which the screenwriters did not return to the proven rhythms of an earlier film, but instead tried to capture the spirit of the literary text.

Enrique Claudin (Claude Rains) is a violinist for the Paris Opera who is enamored with a young soprano, Christine. Enrique is paying for Christine's singing lessons from a smarmy Italian coach, but has arthritis and his job with the Opera is in jeopardy. Enrique hopes his own compositions will garner him enough money to continue to sponsor his young lady friend, but a conniving German music publisher seems to be bootlegging Enrique's scores. (As might be expected, in 1943 the Germans and Italians are not in heroic parts.) When Enrique hears Franz Liszt (!) playing one of his pieces, he concludes that the publisher is a plagiarist and storms into the offices. For his intemperate accusations Enrique receives a face full of acid from the publisher's wife. In horrible pain he seeks refuge, first in the sewers, and then in the catacombs beneath the opera house.

Thus far the 1943 *Phantom* has corrected the narrative flaw of the Chaney version by following the implications of the novel: Enrique has a bond with Christine, a reason to choose her. He passionately loves music. He is much older than Christine (we are told he is fifty), and is being eased into retirement. It is clear that Christine is much too young for him to even think about other than as a mentor. As a matter of fact, she is being courted by the sleazy Italian voice teacher, by the inspector of police, and by the American singer, Nelson Eddy, who looks like Johnny Carson's version of a Southern California car salesman.

The Phantom does what he can to advance the career of his protégée; he drops poison into the wine of the prima donna, and when she refuses to let her understudy, Christine, have her part, he spirits his young lady friend off to his nether world. He wants her to "sing only for me" and he pleads repeatedly, calling her "my child" and "my little one." Unfortunately, although this version cost almost a million dollars more than the Chaney one, Enrique has only a piano downstairs, not the more appropriate organ. When Christine's boyfriends realize that she has been abducted, they try to lure the Phantom up out of his maze by convincing Liszt to play one of Enrique's compositions, hoping that this will be the cheese to entice the mouse out into the open. They guess wrong. Sawing the ceiling chain in time with the music, the Phantom drops the great chandelier.

Escaping again below decks, Enrique plays the concerto just for Christine, and her spirits revive. She recognizes the melody from her childhood; it seems that they both came from the same rural province. What a coincidence! Meanwhile, the police inspector and Nelson Eddy have been following the music and now startle the happy couple (she has just pulled off the Phantom's mask—he is not so badly scarred, after all), and in the ensuing ruckus there is a cave-in and the Phantom suffocates. All that remains is his violin. Says Christine, while fondling the instrument, "I was always drawn to him . . . he was a stranger to me, but I always felt drawn to him."

Nowhere is that attraction explained, but if you recall the Beauty and the Beast tale you have a pretty good idea what Arthur Lupin and his Freudian screenwriters had in mind. This *Phantom* increases our apprehension by implying a familial context between Beauty and the Beast. In the fairy tale, Beauty is allowed happiness with the Beast only after the father is weakened, for only then has she become independent. Only then can the beastliness of interfamilial sexuality be transformed into the loving relationship of nonrelated equals. Only then can the Beast become a prince.

In Hollywood movies of the thirties and forties, especially those with music, every Jack must finally have his Jill, and so we expect that Nelson Eddy will finally win Suzanna Foster. After all, the "Raoul" character has always gotten the girl in both print and film. But no, in this version Christine is clearly not ready to make the separation from the Phantom. After all, she is still clutching Enrique's violin and claiming that she is "drawn to him." So at the end, instead of choosing between the French inspector or the American warbler, Christine goes off with her Paris Opera groupies and the young men wink at each other and go off for a night on the town.

This is arguably the best *Phantom* ever made. In part because, as one can see in *The Wolf Man*, Claude Rains makes a simply perfect father figure. It is all in the voice. As *The Invisible Man* showed, Rains had an extraordinary voice—just a touch of a lisp like Karloff and Price, with a round, dulcet sound. This Phantom is not at all horrible to look at; only half his face is scarred, and when the mask is removed, people in the audience did not faint, as Universal claimed they did watching the Chaney version. The horror here is generated inside the relationships. Why then did Hammer Studios, a few years later, make such a mess out of what they should have recognized as exactly their kind of story? Terence Fisher even saw the Rains version but, perhaps because the 1943 Universal film out-Hammered Hammer (color, lush sets, and especially the incest motif), he decided on something different, much too different.

Hammer's 1962 *Phantom* is a farrago of absurdities. For some inexplicable reason the action is moved from the Paris Opera to the London Opera House, which is about as full of macabre connotations as a shopping mall in Kansas City. The entire production is shoddy; the props look as if they were assembled for a rummage sale at Bray Studios and the mask, with one cyclopean eyehold in the center, looks as if it were made in about fifteen minutes, which it was. The real problem, however, is with John Elder's (Anthony Hind's) screenplay, for although Hammer had legal access to Universal's adaptation and characterization, they thought they could make the Phantom into their version of Frankenstein. The Phantom is played for pathos, becoming old Professor Petrie, who has been disfigured with acid and is tended by yet another Hammer hunchback. This malfeasor commits all the really nasty murders à la Ygor/Fritz, leaving the kind professor time to become paternally close to Christine. So kind, in fact, that the film ends with the professor gamely swinging under the falling chandelier that has been cut by the hunchback, just in time to save Christine from distress. The Phantom was ill-served by becoming D'Artagnan, and the public knew it. Even Hammer finally realized its mistake and tried to salvage the muddle by deleting the hunchback and adding a pair of detectives to the export print. When in doubt, make the Phantom a whodunit, but the American audience, as least, spotted the problem: there can be no whodunit when nothing has been done.

William K. Everson in his *Classics of the Horror Film* (1974) quipped that after Hammer's travesty "we may well get a version in which the ubiquitous phantom kidnaps his Christine and lives happily ever after with her in the Opera House catacombs" (p. 15). That version is still to come, but if the Phantom follows the path of his colleagues—Dracula, Frankenstein, the werewolf, and Dr. Jekyll—it will not be long in coming. For one of the few ways by which the contemporary filmmaker can squeeze shivers out of the old standbys is either to extend their conventions almost to parody or else to turn them inside out. In the mid 1970s, while Terence Fisher was making an especially randy *Frankenstein and the Monster From Hell*, which ranks only with Andy Warhol's *Frankenstein* and vampire movies like *Captain Kronos: Vampire Hunter* (in which the bloodsucker was crossbred with the cheroot-smoking hero of the spaghetti Westerns), Brian De Palma was making his *Phantom of the Paradise* (1974). I mention this film not so much because it continues the turn Hammer was making with the myth (the sympathetic beast relieved of responsibility), but because in this pastiche of horror motifs one can see how supple and exploitable the sequences are. This Phantom is sympathetic, especially to adolescents; he is an ingenuous rock-and-roll composer whose cantata is stolen by a demonic impresario who intends to present it as the highlight of his career. Instead of having acid thrown in his face as in the earlier versions, the composer gets his head stuck into a record-pressing machine and flees into the auditorium to become the Phantom. As the Phantom, he finally prevails on the evil impresario to let his girlfriend sing the lead but, after a series of double- and triple-crosses, he comes swinging down from the rafters mid-performance to destroy the exploiters and save the day. The audience within the movie loved it: they thought it was all part of an acid-rock show. The audience in the theater didn't: the *Phantom of the Paradise* flopped.

This film is of far more interest as a modernization of Grand Guignol set to music than it is as a horror film. It plays off *Caligari* (the sets), *Frankenstein* (the coming to life of "Beef," the male singer), *Dracula* ("Beef's" incisors and hisses, presaging the vampiric effect of KISS, a modern, real-life, rock-and-roll ensemble), and *The Picture of Dorian Gray* (the impresario has eternal life; videotapes in the closet contain his aging persona). De Palma plays on these allusions so artfully that, if one can block out the acoustical assaults and inappropriate dialogue, it is possible to enjoy the manipulation of sequences and motifs by someone who clearly has also enjoyed watching them.

That De Palma's Phantom would be sympathetic is almost a given from the beginning of this film: How can you mistrust someone so young and so victimized? But compassion for the Phantom has certainly not been the usual drift of the myth—the Hunchback of Notre Dame, yes, but not the Phantom. What we see in the more traditional Phantom legend is a tale of suppressed incest, a story line that concentrates on the older patron transgressing the rights of a young woman. The narrative has become almost allegorical: an older man moving too close to a specific young woman who finds that he is a beast under the mask. She may very well pity him; after all, he only wants to guide her career and, goodness knows, she needs guidance. All he asks is that she stay with him and forsake the young men who cluster around her.

In a sense *The Phantom* is the Beauty and the Beast story told from the Beast's point of view. In the fairy tale we follow the girl: her father goes away, she goes to the Beast, her father weakens and then she realizes that the Beast is the proper choice, and, indeed, she is proven right by his transformation. But in the horror version, the Beast searches for this particular girl; he tends her, and even though she wants to go to her Raoul, he actively prohibits her. In the printed text and in the 1943 film we are assured that the Phantom cannot be her father—after all, Christine's father has been dead for years, and was it not he who put her in contact with "the singing teacher" in the first place? As is typical in folklore the "real" father is introduced to calm our suspicions, yet our security is immediately undercut. For clearly, while the emphasis is on older man and younger innocent, we soon realize that the Phantom is an older man who has all the signifiers associated with a beyond-death existence. He is a skeleton. The same kinship phobias that have animated the other horror myths seem to operate here as well. Again, the frisson is in the service of social education. Go into the cellar with that man, even though all he wants to do is help you, and you will find it very difficult to make your way back to the family parlor.

While the vampire has metamorphosed into such independent forms as the zombie, the mummy, the "alien," and an unending procession of deathless types from the "I Eat Your Flesh, I Drink Your Blood" swamps of schlock, the Frankenstein myth has split into the Faustian mad scientist who is "delving too deeply into the secrets of life" and into the sympathetic hulk who often plays out the Beast role in our updating of the Beauty and the Beast fantasy. On either side of the split, however, the concern with forbidden sexuality seems to excite adolescent curiosity, whether it be in the creation and manipulation of life forms as performed by the mad doctor or in the inappropriate mating of forms as in the Ape Man, Creature from Below/Above, Phantom, and Hunchback narratives. In the last of our contemporary horror monsters, the werewolf, this split is concentrated into one form: the schizophrenic. In the last twenty years we have seemed especially fascinated by the Dr. Jekyll/Mr. Wolfman transformation in which one id-driven persona breaks away from its more respectable host and performs acts of sexual aggression that the host may secretly desire.

A generation ago this monster was just starting to find a theater audience, not as a Jack-the-Ripper, but as an aesthete, a man of feeling, or, more exactly, a man of particular feeling. One of the most interesting attempts to animate this monster was a return to an art text, Oscar Wilde's *The Picture of Dorian Gray*. Albert Lewtin's moving-picture of *The Picture* proved desultory, but illuminating. The essential problem was that the Wilde novel is not at all a horror story, but a pretext for sardonic commentary on Victorian affectation and hypocrisy perceived through the eyes of Lord Henry. In the novel, the ostensible protagonist, Dorian Gray, is so contrivedly mythic and amorphous that he really has no life of his own. He has been likened by critics to Faust, Charmides, Narcissus, the Beautiful Princess, and, as I ventured to suggest in *The Living Dead*, to the vampire. Dorian is assuredly not of the misty midnight, extended-incisors variety, yet he does function as a metaphorical bloodsucker, draining the life out of those around him, especially the appropriately named Sibyl Vane (vein). Of course, Dorian is made this way by the Realistic painter, Basil Hallward, who has painted the foppish young man not as he seems, but "as he really is." A "Portrait" of Dorian Gray would have been all right; a "Picture," however, will disturb the balance between life and art. Realism with a capital R simply will not do for Wilde. Art does not imitate life; it creates life, and to try to hold a mirror up to nature, as Basil did, will only risk monstrosity.

There are intimations here of the Frankenstein myth as well, for Basil, the well-meaning but mad doctor, has become the mad artist evoking the romantic dilemma articulated in Hawthorne's *The Artist of the Beautiful*, Poe's *The Oval Portrait*, and James's *The Sacred Fount*. The artist who attempts to make reality out of illusion risks unleashing chaos instead. As opposed to the Frankenstein myth, however, Dorian has the power to hold both sides of his personality together; but, like the transformation monster, he wants to let the buried side loose. Here, five years after Stevenson's novella, Wilde is retelling the Jekyll/Hyde tale and encountering the same problems; namely, how can it first be brought to a climax and, second, how can it end. Stevenson resolved this by having the still highly moral Jekyll assert his righteous personality over Hyde; and Wilde, for all his protestations, is likewise constrained by both propriety and by the inherited tradition of the novel to attempt the same. Since Dorian's "other half" is locked upstairs in the closet, resolution is not so simple. At the end of *The Picture* Dorian finds a simple village girl, Hetty Merton, of whom he becomes fond, but realizing that "his embrace would be fatal," he nobly spares her by repressing his desire. Then suddenly he is hurried to an eleventh-hour conversion, and, true to the conventions of the gothic, he must now destroy himself. So with a knife, almost the same instrument with which he was created (the palette knife), and exactly the same instrument with which he had stabbed his creator (appropriately "in the great vein that is behind the ear"), Dorian's Jekyll goes upstairs to stab his Mr. Hyde. And, having mutilated the painting, he falls to the ground, assuming the "withered, wrinkled and loathsome visage" of his closet counterpart. In a sense this is the exact opposite of the Hollywood ending of the Jekyll/Hyde myth, but the effect is the same. Only in death can the clocks of time be reset and the scales of justice rebalanced.

When *The Picture of Dorian Gray* was brought to the screen in 1945, there was no way that it could capture the insouciance of the text, let alone follow the plot. Still, the enormous financial success of M-G-M's *Dr. Jekyll and Mr. Hyde* with Spencer Tracy made Metro eager to apply the same big-budget formula to another *fin-de-siècle* novel, and this movie is about the best one could expect; it is maudlin, pretentious, and silly. Its only claim to being a horror movie was in the advertising copy. Even as melodrama the film is flat and predictable, in large part because Dorian (Hurd Hatfield) is so postured and unthreatening. To make the causality linear and the theme easily understandable, Dorian must imitate the transformation; yet, true to the Hollywood formula of the forties that anyone so handsome could not be irredeemably nefarious, the adaptors added a patently stupid device. They introduced a fantastic Egyptian statue of a cat with magical powers like the mummy motif of the Scroll of Thoth. The cat seems to trigger Dorian's Faustian bargain to exchange his soul for immortality. All the novel's concern with Realistic versus Romantic art is simply nonexistent, and so the witty repartee is wasted on crumpets and cakes. Sibyl Vane is introduced early on as the fated love interest, but again in the Hollywood grand style, it is Dorian's intention to marry her, not his desire to drain her dry of talent (as in the novel), that sets the transformation in motion. For when she rejects his unspoken proposal (she prefers to remain a virgin until the vows are said) we are supposed to think that he bargains away his soul for an immortality of naughty behavior toward women. With mawkish sentimentality this film would have us believe that Dorian lays waste London sophisticates with clever quips and choice *bons mots*. What little action there is, is proffered against a backdrop of art-deco sets, lisping actors play characters not imagined or implied in the novel (such as a new character, Basil Hallward's invented niece), and there is an earful of awful tinkling music. So that we can't miss the point, the black-and-white film bursts into color for the final scenes with the painting. An unidentified narrator, who has pestered us throughout the entire film with his vapid commentary, finally leaves us with a shriveled-up Dorian and a snippet of Omar Khayyám.

I doubt that *Dorian Gray* can ever be made into a horror film, chiefly because the transformation is not sufficiently atavistic, and Dorian's revenge not sufficiently motivated. Post-portrait Dorian is really pre-portrait Dorian with sarcasm. He is still Young Mr. Gray, too vapid to be taken seriously. He poses no threat to our well-being, let alone to these dim young ladies. He would be no match for a Dorothea Brooke or a Catherine Earnshaw; and certainly an Anna Karenina, a Madame Bovary, a Hetty Sorrell, or a Tess of the D'Urbervilles would make mincemeat of him.

About the same time as Albert Lewin's *Dorian Gray*, another transformation monster was achieving the necessary changes via organ transplants. From *Black Friday* (1940) to the late Hammer *Frankenstein*s in the 1970s, this seemed a promising path to follow. Equipped with the brain of a maniac, an otherwise meek and mild-mannered man (never a woman) might give vent to all manner of tabooed aggressions. Another promising path to this kind

of shock was the ape-serum route by which the pathetic recipient of an injec-
tion of either ape blood or ape glands could lumber out into the world with
his knuckles scraping the ground to commit acts of which he had only
dreamed.[7]

The only instance I can recall in which a woman was made monstrous in
this manner was in *The Jungle Woman/Jungle Captive/Captive Wild
Woman* genre, in which the sex hormones of Paula Dupree were injected
into a circus ape. These transplants and animal mutations are not really the
way to produce the transformation monster, and this may account for the
fact that they never garnered an audience for more than a few pictures. For
the monstrous change to be effective, it seems that it must come from within,
not be administered from without.

Because of his implosive nature, the transformation monster is now almost
totally in the province of popular psychology. He is now usually a psychopathic schizophrenic, pure and simple and vindictive. Aside from such productions as *Altered States* (1980), in which the protagonist regresses into a
simian second self and runs around Cambridge for a few wild nights, the
conversion is the realm not of the Darwinians, but of the Freudians. Certainly the most influential movie of this Jekyll/Hyde ilk was Hitchcock's
Psycho (1960), and it has been played again and again. Here both men and
women transmogrify. On the distaff side there is a continuing theme that
runs through more than a hundred films from *Whatever Happened to Baby
Jane?* (1962) and *Repulsion* (1965) to *Prom Night* (1979), while their unhinged
male counterparts populate hundreds more from *Homicidal* (1961) and
Dementia 13 (1963) to *Alone in the Dark* (1982). The males clearly dominate
the proto-myth and it may well be that one of them, like Michael of *Halloween* or Jason of *Friday the 13th*, will spring loose and generate a saga of his
own. After all, as we see with "Scorpio" in *Dirty Harry*, Luther in *The War-
riors*, and Travis Bickle in *Taxi Driver*, the sadistic psychopath has already
migrated into other genres. Perhaps if we knew more about his victim we
would be more interested in his mindless rage.

For me none of these are real horror stories; they are, instead, rituals of
terror, and most recently the ritual has centered around "undressed women
in distress" being molested by masked, maniacal men. As we have seen, while
terror and horror share many of the same motifs, the manipulation is profoundly different. Terror drives for shock; horror for forbidden knowledge.
To me the most interesting of the lot is a film that may prove more influential
than *Psycho*. It was made in the same year, 1960, by another English director,
and initially suffered the same drubbing in the press. The movie is *Peeping
Tom* and I should like to discuss it briefly, both for what it promises and for

what it delivers in the development of the modern iconography of both terror and horror.

I started this discussion of modern horror by looking at the mid-eighteenth-century engravings of Hogarth, "The Four Stages of Cruelty." If you recall, they traced the decline and fall of one of the first urban beasts, Tom Nero, as he moved from slum to slaughterhouse. Tom is unmythic, uninteresting, and positively banal in the progressively brutal application of his masculine power. However, like the more complex horror monsters that would come in the future, we can see in his actions, especially in his sexual aggression, the direction that romantic shivers were taking. The evolution of the gothic did much to nurture and transport this one eidolon of communal—and more particularly, familial—fears. For Tom became, by turns, the rogue, the villain, and finally the monster.

The energies of his terrifying attacks still animate so much that inheres in modern fright. What makes *Peeping Tom* noteworthy is that here, almost from the first frame, we are forced to confront the relationship between watching and participating. In horror art there is no such thing as a casual observer; detachment is not just impossible, it is fraudulent. As Stella (Thelma Ritter) announces at the beginning of *Rear Window* (1954), "we have become a nation of Peeping Toms." As Brian De Palma has most recently shown in *Body Double* (1984), the eye is the lens of the entire nevous system, letting in information and excitement without understanding and censorship. Like Renaissance views of love, modern horror first enters through the eye: it is visual, then visceral. Little wonder it is so often pornographic. Predictably, *Peeping Tom* has become a favorite of New Wave criticism because it equates the act of seeing with aggression, even sexual aggression, even rape. So here, for instance, Susan Sontag in *On Photography* (1973) isolates one of the film's many facets:

> There is a much stronger sexual fantasy in Michael Powell's extraordinary movie *Peeping Tom* (1960), which is not about a Peeping Tom but about a psychopath who kills women with a weapon concealed in his camera, while photographing them. Not once does he touch his subjects. He doesn't desire their bodies; he wants their presence in the form of filmed images—those showing them experiencing their own death—which he screens at home for his solitary pleasure. The movie assumes connections between impotence and aggression, professionalized looking and cruelty, which point to the central fantasy connected with the camera. The camera as phallus is, at most, a flimsy variant of the inescapable metaphor that everyone unselfconsciously employs. However hazy our awareness of this fantasy, it is named without subtlety whenever we talk about "loading" and "aiming" a camera, about "shooting" a film. (pp. 13–14)

When first displayed, *Peeping Tom* evoked not such sympathy but wrath, and this wrath was so long-lasting that the film was pulled from major American distribution. Here is just a sampling of English dudgeon: "The only really satisfactory way to dispose of *Peeping Tom* would be to shovel it up and flush it swiftly down the nearest sewer. Even then the stench would remain ..." (Derek Hill in the *Tribune*); "*Peeping Tom* stinks more than anything else in British films since *The Stranglers of Bombay*. . . . What worries me is that anyone could entertain this muck and give it commercial shape ..." (William Whitebait in *The New Statesman*); "It is only surprising that while the Marquis' books are still forbidden here after practically two centuries, it is possible within the commercial industry, to produce films like *Peeping Tom*. De Sade at least veiled his enjoyment under the pretence of being a moralist" (David Robinson in the *Monthly Film Bulletin*); and "I was shocked to the core to find a director of his standing befouling the screen with such perverted nonsense. It wallows in the discarded urges of a homicidal pervert. . . . It uses phoney cinema artifice and heavy orchestral music to whip up a debased atmosphere. . . . From its lumbering, mildly salacious beginning to its appallingly masochistic and depraved climax it is wholly evil" (Nina Hibbins in *The Daily Worker*). When American audiences did finally have a chance to see the film in the mid-sixties, it was cut by some seventy minutes and was usually shown as the weak side of a double bill. When next dumped onto television, it was still further truncated, given a new title (*Face of Fear*), and relegated to the middle of the night. *Peeping Tom* would have been forgotten had not Martin Scorcese (*Taxi Driver*, *Raging Bull*) revived it and redistributed it, and had not critical interest in Structuralism, Deconstruction, Reader Response Criticism, and all the recent hullaballoo about "text location" provided a polite vocabulary for discussing images otherwise so disturbing. For this is the kind of film one feels very uneasy about liking and even less easy about discussing.

As with Polanski's *Repulsion*, which was to come five years later, *Peeping Tom* starts by taking us inside the protagonist's eye or, in this case, inside his camera. We see life just as he does, as images on thin-emulsion, 16 mm, black-and-white film. We watch as he trails a prostitute through Prufrockean streets, winding upstairs to her place of business. We are forced, simply by opening our eyes, to conspire with his designs. The camera makes his reality ours. All we know is what it "sees"; our limits are its depth of field, its direction, its speed, its perimeters. And as long as the girl is attractive and the prospects are encouraging, such voyeurism is titillating. She is poised on the cross hairs of the viewfinder. But then, abruptly, we see from her face she is terrified and coming up into the picture from below we see the needle-sharp point of the tripod leg. The chrome leg is becoming a knife. It is a moment not soon forgotten, for what we thought was going to be an act of peeping delight is now transformed into one of sadistic cruelty. We are not just observing; we are participating.

We now jump from 16 to 35 mm film and see the world in Eastman color and hear it complete with the comforting sound track of a jazz piano. We are "back at the movies" and we now see who has been moving us about— whom we have eyed/I'd. His name is Mark Lewis and he is as nice a young man as we could ever hope to meet (Laurence Harvey had tested for the part, but Carl Boehm is just ideal—not a trace of anything stirring below the surface except . . .). In his working hours Mark is a focus-puller at a movie studio and so spends his day setting up "reality" for others. In his spare time he freelances, taking soft-porn stills for magazines, and then for his own amusement he films a few cinéma vérité scenes for himself. He is only content when looking at life through a viewfinder and only secure when the actual pictures have been "taken" from life. Like the vampire he lives off the energies of what he can capture and bleed.

Mark lives in a nicely furnished Victorian house, not the gothic manse of his American counterpart Norman Bates, but with the same, now omnipresent, central staircase. Since his parents have died, he lives upstairs, renting the first floor to a blind woman and her daughter, Helen. Soon Helen and Mark become friendly, or as friendly as a couple can be if one of them is obsessed with seeing everything through a camera lens, and Mark is temporarily able to put his magical glass down for a few minutes. He even asks Helen upstairs to see his apartment. As he gradually feels more secure, he shows her more and more of his life—especially the darkroom where he develops, catalogs, and projects the images of his private life. He even shows Helen films taken by his father, films first of his father and stepmother (a woman whom he regards with disgust and who looks just like all his victims) and then films of himself as a child, especially one in which he is being startled awake by a lizard. Helen watches in terror as she sees the child cringing from the reptile, and Mark reflexively grabs his camera and starts filming her. We now finally realize that the camera is to Mark what the bludgeon is to Tom Nero; it is his chosen instrument of expression and oppression.

As if we didn't already know it, it becomes clear as we see Mark fondling the camera in his lap: the instrument is sexual. We listen as he explains family life to Helen. Mark's father was a biologist studying the effects of fear on the human organism, and to obtain an objective record of terror-habituation he contrived a life of frightening events for his son. He filmed them. Such a medical history might have exculpated Mark if he, himself, had not then proceeded to do exactly the same, only much worse, to others. The next day he sets out to film another victim, this time a stand-in actress who has trou-

Carl Boehm and camera in *Peeping Tom,* 1960 (Anglo-Amalgamated)

bles expressing fright; Mark literally impales her. We watch numbly as he whispers comforting encouragement from behind the camera—you see, he says, you can express fear, you can act, even though it will be your last act.

Back at home, matters with Helen have so warmed that she is now kissing both him and his camera. Her blind mother is suspicious and ventures upstairs into Mark's darkroom. She cannot, of course, see what he has been doing, but she is sensible enough to warn him that "all this filming everything is unhealthy." Mark already knows that. A psychiatrist, called in to investigate the murder of the film actress, has even made the proper diagnosis: scoptophilia, the nursing baby's natural pleasure in watching the nurturing breast, the voyeur's displaced and aggressive sexual excitement. Still Mark is hopelessly trapped by his own inability to become frightened/excited and must compulsively return to repeat the only act he has associated with pleasure: the terrorizing of women.

Helen, meanwhile, has become not so much a lover as a confidante. As a matter of fact, Mark even lets her in to see the shrine of his mother's room. It is clear that Helen's position as mother-substitute has protected her from Mark's aggression, but it is also clear that if she ever strays into becoming the stepmother—that is, a woman—she will be in danger. Helen could have been protected by Mark's Oedipal inhibition had she not ventured, like her mother, into his private world, into the room where he develops and consumes his forbidden images. She catches Mark in an act of self-arousal, staring at his films of women being literally invaded, and he is startled and confused, not at being caught, but at her look of panic. It is the look he associates with those "other" women. He begs her to settle down: "You are safe as long as I can see you, as long as I can't hold my camera," he all but says as she at last realizes the truth. Like Tom Nero, Mark has lost control.

Outside, the police, following the trail Mark has conveniently left from victim to victim, draw closer. By this time we are hoping not to see what is next, for we have grown fond of Helen and had quite enough of this nice-looking, monstrous Mr. Lewis. In preparation for his grand exit Mark has trip-wired his room with all sorts of audio and video devices and even attached a large mirror to the top of his camera so that Helen can see herself seeing him approaching. "Nothing is so frightening as one's own fear," he calmly opines. Mark loads the camera, unclasps the tripod, and starts to fire. First he "shoots" the police from the upstairs window in Hollywood gangster style as they surround the house, then he pans to Helen. As he moves closer to her he trips the remote-controlled still cameras and we hear the focal plane shutters open and shut, his 16-mm camera whir, and see the flash-bulbs pop. In an abrupt series of jump-cuts we are back now inside his movie camera, back in black and white, back where we began in *Peeping Tom*, again moving across a room toward the panic-stricken victim. We see the tripod leg point first toward her, then skewer her, then point back at Mark, at us. In the background we hear the recorded voice of Mark's father coming from one of the many recorders. "Don't be a silly boy. There is nothing to be afraid of." The police break down the door, too late. She is dead and he is dead, stuck on the spike of his tripod. We are exhausted.

Michael Powell has called *Peeping Tom* "a very tender film and a very nice one," and setting aside the obvious irony, there is something horribly sympathetic about Mark Lewis. Admittedly, this is an absolutely gruesome and macabre record of a young man's life; it is totally devoid of humor or relief, and it is unremitting in intensity. The symbolism is often blatant to the point of distraction: when queried, Mark claims to be a photographer of *The Observer*; the "blind" mother "sees"; Helen refers to the camera as Mark's "extra limb"; to say nothing of a scene in which Mark all but performs fellatio on his lens mount. However, if you can view the film as a ritual of family romance, as a rite of passage, as a modern morality play, then *Peeping Tom* is indeed a rather "tender" film, although hardly a "nice" one. The adolescent's family relationships have essentially been elevated to the ferocious; the father has given Mark the code of masculine behavior and disappeared;

the surrogate mother is "blind" to the violation of her son; and Mark is left to apply the code, not with Tom Nero's sticks and knives, but with mirrors and shutters and spikes. That Helen, the sister/mother, should be the ultimate victim is terrible, but predictable.

What is missing from *Peeping Tom*, and what makes this rendition of family romance so unsettling, is any palliative of myth. There are no prisms between the narrative and life, no Transylvanian forests between him and us, no distant island, no magical lab or transforming drug. There is nothing to protect us; worse still, we seem continually drawn into this maelstrom simply by watching it. Once we start to look, we cannot help but see; reality is, after all, in the lens of the director. So we sit watching Mark watching Helen watching Mark watched by us.

I do not argue that *Peeping Tom* is a traditional horror film—it is a thriller; but I would like to suggest that it may point us in the direction in which current horror motifs are moving. When one looks back over the last two decades, it is clear that there has been a domesticating and demythologizing of characters.[8] Here Mark Lewis is indeed another vampire/werewolf violating the privacy of "the ones he loves most in life," and another mindless monster acting out repressed sexual hostilities. Again and again we have seen him return as the stalk-and-slasher in such "wait until dark" forgettables as *When a Stranger Calls, Don't Go in the House, He Knows You're Alone, Maniac, Deadly Blessing, Without Warning, The Bogeyman, I Spit on Your Grave, Maniac,* all of which, thanks to the Steadicam, show us the rampage from the ripper's point of view and, thanks to expert editing, make that viewpoint our own. The influence of Peeping Tom's camera is going to be felt and seen for some time to come. No longer is it *their* family that has problems; it is our own. No longer *him* doing it, but me.

One can certainly see the domestication of horror archetypes all through the 1970s. It is almost as if the old mythic projections— Dracula, Frankenstein, Wolfman—had been caught in Dr. Cyclops' miniaturizing gizmo and been reduced to Lilliputian dimensions. Where the 1950s and 1960s had teenage vampires, Frankenstein monsters, and werewolves (*I Was a Teenage . . .*), the 1970s had the vampire children of *'Salem's Lot*, the zombie kids of *The Children*, the cannibal tots of *Raw Meat*, the telekinetic toddlers of *Village of the Damned*, and their teenage counterparts in *Carrie, Jennifer,* and *Cathy's Curse*. It would be tantalizing to imagine that this "downsizing" of monsters was related to changes in human reproduction habits and shifting demographic patterns, as if the culture were saying "let's think twice about bringing more children into the world." Kids *can* be monstrous. But I suspect these pint-sized monsters were developed to reach a movie audience between eight and twenty-two years old. After all, this was the only audience with enough disposable income and interest to be counted on, and like other audiences they wanted to see themselves in the starring roles. The pubescent monsters of the seventies were not always polite, but they were always sympathetic, at least for a while.

I would not want to attribute too much to audience composition, because there are other monsters developing, seedling monsters, that have no counterpart audience. The infant monster is, however, a fascinating cultural development in part because it is such an inversion of the Victorian victim. For the past two centuries there has been an occasionally strident dialogue embedded in culture about the nature of children. In simplest terms, as Peter Coveney outlined two decades ago in *The Image of Childhood*, the opposing forces of Puritan and Romantic tended to categorize the child in antithetical terms.[9] The Puritan defined the infant in terms of his propensity for evil; the romantic, in terms of his incapacity for evil. Now, admittedly, Blake, Wordsworth, Coleridge, Dickens, George Eliot, and Lewis Carroll tended to emphasize the child's active impulse for goodness, but they were extreme. The usual romantic view is the more temperate position articulated in religious terms by thinkers like Locke, Wesley, Newman, and Spencer—the child is innocence as yet uncorrupted.

What has occurred in our century is curious, for the proposition articulated by Blake and the other romantics, that youth is *active* goodness, has been transposed (at least in some important horror movies) into the Puritanical extreme of child as active evil. The key explicators here are not theologians, but psychologists, especially the Freudians, who have found in the "Darling of a pigmy size" a raging inferno of sexual energies directing libidinous forces with the ferocity of a snarling beast. The literary work that first announces this shift is Henry James' *The Turn of The Screw* (1897). Clearly, in this novella we have no idea if little Miles and little Flora have done something horrible, but the possibility is there. And while that possibility was not exploited in *The Innocents* (1961), a stylish adaptation by Truman Capote that resolved all those Jamesian ambiguities by making much too much of the neurotic governess, it has not been neglected elsewhere. In the late fifties *The Bad Seed* did just the opposite by transforming the William March novel and Maxwell Anderson play into a riveting tale of pint-sized fury. But even in this film Mervyn Le Roy was unwilling to let the story end where it should have: with the lightning bolt zapping the bad seed, young Rhoda. He tacked on a theatrical curtain call in which the actors pass in review and so the last thing we see is Rhoda being spanked by her mother for having been naughty while the cast applauds. As the house lights come up, we are requested not to reveal the ending to friends. Which ending—the movie's or the studio's? A few years later the English adapted John Wyn-

Grave of the Vampire: lobby poster, 1972 (Millenium Productions)

Rick Baker and the *It's Alive* and *It Lives Again* monster baby, 1974-78 (Warner Brothers)

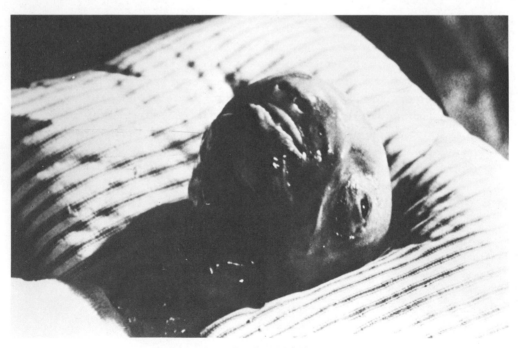

Baby in *Eraserhead*, 1978 (Libra Films)

Children in the *Village of the Damned*, 1960 (M-G-M Studios)

Harvey Stephens as Damien in
The Omen, 1970
(20th Century Fox)

dham's *The Midwitch Cuckoos* and were characteristically more tolerant of the possessed moppets of Midwitch (*Village of the Damned*, 1960, and its sequel, *Children of the Damned*, 1963) by having the children ultimately sympathetic. But there could be no doubting it, in the modern horror tale pedophobia was crowding in on the family of monsters. Almost as if to relieve ourselves of the responsibility, we claimed it was not Dr. Spock but the Devil that made them act that way. So we have entertained the idea that the youngster's body could be a husk for demonic forces in films like *The Exorcist*, *The Devil Within Her*, *Fear No Evil*, *The Haunting of Julia*, *Possession*, *The Omen* (*I, II,* and *III*), *To the Devil ... A Daughter*, all of which have *Rosemary's Baby* as the immediate incubating text. We also like to pretend that the child can be an independent perpetrator of evil, simply a mistake—no fault of our own. The only thing more frightening than the adult brutalizing the cherubic child is that same situation turned inside out—the child systematically brutalizing the loving parent.

Here we may be developing a new image of horror that might become archetypical if it ever finds a stable narrative: the central image is a slithery embryonic creature who gets into the family by invading the female reproductive system and then by reappearing as the demonic, devouring child.

I think that a case could be made that this image starts to find conceptual dimensions in John Hayes' crude *Grave of the Vampire* (1971). Although critically neglected, this film is prescient in its anticipation of contemporary concerns, not the least of which is its concentration on the human baby as literal monster consuming the energies of all who nurture it. In *Grave*, the heroine, Lesley, is raped by a patriarchal vampire just after her beau has proposed marriage. Months later when the medical authorities assure Lesley that she is now incubating a monstrosity ("What is inside you cannot be a human being. It's a parasite. It will kill you."), she refuses to have an abortion. She carries the parasite to term and then, once delivered, it turns on her, draining her lifeblood as milk. Then it moves on to others, all the time exchanging its death for their life. We see the same general situation replayed in David Lynch's *Eraserhead* (1977) and then in still more ferocious detail in Larry Cohen's twins, *It's Alive* (1974) and *It Lives Again* (1978), as well as in David Cronenberg's *The Brood* (1979) and in Andrzej Zulanski's *Possession* (1981). We see the same image of the pint-sized, snaggle-toothed carnivore either stated or implied in such films as *To the Devil ... a Daughter* (1976), *Inseminoid* (1980), *Scared to Death* (1980), and *The Intruder Within* (1981). Admittedly, the image of innocence corrupted runs through the "possession" genre in such films as *The Exorcist*, *The Heretic*, *Audrey Rose*, *The Manitou*, *Demon Witch Child*, *The Stranger Within*, *The Sentinel*, and now Damien of *The Omen* trilogy, but this new mini-monster is shorn of all pseudo-religious explanations. It's alive, and it's out to get us.

Whether or not the miniature demon survives is quite another question, a question beyond the scope of this study. Perhaps it will become the nonmetaphorical mindless bogey of *Alien, The Beast Within, Parasite* ilk. Maybe it will play out the role of miniature Hyde as does Belial in *Basket Case*. Or maybe it will mature into the benign child of fantasy films like the nice little red-coated alien ambassadors of *Close Encounters of the Third Kind*. But, more likely, I think the squid-child will continue as the abdomen-bursting, parent-destroying whelp of evil as it has for the last decade. After all, in 1981 *Humanoids from the Deep* was made, which includes something new among the ritual scenes; here we witness the resurrection of a slew of Creatures from the Black Lagoon (thanks to a leak of "DNA–5" into the water system), the mating of those creatures with the requisite young teenage girls, and the bashing of the creatures by the townspeople. The last frames of this film show a struggling schoolgirl in the maternity ward experiencing the tortures of extraordinary contractions. We see the bug-eyed doctor and frantic nurses as her belly explodes and there it is—the little hellion is out again.

I suspect that while we are clearly tiring of the maniacal slasher (there have been a number of recent movies like *The Seduction*, 1982, in which the female out-slashes her assailant), we are only starting to be plagued by this miniature cannibal. It is debatable whether the irredeemable brat will gain a toehold in popular culture. This much, however, is clear: the dominant monsters of the modern imagination—the vampire, the hulk-with-no-name, and the transformation monster—will endure for some time to come. They will endure, while other beasts come and go, because we will continue to search them out in the dark, continue to listen to what they have to say and watch what they do, and continue to be terrified by them out of ignorance. We may not appreciate them, let alone want to have them around, but they have been with us for a long time, and for good reasons. Unless these reasons change, we had best be prepared to see them again and again, illumined by the full moon of adolescent curiosity.

Notes

Chapter 1

1. This technique of forcing an audience to beg for the privilege of being terrified has not been lost on Hollywood distributors just as it was never lost on camp counselors sitting around the fire or on Victorian serial novelists. Doubtless the bard singing *Beowulf* did the same thing. Right now many B-pictures have joined *The Rocky Horror Picture Show* in being shown *only* at midnight and *only* on weekends. It seems that the more difficult horror images are to reach, the more startling their effect. *Rocky Horror* has now grossed more than $430 million in this manner and it is only a matter of time before *Variety* will refer to Tom Deegan, director of advertising at Twentieth-Century Fox, as a "genius in the state of the art." "Limited-audience films," as they are called, are usually re-releases of films that did not do well during normal hours, but explode financially when confined. Movies like *Night of the Living Dead*, *Pink Flamingos*, *Eraserhead*, *The Harder They Come*, *The Texas Chainsaw Massacre*, and *The Last House on the Left* are becoming genuine cult films, and why cultism is so important in horror art, I will try to explain in the next chapter.

2. This distinction between horror and terror was not at all what Mrs. Radcliffe had in mind when she and others attempted to construct a crude paradigm of frightful events. In the eighteenth century, terror was the sensation of something loathsome while horror was its direct apprehension. Here is the usual metapsychology made modern by Dorothy Scarborough: "Seeing a supernatural visitant is terrible, hearing him is direful, smelling him is loathsome, but having him touch you is the climax of

horror." So presumably if you are lying in darkness and you hear stirrings in the attic—that's terror; if you hear creaking stairs—it's still terror; and if you see your door slowly open—yet more terror. But when the thing pounces on you—ah, now, that's horror. But if it misses, only more terror. Stephen King in *Danse Macabre* (1981) echoes this anatomy by considering terror the stuff that sets the skin a-crawling, horror what is subcutaneous, so to speak, and then "lowest of all, the gag reflex of revulsion." He continues, "I recognize terror as the finest . . . emotion, and so I will try to terrorize the reader. But if I find I cannot terrify him/her, I will try to horrify; and if I find I cannot horrify, I'll go for the gross-out. I'm not proud" (p. 37). Although I disagree with Mr. King, he would not be without academic supporters. Here is Professor Rictor Norton's explanation in "Aesthetic Gothic Horror":

> A statistical survey of the pertinent diction in Gothic novels would indicate that "horror" is indeed often associated with physicality, but it would also indicate that there is nevertheless a definite difference between horror and disgust. Edgar Allan Poe, who cannot be overlooked in a discussion of horror fiction, indicates in *The Masque of the Red Death* the cumulative series-relationship of such terms: at the appearance of the mummer "there arose at length from the whole company a buzz, or murmur, expressive of disapprobation and surprise—then finally, of terror, of horror, and of disgust." "Horror" almost always follows "terror" and precedes "disgust" and, most important, is brought about by a succession of structured enclosures similar to Prince Prospero's chambers. Terror is a psychological reaction that exists when the terror-inspiring object is still at some distance from oneself and there is the possibility of fleeing it; horror is an aesthetic experience which exists when the terror-inspiring object is in very close proximity to oneself and there is no possibility of escaping it. (p. 35)

3. A good case could be made that modern monsters have Milton's Satan as their great progenitor. As Blake knew, there was something revolutionary in Milton's demon—something modern. What modern horrors have is different from all that went before: they have their own unique existences, their own solipsistic codes, not just "a room of their own" but their own self-contained worlds. They are not in the text to illuminate their opponent, but to establish their own *raison d'êtres* at his expense. Destroying them is still important, but we now know we will never be successful, for like Antaeus they will only rise up again with more strength. We can never defeat horror monsters so we must learn to live with them. As the newspaperman says at the end of *The Thing*, "Keep watching the skies!" There are a lot more of those things with no name around than we can ever control.

4. In fact, the next possible breakthrough is a 4- by 5-foot black machine called Introvision that fits onto the camera and allows the picture to be dissected so that objects can be photographed in wildly improbable scenes with no loss of verisimilitude. It has already been used in movies like *Outland* and *Megaforce* and promises to cut the cost of production by millions as it essentially does the work of mattes and front and rear projection.

5. The background of wigged dignitaries has been lifted *in toto* from another engraving, but no matter; what is interesting to note is that in 1745 the surgeons separated from the barbers to form their own consortium, complete with operating theater, right next door to Newgate Gaol. If only Sweeney Todd had been on the

other side, they might have been well provided for. This is, I think, the first scene in English art where the surgeon actively participates in the horror of dismemberment. Medicos can now look forward to a long and productive career in fabricated fright, for the overenthusiastic surgeon will soon become archetypal: Drs. Frankenstein, Gogal, X, Death, Phibes, Butcher, and a host of healers will continue to act out our secret suspicions about what they are really like under their bedside manners. The surgeons here are clearly enjoying themselves, but soon they will have to seek elsewhere for bodies, thus initiating a subtext of medicine-become-horrible: the story of Burke and Hare, the body snatchers. Anyone who has ever heard Karloff's "You'll never get rid of me" can never forget the Val Lewton movie, but why is it that the villains in grave-robbing movies are always so likable? Is it because they are "resurrectionists" and the dead have nothing to lose; are they vampires in reverse? And what about the "transfusers" who, until recently, had the improvement of the race as the noble object of their experiments and would have succeeded if only Ygor had returned with the proper organ? How can we dislike someone whose intentions are to straighten the tracks of evolutionary progress? Or the re-builders like Dr. Moreau, the notorious vivisector, who is strangely sympathetic in both the novel and films. How can you blame him for the fact that those animals prefer to be savage?

6. I'll say something about his works of fantastic horror— *Christabel, The Rime of the Ancient Mariner, Kubla Khan*—later. We tend to treat them as *sui generis*, but they derive in part from high gothic and are some of the first poetic works of "modern horror."

7. To see how long that list could be, see David Punter, *The Literature of Terror*, Chapter 14, Stephen King, *Danse Macabre*, Appendix 2 (a list of some hundred contemporary practitioners), Glen St. John Barclay, *Anatomy of Horror: The Masters of Occult Fiction* (J. Sheridan Le Fanu to Dennis Wheatley), Irving Malin, *New American Gothic* (O'Connor, Purdy, McCullers, Capote, Hawkes, and Salinger), and for real excess see Elsa J. Radcliffe, *Gothic Novels of the Twentieth Century: An Annotated Bibliography* (1979) which has a census of 1,973 items.

8. Distinct Italian, Mexican, Scandinavian, Germanic, French, and especially Japanese, cycles of horror have evolved in dramatically different ethnic ways. Scandinavians and Germans have had a literary history much like our own, so they never had to go far beyond the printed text to capture the popular audience. But the Mexicans and Japanese, almost without a history of horror texts, have had to develop an entourage of resident monsters (Santo and Godzilla are the most famous) and involve them in specifically nationalistic plots. These historical and cultural differences still show— northern European horror almost unremittingly is intellectual and obscure (Bergman's *Hour of the Wolf*, Dreyer's *Vampyr*); Mexican and Japanese, wild and sensual. Oddly enough, it is the Italian *Giallo* film, from Maria Bava in the forties to a new generation of simple-minded directors who revel in really gratuitous terrors (*City of the Living Dead, Zombie II* . . .), that is giving Hollywood the financial jitters. These Italian horrors take the European literary themes and treat them with a lustiness reminiscent of the Mexicans and the naive exuberance of the Japanese. The other up-and-coming producers of horror are the Canadians and the Australians, whose movies like *They Came from Within* or *The Last Wave* in the last decade promise much more than they have so far delivered. What usually happens is that the best Canadians and Australians end up in Hollywood making American movies.

Chapter 2

1. Although discussing the procreative anxieties inherent in horror myths may belabor the obvious, excellent articles have been written on this subject by Walter Evans, "Monster Movies and Rites of Initiation" and "Monster Movies: A Sexual Theory" and by Robin Wood, "Gods and Monsters" and "Return of the Repressed."

2. In the grocery store of myth I know just where to look to find the tonic water, while my children know just where *Count Chocula* and *Frankenberry* are. Movie producers are as knowledgeable about "hunger and thirst" as marketing executives at the A&P; they are, in fact, largely supported by it. Since the 1960s the transmission of horror has become, in terms of the trade, "a primary profit center." Horror movies are not just top money-makers year in and year out, and not just among the top grossers of all time; they have become one of the least risky of all genres. It currently (1985) costs about $10 million to make an average movie and then another $6 million to market it. The average horror film costs half that much. Who can afford to take a chance even when the market is saturated as it is now. Certainly not George Litto, who announced when he took over Filmways (the conglomerate where the old warhorse American International Pictures is now stabled): "Making films doesn't have to be like going to Las Vegas. You just sit down with your distributors in Japan, Spain, and Germany, and ask them what their audiences want to see. You find out what the people want, and you fulfill that" (*Wall Street Journal*, March 11, 1981, p. 12). What has been Filmways' major success since Mr. Litto took over control from the trustees at Chase Manhattan? *The Amityville Horror*, a mediocre horror film still making money even with terrible sequels.

The reason the grocery store at Hollywood and Vine is so full of the junkfood of horror schlock is that this is the stuff that sells. The producer takes a chance investing in *Kramer vs. Kramer*, *Ordinary People*, *The Four Seasons*, *Chapter Two*, or *Terms of Endearment*, but the horror movie is almost sure to be consumed at a profit: it is simply a matter of demographics and disposable income. Although surveys vary slightly, the only audience that can be counted on, or rather, banked on, is now between twelve and twenty years old. In the late seventies this audience was between fifteen and twenty-four. Ironically, the only people who have both the desire and the money to go to the movies are teenagers. So if you think "they're not making movies like they used to," you're right. And chances are they won't for quite a while. Certainly not as long as a forgettable movie like *Maniac* can gross $1.4 million in its first week in New York City or an equally nonsensical *Blood Beach* $3.1 million. These are low-quality productions even by industry standards. When the film is well done, the sky's the limit: Irwin Yablans spent $320,000 to make *Halloween* in 1978 and so far it's made over $75 million; Stanley Kubrick spent $15 million on *The Shining*, which has returned more than $120 million. It seems that the most important thing for a producer to worry about is to be sure his movie is rated not "X" or "PG" but "R" (supposedly no one under seventeen admitted without an adult, but, as even the industry admits, as it did in *The Report of the U.S. Commission on Obscenity and Pornography*, only children are kept out of "R" horror films). A 1982 Gallup Youth Survey found 83 percent of 1,012 respondents in the 13 to 15 age group had seen an "R" film. The long range influence of "PG–13" remains to be seen, but it already has had its first impact on thrillers. *Dreamscape*, the first movie so rated, was trimmed of twenty seconds to avoid an "R." Ironically, while the "soft R" films may be tempered, the "hard R" slashers may become more gruesome as the producers argue that the kiddies can't see it anyway so the imagery and action can be closer to "X."

3. The closest thing to an in-depth audience study was Leo A. Handel's *Hollywood Looks at Its Audience* (1950), which has been updated with studies like: Stuart H. Britt, "What Is the Nature of the Drive-In Theater Audience?"; Harry Carlson, "Movies and Teenagers"; K. A. Kaufman, "Why Do People Go to the Movies? A Study of Attendance"; and A. D. Murphy, "Audience Demographics, Film Future." As yet there has been no detailed study of the horror-movie audience.

4. In "Why Movie Audiences Aren't Safe Any More," Roger Ebert expands on this shift of sensibility:

> The lust to kill and rape becomes the true subject of [these] movies. And the lust is not placed on the screen, where it can be attached to the killer-character; it is placed in the audience. The missing character in so many of these films can be found in the audience; we are all invited to be him, and some (such as my white-haired neighbor) gladly accept the role. (p. 56)

Janet Maslin, "Bloodbaths Debase Movies and Audiences," concurs:

> And this kind of horror film, in addition to inuring its audience to genuine violence, has a debasing effect as well. In this respect it harkens back to hard-core sexual pornography, the tactics of which it carries to the most extreme degree. Years ago, when sexual explicitness on screen seemed to have advanced as far as it possibly could go, it was often remarked that only by actually penetrating the body could the camera go farther. That, in a sense, is what the camera does now. (*New York Times*, November 21, 1982, p. 13)

In "The Effects of Multiple Exposures to Filmed Violence Against Women," David Linz and two colleagues in the Psychology department at the University of Wisconsin contend such films "desensitize" the audience to acts of male barbarism. Over a five day period twenty-four male students, divided into equal groups, watched *Texas Chainsaw Massacre, Maniac, I Spit on Your Grave,* and *Toolbox Murders* in different order. They were then asked to rate the films in terms of degradation and violence. The films watched last were generally considered less debased. This suggested to the psychologists that the viewers were becoming immune to such sequences. Then a control group and a group that had consumed the images of misogyny watched a videotaped trial of a man accused of raping a young woman. The group that had seen the thrillers were less sympathetic with the female victim, and thought she had suffered less harm, than the group that had not seen the films.

5. There is an anecdote that explains the almost compulsive repetition of horror sagas. Here it is as told by Saul Bellow:

> One of my [favorite stories] is about an American singer who makes his debut at La Scala. He sings his first aria to great applause. And the crowd calls "Ancora, vita, vita." He sings it a second time, and again they call for an encore. Then a third time and a fourth .... Finally, panting and exhausted, he asks, "How many times must I sing this aria?" Then someone tells him, "Until you get it right."

Harvey M. Greenberg, M.D., also concurs in *The Movies on Your Mind* (1975) that it is the audience's feelings that they haven't "got it quite right", and so demands that the "singer" of the horror tale repeat the same "song" until either he gets it right or the audience becomes interested in other "songs."

6. Here the sense of collective unconscious seems implied by Freud and it is noteworthy that, although Jung never dealt with modern horror myths per se (wisely preferring to examine more stable images), it is no accident that he glosses a picture of Godzilla in *Man and His Symbols*: "Perhaps the monsters of modern 'horror' films are distorted versions of archetypes that will no longer be repressed" (p. 92).

7. The special effects here are remarkable. Although the original plans called for the monster to announce his presence only with heavy breathing, the front office at M-G-M felt constrained to show something anyway. But what should that something look like? M-G-M subcontracted with Disney to use the talents of Joshua Lawrence Meador who, after some false starts, produced a monster that looks less like a tiger than a lion—in fact, somewhat like M-G-M's Leo the Lion trademark.

8. I may exaggerate the importance of my topic in contending that the myths of early adolescence are as important as the tales of childhood, but who could have foreseen a generation ago how much children's "literature" could hold in the way of important messages? In contemporary academia "kiddie lit" is a veritable growth industry complete with scholarly journals (*Children's Literature, The Lion and the Unicorn, The Horn Book*), scholarly books (since Harvard University Press's 1978 publishing of Roger Sale's *Fairy Tales and After: From Snow White to E. B. White*, it has become de rigueur for a university press to have such a book on its list), and finally, the true mark of scholarly acceptance, the Modern Language Association has raised children's literature to "division status" along with Renaissance Literature and Victorian Novel. One quick fact says even more: from 1930 until 1970 two hundred theses were written about children's literature; in the 1970s alone more than eight hundred dissertations.

9. The often acrimonious battle over Freud's changing views on incest resulted from Jeffrey Masson's exposé, *The Assault on Truth* (1984) and was widely reported in the national media. The best explanation of the controversy is in Janet Malcom's *In the Freud Archives*.

10. Here is Masao Miyoshi's clear-headed explanation for the romantic's fascination with what will become the central convention of modern horror:

> The incest theme has a lineage as long as the Western literary tradition, but its appearance at this time, after a noticeable hiatus in the neoclassic period, and its frequent use since, takes on special significance. Violation of a taboo of this sort, even in fiction, tells as much about the temper of the time as about the author's own psychology. As perhaps the extreme expression of social defiance, incest was a serviceable symbol for the Romantics, who took seriously their obligation as rebels and social critics. What society finds distasteful or dangerous is often for that reason alone attractive to those who see that same society as corrupt and contemptible. Moreover, the sheer shock effect of violating in print such a strong taboo prepared the way for the attack on a whole range of other customs and complacencies. Incest was thus probably the most versatile weapon in the Romantics' antisocial arsenal. It was also, so they were discovering, a metaphor of the most astonishing correspondence to their own state of dual and undecided identity. The

incestuous relation, in dissolving the usual familial as well as extrafamilial bonds between individuals, finally dissolves the identifying masks distinguishing one individual from another. Given the time-honored sense of the family as an extension of self, a larger self in a sense, the incestuous act becomes the moment for the self meeting with itself. At the same time, it provides a temporary escape from roles assigned by fate or society and now unwanted. In embracing his daughter as his mistress, the incestuous father denies his paternity. One can be, through incest, other than oneself, yet strangely, by virtue of this sense of the family as a "larger self," more completely oneself. The new role provides a freedom denied in everyday family experience. In this double perspective, clear border lines of things shift and blur. Not only the familial identities of persons, which shift from daughter to mistress, or son to lover, in relation to the incestuous parent, but the moral categories derived from the family structure begin to transfuse—love into lust, kindness into cruelty. (*The Divided Self: A Perspective on the Literature of the Victorians*, pp. 11–12)

11. In Sweden, long the home of supposed sexual permissiveness, legislators have proposed dropping legal restrictions for an act not uncommon and—as we will see—not necessarily genetically destructive. Canada also seems to be considering publicly acknowledging the inappropriateness of legal punishment for incest. The social ban, of course, is still in effect as well as legal protections for minors. Since the law itself is not clear if the crime is to marry a relative or to fornicate with one, justice may be more appropriately served by prosecuting acts of rape, fornication, seduction, or sexual battery than by making a legal case of incest.

12. Recently there have been some reputable psychologists who have suggested that latency is a period of "sexual rehearsal" and that incest may not be disastrous, but as Wardell Pomeroy, a co-author of the Kinsey report, stated, "sometimes beneficial." Then, in 1979, the Sex Information and Education Council of the United States (SIECUS) released a paper that questioned the "moral and religious pronouncements with respect to incest." Sexologists historically have made their marks by attacking taboos and here was the only one left, now that masturbation, homosexuality, and "a full sex life" were passé. This hubbub has produced a shocking phrase, "positive incest," which has been written about by Ann Landers, talked about by Phil Donahue, and shown on the silver screen by Bernardo Bertolucci in *Luna*. It has also produced outrage articulated by the likes of Benjamin De Mott, in "The Pro-Incest Lobby," and Elizabeth Janeway, in "Incest: A Rational Look at the Oldest Taboo." I would venture to suggest that one of the bits of social information we may be able to glean from the horror movie, from Ulmer's *The Black Cat* (1934) to Cronenberg's *Shivers* (1975), is that there is no such thing as "positive incest."

13. For more on these and other such examples, see Y. A. Cohen, *The Transition from Childhood to Adolescence* (1964); S. N. Eisenstadt, *From Generation to Generation* (1956); Mircea Eliade, *Rites and Symbols of Initiation* (1965); Robin Fox, *The Red Lamp of Incest* (1980); H. Garfinkle, "Conditions of Successful Degradation Ceremonies" (1956); M. Gluckman, ed., *Essays on the Ritual of Social Relations* (1962); Marjorie Shostak, *Nisa: The Life and Words of a !Kung Woman* (1981); A. Van Gennep, *The Rites of Passage* (1909); J. W. M. Whiting, R. Kluckhohn, and A. S. Anthony, "The Function of Male Initiation Ceremonies at Puberty" (1958); and F. Young, *Initiation Ceremonies: A Cross-Cultural Study of Status Dramatization* (1965).

14. As a result of greater awareness about child molestation, but still ignorance about the social utility of horror, these lines were recently removed from the "Monster Song" on *Sesame Street*:

> *If I make friends with a friendly monster,*
> *I'll let him bounce me on his knee.*
> *I'll let him do whatever he wanster,*
> *Especially if he's bigger than me.*

I think this was a proper deletion although Edward Palmer of the Children's Television Workshop said that the song was intended to help children learn that they "need not fear the different kinds of monster images which their fantasies might conjure up" (*New York Times*, April 9, 1984, p. 16).

15. Fox's theory is not without ramifications also implied in horror myt' that the nuclear family is not of primary importance nor is monogamy—what is important is the successful (i.e., reproductive) pairing; that adolescent male hostility is not necessarily Oedipal, but the result of thwarted sexual desire for women; and finally that nonreproductive characters of either sex, be they independent females or homosexual males, are ruthlessly treated in these myths, the former by being the victim of brutal rape, the latter by being the object of ridicule. The people who are always safe in horror stories are mothers who already have children and older men; those most in danger are the sexually active, the young.

Chapter 3

1. It is noteworthy that in both German *Nosferatu* movies, Murnau's in 1922 and Herzog's remake in 1979, the fiend moves with an entourage of invading rats. Since there is no American cultural memory of the plague, the rat is used in the Dracula myth sparingly, like the wolf, to suggest bestial control.

2. In "real life" Dracula has not fared so well. To the 35,000 people who responded to a questionnaire at Madame Tussaud's waxworks museum from 1970 to 1979, Dracula finished fourth in a list of persons, real or fictional, they hated most, behind Hitler, Idi Amin, and Nixon.

3. The folk may be able to pass this contradiction by; however, artists have enjoyed exploiting it and the theme of "in a land of vampires the non-vampire is a monster" has now become almost a subgenre. Taken from Richard Matheson's text, *I Am Legend* (1954), this theme has been exploited on film first in *The Last Man on Earth* (1967) with Vincent Price and then in *The Omega Man* (1971) with Charlton Heston.

4. In *The Living Dead: A Study of the Vampire in Romanticism* (1981), I have tried to make the case that these and other prominent figures in romanticism were, in part, metaphorical vampires based on the newly emerging folk archetype.

5. By no means was this interest in the vampire restricted to Anglo-American literature: think only of de Maupassant's *The Horla*, Tieck's *Wake Not the Dead*, Hoffman's "Aureila" from *The Serapion Brothers*, Nodier's *Smarra*, Gautier's *Clairmonde*, as well as many of Baudelaire's poems such as *Metamorphosis* and Mérimée's ballads in *La Guzla*.

6. Byron, however, did have more than a passing familiarity with the vampire. For instance, in his incredibly popular *Giaour* (a first edition in 1813; the fourteenth edi-

tion in 1815!) he composed the famous "Giaour curse" (which may incidentally have influenced Shelley's *Cenci*):

> But first on earth, as Vampyre sent,
> Thy corpse shall from its tomb be rent;
> Then ghastly haunt thy native place,
> And suck the blood of all thy race;
> There from thy daughter, sister, wife,
> At midnight drain the stream of life;
> Yet loathe the banquet, which perforce
> Must feed thy living corpse,
> Thy victims, ere they yet expire,
> Shall know the demon for their sire;
> As cursing thee, thou cursing them,
> Thy flowers are withered on the stem.
> But one that for thy crime must fall,
> Thy youngest, best beloved of all.
> Shall bless thee with a father's name—
> That word shall wrap thy heart in flame!
> Yet thou must end thy task and mark
> Her cheek's last tinge—her eye's last spark.
> And the last glassy glance must view
> Which freezes o'er its lifeless blue;
> Then with unhallowed hand shall tear
> The tresses of her yellow hair,
> Of which, in life a lock was shorn
> Affection's fondest pledge was worn—
> But now is borne away by thee
> Memorial to thine agony!
> Yet with thine own best blood shall drip
> Thy gnashing tooth, and haggard lip;
> Then stalking to thy sullen grave
> Go—and with Ghouls and Afrits rave.
> Till these in horror shrink away
> From spectre more accursed than they.

7. See especially Act II, i, 21–30; Act II, ii, 50–59 and 118–22 in which the relationship between Manfred and Astarte is established and the connections made between blood and forbidden sex. This was, incidentally, the standard interpretation in the nineteenth century and one reason why the play was never performed.

8. This vampiric interpretation occurred almost by spontaneous combustion to two critics back in the 1960s: Lyle Kendall, "The Vampire Motif in *The Fall of the House of Usher*," and J. O. Bailey, "What Happens in *The Fall of the House of Usher*."

9. The wolf transformation (lycanthropy) is ancient, resulting from the belief that "berserk" people were possessed by wolf spirits and that the vampire with his snarling, biting, and howling was nothing if not berserk. But the bat transformation is recent. During the Spanish conquest of Mexico the conquistadores found a bat (*Desmodus rotundus*) that seemed to drink blood, and returned home with the story. Actually, they do not drink blood; they remove a small plug of skin and lap the blood, but too late—the image by the nineteenth century was already in place. Hence the

red eyes, pallid face, pointed ears, widow's peak, winglike cape, and cowl of the "modern" vampire.

10. *Varney* has now reappeared once again both as a Dover reprint and as a New York Graphic Society reprint.

11. I am not the first to believe this. The argument has been proffered first by Maurice Richardson in "The Psychoanalysis of Ghost Stories" and then quickly reaffirmed in Royce Macgillivary, "*Dracula*: Bram Stoker's Spoiled Masterpiece," Leonard Wolf, *A Dream of Dracula* (chapter 6), C. F. Bentley, "The Monster in the Bedroom: Sexual Symbolism in *Dracula*," Phyllis R. Roth, "Suddenly Sexual Women in Bram Stoker's *Dracula*," and Carrol L. Fry, "Fictional Connections and Sexuality in *Dracula*." It is now rare to find the psychosexual reading not routinely invoked. I expressed my own views more fully in "The Vampire Myth" (1980).

12. Page numbers in parentheses refer to Bram Stoker's *Dracula* (1897), reprinted in Signet paperback (1965).

13. The most scandalous episode in this version, as tasteless today as it was twenty years ago, involves the up-ending of a victim, the cutting of his throat, then the hanging of his body upside down so that his dripping blood might nourish Dracula's dusty remains and let him live . . . again.

14. Does her passive, even conspiratorial, role support a chauvinist view of rape, in which the raped secretly encourages the rapist? Although this Reichian view has been recently debunked by feminists, most notably in Susan Brownmiller's *Against Our Will*, it may indeed be supported by this myth. It is probably best, however, to keep in mind that there is a considerable body of psychological thought, also from the female point of view, that would contradict Brownmiller. These studies are clearly dated: see, for instance, Helene Deutsch, *The Psychology of Women* (1944), vol. I, chapter 4, "The Psychology of the Sexual Act," and Karen Horney, "The Problem of Feminine Masochism" (1935) in *Feminine Psychology* (1967), *The Neurotic Personality in Our Time* (1937), and *New Ways in Psychoanalysis* (1939). For Horney on young girls' "instinctive" rape dreams, see "The Denial of the Vagina," in *Feminine Psychology* (1967).

15. In many "primitive" cultures, the rupturing of the hymen is performed by a surrogate father during a stylized ceremony. As Freud explains in "The Taboo of Virginity,"

> The customs of primitive peoples seem to take account of this *motif* of the early sexual wish by handing over the task of defloration to an elder, priest or holy man, that is, to a substitute for the father. There seems to be a direct path leading from this custom to the highly vexed question of the *jus primae noctis* of the medieval lord of the manor." (*The Complete Works*, Vol. 11, p. 204)

16. After Dracula's 133 full-length feature films, *The Guinness Book of Film Facts* (1980) lists the legendary Frankenstein (91), and then in rapidly descending order Tarzan (83), Hopalong Cassidy (66), Zorro (65), Charlie Chan (49), and Robin Hood (48), which gives some idea of the overwhelmingly adolescent audience for films. Of the spate of recent books on the vampire film, the best are by David Pirie, *The Vampire Cinema* (1977), and James Ursini and Alan Silver, *The Vampire Film* (1975); the most comprehensive for chronology and summary are by Donald Glut, *The Dracula Book*

(1975), and Michael Murphy, *The Celluloid Vampires* (1979); and the best on Hammer Studios are David Pirie's *A Heritage of Horror* (1973) and Allen Eyles et al., *The House of Horror* (1973).

17. The following is by no means a comprehensive listing, but it does testify to the vampire's current good health: Ray Bradbury has written a number of vampire stories ("The Crowd," "The Man Upstairs," and "Homecoming," for example) and a novel (*Something Wicked This Way Comes*); Robert Bloch has also written many stories of this nature (see "The Bat Is My Brother," "The Living Dead,"); F. F. Benson's "Mrs. Amworth" is a small gem in the genre; H. P. Lovecraft wrote many vampire stories that appeared in *Weird Tales*, such as "The Thing on the Doorstep" and "The Case of Charles Dexter Ward"; Richard Matheson's *I Am Legend* is often anthologized as an excellent example of a compact and terrifying vampire story; Peter Saxon has written many vampire novels (e.g., *The Darkest Night, Scream and Scream Again, Vampire's Moon*) that are forgettable; the same is true of Virginia Coffman's *The Vampire of Moura*. The best vampire novels are recent: Theodore Sturgeon, *Some of Your Blood* (1961); John Rechy, *The Vampires* (1971); Fred Saberhagen, *The Dracula Tapes* (1975); Desmond Steward, *The Vampire of Mons* (1976); Colin Wilson, *The Space Vampires* (1976); Stephen King, *'Salem's Lot* (1975); Chelsea Quinn Yarboro, *Hotel Transylvania* (1978); and Anne Rice, *Interview with the Vampire* (1976).

18. In fact, one of the most important unstudied images in the early cinema was that of the vampiress herself—namely, Theda Bara (an anagram for Arab death). Of all Hollywood's starlets, she was probably the most improbable and influential. It's hard to believe that *A Fool There Was* (1915), in which Theda plays "a hellcat" who ruins men with sex, could cause anything other than hysterical hooting, but it did. It stunned—in some cases, literally—audiences. Almost overnight the world knew what a vamp was, and for the next five years Theda starred in many movies to make sure they wouldn't forget. Little did the audience realize that her famous faraway gaze was the result of near-sightedness but, then again, few knew that her counterpart, Bela Lugosi, had that rolling diction because his cue cards were written phonetically.

19. Quite possibly, the most important positive contribution of *Son of Dracula* was that Universal finally got the bat to fly properly. Not only do you not see the piano wires, but John P. Fulton's use of the traveling matte made the porcine Mr. Chaney into a squealing little bat with what seemed to be just a flip of the cape.

20. Universal's scariest movie, I think, they luckily stumbled into: *Abbott and Costello Meet Frankenstein*. Not only was it well-written and well-produced, but all the monsters—Dracula, the Frankenstein monster, and the Wolfman—finally were properly cast: Bela Lugosi, Glenn Strange, and Lon Chaney, Jr.

21. Bettelheim's case, however, is not convincing to Robert Darton who contends, in *The Great Cat Massacre and Other Episodes in French Cultural History* (1984), that the wolf's hunger and LRRH's carelessness with food reflect conditions in a near-starvation society. Yet literal appetites and sexual appetites are often combined in this myth as well as in many others. On the subject of incest in fairy tales Judith Lewis Herman, in *Father-Daughter Incest* (1981), makes the case that in many of the pre-Disney versions of Cinderella the story tells of how the girl's mother died, leaving her alone with a widowed father. Today, the father has been replaced by a cruel stepmother, but in many earlier renditions "the daughter suffers because the father wishes to marry her himself" (p. 1).

Chapter 4

1. So far I've only dealt with two myths. One could easily get lost in the shuttlecock interchanges of modern horror myths if one added, say, all the Mummy, Dr. Jekyll, and Wolfman films, for then the migrations become bewildering: Lugosi is "Bela" in *The Wolf Man*, Karloff is the bandaged one in *The Mummy*, Christopher Lee is all over the place: Dr. Jekyll, the Mummy, Fu Manchu, among many others. These inner and outer transpositions inspired John Carpenter to cast Jamie Lee Curtis in *Halloween* precisely because he knew that his audience would know that she was the real-life daughter of Janet Leigh, the cinematic victim of the psycho-killer in Hitchcock's 1960 movie.

2. The problem of an authoritative text is complicated because we really do not know Mary Shelley's intentions. For those who like the 1818 text there is James Rieger's edition of *Frankenstein* (1974), which gives the variant readings, and for those who don't really care there is a spate of popular reprints of the 1831 book. The most important shift between the two is that in the 1818 text Elizabeth is Victor's first cousin while in 1831, to avoid any hint of consanguinity, she is an aristocratic foundling. I will be glossing quotations from Harold Bloom's Signet edition (1965), which is not only the most popular current edition, but also includes Bloom's provocative Afterword. My major complaint with the edition is that for some reason the publisher "normalized" the spelling of "daemon" to "demon," thereby destroying an important distinction. Even Bloom seems to realize this mistake, for in his Afterword he properly refers to the creature the way Victor does, as a "daemon," in other words, as a spirit not necessarily evil.

3. Victor's creature, which, since the movies, is invariably referred to as a "monster," is most often referred to by Victor as "daemon." In the M. K. Joseph edition of the 1831 *Frankenstein* (1969), the spelling "daemon" properly indicates Mary Shelley's intention that the creature represent life that is "other" than human (e.g., pp. 26, 76, 165, 166, 203, 204, 219). Unfortunately, the Signet edition, edited by Harold Bloom, changes it to "demon," which means an evil spirit in the Christian mythology, and does real damage to the characterization of both protagonist and his creation. Admittedly, the daemon becomes a demon, but this, in part, is because of the way he is treated.

4. It is interesting to speculate on the possible influence of Coleridge's *Christabel* on Mary Shelley's imagination. It is clear, especially in her note acknowledging Coleridge in the 1831 edition, that *The Rime of the Ancient Mariner* impressed her, but we also know that she heard *Christabel* not once, but twice, during the summer of 1816. The reason I find this interesting is that I think both works generate horror by showing a displaced protagonist acting out forbidden Oedipal desires; see my " 'Desire with Loathing Strangely Mix'd': The Dreamwork of *Christabel*."

5. Although the doppelgänger transformation has been extensively discussed in Masao Miyoshi, *The Divided Self: A Perspective on the Literature of the Double* (1970), Carl F. Keppler, *The Literature of the Second Self* (1972), Irving Massey, *The Gaping Pig: Literature and Metamorphosis* (1969), and elsewhere, the best psychoanalytic interpretation of the monster as Victor's double is in Morton Kaplan, "Fantasy of Paternity and the Doppelgänger: Mary Shelley's *Frankenstein*" in *The Unspoken Motive: A Guide to Psychoanalytic Criticism*, eds. Morton Kaplan and Robert Kloss (1973), and Robert Kiely, *The Romantic Novel in England* (1972).

6. The relationship between Robert Walton and his sister Mrs. Savile (is there a pun here?) mimics the role of Victor Frankenstein and his "sister" Elizabeth. Once again, the doppelgänger transformations and implied incestuous relationships indicate not so much the author's weakness at delineating character as they do her almost obsessive compulsion to rework the familial relationships until she "gets it right." For more on this aspect of the novel, see Gordon D. Hirsch, "The Monster Was a Lady: On the Psychology of Mary Shelley's *Frankenstein*," and Susan Harris Smith, "*Frankenstein*: Mary Shelley's Psychic Divisiveness."

7. See, for instance, Sandra M. Gilbert and Susan Gubar, *The Madwoman in the Attic* (1979); Marc A. Rubenstein, "'My Accursed Origin': The Search for the Mother in *Frankenstein*"; and Ellen Moers, "Female Gothic: The Monster's Mother," first appearing in the *New York Review of Books* (March 24, 1974) but subsequently reprinted with minor changes as "Female Gothic" in *The Endurance of "Frankenstein*" (1979), eds. George Levine and U. C. Knoepflmacher.

8. From a psychoanalytic point of view it is curious that William, the creature's first victim in *Frankenstein*, has the same name as Mary Shelley's father, brother, and infant son (six months old while she was writing his name into her story). This child was to die two years later, and it must have been difficult indeed for Mary to revise the text for the second edition.

9. Ellen Moers in "Female Gothic" cleverly compares Victor's description of his newly created being with Dr. Spock's description (*Baby and Child Care*) of the newborn human:

> A baby at birth is usually disappointing-looking to a parent who hasn't seen one before. His skin is coated with wax, which, if left on, will be absorbed slowly and will lessen the chance of rashes. His skin underneath is apt to be very red. His face tends to be puffy and lumpy, and there may be black-and-blue marks .... The head is misshapen ... low in the forehead, elongated at the back, and quite lopsided. Occasionally there may be, in addition, a hematoma, a localized hemorrhage under the scalp that sticks out as a distinct bump and takes weeks to go away. A couple of days after birth there may be a touch of jaundice, which is visible for about a week. ... The baby's body is covered all over with fuzzy hair. ... For a couple of weeks afterward there is apt to be a dry scaling of the skin, which is also shed. Some babies have black hair on the scalp at first, which may come far down the forehead. (p. 77)

10. For extended information about *Frankenstein* on film see Donald F. Glut, *The Frankenstein Legend* (1973) and *The Frankenstein Catalog* (1984), which record almost every appearance of the Frankenstein monster from the novel to the breakfast cereal ("Frankenberry"); Martin Tropp, *Mary Shelley's Monster* (1977), chapters 6–8; Albert J. Lavalley, "The Stage and Film Children of *Frankenstein*" in *The Endurance of "Frankenstein*" (1979); John Stoker, *The Illustrated Frankenstein* (1980); and Gregory William Mank, *It's Alive!: The Classic Cinema Saga of Frankenstein* (1981).

11. But this scene is not enough to carry the saga, as the producers of the most recent *Frankenstein* (1981) on Broadway recently learned. It cost them $2 million to find out that brilliant sparks, huge beakers of colored water bubbling with foam,

cyclotrons, bolts of lightning, booming organ music, and disco lighting were not all what the story was about. This incredibly visual and expensive show opened and closed in one night (January 11, 1981), as well it should have, for the adapter, Victor Gialanella, did not realize that the real *son et lumière* of the play comes from Victor's interactions with his family.

12. The scene is still missing from most prints and the movie suffers from this excision. It now seems as if the monster was sexually bestial with the child, for the next scene shows Maria dead in the arms of her distraught father.

13. Elizabeth was not the only one who had trouble accepting this line; the movie censor at the Hays office did, too. The embarrassment has been resolved by an abrupt jump-cut from the laboratory to the living room of the Baron (Henry's father) where the Baron claims Henry's problem is with another woman; in a way the dotty Baron is right.

14. The best thing about this movie is the story told by Curt Siodmak about how it came to be. Here is how Siodmak recalled it for Gregory William Mank's *It's Alive!: The Classic Cinema Saga of Frankenstein* (1981):

> My producer at Universal was George Waggner. He was very nice, and he made lots of money for Universal. He was very German in his tastes, and his fun was to drink beer and sing songs—a typical German-American.
>
> Well, I went to his office once a week, and gave him all the honey I could think of, telling him what a great man he was. I thought, "One day he must find out that I'm kidding!" He never found out, of course. He *never* found out. Anyway, with *Frankenstein Meets the Wolf Man*, what really happened was this: I was sitting in the Universal commissary, and George Waggner came by, and we had lunch together. And I made a joke. I said, "George, why don't you make a picture, *Frankenstein Wolfs the Meat Man*—er, I mean *Frankenstein Meets the Wolf Man*?" He didn't laugh.
>
> So, it was during the war, and I wanted to buy an automobile, and I wanted to get a new assignment so I could afford it. George would talk to me every day, and say, "Did you get the new car?" And I'd say, "No! What's my new job?" And George would say, "Never mind, get the car."
>
> Well, one day I had to pay to get the car. George said, "Did you buy it?" and I said, "Yes, I bought it." George said, "Okay! Your job is *Frankenstein Wolfs the Meat Man*, er, I mean *Frankenstein Meets the Wolf Man*. I give you two hours to accept!" (p. 112)

15. Actually, Universal had already poked fun at these monster-mash movies by letting "the boys" at them in *Abbott and Costello Meet Frankenstein* (1948). If one took Lou and Bud out of this movie it would be a logical successor to *House of Dracula* (1945), as it maintains the same characterizations (now copyrighted), the same production values (in fact, even better), the same plot (except the transfusions involve getting Bud's brain into the monster's skull), and the same "feel" of a Universal production. In contrast to the English attempt in *Carry on Screaming* (1966), Universal knew better than to change the stereotypes. They were right: *Abbott and Costello Meet Frankenstein* was the biggest money-maker of the year and the most successful film of the series.

16. The best accounts of these Hammer "epics" are *The House of Horror: The Story of Hammer Films*, eds. Allen Eyles, Robert Adkinson, and Nicholas Fry (1973),

and David Pirie, *A Heritage of Horror: The English Gothic Cinema, 1964–1972* (1973).

17. In 1983 two books appeared within months of each other discussing this phenomenon, both with the same title: *Midnight Movies*; one by J. Hoberman and Jonathan Rosenbaum and the other by Stuart Samuels. Both also discuss such cult movies as *Eraserhead*, *El Topo*, and the films of John Waters and George Romero.

18. Tim Curry's talent for portraying androgyny was not lost on the critics: he was considered "half Auntie Mame, half Bela Lugosi," "a cross between Greer Garson and Steve Reeves," "a hybrid of Sophie Tucker and Mick Jagger," "a combination of early Joan Crawford, Francis Lederer, and Carmen Miranda," "Little Richard meet Elsie Tanner," "part David Bowie, part Joan Crawford, part Basil Rathbone," "Imagine Liza Minelli in *Cabaret*, Alice Cooper at his most demonic, Jagger at his most sensual. Then throw in Vincent Price and Bowie's drive for neuter sex," and "Charles Laughton doing Captain Bligh and Nita Naldi at the same time." See Bill Henkin, *The Rocky Horror Picture Show Book*, p. 133.

19. Here is what Bruce A. Austin concludes about the audience in "Portrait of a Cult Film Audience: *The Rocky Horror Picture Show*":

> While the range of ages reported was from 13 to 50, generally the *Rocky Horror* audience was a relatively young one. Most individuals were between 17 and 22. Overall, veterans tended to be the youngest and regulars the oldest audience groups. Further, an analysis of variance showed that each of the three groups differed significantly ($p < .001$) in age. Seventeen percent of the audience was under 17 years old even though *Rocky Horror* is rated R (restricted for such individuals without accompanying parent or guardian). Given the youthfulness of the audience, it is not surprising to find that few (6.3 percent) were married. Nor is it surprising that more than half of the audience (61.9 percent) reported their occupation as either high school or college students. (pp. 48–49)

Chapter 5

1. We have never lacked for studies on the wolf or, for that matter, the werewolf. Even Byron felt secure on this subject:

> *Oh! ye immortal Gods! What is Theogony?*
> *Oh! thou, too, mortal man! what is Philosophy?*
> *Oh! World, which was and is, what is Cosmogony?*
> *Some people have accused me of Misanthropy;*
> *And yet I know no more than the mahogany*
> *That forms this desk, of what they mean:—Lycanthropy*
> *I comprehend, for without transformation*
> *Men become wolves on any slight occasion. (Don Juan, 9, 20)*

The best recent semi-scholarly work on the werewolf is Ian Woodward, *The Werewolf Delusion* (1979); the most academic is Robert Eisler, *Man into Wolf* (1952); the most pedantic, but still very interesting, is Montague Summers, *The Werewolf* (1933); the best for children, Nancy Garden, *Werewolves* (1977); the most inaccurate, Sabine Baring-Gould, *The Book of Were-Wolves* (1865); and there are plenty of other less important works, such as Elliott O'Donnell, *Werewolves* (1912) or Caroline Stewart, *The Origin of the Werewolf Superstition* (1909) for the nondiscerning enthusiasts. Very little has been written on the Wolfman; see, for instance, appropriate chapters in Donald Glut, *Classic Movie Monsters* (1978), R. H. W. Dillard, *Horror Films* (1976), William Everson, *Classics of the Horror Film* (1974), Alan Frank, *The Movie Treasury: Horror Movies* (1974), and Richard Davis, ed., *The Encyclopedia of Horror* (1981).

2. The exception is where you would expect it—in the "blood and thunder" of Jacobean drama. In John Webster's *The Dutchess of Malfi* a nefarious noble is described:

> One met the duke 'bout midnight in a lane
> Behind Saint Mark's church, with the leg of a man
> Upon his shoulder; and he howled fearfully;
> Said he was a wolf, only the difference
> Was, a wolf's skin was hairy on the outside,
> His on the inside.

We never meet the maniac on stage, so the description is safe, but the werewolf, or *loup-garou*, is also one of the staples of seventeenth-century French fiction.

3. The aforementioned and many other werewolf stories are collected in Bill Pronzini's *Werewolf!* (1979). To have some idea of how popular this horror subgenre was around the turn of the century, one need only be reminded of such works as: H. Beaugrand's *The Werewolves* (1898), Count Eric Stenbok's *The Other Side* (1893), Algernon Blackwood's *Strange Adventure* (1906), and with Wilfred Wilson, *The Empty Sleeve* (1921), the Hon. Mrs. Greene's *Bound by a Spell* (1885), Eden Phillpotts' *Loup-Garou!* (1899), and Hugh Walpole's *Tarnheim; or, The Death of My Uncle Robert*. By the 1930s there was such a glut of were-mutations that pulp magazines like *Weird Tales* were almost supported by the same tale endlessly told.

4. Much in this movie was just silly: the victim can only be relieved by a mysterious plant from Tibet and there is a heady mix of Fu Manchu in the antagonist Yogami. It did play up the most important aspect of the myth: the werewolf by instinct kills the ones he loves most. This motif, so central to the vampire as well, has been more usually neglected in modern versions.

5. Actually, Rob Bottin made the masks for *The Howling*, and both Bottin and Baker learned the intricacies of the air bladder and cable work from the man who has masterminded so many revolutionary effects, Dick Smith. Smith, who started his career doing special effects for NBC, reached a pinnacle of sorts spinning Regan's head in *The Exorcist*, giving hefty breasts to Katherine Ross in *The Stepford Wives*, and making Dustin Hoffman into a prune-faced ancient in *Little Big Man*. Smith most recently created the dazzling transformations in *Altered States*. That *Cinefantastique*, a magazine devoted to the fantasy and horror film, dedicated an entire issue (2, No. 1) to Smith, and the fact that he has been imitated so often, certainly intimates that he is well on his way to becoming the Jack Pierce of our times.

6. This isn't the only refashioning of the myth. It seems that silver bullets are to no avail, that the villagers are in cahoots with the werewolf like the villagers in vampire films, and that the "living dead" (those killed by the werewolf) have a prankish, *Animal House*-type sense of humor. Unfortunately, however, although Landis initially

holds with the motif that the beast can only be killed "by a loved one," it is left to Scotland Yard to do the job with machine guns.

7. This mother-son relationship becomes even clearer in the sequel, *Frankenstein Meets the Wolf Man*, in which Malvena "adopts" Larry as "my son" and takes him to the doctor for help.

8. I am quite sure Curt Siodmak did not know of this, but there is a tantalizing analog to his Wolfman story told in the ancient *Volsunga Saga* (chapter 8). A long time ago Sigmund and his son Sinfjötli were hunting in the woods and came on a cottage in which there were men sleeping under wolf skins. These men were shape-shifters at night, and father and son took the wolf skins. When they tried them on, they themselves turned into wolves. Although they made a pact to help each other out in the event of an attack, the son was soon attacked and did not howl, but instead killed his attackers. When the father heard that the son breached the agreement, he bit him savagely.

> Then he realized what he had done and, manlike, was sorry; Sinfjötli was, after all, his son. He picked Sinfjötli up and carried him home on his back, cursing the evil wolf-shapes for making him act so inhuman. And when he finally regained human shape, at the end of ten days, he burned both the skins so he and his son would never be tempted to become wolves again.

It is not unusual to have aspects of Oedipal struggles played out in folklore, but this time it is done in the guise of werewolves.

9. The text I am using is the most accessible, marred as most popular texts are by the Fredric March Hyde on the cover, published in paper by Bantam Books, 1967. For a comprehensive collection of Dr. Jekyll/Mr. Hyde information, see Harry M. Geduld, ed., *The Definitive "Dr. Jekyll and Hyde" Companion* (1983).

10. This young girl is the Jamie Lee Curtis of Victorian horror and her appearance in the story is no mere happenstance. David Daiches in *Robert Louis Stevenson and His World* (1973) claims that Hyde's sadism was indeed sexual, and the movies true to the story's spirit express it as such. This sexual aggression is not expressed overtly in the novella because the audience of the 1880s would never have stood for such pornography, at least not in a work purported to be family reading. But another explanation may be even simpler. Stevenson himself did not believe in his protagonist's sexuality. In the Beinecke Library at Yale there are a number of letters from F. W. H. Myers, a founder of the Society for Psychical Research, to Stevenson imploring the author to better explain Hyde's behavior in sexual terms. Myers wanted Hyde's crimes "developed from lust . . . not mere madness and savagery" (B, #7271). Myers understood that the walking stick was no inappropriate prop. He may have been twittish in his effrontery, but may well have understood the story better than the author, for Stevenson long insisted that Jekyll was not a sexually motivated creature at all. He explained in a letter to John Paul Bocock now in the Huntington Library:

> The harm was in Jekyll, because he was a hypocrite—not because he was fond of women; he says so himself; but people are so filled full of folly and inverted lust, that they can think of nothing but sexuality. The hypocrite let out the beast Hyde—who is no more sensual than another, but who is the essence of cruelty and malice, and selfishness and cowardice: and these are

the diabolic in man—not this poor wish to have a woman, that they make such a cry about. (H, #2414)

11. There is no script record extant for the Sullivan play; what we know about it comes from William Winter's biography, *The Life and Art of Richard Mansfield* (1910). We know that matinee idol Richard Mansfield urged his friend Thomas Sullivan to write the adaptation especially for him, and we know that Stevenson accepted the idea and that the play was a sensation on both sides of the Atlantic. Sullivan ran into some competition, since he had improperly covered his work by copyright; however, the London production was closed after ten weeks not by legalisms or by reviews but by the coincidence that the real-life Jack-the-Ripper was proving it unpopular to portray Hyde in public. Mansfield's name was high on the police list of suspects.

12. While the best commentary on this film is recent: William Luhr and Peter Lehman, *Authorship and Narrative in the Cinema* (1977), chapters 6–8; S. S. Prawer, *Caligari's Children* (1980), chapter 3; and Janice R. Welsch, "The Horrific and the Tragic" in Michael Klein and Gillian Parker, *The English Novel and the Movies* (1981)—I am interested in narrative development and plot rearrangement.

13. Although Mamoulian has repeatedly refused to divulge how he did this (see, for example, Thomas R. Atkins, "An Interview with Rouben Mamoulian"), it is clearly done with colored filters, changed to reveal different layers of makeup.

14. The English production company Amicus was always trying to capture Hammer's audience at the box office, and in *I Monster* (1970) they tried what has always failed with horror movies: an attempted return to the sacred text. Amicus even hired Hammer's star, Christopher Lee, to do the horrors, but the movie flopped, in large part because in returning to the printed story sexual violence was sacrificed. Who wants to watch a "whodunit" when any schoolboy knows whodidit? Jean Renoir also experimented with an arty version, *Le Testament du Dr. Cordelier* (1959), which wasn't much better. It, too, "attempted" to be faithful to the text, but is more interesting because Hyde is played as a finger-snapping, gum-chewing teenager of the 1950s.

Chapter 6

1. I don't mean to belittle these unsophisticated monsters, for they clearly have carved out a niche in popular culture. The oversized green lizard has starred in sixteen feature films and has been so impressive that it is one of the first images Westerners think of when they hear the word "Japan." In 1982 a likeness of Godzilla appeared on garbage bags sold by Sears and Roebuck under the name "Bagzilla." The bags depicted "a comic, helpful, personified reptilian creature" indicating "Monstrously Strong Bags" and also creating "unfair competition" and "unjust enrichment," at least according to the lawyers for the Toho Co., Ltd., which was responsible for those grade Z films. The 9th U.S. Circuit Court of Appeals dismissed the case, holding that Sears had not "impaired the effectiveness of the name or image of Godzilla." Nothing could do that.

2. Balderson, also one of the scriptwriters for *The Bride of Frankenstein*, had been the London correspondent of *The New York World* and was up-to-date on the recent archeological finds in Egypt. It is his scenario that has been replayed, even though there have been a number of mummy vignettes in literature, such as Theophile Gautier's *The Foot of the Mummy*, Conan Doyle's *Lot 249* and *The Ring of Toth*, Alger-

non Blackwood's *A Descent into Egypt*, and more recently, Richard Marsh's novel, *The Beetle*. Only Bram Stoker's *Jewel of the Seven Stars* has made it to the screen in Hammer's *Blood from the Mummy's Tomb* (1971), which was interesting for the incest motif: the mummified princess is reincarnated as the daughter of the archeologist, whom she seduces. In 1980 this story was remade into Charlton Heston's *The Awakening*, with mediocre results.

3. Equally tantalizing is an updating of a botanical theory most recently put forward by Harvard botanist E. Wade Davis in the *Journal of Ethnopharmacology*. Davis explains the myth in terms of group ingestion of certain hallucinogens indigenous to Haiti. The nerve poison, tetrodotoxin, found in the New World toad (*Bufo marinus*) and in the puffer fish, may cause the glassy-eyed stare and death-like coma characteristic of the zombie trance.

4. It is hard to see almost any carefully made horror film since the 1960s and not be aware that the modern family is its implied or stated center. Take Tobe Hooper's *Texas Chainsaw Massacre* (1974), for example. Here we follow a van-load of teen-agers who, having checked the family burial grounds to see if the graves of their relatives have been disturbed, are now "going home" to the family farm of one of their group. They leave the metaphoric highway, cross an overgrown meadow, and find that, as with Dracula's castle and Frankenstein's laboratory, the house is now populated with the monsters of childhood. Upstairs is a bloodsucking grandfather; downstairs a Frankenstein monster (Leatherface) and his cannabalistic brother. This grotesque family of males wants the teenage females and almost succeeds in literally having them. There is no mother figure in either family, and so the adolescents must fend for themselves. They do so with predictably mixed results. *Texas Chainsaw Massacre* was the best-selling video of 1982 and still draws crowds on college campuses and as a "midnight movie." The conscious drift toward portraying the breakdown of the American family in horror films has been briefly discussed by Tony Williams, "American Films in the '70's: Family Horror," and was one of the recurring topics at a conference on contemporary horror films held in Toronto in 1979. The conference papers, many of which had been published earlier in *Film Comment* and *Movie*, were edited by Andrew Britton and published as *American Nightmares: Essays on the Horror Film* (1979).

5. Browning's film was banned by the British censors for almost forty years and was rarely shown in this country. The objectionable scene occurs at the end when freaks from a circus troop overwhelm a "normal" but conniving female trapeze artist and somehow connect her upper torso and head to what looks like the rump of a huge hen. Most critics have contended that the film's commercial failure was not so much caused by this final scene, as by Browning's use of real freaks. Rondo Hatton, who was a real freak (suffering from acromegaly), was a minor sensation as the monster "creeper" in films that ought to have been lost, like *House of Horrors* (1946) and *The Brute Man* (1946). I suspect that it is not freakishness that frightens as much as the process of mutation from "one of us" to "one of them." For more on the role of freaks in American culture, see Leslie Fiedler, *Freaks: Myths and Images of the Secret Self* (1978).

6. For this and the variant tellings, see Bruno Bettelheim, *The Uses of Enchantment: The Meanings and Importance of Fairy Tales* (1975), pp. 303–310, and for literary interpretations, see Roger Sale, *Fairy Tales and After* (1978), pp. 58–63.

7. Darwin was certainly right: the jungle was full of unexpected surprises, and Freud was equally perspicacious in describing exactly where they were. However,

Norbert Wiener may have the last word, at least in the 1980s. Since Hal 9000 in *2001:
A Space Odyssey*, we have been plagued by computer-on-the-loose monsters, as in
Westworld, Colossus: The Forbin Project, or, better yet, *Demon Seed*, in which a sentient computer rapes Julie Christie and forces her to give birth to what looks like a
human fetus except that it has a strange internal hum and moments of ferocity.
Demon Seed is clearly a hybrid of *Rosemary's Baby, It's Alive*, and *Jaws*, and it may
well set a new pattern for contemporary phobias—computer intrusion.

8. I am not sure this domestication of horror scenarios is a conscious design in the
major studio productions, but it certainly is among the new auteurs of horror like
George Romero, Bob Clark, David Cronenberg, and Wes Craven. Here, for instance,
is Mr. Craven (*Last House on the Left, The Hills Have Eyes, Swamp Thing, Nightmare on Elm Street*), an ex-Professor of English:

> The family is the best microcosm to work with. If you go much beyond that
> you're getting away from a lot of the roots of our own primeval feelings.
> Let's face it, most of the basic stories and the basic feelings involve very few
> people: Mommy, Daddy, me, siblings, and the people in the other room. I
> like to stay within that circle. It's very much where most of our strong emo-
> tions or gut feelings come from. It's from those very early experiences and
> how they are worked out. (as quoted in Robin Wood, "Neglected Night-
> mares," p. 28)

9. Coveney's thesis has recently been updated in David Grylls, *Guardians and
Angels: Parents and Children in Nineteenth-Century Literature* (1978), Robert Pattison *The Child Figure in English Literature* (1978), and Laura A. Pollock, *Forgotten
Children: Parent-Child Relations from 1500 to 1900*. A fascinating study is yet to be
done on the representation of the young child in the movies, and certainly infant
monsters would play a major part.

Select Bibliography

This Bibliography is by no means complete or even comprehensive, but it does reflect the bias of my thesis. For the sake of brevity I have omitted some articles from major magazines devoted to the fantasy/horror genre as well as separate issues of cinema periodicals, like volume 19 of *Photon*, volume 2 (no. 2) of *Film Journal*, and volume 6 (no. 1) of *Film Criticism*, which were devoted exclusively to horror films. Newspaper citations are given only within the text. I have also omitted gothic novels which I referred to, but did not quote from. Not only do I owe a considerable debt to academic scholars, but I also have been informed by that often enlightening medium of popular culture, the "fanzine." There have been many such magazines for the horror film fan from Forrest J Ackerman's playful *Famous Monsters of Filmland* to the relatively learned French *Midi-Minuit Fantastique*, but the American *Cinefantastique* is quickly establishing itself as the most dependable journal on cineteratology and I am particularly indebted to it.

Alexander, Alex E. "Stephen King's *Carrie*: A Universal Fairy Tale." *Journal of Popular Culture* 13 (1979): 282–88.

Alexander, Richard D. *Darwinism and Human Affairs*. Seattle: University of Washington Press, 1979.

Alloway, Lawrence. "Monster Films." In *Focus on the Horror Film*, edited by Roy Huss and T. J. Ross. Englewood Cliffs, N.J.: Prentice-Hall, 1972.

Allen, Woody. "Count Dracula." In *Getting Even*. New York: Random House, 1971.

Altick, Richard Daniel. *The English Common Reader: A Social History of the Mass Reading Public 1800-1900*. Chicago: University of Chicago Press, 1957.

Amis, Kingsley. "Dracula, Frankenstein, Sons and Co." In *What Became of Jane Austen?* New York: Harcourt Brace Jovanovich, 1970.

Andrews, Nigel. "Dracula in Delft." *American Film* 4, no. 1 (1978): 32–38.

Anglo, Michael. *Penny Dreadfuls and Other Victorian Horrors*. London: Jupiter, 1978.

Annan, David. *Movie Fantastic: Beyond the Dream Machine*. New York: Bounty, 1974.

Anobile, Richard J. *James Whale's Frankenstein*. New York: Universe Books, 1974.

———. *The Offical Rocky Horror Picture Show Novel*. New York: A. & W. Visual Library, 1980.

Armes, Roy. *A Critical History of English Cinema*. New York: Oxford University Press, 1978.

Ashley, Mike. *Who's Who in Horror and Fantasy Fiction*. New York: Taplinger, 1977.

Astle, Richard. "Dracula as Totemic Monster: Lacan, Freud, Oedipus and History." *Sub-stance* 25 (1980): 98–105.

Atkins, Thomas R. "An Interview with Rouben Mamoulian." *Film Journal* 2 (1973): 37–44.

Austin, Bruce A. "Film Audience Research: 1960–1980, An Update." *Journal of Popular Film and Television* 8, no. 2 (1981): 53–60 and 8, no. 4 (1981): 57–59.

———. "Portrait of a Cult Film Audience: *The Rocky Horror Picture Show*." *Journal of Communication* 31, no. 2 (1981): 43–54.

Aylesworth, Thomas G. *Monsters From the Movies*. Philadelphia, Pa.: J. P. Lippincott, 1972.

Bailey, J. O. "What Happens in *The Fall of the House of Usher*." *American Literature* 35 (1964): 445–66.

Balun, Charles. *The Connoisseur's Guide to the Contemporary Horror Film*. Westminster, Ca.: Privately printed, 1983.

Barber, Dulan. *Monsters Who's Who*. New York: Crescent Books, 1975.

Barclay, Glen St. John. *Anatomy of Horror: The Masters of Occult Fiction*. New York: St. Martin's Press, 1979.

Baring-Gould, Rev. Sabine. *The Book of Were-Wolves*. London: Smith-Elder and Co., 1865.

Bean, Robin. "Muscle Mayhem." *Films and Filming* 10, no. 9 (1974): 13–18.

Beck, Calvin Thomas. *Heroes of the Horrors*. New York: Macmillan, 1975.

Bentley, C. F. "The Monster in the Bedroom: Sexual Symbolism in *Dracula*." *Literature and Psychology* 22 (1972): 27–34.

Bettelheim, Bruno. *The Uses of Enchantment: The Meaning and Importance of Fairy Tales*. New York: Alfred A. Knopf, 1975.

Beyer-Berenbaum, Linda. *The Gothic Imagination: Expansion in Gothic Literature and Art*. Rutherford, N.J.: Fairleigh Dickenson University Press, 1982.

Bierman, Joseph S. "*Dracula*: Prolonged Childhood Illness and the Oral Triad." *American Imago* 29 (1972): 186–98.

Birkhead, Edith. *The Tale of Terror*. 1927; rpt. London: Russell and Russell, 1963.

Blinderman, Charles S. "Vampirella: Darwin and Count Dracula." *The Massachusetts Review* 21 (1980): 411–28.

Bloom, Harold. "*Frankenstein, Or the Modern Prometheus*: A Review." *Partisan Review*, 32 (1965): 611–618. Rpt. as "Afterword" to *Frankenstein*, by Mary Shelley. New York: New American Library, 1965.

Bond, Douglas D. "The Bride of Frankenstein." *Psychiatric Annals* 3, no. 12 (1973): 10–22.

Briggs, Julia. *Night Vistors: The Rise and Fall of the English Ghost Story*. London: Faber, 1977.

Britt, Stuart H. "What Is the Nature of the Drive-in Theater Audience?" *Media/Scope* 4 (1960): 100–102.

Britton, Andrew, et al. eds. *American Nightmare: Essays on the Horror Film*. Toronto: Festival of Festivals, 1979.

Brock, Brower. "The Vulgarization of American Demonology." *Esquire*, June 1964, 94–99

Brokaw, Kurt. *A Night in Transylvania: The Dracula Scrapbook*. New York: Grosset & Dunlap, 1976.

Brosnan, John. *The Horror People*. New York: St. Martin's Press, 1976.

———. *Movie Magic: The Story of Special Effects in the Cinema*. New York: St. Martin's Press, 1974.

Brownell, M. R. "Pope and the Vampires in Germany." *Eighteenth Century Life* 2 (1976): 96–97.

Brownmiller, Susan. *Against Our Will: Men, Women, and Rape*. New York: Simon and Schuster, 1975.

Brustein, Robert. "Reflections on Horror Movies." *Partisan Review* 25 (1958): 288–96.

Buckley, Jerome Hamilton. *The Victorian Temper: A Study in Literary Culture*. Cambridge, Mass.: Harvard University Press, 1951.

Burke, Edmund. *A Philosophical Enquiry into the Origin of our Ideas of the Sublime and Beautiful*. Edited by J. T. Boulton. London: Routledge and Paul, 1958.

Butler, Ian. *Horror in the Cinema*. New York: A. S. Barnes, 1970.

———. *The Horror Film*. New York: A. S. Barnes, 1967.

Byron, Lord (George Gordon). "The Vampire" [a fragment]. Rpt. in *Three Gothic Novels*, edited by E. F. Bleiler. New York: Dover, 1977.

Calmet, Dom Augustin. *Dissertation upon the Apparitions of Angels, Daemons and Ghosts and Concerning Vampires*. 1746; rpt. London: M. Cooper, 1759.

Carlson, Harry. "Movies and Teenagers." *Journal of Screen Producers Guild*, March 1973, 23–26.

Carroll, Noel. "Nightmare and the Horror Film: The Symbolic Biology of Fantastic Beings." *Film Quarterly* 34, no. 3 (1981): 16–25.

Carter, Margaret L. *Shadow of a Shade: A Survey of Vampirism in Literature*. New York: Gordon Press, 1975.

Chesterton, Gilbert Keith. *Robert Louis Stevenson*. 1928; rpt. New York: Sheed and Ward, 1955.

Clarens, Carlos. *An Illustrated History of the Horror Film*. New York: Putnam, 1967.

———. "Horror Films." In *Rediscovering the American Cinema*, edited by Douglas J. Lemza. New York: Pioneer Press, 1977.

Cohen, Yehudi. *The Transition from Childhood to Adolescence: Cross-Cultural Studies of Initiation Ceremonies, Legal Systems, and Incest Taboos*. Chicago: Aldine, 1964.

Copper, Basil. *The Vampire in Legend, Fact and Art*. New York: Citadel, 1974.

Coveney, Peter. *The Image of Childhood: The Individual and Society: A Study of the Theme in English Literature*. Rev. ed. with an intro. by F. R. Leavis. Baltimore, Md.: Penguin Books, 1967.

Daiches, David. *Robert Louis Stevenson and His World*. London: Thames and Hudson, 1973.

Dalziel, Margaret. *Popular Fiction 100 Years Ago: An Unexplored Tract of Literary History*. London: Cohen & West, 1957.

Daniels, Les. *Living in Fear: A History of Horror in the Mass Media*. New York: Scribner's, 1975.

Darton, Robert. *The Great Cat Massacre and Other Episodes in French Cultural History*. New York: Basic Books, 1984.

Davis, E. Wade. "The Ethnobiology of the Haitian Zombie." *Journal of Ethnopharmacology* 9, no. 1 (1983): 85–104.

Davis, Richard. *The Encyclopedia of Horror*. London: Octopus, 1981.

Deane, Hamilton, and Balderston, John. *Dracula: The Vampire Play in Three Acts*. New York: Samuel French, Inc., 1960.

Demetrakopoulos, Stephanie. "Feminism, Sex, Role Exchanges and other Subliminal Fantasies in Bram Stoker's *Dracula*." *Frontiers* 11 (1977): 106–7.

De Mott, Benjamin. "The Pro-Incest Lobby." *Psychology Today*, March 1980, 11–16.

Derry, Charles. *Dark Dreams: A Psychological History of the Modern Horror Film*. New York: A. S. Barnes, 1977.

Dettman, Bruce, and Michael Bedford. *The Horror Factory: The Horror Films of Universal*. New York: Gordon Press, 1976.

Deutsch, Helene. *The Psychology of Women: A Psychoanalytic Interpretation*. New York: Grune & Stratton, 1944.

Dickstein, Morris. "The Aesthetics of Fright." *American Film* 5, no. 10 (1980): 32–37, 56–59.

Dillard, R. H. W. "Drawing the Circle: A Devolution of Values in Three Horror Films." *The Film Journal* 2, no. 2 (1973): 6–36.

———. "Even a Man Who Is Pure at Heart." In *Man and the Movies*, edited by W. R. Robinson. Baltimore, Md.: Penguin Books, 1967.

———. *Horror Films*. New York: Monarch Press, 1976.

Douglas, Drake [pseud.]. *Horror!* New York: Macmillan, 1966.

Dowse, Robert E. "*Dracula*: The Book of Blood." *The Listener*, March 7, 1963, 428–29.

Durgnant, Raymond. "Scream Louder, Live Longer: An Introduction to Screen Violence." *The Listener*, December 3, 1964, 880–82.

Ebert, Roger. "Just Another Horror Film—Or Is It?" *Reader's Digest*, June 1969, 127–28.

———. "Why Movie Audiences Aren't Safe Anymore." *American Film* 6, no. 5 (1981): 54–56.

Edelson, Edward. *Great Monsters of the Movies*. Garden City, N.Y.: Doubleday, 1973.

Eigner, Edwin. *Robert Louis Stevenson and Romantic Tradition.* Princeton,N.J.: Princeton University Press, 1966.

Eisenstadt, Shmuel Noah. *From Generation to Generation: Age Groups and Social Structure.* Glencoe, Ill.: Free Press, 1955.

Eisler, Robert. *Man into Wolf.* New York: Philosophical Library, 1951.

Eisner, Lotte H. *The Haunted Screen: Expressionism in the German Cinema.* 1952; rpt. Berkeley: University of California Press, 1973.

———. *Murnau.* 1964; rpt. Berkeley: University of California Press, 1973.

Eliade, Mircea. *Rites and Symbols of Initiation: The Mysteries of Birth and Rebirth.* Translated by Willard R. Trask. New York: Harper & Row, 1965.

Endore, Guy. *Werewolf of Paris.* New York: Ace Books 1933.

Evans, Walter. "Monster Movies and Rites of Initiation." *Journal of Popular Culture* 4 (1975): 124–42.

———. "Monster Movies: A Sexual Theory." *Journal of Popular Culture* 11 (1973): 353–65.

Everson, William K. *Classics of the Horror Film.* Secaucus, N.J.: Citadel Press, 1974.

———. "A Family Tree of Monsters." *Film Culture* 1, no. 1 (1955): 24–30.

———. "Horror Films." *Films in Review* 5, no. 1 (1954): 12–23.

Eyles, Allen, Robert Adkinson, and Nicolas Fry. *The House of Horror: The Story of Hammer Films.* London: Lorrimer Publishing Ltd., 1973.

Farber, Stephen. "The New American Gothic." *Film Quarterly* 20, no. 1 (1966): 22–27.

———. "Why Critics Love Trashy Movies." *American Film* 6, no. 6 (1981): 65–68.

Fiedler, Leslie. *Freaks: Myths and Images of the Secret Self.* New York: Simon and Schuster, 1978.

———. *What Was Literature: Class Culture and Mass Society.* New York: Simon and Schuster, 1982.

Figenshu, Tom. "Screams of a Summer Night." *Film Comment* 15, no. 5 (1979): 49–53.

Fisher, Terence. "Horror Is My Business." *Films and Filming* 10 (1964): 7–8.

Fleishman, Avrom. *The English Historical Novel: Walter Scott to Virginia Woolf.* Baltimore, Md.: Johns Hopkins University Press, 1971.

Florescu, Radu. *In Search of Frankenstein.* Greenwich, Conn.: New York Graphic Society, 1975.

Fowles, John. *The French Lieutenant's Woman.* Boston: Little, Brown, 1969.

Fox, Robin. *Kinship and Marriage: An Anthropological Perspective.* Baltimore, Md.: Penguin Books, 1967.

———. *The Red Lamp of Incest.* New York: Dutton, 1980.

Fox, Robin, and Lionel Tiger. *The Imperial Animal.* New York: Holt, Rinehart and Winston, 1971.

Frank, Alan G. *The Movie Treasury: Horror Movies: Tales of Terror in the Cinema.* London: Octopus, 1974.

———. *The Horror Film Handbook.* Totowa, N.J.: Barnes & Noble, 1982.

Fraser, John. *Violence in the Arts.* Cambridge, Eng.: Cambridge University Press, 1974.

Frayling, Christopher. "Introduction: to *The Vampyre: A Bedside Companion.* New York: Scribners, 1978.

Freeman, Daniel. *Human Sociobiology.* New York: The Free Press, 1979.

Freud, Sigmund. "The Dissolution of the Oedipus Complex." In vol. 19 of *The Complete Works of Sigmund Freud*, edited by James Strachey. London: The Hogarth Press, 1955.

——. *Moses and Monotheism*. Translated by James Strachey. New York: W. W. Norton and Co., 1952.

——. "On the Universal Tendency to Debasement in the Sphere of Love." In vol. 11 of *The Complete Works . . .*, edited by James Strachey. London: The Hogarth Press, 1955.

——. "The Taboo of Virginity." In vol. 11 of *The Complete Works . . .*, edited by James Strachey. London: The Hogarth Press, 1955.

——. "The Transformations of Puberty." In vol. 7 of *The Complete Works . . .*, edited by James Strachey. London: The Hogarth Press, 1955.

——. "The Uncanny." In vol. 17 of *The Complete Works . . .*, edited by James Strachey. London: The Hogarth Press, 1955.

Fry, Carrol L. "Fictional Connections and Sexuality in *Dracula*." *Victorian Newsletter* 42 (1972): 20–22.

Fry, Ron, and Pamela Fourzon. *The Saga of Special Effects*. Englewood Cliffs, N.J.: Prentice-Hall, 1977.

Furnas, J. C. *Voyage to Windward: The Life of Robert Louis Stevenson*. New York: William Sloane, 1951.

Garden, Nancy. *Werewolves*. New York: Bantam, 1977.

Garfinkle, Harold. "Conditions of Successful Degradation Ceremonies." *American Journal of Sociology* 61, no. 5 (1956): 420–24.

Geduld, Harry M. *The Definitive "Dr. Jekyll and Mr. Hyde" Companion*. New York: Garland, 1983.

Gerard, Emily. *The Land Beyond the Forest*. New York: Harper and Bros., 1888.

Gifford, Denis. *Karloff: The Man, the Monster, the Movies*. New York: Curtis, 1973.

——. *Movie Monsters*. New York: Dutton, 1969.

——. *A Pictorial History of Horror Movies*. New York: Hamlyn, 1973.

Gilbert, Sandra M., and Susan Gubar. *The Madwoman in the Attic: The Woman Writer and the Nineteenth-Century Literary Imagination*. New Haven, Conn.: Yale University Press, 1979.

Gluckman, Max, ed. *Essays on the Ritual of Social Relations*. Manchester, Eng.: Manchester University Press, 1962.

Glut, Donald F. *The Dracula Book*. Metuchen, N.J.: Scarecrow Press, 1975.

——. *Classic Movie Monsters*. Metuchen, N.J.: Scarecrow Press, 1978.

——. *The Frankenstein Catalog*. Jefferson, N.C.: McFarland & Co. 1984.

——. *The Frankenstein Legend: A Tribute to Mary Shelley and Boris Karloff*. Metuchen, N.J.: Scarecrow Press, 1973.

Goldberg, Gerry, et al., eds. *Nighttouch: Journeying into the Realms of Nightmare*. New York: St. Martin's, 1977.

Grant, Marcus. *Horror: A Modern Myth*. London: Heineman, 1974.

Greenberg, Harvey R. *The Movies on Your Mind*. New York: Dutton, 1975.

Griffin, Gail. "'Your girls that you all love are mine': *Dracula* and the Victorian Male Sexual Imagination." *International Journal of Women's Studies* 3, no. 5 (1980): 454–64.

Grotjahn, Martin. "Horror—Yes, It Can Do You Good." *Films and Filming* 5 (1958): 9.

Grylls, David. *Guardians and Angels: Parents and Children in Nineteenth-Century Literature.* Boston: Faber, 1978.

Gussow, Mel. "Gorey Goes Batty." [an extended discussion of the 1977 Broadway production of *Dracula*] *New York Times Magazine*, October, 16, 1977, 40–42, 71, 74–76.

Hadfield, James Arthur. *Dreams and Nightmares.* Baltimore, Md.: Penguin Books, 1954.

Haining, Peter. *The Dracula Scrapbook.* London: New English Library, 1976.

———. *The Ghouls.* New York: Stein and Day, 1971.

———. *Terror!: A History of Horror Illustrations from the Pulp Magazines.* New York: A & W Visual, 1976.

Halliwell, Leslie. "The Baron, the Count and Their Ghoul Friends." *Films and Filming* 15, no. 9 (1969): 13–16 and, no. 10 (1969): 12–16.

Handel, Leo A. *Hollywood Looks at Its Audience: A Report of Film Audience Research.* Urbana: University of Illinois Press, 1950.

Handling, Piers, ed. *The Shape of Rage: The Films of David Cronenberg.* New York: Zoetrope, 1983.

Harrington, Curtis. "Ghoulies and Ghosties." In *Focus on the Horror Film*, edited by Roy Huss and T. J. Ross. Englewood Cliffs, N.J.: Prentice-Hall, 1972.

Heimel, Cynthia. "Interview with an Ex-Vampire." *New York*, April 24, 1978, 56–58.

Henderson, Joseph. *Thresholds of Initiation.* Middletown, Conn.: Wesleyan University Press, 1967.

Henkin, Bill. *The Rocky Horror Picture Show Book.* New York: Hawthorne Books, 1979.

Hennelly, Mark M. "*Dracula*: The Gnostic Quest and Victorian Wasteland." *English Literature in Transition* 20, no. 1 (1977): 13–26.

Herman, Judith Lewis. *Father-Daughter Incest.* Cambridge, Mass.: Harvard University Press, 1981.

Higashi, Sumiko. *Virgins, Vamps and Flappers: The American Silent Movie Heroines.* St. Albans, Vt.: Eden Press, 1978.

Hill, Derek. "The Face of Horror." *Sight and Sound* 28, no. 1 (1958/9): 6–11.

Hill, John M. "*Frankenstein* and the Physiognomy of Desire." *American Imago* 37 (1975): 335–58.

Hinds, Michael de Courey. "The Child Victim of Incest." *New York Times*, June 15, 1981, p. 22.

Hirsh, Gordon. "The Monster Was a Lady: On the Psychology of Mary Shelley's *Frankenstein.*" *Hartford Studies in Literature* 7 (1975): 116–53.

Hoberman, J., and Jonathan Rosenbaum. *Midnight Movies.* New York: Harper & Row, 1983.

Horney, Karen. *Feminine Psychology.* Edited by Harold Kelman. New York: W. W. Norton, 1967.

———. *The Neurotic Personality in Our Time.* New York: W. W. Norton, 1937.

———. *New Ways in Psychoanalysis.* London: Routledge & Paul, 1939.

Howells, Coral Ann. *Love, Mystery and Misery: Feeling in Gothic Fiction.* London: Athlone Press, 1978.

Hubler, R. G. "Scare 'Em to Death and Cash In: What Makes the Movie Horror-Thriller Scary and Why." *Saturday Evening Post*, May 23, 1942, 20–21.

Hufford, David J. *The Terror That Comes in the Night: An Experience Centered Study of Supernatural Assault Traditions*. Philadelphia: University of Pennsylvania Press, 1982.

Hughes, Winifred. *The Maniac in the Cellar: Sensation Novels of the 1860s*. Princeton, N.J.: Princeton University Press, 1980.

Hugo, Victor. *The Hunchback of Notre Dame*. New York: The Modern Library, 1941.

Hume, Robert D. "Gothic Versus Romantic: A Reevaluation of the Gothic Novel." *PMLA* 84 (1969): 282–290.

Huss, Roy. "Almost Eve: The Creation Scene in *The Bride of Frankenstein*." In *Focus on the Horror Film*, edited by Roy Huss and T. J. Ross. Englewood Cliffs, N.J.: Prentice-Hall, 1972.

Huss, Roy, and T. J. Ross, eds. *Focus on the Horror Film*. Englwood Cliffs, N.J. Prentice Hall, 1972.

Hutchinson, Tom. *Horror and Fantasy in the Cinema*. London: Macmillan, 1974.

Huxley, Francis. *The Invisibles*. London: Hart-Davis, 1966.

Irvin, Eric. "Dracula's Friends and Forerunners." *Quadrant* 135 (1978): 42–44.

Isherwood, Christopher, and Don Bachardy. *Frankenstein: The True Story*. New York: Avon, 1973.

Jackson, Rosemary. *Fantasy: The Literature of Subversion*. London: Methuen, 1981.

Jacobs, Joseph. *Literary Studies*. London: D. Nutt, 1895.

Janeway, Elizabeth. "Incest: A Rational Look at the Oldest Taboo." *Ms.*, November 1981, 61–64, 78–81, 109.

Johnson, Glen M. "'We'd Fight ... We Had to': *The Body Snatchers* as Novel and Film." *Journal of Popular Culture* 13 (1979): 5–16.

Jones, Ernest. *On the Nightmare*. 1931; rpt. New York: Liveright Publications, 1971.

Joseph, M. K., ed. *Frankenstein*. By Mary Shelley. London: Oxford University Press, 1969.

Jung, Carl G., et al. *Man and His Symbols*. New York: Dell, 1972.

———. *Psyche and Symbol*. Edited by Violet S. de Lazio. Garden City, N. J.: Doubleday, 1958.

Kaminsky, Stewart. *American Film Genres: Approaches to a Critical Theory of Popular Film*. New York: Dell, 1977.

Kane, Joe. "Beauties, Beasts, and Male Chauvinist Monsters: The Plight of Women in the Horror Film." *Take One* 4 (1973): 8–10.

Kaplan, Morton. "Fantasy of Paternity and the Doppelgänger: Mary Shelley's *Frankenstein*." In *The Unspoken Motive: A Guide to Psychoanalytic Criticism*, edited by Morton Kaplan and Robert Kloss. New York: The Free Press, 1973.

Kapsis, Robert. "Dressed to Kill." *American Film* 7, no. 5 (1982): 3–56.

Kaufman, K. A. "Why Do People go to the Movies? A Study of Attendance." Master's thesis, University of Pennsylvania, 1983.

Kayser, Wolfgang. *The Grotesque in Art and Literature*. Translated by Ulrich Weisstein. 1957; rpt. New York: McGraw-Hill, 1966.

Kayton, Lawrence. "The Relationship of the Vampire Legend to Schizophrenia." *Journal of Youth and Adolescence* 1, no. 4 (1972): 303–14.

Kendall, Lyle H. "The Vampire Motif in *The Fall of the House of Usher*." *College English* 24 (1963): 450–53.

Keppler, Carl F. *The Literature of the Second Self.* Tucson: University of Arizona Press, 1972.

Ketterer, David. *Frankenstein's Creation: The Book, the Monster, and Human Reality.* English Literary Studies Monograph Series, no. 16. Victoria, B.C.: University of Victoria Press, 1979.

Kiely, Robert. *The Romantic Novel in England.* Cambridge, Mass.: Harvard University Press, 1972.

King, Stephen. *Danse Macabre.* New York: Everest House, 1981.

Knight, Arthur. *The Liveliest Art: A Panoramic History of the Movies,* rev. ed. New York: Macmillan, 1978.

Koch, Stephen. "Fashions in Pornography: Murder as Cinematic Chic." *Harper's,* November 1976, 108–111.

Kracauer, Siegfried. *From Caligari to Hitler: A Psychological History of the German Film.* 1947; rpt. Princeton, N.J.: Princeton University Press, 1971.

———. "Hollywood's Terror Films: Do They Reflect an American State of Mind?" *Commentary,* August 1946, 132–36.

Kristeva, Julia. *Powers of Horror: An Essay on Abjection.* Translated by Leon S. Roudiez. New York: Columbia University Press, 1982.

Kroeber, A. L. "*Totem and Taboo*: An Ethnologic Psychoanalysis." *American Anthropologist* 22 (1920): 48–55.

———. "*Totem and Taboo* in Retrospect." *American Journal of Sociology* 55 (1939): 446–451.

Laclos, Michel. *Le Fantastique au cinéma.* Paris: Jean-Jacques Pauvert, 1953.

Laing, R. D. *The Divided Self: An Existential Study of Sanity and Madness.* Baltimore, Md.: Penguin, 1971.

Lavalley, Albert J. "The Stage and Film Children of Frankenstein." In *The Endurance of "Frankenstein,"* edited by George Levine and V. C. Knoepflmacher. Berkeley: University of California Press, 1979.

Lawrence, D. H. "Edgar Allan Poe." In *Selected Literary Criticism,"* edited by Anthony Beal. 1932; rpt. New York: Viking Press, 1966.

Leavis, Queenie Dorothy. *Fiction and the Reading Public.* New York: Russell and Russell, 1965.

Lee, Walt, ed. *Reference Guide to Fantastic Films: Science Fiction, Fantasy and Horror,* 3 vols. Los Angeles: Chelsea-Lee Books, 1972.

Le Fanu, J. Sheridan. "Carmilla." In *Carmilla and the Haunted Baronet.* New York: Warner, 1974.

Lenne, Gérard. *Le Cinéma "fantastique" et ses mythologies.* Paris: Editions du Cerf, 1970.

Lennig, Arthur. *The Count: The Life and Films of Bela "Dracula" Lugosi.* New York: Putnam, 1974.

Lentz, David, Edward Donnerstein, and Steven Penrod. "The Effects of Multiple Exposures to Filmed Violence Against Women." *Journal of Communication* 34, no. 3 (1984): 130–147.

Leroux, Gaston. *The Phantom of the Opera.* Indianapolis, Ind.: Bobbs-Merrill, 1911.

Levine, George. "*Frankenstein* and the Tradition of Realism." *Novel* 7 (1973): 14–30.

Levine, George, and U. C. Knoepflmacher, eds. *The Endurance of "Frankenstein."* Berkeley: University of California Press, 1979.

Lévi-Strauss, Claude. "The Family." In *Man, Culture and Society*, edited by Harry Lionel Shapiro. New York: Oxford University Press, 1956.

Lockwood, Charles. "Priestess of Sin: Theda Bara." *Horizon*, January 1981, 65–69.

London, Rose. *Zombie: The Living Dead*. New York: Bounty, 1976.

Losano, Wayne A. "The Vampire Rises Again in Films of the Seventies." *The Film Journal* 2, no. 2 (1973): 60–62.

Ludlam, Harry. *A Biography of Dracula*. London: W. Foulsham and Co., 1962.

Luhr, William, and Peter Lehman. *Authorship and Narrative in the Cinema: Issues in Contemporary Aesthetics and Criticism*. New York: Putnam, 1977.

Lund, Mary Graham. "Mary Godwin Shelley and the Monster." *The University of Kansas City Review* 28 (1962): 253–58.

MacAndrew, Elizabeth. *The Gothic Tradition in Fiction*. New York: Columbia University Press, 1979.

MacGillivary, Royce. "*Dracula*: Bram Stoker's Spoiled Masterpiece." *Queens Quarterly* 79, no. 4 (1972): 518–27.

Mack, John E. *Nightmares and Human Conflict*. Boston: Houghton Mifflin, 1974.

Maixner, Paul, ed. *Robert Louis Stevenson: The Critical Heritage*. London: Routledge and Kegan Paul, 1981.

Malcom, Janet. *In The Freud Archives*. New York: Knopf, 1984.

Malin, Irving. *New American Gothic*. Carbondale: Southern Illinois University Press, 1962.

Manchel, Frank. *Terrors of the Screen*. Englewood Cliffs, N.J.: Prentice-Hall, 1970.

Mank, Gregory William. *It's Alive!: The Classic Cinema Saga of Frankenstein*. New York: A. S. Barnes, 1981.

Manvell, Roger, and Heinrich Fraenkel. *The German Cinema*. New York: Praeger, 1971.

Marcus, Steven. *The Other Victorians: A Study of Sexuality and Pornography in Mid-Nineteenth-Century England*. New York: Basic Books, 1964.

Massey, Irving. *The Gaping Pig: Literature and Metamorphosis*. Berkeley: University of California Press, 1969.

Masson, Jeffrey Moussaieff. *The Assault on Truth: Freud's Suppression of the Seduction Theory*. New York: Farrar, Straus and Giroux, 1984.

Masters, Anthony. *The Natural History of the Vampire*. New York: Putnam, 1972.

Matheson, Richard. *I Am Legend*. New York: Fawcett Publications, 1954.

McCarty, John. *Splatter Movies*. New York: St. Martin's, 1981.

McClelland, Douglas. *The Golden Age of "B" Movies*. Nashville, Tenn: Charter House, 1978.

McConnell, Frank. "Rough Beast Slouching: A Note on Horror Films." *Kenyon Review* 32 (1970): 109–20.

———. "Song of Innocence: *The Creature from the Black Lagoon*." *Journal of Popular Film* 2, no. 1 (1973): 15–28.

———. *The Spoken Seen: Film and the Romantic Imagination*. Baltimore, Md.: Johns Hopkins University Press, 1975.

McNally, Raymond T. *A Clutch of Vampires*. New York: Warner, 1975.

———. *Dracula Was a Woman*. New York: McGraw-Hill, 1983.

McNally, Raymond T., and Radu Florescu. *In Search of Dracula*. New York: Warner, 1973.

Messent, Peter B., ed. *Literature of the Occult*. Englewood Cliffs, N.J.: Prentice-Hall, 1981.

Meyers, F. W. H. Letter to Robert Louis Stevenson. February 21, 1886. MS. 5260, Stevenson Collection, Beinecke Library. New Haven, Conn.

———. Letter to Robert Louis Stevenson. February 28, 1886. MS. 7271, Stevenson Collection, Beinecke Library. New Haven, Conn.

Meyers, Richard. *The World of Fantasy Films*. Cranbury, N.J.: A. S. Barnes, 1980.

Milne, Tom. *The Cinema of Carl Dreyer*. New York: A. C. Barnes, 1971.

Miyoshi, Masao. *The Divided Self: A Perspective on the Literature of the Victorians*. New York: New York University Press, 1969.

Moers, Ellen. "Female Gothic: The Monster's Mother." *New York Review of Books*, March 24, 1974, pp. 24–28.

Monaco, James. "Aieargh!" *Sight and Sound* 48, no. 2 (1980): 80–82.

Moore, Darrell. *The Best, Worst, and Most Unusual Horror Movies*. New York: Beekman House, 1983.

Moretti, Franco. "The Dialectic of Fear." *New Left Review* 136 (1982): 67–85.

Moss, Robert F. *Karloff and Company: The Horror Film*. New York: Pyramid, 1974.

Murphey, A. D. "Audience Demographics, Film Future." *Variety*, August 1975, pp. 3, 74.

Murphy, Brian. "Monster Movies: They Came from Beneath the Fifties." *Journal of Popular Film* 1, no. 1 (1972): 31–44.

Murphy, Michael. *The Celluloid Vampires: A History and Filmography 1897-1979*. Ann Arbor, Mich.: Pierian Press, 1979.

Murray, John. Letter to Lord Byron, 27 April 1819. In vol. 4 of *The Works of Lord Byron*, edited by Roland Prothero. London: John Murray, 1900.

Nabokov, Vladimir. *Lectures on Literature*. New York: Harcourt Brace Jovanovich, 1980.

Naha, Ed. *Horrors From Screen to Scream*. New York: Avon, 1975.

Nelson, Lowry, Jr. "Night Thoughts on the Gothic Novel." *Yale Review* 52 (1962): 236–257.

Norton, Rictor. "Aesthetic Gothic Horror." *Yearbook of Comparative and General Literature* 21 (1972): 31–40.

Novak, Maximillian E. "Gothic Fiction and the Grotesque." *Novel* 13 (1979): 50–67.

O'Donnell, Elliott. *Werewolves*. New York: Longvue Press, 1965.

Otto, Rudolf. *The Idea of Holy: An Inquiry into the Non-Rational Factor in the Idea of the Divine and Its Relation to the Rational*. Translated by John W. Harvey. New York: Oxford University Press, 1958.

Pattison, Barrie. *The Seal of Dracula*. New York: Bounty, 1975.

Pattison, Robert. *The Child Figure in English Literature*. Athens: University of Georgia Press, 1978.

Peake, Richard B. *Presumption, Or the Fate of Frankenstein, A Romantic Drama in Two Acts."* London: J. Duncombe, 1824.

Peary, Danny. *Cult Movies*. New York: Dell, 1981.

Pendo, Stephen. "Universal's Golden Age of Horror: 1931–1941." *Films in Review* 26 (1975): 155–161.

Perry, J. Douglas. "Gothic as Vortex: The Form of Horror in Capote, Faulkner and Styron." *Modern Fiction Studies* 19 (1973): 153–67.

Petronius Arbiter. *The Satyricon*. Translated by William Arrowsmith. Ann Arbor: University of Michigan Press, 1959.

Pirie, David. *A Heritage of Horror: The English Gothic Cinema, 1946–1972*. New York: Avon Books, 1973.

———. *The Vampire Cinema*. New York: Crescent Books, 1977.

Plumb, J. H. "Can Society Banish Cruelty." *Horizon* 18, no. 3 (1976): 84–85.

Polidori, John. *Ernestus Brechtold; or, The Modern Oedipus, A Tale*. London: Longman, Hurst, Rees, Orme and Brown, 1819.

———. "The Vampyre." In *Three Gothic Novels*, edited by E. F. Bleiler. New York: Dover, 1966.

Pollock, Linda A. *Forgotten Children: Parent-Child Relations from 1500 to 1900*. Cambridge, Eng.: Cambridge University Press, 1984.

Powell, Nicolas. *Fuseli: "The Nightmare."* New York: Viking Press, 1972.

Pratt, George C. *Spellbound in Darkness*, 2nd rev. ed. Greenwich, Conn.: New York Graphic Society, 1973.

Prawer, S. S. *Caligari's Children: The Film as Tale of Terror*. New York: Oxford University Press, 1980.

Praz, Mario. *The Romantic Agony*. Translated by Angus Davidson with introd. by Frank Kermode. London: Oxford University Press, 1970.

Prest, Thomas Pecket. *Varney the Vampyre, or, the Feast of Blood*. 1847; rpt. New York: Dover, 1970.

Price, Vincent, and V. B. Price. *Monsters*. New York: Grosset & Dunlap, 1981.

Pronzini, Bill, ed. *Werewolf!* New York: Arbor House, 1979.

Pückler-Muskau, Prince Hermann. *Tour in England, Ireland, and France in the Years 1828 and 1829*. 1826; rpt. Philadelphia, Pa.: Carey & Lea, 1833.

Punter, David. *The Literature of Terror: A History of Gothic Fictions from 1765 to the Present Day*. New York: Longman, 1980.

Radcliffe, Elsa J. *Gothic Novels of the Twentieth Century: An Annotated Bibliography*. Metuchen, N.J.: Scarecrow Press, 1979.

Railo, Eino. *The Haunted Castle: A Study of the Elements of English Romanticism*. London: George Routledge and Sons, 1927.

Rank, Otto. *The Double: A Psychoanalytic Study*. Translated and edited by Harry Tucker, Jr. Chapel Hill: University of North Carolina Press, 1971.

Reed, Donald A. *The Vampire on the Screen*. Inglewood, Calif.: Wagon and Star Publishers, 1965.

Reik, Theodor. *Ritual: Psychoanalytic Studies*. 1931; rpt. New York: International Universities Press, 1946.

Reynolds, G. W. M. *Wagner, the Wehr-Wolf*. 1857; rpt. New York: Dover, 1975.

Richardson, Maurice. "The Psychoanalysis of Ghost Stories." *The Twentieth Century* 166 (1959): 419–31.

Rieger, James. "Dr. Polidori and the Genesis of *Frankenstein*." *Studies in English Literature* 3 (1963): 461–72.

———, ed. *Frankenstein*. By Mary Shelley. Indianapolis, Ind.: Bobbs-Merrill, 1974.

Ringel, Harry. "A Hank of Hair and a Piece of Bone." *Film Journal* 2, no. 4 (1975): 14–18.

———. "Interview with Terence Fisher." *Cinfantastique* 4, no. 3 (1975): 24–26.

———. "Terence Fisher: The Human Side." *Cinefantastique* 4, no. 3 (1975): 5–16.

———. "Terence Fisher: Underling." *Cinefantastique* 4, no. 3 (1975): 19–28.

———. "The Horrible Hammer Films of Terence Fisher." *Take One* 3, no. 9 (1972): 8–12.

Robertson, Patrick, ed. *The Guinness Book of Film Facts and Feats.* Enfield, Eng.: Guinness Superlatives, 1980.

Robinson, William R. *Man and the Movies.* Baltimore, Md.: Penquin, 1967.

Rogers, Robert. *A Psychoanalytic Study of the Double in Literature.* Detroit, Mich.: Wayne State University Press, 1970.

Ronay, Gabriel. *The Truth About Dracula.* New York: Stein and Day, 1974.

Rosenbaum, Jonathan. "The Rocky Horror Picture Cult." *Sight and Sound* 42, no. 2 (1980): 78–9.

Rosenbaum, Ron. "Gooseflesh." *Harper's,* September 1979, 86–92.

Rosenberg, Samuel. "*Frankenstein* or Daddy's Little Monster." In *Confessions of a Trivialist.* Baltimore, Md.: Penguin, 1972.

Roth, Phyllis R. "Suddenly Sexual Women in Bram Stoker's *Dracula.*" *Literature and Psychology* 27 (1977): 113–21.

Rovin, Jeff. *Movie Special Effects.* New York: A. S. Barnes, 1977.

Rubenstein, Marc A. "'My Accursed Origin': The Search for the Mother in *Frankenstein.*" *Studies in Romanticism* 15 (1976): 165–94.

Sale, Roger. *Fairy Tales and After: From Snow White to E. B. White.* Cambridge, Mass.: Harvard University Press, 1978.

Samuels, Stuart. *Midnight Movies.* New York: Collier, 1983.

Saposnik, Irving R. *Robert Louis Stevenson.* New York: Twayne, 1974.

Sayre, Norma. "Look to the Skies." In *Running Time.* New York: Dial, 1982.

Scarborough, Dorothy. *The Supernatural in Modern English Fiction.* 1917; rpt. New York: Octagon Books, 1967.

Schiff, Gert. *Images of Horror and Fantasy.* New York: Harry N. Abrams, Inc., 1978.

Scholer, Franz. "Die Erben des Marquis de Sade," (Horrorfilm, part 1: Vampirismus in Literatur und Film) *Film* 5, no. 8 (1967): 10–17.

———. "Horror-Bilderbuch und Materialien zu den Literarischer Dorlauferern des Horror-Films," *Film,* 5, no. 11 (1967): 41–51.

Seabrook, William. *Magic Island.* New York: Harcourt Brace and Company, 1929.

Searle, John. "Sociobiology and the Explanation of Human Behavior." In *Sociobiology and Human Nature,* edited by Michael Gregory. San Francisco: Jossey Bass Publications, 1978.

Sedgwick, Eve Kosofsky. *The Coherence of Gothic Convention.* New York: Arno Press, 1980.

Shelley, Mary. *Frankenstein.* 1831; rpt. New York: New American Library, 1965.

———. *Journals.* Edited by Frederick L. Jones. Norman: University of Oklahoma Press, 1947.

Shostak, Marjorie. *Nisa: The Life and Words of a !Kung Woman.* Cambridge, Mass: Harvard University Press, 1981.

Siegel, Joel E. *Val Lewton: The Reality of Terror.* New York: Viking, 1973.

Simon, John. "Rev. of *An Illustrated History of the Horror Film.*" In *Movies into Film: Film Criticism, 1967–1970.* New York: Dial Press, 1971.

Small, Christopher. *Mary Shelley's "Frankenstein": Tracing the Myth.* Pittsburgh, Pa.: University of Pittsburgh Press, 1973.

Smith, Susan Harris. "*Frankenstein*: Mary Shelley's Psychic Divisiveness." *Women and Literature* 5 (1977): 42–53.

Solomon, Stanley. "The Nightmare World." In *Beyond Formula: American Film Genre*. New York: Harcourt Brace, 1976.

Sontag, Susan. "Dr. Jekyll." In *I, Etcetera*. New York: Vintage, 1978.

———. "Notes on Camp." In *Against Interpretation*. New York: Dell, 1966.

———. *On Photography*. New York: Farrar, Straus and Giroux, 1973.

Soren, David. *The Rise and Fall of the Horror Film: An Art Historical Approach to Fantasy Cinema*. Columbia, Mo.: Lucas Brothers, 1977.

Spacks, Patricia Meyer. *The Insistence of Horror: Aspects of the Supernatural in Eighteenth-Century Poetry*. Cambridge, Mass.: Harvard University Press, 1962.

Stacy, Jan, and Ryder Syvertsen. *The Great Book of Movie Monsters*. Chicago: Contemporary Books, 1983.

Stanley, John. *The Creature Features Movie Guide*. 1981; rev. New York: Warner Books, 1984.

Steiger, Brad. *Master Movie Monsters*. New York: Merit, 1965.

———. *Monsters, Maidens and Mayhem: A Pictorial History of Horror Film Monsters*. New York: Merit, 1965.

Stein, Elliot. "'A Very Tender Film, a Very Nice One': Michael Powell's *Peeping Tom*." *Film Comment* 15, no. 5 (1979): 57–59.

Steinbrunner, Chris, and Burt Goldblatt. *Cinema of the Fantastic*. New York: Saturday Review Press, 1972.

Stevenson, Robert Louis. *The Strange Case of Dr. Jekyll and Mr. Hyde*. 1886; rpt. New York: Bantam Books, 1967.

Stewart, Caroline. *The Origin of the Werewolf Superstition*. Columbia: University of Missouri Press, 1909.

Stoker, Bram. *Dracula*. 1897; rpt. New York: Signet, 1965.

Stoker, John. *The Illustrated Frankenstein*. New York: Sterling Publishing, 1980.

Strout, Andrea. "In the Midnight Hour." *American Film* 6, no. 4 (1981): 35–74.

Sullivan, Jack. *Elegant Nightmares: The English Ghost Story from Le Fanu to Blackwood*. Athens, Ohio University Press, 1978.

Summers, Montague. *The Gothic Quest*. 1938; rpt. London: Russell and Russell, 1964.

———. *The Vampire: His Kith and Kin*. 1928; rpt. New Hyde Park, N.Y.: University Books, 1960.

———. *The Werewolf*. 1933; rpt. New Hyde Park, N.Y.: University Books, 1966.

———. *The Vampire in Europe*. 1929; rpt. New Hyde Park, N.Y.: University Books, 1968.

———. Trans. *Malleus Maleficarum*. 1928; rpt. New York: Benjamin Bloom, 1970.

Tallant, Robert. *Voodoo in New Orleans*. New York: Macmillan, 1946.

Tarratt, Margaret. "Monsters from the Id." *Films and Filming* 17, no. 3 (1970): 38–42, and no. 4 (1971): 40–2.

Telotte, Jay P. "Faith and Idolatry in the Horror Film." *Film and Literature Quarterly* 8, no. 3 (1980): 143–55.

Thomas, John. "Gobble, Gobble . . . One of Us." In *Focus on the Horror Film*, edited by Roy Huss and T. J. Ross. Englewood Cliffs, N.J.: Prentice-Hall, 1972.

Thompson, David. "Mark of the Red Death." *Sight and Sound* 49, no. 4 (1980): 258–62.

Thompson, Gary Richard, ed. *The Gothic Imagination: Essays in Dark Romanticism*. Pullman: Washington State University Press, 1974.

Thompson, Richard G. *Romantic Gothic Tales*. New York: Harper & Row, 1979.

Thorslev, Peter L., Jr. "The Wild Man's Revenge." In *The Wild Man Within: An Image of Western Thought from the Renaissance to Romanticism*, edited by Edward Dudley and Maximillian Novak. Pittsburgh, Pa.: University of Pittsburgh Press, 1972.

Todorov, Tzvetan. *The Fantastic: A Structural Approach to a Literary Genre*. Translated by Richard Howard. Cleveland, Ohio: Case Western Reserve University Press, 1973.

Tompkins, Joyce Marjorie Sanxter. *The Popular Novel in England 1770–1800*. Lincoln: University of Nebraska Press, 1961.

Tropp, Martin. *Mary Shelley's Monster*. Boston: Houghton Mifflin, 1977.

Tudor, Andrew. *Image and Influence: Studies in the Sociology of Film*. New York: St. Martin's Press, 1974.

Turan, Kenneth. "Horrors!" *The Progressive* 43 (1979): 38–39.

Twitchell, James B. "'Desire with Loathing Strangely Mix'd': The Dreamwork of *Christabel*." *The Psychoanalytic Review* 61 (1974): 33–44.

———. *The Living Dead: A Study of the Vampire in Romantic Literature*. Durham, N.C.: Duke University Press, 1981.

———. "The Vampire Myth." *American Imago* 37 (1980): 83–92.

Tymms, Ralph. *Doubles in Literary Psychology*. Cambridge, Eng.: Bowes and Bowes, 1949.

Tymn, Marshall, B. *Horror Literature: A Core Collection and Reference Guide*. New York: R. R. Bowker, 1981.

Underwood, Peter Karloff: *The Life of Boris Karloff*. New York: Drake, 1972.

———, ed. *The Vampire's Bedside Companion*. London: Leslie Frewin, 1979.

Ursini, James, and Alain Silver. *The Vampire Film*. New York: A. S. Barnes, 1975.

Van Gennep, Arnold. *The Rites of Passage*. 1909; rpt. Chicago: University of Chicago Press, 1960.

Varma, Devendra P. *The Gothic Flame*. 1957; rpt. New York: Russell and Russell, 1964.

Veeder, William. "*Carmilla*: The Arts of Repression." *Texas Studies in Language and Literature* 22 (1980): 197–223,

Walsh, Thomas P. "*Dracula*: Logos and Myth." *Research Studies* 47 (1979): 229–37.

Waters, John. *Shock Value: A Tasteful Book about Bad Taste*. New York: Dell, 1981.

Welsch, Janice R. "The Horrific and the Tragic: Mamoulian's *Dr. Jekyll and Mr. Hyde*." In *The English Novel and the Movies*, edited by Michael Klein and Gillian Parker. New York: Unger, 1981.

Wharton, Lawrence. "Godzilla to Latitude Zero: The Cycle of the Technological Monster." *Journal of Popular Film* 3 (1974): 31–38.

White, Dennis L. "The Poetics of Horror." *Cinema Journal* 10, no. 2 (1971): 1–18.

White, Timothy. "*Dracula*: The Warmblooded Revival of the Debonaire King of the Undead." *Crawdaddy*, June 1978, 26–33.

Whiting, J. W. M., R. Kluckhohn, and A. S. Anthony. "The Function of Male Initiation Ceremonies at Puberty." In *Readings in Social Psychology*, edited by Eleanor E. Maccoby et al. New York: Holt, Rinehart and Winston, 1958.

Williams, Tony. "American Films in the '70's: Family Horror." *Movie* 27/28 (1981): 117–126.

Willis, Don. *A Checklist of Horror and Science Fiction Films*. Metuchen, N.J.: Scarecrow Press, 1972.

Wilson, Edward O. *Sociobiology*. Cambridge, Mass.: Harvard University Press, 1980.

Winter, William. *The Life and Art of Richard Mansfield*. New York: Moffat, Yard and Company, 1910.

Wolf, Leonard. *A Dream of Dracula: In Search of the Living Dead*. Boston, Mass.: Little, Brown, 1972.

———, annotator. *The Annotated "Dracula."* By Bram Stoker. New York: Clarkson N. Potter, 1975.

———, annotator. *The Annotated "Frankenstein."* By Mary Shelley. New York: Clarkson N. Potter, 1977.

Wood, Robin. "Beauty Bests the Beast." *American Film* 8, no. 10 (1983): 63–65.

———. "Gods and Monsters." *Film Comment* 14, no. 5 (1978): 19–25.

———. "Neglected Nightmares." *Film Comment* 16, no. 2 (1980): 24–32.

———. "Return of the Repressed." *Film Comment* 14, no. 4 (1978): 24–32.

Woodward, Ian. *The Werewolf Delusion*. New York: Paddington Press, 1979.

Woolfolk, William. *Daddy's Little Girl: The Unspoken Bargain Between Fathers and Their Daughters*. Englewood Cliffs, N.J.: Prentice-Hall, 1982.

Young, Frank Wilbur. *Initiation Ceremonies: A Cross Cultural Study of Status Dramatization*. Indianapolis, Ind.: Bobbs-Merrill, 1965.

Zambrano, A. L. *Horror in Film and Literature*, 2 vols. New York: Gordon Press, 1978.

Zaphiris, Alexander G. *Incest: The Family with Two Known Victims*. Englewood, Colo.: The American Humane Society, 1978.

Ziolkowski, Theodore. *Disenchanted Images: A Literary Iconology*. Princeton, N.J.: Princeton University Press, 1977.

Zipes, Jack. *The Trials and Tribulations of Little Red Riding Hood: Versions of the Tale in Sociocultural Context*. South Hadley, Mass.: Bergin & Garvey, 1983.

Index